Contents

How to use this book

The American Express Pocket Guide to New York is an encyclopedia of travel information, organized in the sections listed on the previous page. There is also a comprehensive **index** (pages 196–203), which is accompanied by a **gazetteer** (pages 204–208) of the most important streets that are shown in the full-color **maps** at the end of the book.

For easy reference, all major sections (**Sights and places of interest, Hotels, Restaurants**) and other sections as far as possible are arranged alphabetically. For the organization of the book as a whole, see *Contents*. For individual places that do not have separate entries in *Sights and places of interest*, see the *Index*.

Abbreviations

As far as possible only standard abbreviations have been used. These include days of the week and months, points of the compass (N, S, E and W), street names (Ave., Pl., Sq., St.), Saint (St), century (C), and measurements.

Bold type

Bold type is used in running text primarily for emphasis, to draw attention to something of special interest or importance. It is also used in this way to pick out places – shops or minor museums, for instance – that do not have full entries of their own. In such cases it is usually followed in brackets by the address, telephone number, and details of opening times, printed in italics. Similarly, in *Hotels* and *Restaurants*, it is used to identify places mentioned in one entry which have an entry of their own elsewhere in these sections.

Cross-references

A special type has been used for cross-references. Whenever a place or section title is printed in sans serif italics (for example *Audubon Terrace* or *Basic information*) in the text, this indicates that you can turn to the appropriate heading for further information. For added convenience, the running

---

How entries are organized

Citicorp Center ▥ ☆

153 E 53rd St. (Lexington Ave.), NY 10022 ☎ *559–4259. Map 5N4* ◘ *Open 8am – midnight.*

Posterity has yet to render its verdict on this building. Its distinctive sloping roof line moves it into the Post-Modernist category of skyscraper design, away from the rectangular glass boxes of the Bauhaus school. The roof was intended to house solar energy collectors, a good intention sacrificed to the gods of cost accounting. Quibbles aside, the 1978 building brought life to a dreary block and accommodated into its design the modest but striking **St Peter's Lutheran Church**. Office floors begin at 127ft (39m), clearing the church steeple and providing a public atrium embracing 22 shops and restaurants. The interior plaza is filled with trees and tables, and live music is often laid on by the management. Co-operating were Hugh Stubbins and Emery Roth & Sons – the latter firm was also partly responsible for such looming local monoliths as the *World Trade Center* and *Pan Am Building*.

heads, printed at the top corner of the page, always correspond
with these cross-references.

Cross-references always refer either to sections of the book –
Basic information, Planning, Hotels, Shopping – or to
individual entries in **Sights and places of interest**, such as
Audubon Terrace or *Yorkville*. Ordinary italics are used to
identify sub-sections. For instance: see *Architecture* in *Culture,
history and background*.

Map references

Each page of the color maps at the end of the book has a page
number (2–16), and each map is divided into a grid of squares,
which are identified vertically by letters (A, B, C, D, etc.) and
horizontally by numbers (1, 2, 3, 4, etc.). A map reference
identifies the page and square in which the street or place can be
found – thus **Audubon Terrace** is located in the square
identified as Map **8F2**.

Price categories

Price categories are denoted by the symbols □ ⫽□ ⫽□▯ ⫽▯▯ and
⫽▯▯▯ which signify cheap, inexpensive, moderately priced,
expensive and very expensive, respectively. In the cases of
hotels and restaurants these correspond approximately with the
following actual prices, which give a guideline at the time of
printing. Although actual prices will inevitably increase, in
most cases the relative price category – for example, expensive
or cheap – will be likely to remain more or less the same.

Price categories	Corresponding to approximate prices for **hotels** *double room with bath; single slightly cheaper*	for **restaurants** *meal for one with service, taxes and house wine*
□ cheap	under $40	under $10
⫽□ inexpensive	$40–80	$10–25
⫽▯▯ moderate	$65–100	$20–35
⫽▯▯▯ expensive	$85–130	$30–50
⫽▯▯▯ very expensive	over $130	over $50

— Bold blue type for entry headings.

— Blue italics for address, practical information and symbols,
encapsulating standard information and special recommendations.
For list of symbols see p6.

— Black text for description.
Bold type used for emphasis.
— Sans serif italics used for cross-
references to other entries.

Entries for hotels, restaurants,
shops, etc. follow the same
organization, and are usually
printed across a narrow
measure.
In hotels, symbols indicating
special facilities appear at the
end of the entry. —

Howard Johnson's ✿
*851 8th Ave. (near 51st St.), NY
10019* ☎ *581–4100* ☎ *147183.
Map 4N3* ▮▮▮ ☎ *300* 🛏 *300* 📺
🖼 🍴 AE CB ◉ ◉ VISA
*Location: w of the midtown Theater
District.* One of a trio of relatively
new midtown motels, it shares the
virtues and the liabilities of the
others – ready access by car,
walking distance from the major
theaters and moderate tariffs; but
charmless rooms and a bleak
neighborhood.
‡ □ 🖼 🦽

Key to symbols

- ☎ Telephone
- ⊤ Telex
- ★ Not to be missed
- ☆ Worth a visit
- ✿ Good value (in its class)
- 🚗 Car parking
- 🏨 Simple (hotel)
- 🏩 Luxury (hotel)
- □ Cheap
- ▮▯ Inexpensive
- ▮▮▯ Moderately priced
- ▮▮▮ Expensive
- ▮▮▮▮ Very expensive
- 🛏 Number of rooms
- 🛁 Rooms with private bathroom
- ▤ Air conditioning
- 🏠 Residential terms available
- AE American Express
- CB Carte Blanche
- ◑ Diners Club
- ◐ MasterCard
- VISA Visa
- 🚪 Secure garage
- 🍴 Own restaurant
- ☁ Quiet hotel
- ⬍ Elevator
- ♿ Facilities for the disabled
- 📺 TV in each room
- ☏ Telephone in each room

- 🐕 Dogs not allowed
- ⇺ Outstanding views
- ⇌ Swimming pool
- ⚲ Tennis court(s)
- 👥 Conference facilities
- R Restaurant
- 🍽 Simple (restaurant)
- △ Luxury (restaurant)
- ⊐ À la carte available
- ▬ Set (fixed price) menu available
- ═ Good for wines
- ◈ Open-air dining available
- 🏛 Building of architectural interest
- † Church or cathedral
- ⊡ Entrance free
- ⊠ Entrance fee payable
- ⊞ Entrance expensive
- 📷🚫 Photography not permitted
- 𝒴 Guided tour available
- 🔍 Guided tour compulsory
- 🍵 Cafeteria
- ✳ Special interest for children
- 𝒴 Bar
- ● Disco
- 🔲 Nightclub
- ♫ Live music
- ♧ Dancing
- 🔊 Revue

6

Before you go

Documents required

To rent a car, you need a valid driver's license. If you are arriving by private car from other states and countries you should bring the car registration and certificate of insurance with you. It is also wise to take out short-term extra coverage as the accident rate in New York City is higher than average.

Senior citizens are eligible for a discount in some hotels but must be able to show identification in order to claim it.

Travel and medical insurance

Medical care is good to excellent, but costly. Theft is also more common than average. Extra medical and baggage insurance is therefore strongly recommended. If you are a member of an automobile association this can be arranged through them. Larger hotels have doctors on call but visits are expensive.

Money

It is wise to carry cash in small amounts only, keeping the remainder in travelers cheques. For buying travelers cheques the best-known issuing companies are American Express, Bank of America, Barclays, Citibank and Thomas Cook. The credit card firms MasterCard and Visa have also introduced their own versions. Many shops accept dollar travelers cheques. Credit cards are welcomed by nearly all hotels, airlines and car rental agencies, most restaurants and garages and many shops. American Express, Diners Club, MasterCard and Visa are the major cards in common use. Carte Blanche has less comprehensive coverage. While personal checks drawing on out-of-town banks are not normally accepted, many hotels will cash small amounts in conjunction with a credit card.

Getting there

Kennedy airport is the largest of New York's three airports, but as it deals mainly with international flights it is best avoided if you have a choice. Most national airlines serve both the other airports – LaGuardia which is the smallest and closest to the center (30min) and Newark which is on the other side of the Hudson River in New Jersey (45min). Private planes can land at Teterboro in NE New Jersey.

Long distance and commuter trains arrive at Pennsylvania Station (7th Ave. and 32nd St.), or Grand Central Terminal (Park Ave. and 42nd St.).

All buses, both long distance and commuter, arrive at the recently refurbished Port Authority Bus Terminal (8th Ave. and 41st St.). The long-distance buses have their platforms below street level; passengers from local buses arrive at the upper stories.

From the W and S, interstate highways I-78, I-80 and I-95 connect with Manhattan via the George Washington Bridge (for upper Manhattan), the Lincoln Tunnel (for mid-Manhattan) and the Holland Tunnel (for lower Manhattan). From the N, I-87 (Governor Thomas E. Dewey Thruway) and I-95 (New England Thruway) lead to the Triborough Bridge and other Harlem River and East River crossings. Most of these funnel into the FDR Drive, which parallels the East River. Tolls across the Hudson River are paid when entering the city, but not when leaving. Automobile clubs will suggest the best route from your point of departure.

Basic information

Climate

May, June, Sept and Oct are the agreeable months, incorporating the best days of the short and unpredictable Spring and Fall seasons. Extended periods of oppressive humidity and temperatures of 90°F (32°C) and more characterize July and Aug, while Dec through Feb feature cold rains, occasional snow and readings at or near freezing point. True extremes are rare, however. Temperatures infrequently drop below freezing point or exceed 100°F (38°C), and a snowfall of more than four inches is unusual.

Clothes

A raincoat with a zip-out lining is a good investment for an Oct-Apr visit, as are collapsible rubber boots and a waterproof hat. The winds that accompany rain often turn umbrellas inside-out. High settings of interior heating and air conditioning mean that layering of clothes is advisable.

New Yorkers have grown less formal in dress in recent years. Men feel most comfortable with a jacket at medium-priced and luxury restaurants, but a tie is mandatory at relatively few establishments. Pants may be worn by women at all but a handful of the same places. Denim clothing is sometimes barred by smarter discos and clubs.

General Delivery

A letter marked 'General Delivery,' addressed to a specific post office, will be held there until collected. Identification is usually required when you collect your mail and a fee may be charged. Some commercial firms also provide this service for their customers. The following are centrally located: **American Express** (*150 E 42nd St., New York, New York, NY 10017*), **Central Post Office** (*42 8th Ave., New York, NY 10001*), **Thomas Cook** (*18 E 48th St. New York, NY 10017*).

Getting around

From the airport to the city

Express Carey buses depart Kennedy (1hr ride) and LaGuardia (30min ride) every 20–30min between early morning and midnight, less frequently at other times. All buses stop at East Side Airlines Terminal (1st Ave. and 37th St.). LaGuardia buses also stop near Grand Central Terminal. On weekdays (11am-6pm) Carey buses provide a free shuttle service from the terminal to certain midtown hotels and to the Port Authority Bus Terminal.

Buses from Newark (45min ride) go to the Port Authority Bus Terminal and also run every 20–30min. Mini Bus Tours operate a half-hourly service (7–10am, 3:30–11pm), and less frequently at other times, directly to selected Manhattan hotels.

Most bus-subway connections into the city are confusing but the relatively new JFK Express subway from Kennedy airport to Manhattan is an exception and takes approximately 1hr. For details ☎330–1234.

Taxis from Kennedy and LaGuardia to destinations within the city are metered. From Newark, however, the fare is twice the meter toll. In all cases bridge and tunnel tolls are extra, and traveling in the rush hour can double the fare and time taken.

Helicopters fly between the three airports and between Kennedy and the heliport near the World Trade Center. Operations are sometimes suspended due to bad weather so keep alternative arrangements in mind.

Private limousines are clean, comfortable and often cost little more than taxis as they charge a flat rate and can be shared. You can arrange in advance to have one waiting for you (see *Other transport p11*).

Cars can be rented at all airports. (See *Renting a car p10*.)

Public transport

Subways and buses are often dirty, noisy, defaced by graffiti and subject to unexplained delays, as New Yorkers bitterly declaim. They do however operate 24hr a day with reduced frequency between midnight and 6am, and some are air-conditioned. A single fare lets you journey for as far as you like along any one line. Peak rush hours, to be avoided if possible, are 8–9am and 5–6pm.

For information on subways and buses ☎330–1234. Free maps are available at most token booths.

Subways

The system began as three privately owned lines that went pretty much where they wished. They are still known unofficially as the IRT, (running from N to S on the E and W sides of Manhattan), IND (running along 6th and 8th Aves.), and BMT (running roughly from lower Manhattan to Brooklyn and Queens).

To use the subway, buy a token at the booth near the entrance. Free transfers can be made at 25 intersections with other lines. In order to get on the right train going in the right direction, first note whether you must go uptown, downtown or crosstown, and whether your final station is a local or express stop (*Map 14–15*).

Insert the token into the turnstile, then follow directional signs to the correct platform. Once there, look for signs to indicate whether express and local trains stop on the same or on opposite sides of the platform. The front and sides of a train have signs indicating the route number, whether the train is express or local, and the last station on the route.

Buses

Upon boarding, deposit a subway token or the equivalent in coins in the box next to the driver. He cannot give change, but can sell 'Add-a-ride' transfers to intersecting lines. Routes roughly follow the major N-S avenues (*Map 16*). E-W cross town routes serve as connections between subway lines, which are primarily N-S.

'Culture Bus Loops' stop at major attractions in Manhattan and downtown Brooklyn, at 20–30min intervals on weekends and most holidays. The inclusive fare permits passengers to embark and disembark repeatedly. Descriptive pamphlets are available on the bus.

Taxis

Licensed taxis are painted yellow and, in most cases, have electronic digital meters. They can be hailed anywhere if the sign on the roof is illuminated or can be found in ranks outside major hotels. Drivers are required to take passengers to any destination in the city. Within the five boroughs there is a set

rate for the first ninth of a mile and for every additional ninth.
Bridge and tunnel tolls are extra. If you are going to an unusual
destination it is wise to give the full address and the nearest
cross street – orientation examinations of the drivers are lax and
some drivers speak little English. Tip 20% of total fare.

For lost articles ☎ 825–0416.

Getting around by car

Using a car in the city borders on irrationality. Street parking is
often nonexistent and garage parking is very expensive. One
alternative is to drive to a municipal garage (8th Ave. and W
52nd St.; Leonard St. at Lafayette St.; Delancey St. at Essex
St.; Park Row and Pearl St.; or Washington St. and Greenwich
Ave.) and then use public transport. Most large hotels have
garages, but these are often expensive and a fee may be charged
every time a car is taken out and returned. If you must bring a
car to New York, at least try to confine its use to evenings after
9pm and weekends, or to touring the countryside. When
parking, do not exceed the time limit in a metered parking
space, or your car could be towed away to a pound.

Most cross-streets and many avenues are one-way, the
direction alternating from one street or avenue to the next. In
New York City, unlike the rest of the state, right turns are not
permitted at red traffic lights unless stated. Speeds are sign-
posted, usually 35mph (55mph in New York State) or less.

For further details, contact the American Automobile
Association, or seek advice from your own automobile club.

Renting a car

Car rental agencies are located at airline terminals and at offices
throughout the city. See also Yellow Pages under *Automobile
Renting and Leasing*. Most vehicles are equipped with radios
and air conditioning at no extra charge. A credit card can be
presented in lieu of a deposit, in which case the driver may be as
young as 18. Otherwise, a cash deposit is required, and the
driver must be over 21. Rent-it-here-leave-it-there, weekend
and unlimited-mileage packages are also available.

Getting around on foot

The best, and most colorful, way to cover short distances in
Manhattan is on foot. Above 14th St., it is difficult to lose your
way. Streets are laid out in a straight grid. Named and
numbered avenues run N-S, from 1st Ave. in the E to 11th Ave.
in the W. Cross streets run E–W from 14th St. in the S to 225th
St. in the N. 5th Ave. is the dividing line between E and W.
Building numbers mount from one to the mid-hundreds to the
E, and in the same way to the W. On the avenues, numbers
increase as they proceed N. Because the avenues and Broadway
are so long, the nearest cross street is often mentioned when
asking for a main avenue address. Avenue of the Americas is
always spoken of as 6th Ave., although the grander name is still
used for addresses.

The Manhattan grid is not perfect, of course. Broadway cuts
diagonally across the island from Park Ave. and 14th St. to the
W of Central Park. Below 14th St., in the older part of the city,
the grid goes awry. Down there a map is essential.

Railway services

Both long-distance and commuter trains arrive at Grand
Central Terminal (Park Ave. and 42nd St.) and Pennsylvania

(Penn) Station (7th Ave. and 32nd St.). The Harlem, Hudson and New Haven commuter lines feed into Grand Central from up to 100 miles N, while the Long Island and New Jersey commuter lines use Penn Station.

Amtrak trains from Canada, Boston, Chicago, Washington, Florida and intermediate points use both terminals.

Amtrak ☎ 736–3967 (Metroliners), ☎ 736–4545 (all others)
Conrail (commuter) ☎ 532–4900 (upstate NY), ☎ 736–6000 (New Jersey)
MTA (commuter) ☎ 532–4900 (Westchester County and Connecticut)

Domestic airlines

Domestic flights leave and arrive at all three airports. The Eastern Airlines' shuttle to Washington and Boston has a separate terminal at LaGuardia. This service has hourly flights (more or less) throughout the day and early evening. Reservations are not required and tickets are paid for on board. New York Air runs a similar shuttle, with lower fares. PEOPLExpress operates cheap flights from Newark to the East Coast and Mid-West.

Air Canada 600 Madison Ave. ☎ 935–4141
American 405 Lexington Ave. ☎ 557–1234
Delta 1 Pennsylvania Plaza ☎ 868–2300
Eastern 10 Rockefeller Plaza ☎ 397–4610
New York Air LaGuardia Airport ☎ 565–1100
Northwest 537 5th Ave. ☎ 594–0320
Pan Am 200 Park Ave. ☎ 880–1234
PEOPLExpress Newark Airport ☎ 772–0344
Piedmont 1290 Ave. of the Americas ☎ 765–7088
Republic 630 5th Ave. ☎ 489–0784
TWA 2 Pennsylvania Plaza ☎ 695–6000
United 1221 Ave. of the Americas ☎ 764–2800
US Air 535 5th Ave. ☎ 736–3200

For further information contact *The Central Airlines Ticket Office* 100 E 42nd St. ☎ 986–0888.

Ferry services

America's favorite boat ride – the Staten Island Ferry – is still the biggest bargain in town, serving up spectacular views and bracing breezes. It departs from the Whitehall St. pier at downtown Battery Park every 20–30min, 24 hours a day, seven days a week. The Ellis Island Ferry sails from the Battery four times daily, Apr-Oct. The price of the ride includes a guided tour of the museum. The Statue of Liberty ferry also leaves from Battery Park.

Other transport

Hourly rates for private limousines are high, but there are special airport and theater-dinner flat rates that can total little more than taxi fares.
Among the reputable firms:
Alex Limousines 500 E 77th St. ☎ 535–5553
Cooper Rolls-Royce 132 Perry St. ☎ 929–0094
Dav-El 219 W 77th St. ☎ 580–6500
London Towncars 40–14 23rd St. (Long Island City) ☎ 988–9700
Manhattan Limousine 13–05 43rd Ave. (Long Island City) ☎786–0800
Villela Limousine 30 E 40th St. ☎ 225–5227

Basic information

Rent a rowboat or bicycle at the 72nd St. boathouse in Central Park. Bicycles and mopeds can be hired from the following:

Metro Bicycles 1311 Lexington Ave. (88th St.) ☎ 427–4450
6th Ave. Bicycles 546 Ave. of the Americas (15th St.) ☎ 255–5100
Stuyvesant Bicycle 349 W 14th St. ☎ 254–5200
West Side Bicycle 231 W 96th St. ☎ 663–7531

Rides in horse-drawn hansom cabs begin from near the 5th Ave. and 59th St. corner of Central Park, day or night. Most rides take 30min. Establish the rate in advance.

On-the-spot information

Public holidays

Jan 1; President's Day, celebrated on a three-day weekend in mid-Feb; Memorial Day, a three-day weekend at the end of May; Independence Day, July 4; Labor Day, first Mon in Sept; Columbus Day, second Mon in Oct; Election Day, first Tues in Nov; Veterans Day, Nov 11; Thanksgiving, last Thurs in Nov; Dec 25.

As in the rest of the country, shops, schools, banks, post offices and most public services are usually closed on these days, although some shops stay open on the three-day weekends.

A number of other special days are observed with religious services, parades, gift-giving, or other celebrations. These include: Chinese New Year, Jan/Feb; St. Patrick's Day, Mar 17; Easter and Passover, Apr; Mother's Day, May; Martin Luther King Memorial Day, May; Puerto Rican Day, June; Rosh Hashanah, Sept; Halloween, Oct 31; Hanukah, Dec.

Time zones

New York is in the US Eastern Time Zone, 1hr ahead of Central Time Zone, 2hr ahead of Mountain Time Zone and 3hr ahead of Pacific Time Zone. All zones abiding by Daylight Saving Time put their clocks forward one hour Apr-Oct to take advantage of extra daylight.

Banks

Customary business hours for banks are 9am-3pm, Mon-Fri; some close at 4pm and some are open on Thurs evenings or Sat mornings. Travelers cheques can be cashed at all banks.

Shopping hours

Department stores, clothes and sports equipment shops usually open between 9-10am and close at 6pm. Late night shopping is on Mon and Thurs, usually until 9pm. Although many fast-food stands, coffee shops and delicatessens open by 8am and don't close until 10pm or later, more formal restaurants confine themselves to noon-3pm and 6-11pm, with slight variations. Bars and discos do not have to close until 4am. In sections of the city where merchants are predominantly Jewish, stores often close on Sat and open on Sun. In Greenwich Village and SoHo, you may find that boutiques and galleries do not get going until noon.

Rush hours

Driving or using public transport between 8-9am and 5-6pm

could be considered an exercise in masochism, and the situation is almost as bad for an hour before and after these times. Avoiding lunch between noon and 2pm is canny, as is making dinner reservations before 7:30pm or after 8:30pm.

Post and telephone services

Post offices are open 8am-5pm Mon-Fri, 8am-noon Sat. The main post office at 8th Ave. and 33rd St. is open 24hr.

Telephones are everywhere. Try to use those in shops or public buildings – the ones installed on street corners are often out of order. All New York City is in area code 212. Local calls need only their seven-digit number. When calling an out-of-town number, dial 1, then the area code, and finally the seven-digit number. Direct dialing to all US numbers and many foreign countries is available, but these are best made from hotel rooms, considering the amount of coins required for a pay phone. Remember, however, that hotels typically add surcharges. Cheap rates apply after 5pm and on weekends.

Telegrams are fast disappearing as a means of communication. Money can still be wired from one Western Union office to another, though, and a mailgram might arrive sooner than a letter. ☎ 797–3311 for ITT, the primary international cable service.

Public rest rooms

These are to be avoided at all times in subway stations. Those in museums and public buildings are usually satisfactory. In extremis, duck into the nearest hotel.

Tipping

In restaurants tip the waiter at least 15% of the check before tax; 20% is more usual in luxury establishments or if the service warrants. An easy way to compute the minimum is to double the 8% sales tax. Some restaurants have taken to adding a service charge, so don't tip twice. Bellmen, doormen and chambermaids should be tipped, too. Rest room attendants should be given something, to be left on the conspicuous plate. When there is a stated fee for checking coats and parcels that is sufficient. Otherwise give half a dollar per item. Tour guides expect a dollar or two.

Disabled travelers

Federal regulations have brought about some improvements in access to most places. Many rest rooms provide special facilities for the disabled and certain buses are equipped with motorized platforms. Most hotels have specially converted rooms. Subways offer reduced fares for disabled passengers but are nearly impossible to negotiate without help. Seeing-eye dogs are permitted everywhere. For further details contact *Rehabilitation International USA*, 20 W 40th St., NY 10018 or obtain *Access New York* from New York University Medical Center, 400 E 34th St., NY 10016.

Local publications

Special arts and leisure sections appear Fri and Sun in the *New York Times* and in the weekly magazines *New York* and *The New Yorker*. They provide useful reviews and listings of current plays, concerts, films, exhibitions, ballets and operas; *The New York Times* includes ticket availability. *The Village Voice* and *SoHo News* are weeklies emphasizing the offbeat arts and presentations. *The Daily News* and *New York Post* have expansive sports coverage.

Basic information

Useful addresses

Tourist information

NY Convention and Visitors Bureau 2 Columbus Circle
☎ 397–8222
Times Square Information Center Broadway (42nd St.)
☎ 221–9869

Main post offices

8th Ave. (33rd St.)
Lexington Ave. (45th St.)

Telephone services

Daily events ☎ 976–2323
Free daily cultural events ☎ 755–4100
International calls – dial operator
Sportsphone ☎ 976–1313 or ☎ 976–2525
Telephone information ☎ 555–1212
Time ☎ 976–1616
Traffic report (during rush hours) ☎ 976–2323

Tour operators

Circle Line Pier 83, foot of W 43rd St. ☎ 563–3200. 3-hr boat
cruises around Manhattan. Apr-Nov: Eight sailings weekdays,
ten on Sat and Sun – to be recommended.
Crossroads Sightseeing 900 8th Ave. (47th St.) ☎ 581–2828.
Several motorcoach tours.
Gray Line 900 8th Ave. (54th St.) ☎ 397–2600. Long-
established company offering ten half-day bus tours.
Greenwich Village Walking Tours ☎ 226–1426. 2½-hr guided
tours on foot.
Island Helicopters. Heliport at foot of E 34th St. ☎ 895–5374.
5–45min flights, daily. Expensive, but worth it.
Manhattan Sightseeing Bus Tours 150 W 49th St. ☎ 245–6641.
Several tours of varying length and coverage.
New York Big Apple Tours 162 W 56th St. ☎ 582–6339. Over a
dozen bus tours.
Penny Sightseeing Company 303 W 42nd St. ☎ 247–2860.
Short Line 168 W 46th St. ☎ 246–5550.

Major places of worship

Baptist Calvary Baptist, 123 W 57th St.
Catholic St Patrick's Cathedral, 5th Ave. (51st St.)
Episcopal St Thomas' Church, 1 W 53rd St. (Entrance on 5th
Ave.)
Jewish Temple Emanu-El, 5th Ave. (65th St.)
Lutheran Holy Trinity, Central Park West (65th St.)
Methodist Lexington United Methodist Church, 150 E 62nd St.
Presbyterian Presbyterian Church, 5th Ave. (55th St.)

Libraries

American Bible Society 1865 Broadway ☎ 581–7400
Donnell Library Center 20 W 53rd St. ☎ 790–6463
Library for the Blind and Physically Handicapped 166 Ave. of the
Americas ☎ 925–1011
Lincoln Center Library (music, theater) 11 Amsterdam Ave. ☎
799–2200
Mercantile Library (contemporary books) 17 E 47th St. ☎
755–6710
New York Public Library 5th Ave. (42nd St.) ☎ 790–6262.
Schomburg Center (research in black studies) 103 W 135th St. ☎
862–4000

Emergency information

Emergency services

Police
Ambulance } ☎ 911 (10¢ needed from a phone booth)
Fire

Hospitals with emergency rooms

Ambulances called on 911 carry the patient to the nearest municipal hospital. Private hospitals are preferable, however, so if possible take a taxi to one of these: *Financial District*, Beekman Downtown Hosp., 170 William St. ☎ 233–5300. *Greenwich Village*, St. Vincent's Hosp., 7th Ave. (11th St.) ☎ 790–7000. *Lower East Side*, Bellevue Hosp., 1st Ave (29th St.) ☎ 561–4141. *Midtown East*, New York University Med. Center, 1st Ave. (30th St.) ☎ 674–3200. *Midtown West*, Roosevelt Hosp., 9th Ave. (58th St.) ☎ 554–7000. *Upper East Side*, New York Hosp., York Ave. (70th St.) ☎ 472–5454. *Upper East Side and East Harlem*, Flower-Fifth Ave. Hosp., 5th Ave. (103rd St.) ☎ 860–8000. *West Harlem*, Columbia Presbyterian Med. Center, 622 W 168th St. ☎ 694–2500.

Other emergencies

Doctors Emergency Service ☎ 328–1000
Dentists Emergency Service ☎ 679–3966 (9am-8pm)
                              ☎ 679–4172 (8pm-9am)

Late-night drugstores (pharmacies)

Kaufman 557 Lexington Ave. (50th St.) ☎ 755–2266
Manhattan Garden 1632 Broadway (W 50th St.)
☎ 265–3546

Help lines

Crime Victim Hotline ☎ 577–7777
Help line (personal counseling) ☎ 481–1070
Rape Help Line ☎ 233–3000
Suicide Prevention League ☎ 736–6191/6192/6193.
Travelers Aid Society ☎ 679–0200

Automobile accidents

– Call the police immediately
– If car is rented, call number in rental agreement
– Do not admit liability or incriminate yourself
– Ask witnesses to stay and give statements
– Exchange names, addresses, car details, insurance companies and three-digit insurance company codes
– Remain to give your statement to the police

Car breakdowns

Call one of the following from nearest telephone.
– Number indicated in car rental agreement
– Local office of AAA (if you are a member)
– Nearest garage or towing service.

Lost travelers cheques

Contact police immediately, then issuing bank or company, giving serial numbers and identification. Travelers cheque refund information numbers:
American Express ☎ 248–4584
Barclays ☎ 233–1511
Thomas Cook ☎ 754–2868

Introduction

New York is not America. A world city – *the* world city, by any reasonable measure – it cannot be contained within geopolitical boundaries. Every language is spoken in New York, every cuisine prepared, every nation and race represented, every dream conjured, every depredation performed. If an idea, an object, a hope, a taste, a scent, a sin cannot be found here, the likely conclusion is that it does not exist. The only emotion New York cannot arouse is indifference. No other place created by man provokes such adoration and abhorrence, often at the same time, in the same individual. Few words applied to this city can be dismissed as hyperbole. It is an entity of exhilarating, numbing, horrifying, glorious excess.

Ethnic diversity

Although among the greatest of cities, it can no longer claim to be the largest. New York covers nearly 300 square miles and has a population of over 7,000,000 people. A recent census recorded 4,293,695 whites, 1,784,124 blacks, 11,824 Native Americans, 231,505 Asians, and an astonishing 749,882 regarded as racially unclassifiable.

The largest ethnic minority is probably that of Hispanic origin, but there is no ethnic majority. People of Italian, Irish and East European origins are present in enormously influential numbers. Germans and other North Europeans were among the earliest immigrants and were quickly assimilated. Puerto Ricans and others of Caribbean background continue as largely unified groups, as do the Chinese. Refugees from Southeast Asia, Haiti, Central America, Greece and the Indian subcontinent are becoming increasingly apparent.

City of villages

Water-girt New York comprises five distinct divisions called boroughs, only one of which – The Bronx – is situated on the North American continent. The island of Manhattan is, of course, the central borough. Brooklyn (largest in population) and Queens (largest in area) take up the western tip of Long Island, which itself stretches 125 miles into the Atlantic. Staten Island, to the S of its sisters, snuggles up to New Jersey.

When approached from the E through the outlying industrial dross, the famous Manhattan skyline appears somehow diminutive. At the southern tip of the island, the concrete spires and glass slabs of the Financial District are dominated by the twin pillars of the World Trade Center. The profile then dips to the lower heights of converted warehouses ('loft' buildings) and tenements, lifting gradually once more to midtown and the peak of the instantly recognizable Empire State Building. After another two miles, the skyline dips again, nearly meeting the rising ground that continues for another six miles, terminating at the lip of the inky tidal course known as the Spuyten Duyvil.

Once you plunge into the street canyons, warring stimuli battle for attention: the noise of the traffic seems trapped between the high walls of buildings. From time to time, clouds of steam billow from manholes as if from an inferno just below. Rivers of people press forward on apparently urgent tasks. Traffic jerks and clogs along congested arteries. All the senses are staggered and continue to be bombarded even when the newcomer has begun to adapt to the pace.

But there are quiet places, too. Side streets end in shaded

cul-de-sacs, more than 50 museums muffle the clamor beyond their walls, and there are nearly 37,000 acres of parks. The most important of these is Central Park, in the heart of Manhattan. Two Monacos could be contained within its borders, with room left over for a chunk of Nice.

A brief history

The broad protected harbor was first discovered in 1524, but permanent settlement did not take place until a century later. The English took New Amsterdam from the Dutch in 1664, and the city was renamed New York. Resentment against British rule culminated in the War of Independence in 1775, and New York was for a time the capital of the infant nation.

The population was then slightly over 30,000. It multiplied dramatically with the mass immigrations of the 19thC, and those who prospered moved uptown. In the 40 years following the Civil War (1861–65), Central Park was finished and the first skyscrapers erected. In 1898, the four outer boroughs were annexed to Manhattan, instantly fashioning the largest city in the world. The population was then over 3 million.

Despite the Wall Street Crash of 1929, construction of the Empire State Building began. Twenty years later, the city's population reached 8 million, and the United Nations moved into its new headquarters on the East River. The city was at its zenith – the capital of the world, untouched by war.

Since then there has been a gradual decline, evidenced by fiscal crises, deteriorating public services, accelerating crime rates and loss of industry and workers. But signs of recovery are visible. Tourism continues to grow, as Americans and foreigners alike rediscover New York. And while the demise of Broadway has been proclaimed with tedious regularity since the Depression and The Talkies, it continues to flourish. New York remains the center for those intent on careers in publishing, finance, advertising, ballet, opera and the visual arts.

Safety first

To avoid a visit to New York on the basis of out-of-proportion stories of crime is akin to denying oneself Naples because of garbage in the streets. Still, prudence is in order. After dark, for example, women and older people are wise to travel in groups or with escorts. Although the odds are that a nightly walk across the nearest park or along deserted streets would be uneventful, there is no reason to tempt fate. Expensive-looking jewelry and clothing should be avoided when traveling by foot. Grip handbags firmly and keep wallets in a safe place. When in the subways at night, ride in the crowded central cars.

New Yorkers

The reputation New Yorkers have earned for rudeness and pugnacity is not without foundation. Yet beneath their often brusque exterior lies an enviable openness to new experiences and relationships. There is no fad, art form, lifestyle or ideology that they will not sample, or at least tolerate. Outside of working hours – and, in a 24hr city, that means any time – they can be seen jogging, cycling, flipping Frisbees, roller or ice-skating, dancing in nightclubs, demonstrating at the UN, taking the sun on Hudson River piers or watching it set from Riverside Park. Of all the surprises of a first visit to this city, one of the most agreeable can be the New Yorkers themselves.

17

Time chart

1524	Italian explorer Giovanni da Verrazano discovered New York Bay while searching for a NW passage.
1609	Henry Hudson sailed his *Half Moon* up the river that was eventually given his name.
1623	New Netherland became a province of the Dutch West India Company and the cluster of huts at the S tip of Manhattan was called New Amsterdam.
1626	Provincial Director-General Peter Minuit bought the island from the Algonquin Indians.
1643	Population grew to about 500 people speaking 18 different languages. During the tenure of Governor Peter Stuyvesant, settlements were established in the areas eventually known as The Bronx, Queens, Brooklyn and Staten Island.
1664	The Duke of York sent a fleet into the harbor. Abandoned by the burgomasters who chafed under his authoritarian rule, Stuyvesant surrendered the city to the English. It was renamed New York.
1674	After extended hostilities between the English and Dutch – and one brief reoccupation by the Dutch – the city and province were ceded by treaty to the English.
1689	A German merchant, Jacob Leisler, led a revolt against oligarchic trade monopolies when he learned of the overthrow of James II. He was hanged for treason.
1712	Slaves now constituted a substantial segment of the population. Despite ordinances denying them weapons and the right of assembly, a number of blacks set fire to a building near Maiden Lane and killed nine whites who attempted to stop the blaze. When soldiers arrived, six of the blacks committed suicide; 21 others were captured and executed.
1725	The New York *Gazette* was founded.
1734	John Peter Zenger, publisher of the *New York Weekly Journal*, was charged with libel of the Government. He was acquitted in the first test of the principle of freedom of the press in the colonies.
1754 –63	Population now 16,000. King's College founded. Benjamin Franklin proposed union of the colonies for common defence during the French and Indian War, but was rejected. A force led by George Washington was defeated by the French at Fort Necessity in Pennsylvania. The conflict, part of the worldwide Seven Years War, ended with the Treaty of Paris. English sovereignty over most of explored North America was thereby conceded.
1764 –70	Colonial grumbling over British rule escalated into sporadic demonstrations and protests with the passage of the punitive Sugar, Stamp, and Colonial Currency Acts. The Quartering Act permitted British troops to requisition private dwellings and inns, their rent to be paid by the colonies. At the Stamp Act Congress held in Manhattan, delegates of nine colonies passed a Declaration of Rights and Liberties. Skirmishes between soldiers and the insurrectionist Sons of Liberty culminated in January 1770 in the killing of a colonial and the wounding of several others. The Boston Massacre, in which British troops fired upon taunting protesters, occurred seven weeks later.

1775 The American Revolution. The Continental Congress
−83 appointed Washington Commander-in-Chief and, on
July 4, 1776, adopted the Declaration of Independence.
After early battles ranging from Manhattan to Long
Island, most of which he lost, Washington withdrew.
New York was occupied by the British for the remainder
of the war. With the Treaty of Versailles in September
1783, the British troops left the city.

1789 Washington was sworn in as first President at Federal
Hall in New York, the first capital of the Federal
Government.

1790 An official census recorded the population at 33,000.

1807 Robert Fulton made a round trip from New York to
−09 Albany in his steamboat *Clermont*. In reaction to British
and French seizure of American ships at sea, Congress
prohibited export of most goods. This Act did more
harm to New York and New England agriculture and
commerce than to the other side, and was repealed.

1812 War declared against Britain. New York blockaded.

1814 Peace treaty signed at Ghent.

1825 Erie Canal opened, enhancing New York's role as a port.

1832 New York and Harlem railway completed.

1830 The influx of immigrants – largely German and Irish –
−60 rose to flood proportions. Epidemics of yellow fever and
cholera ensued, exacerbated by poor water supplies,
insanitary conditions and the poverty of most of the
newcomers. Yet on the eve of the Civil War, the
population neared 750,000.

1861 Civil War, caused by growing differences between
−65 northern and southern states, notably the slavery issue.
New York on the side of the Union (N) against the
Confederates (S).

1863 Draft Riots, following a conscription law that permitted
the rich to buy deferment. New Yorkers set fire to
buildings and looted shops and homes. Over 1,000 died.

1868 The first waves of Italian and East European immigrants
−98 arrived, many of them working on the new elevated
railway, Brooklyn Bridge and early skyscrapers. The
Statue of Liberty, a Franco-American project, was
inaugurated in 1886. At the culmination of a period of
annexation and expansion, New York assumed its
present boundaries. There were now more than
3 million inhabitants.

1900 Immigration continued unabated, despite growing
−29 pressure for its curtailment. The railway system was
extended, now underground as well as above. The
decade after World War I brought Prohibition, women's
suffrage, economic prosperity, and a Federal Act
cutting immigration (1924).

1929 The Wall Street Crash and the start of the Great
−39 Depression. The worst of the Depression was over by
1936, but it did not end until 1939 when the country
began to prepare for war.

1941 Apart from rationing, blackouts and shortages, New
−45 York was not greatly affected by World War II. It grew
more prosperous, as did the rest of the country.

1948 Idlewild Airport opened in Queens (renamed Kennedy
in 1963).

1952 United Nations headquarters complex opened.

1973 World Trade Center opened.

19

Culture, history and background

Architecture

Were the existing 18thC structures of New York grouped
together, they would constitute a sizeable and quite handsome
village. As it is, they are scattered throughout the city, largely
neglected survivors of the Great Fires of 1776 and 1835.
Most are Georgian Colonial or Federal, corresponding to the
style prevalent in England during the successive reigns of the
four Georges.

Although Georgian was itself imitative of Classical Greco-
Roman themes, the first half of the 19thC saw a heightened
enthusiasm for Greek and Gothic Revival. These overlapping
modes dominated from 1830–55, manifest in the Athenian
'temple' that is the Federal Hall National Memorial (1842), and
that homage to medieval workmanship, Trinity Church (1846).
In the increasingly popular terraced town houses, Greek
Revival was largely confined to decorative facades.

After the Civil War, an unabashed exuberance for virtually
all European styles took hold. Motifs ranging from Venetian
Renaissance to French Second Empire to Tudor to

◀ **St Paul's Chapel (1766)** The only
Colonial church left in New York.
Interior is noted for its fluted Corinthian
columns and Palladian window.

**Morris-Jumel Mansion
(1768)** Georgian Colonial, remodeled
in Federal style in 1810. Tuscan-
columned portico and wooden quoins are
typical Federal features.

Trinity Church (1846) A landmark at
the end of Wall Street, Richard Upjohn's
church is the city's best-known example of
Gothic Revivalism.

**Federal Hall National Memorial
(1842)** This Neo-Greek temple is
perhaps the purest example of Greek
Revival architecture in New York.

20

Romanesque were used, not infrequently all on the same building. The result was often called 'Kitchen Sink', for obvious reasons. The fashionable architectural firm of the time was McKim, Mead and White, whose fondness for the Italian Renaissance is best seen in the Villard Houses (1886).

Technology was prompting fresh looks at old design assumptions. The Brooklyn Bridge (1883) employed Gothic granite towers, but also spidery cables of woven steel. The invention of the hydraulic elevator and the presence of a sturdy bedrock, known as Manhattan schist, made skyscrapers possible. By 1900, commercial buildings of 20 floors and higher were routine.

The row house persisted as the favored residential mode, however, now embellished with Italianate carving around arched doors and pediments. Red sandstone, widely used as a facing material, gave this style the name of brownstone. Blocks of brownstones remain throughout Manhattan and Brooklyn, lending a Parisian flavor to their neighborhoods. Luxury high-rise apartment buildings made their appearance with the Chelsea and the Dakota in 1884, but they were resisted

Washington Square North (c. 1832) Ionic porticos reflect the mid-19thC rage for Greek Revivalism.

Villard Houses (1886) Now incorporated into the Palace Hotel, a complex of six houses inspired by the Palazzo della Cancelleria in Rome.

Flatiron Building (1902) The revolutionary steel frame is disguised by rusticated stone facades.

Metropolitan Museum of Art (1902) Rich, Neo-Classical decoration typical of the Beaux Arts movement.

21

Culture, history and background

by the wealthy for decades. The turn of the century brought a flirtation with the voluptuous Beaux Arts style and related neo-chateau fancies, best seen in the Metropolitan Museum of Art (1902).

Meanwhile commercial architecture was entering the Modernist phase with the form-follows-function theories of Louis Sullivan. His work in Chicago proved to his successors that tall structures need not simulate stacked neo-Georgian or Romanesque tiers. The next major influence was Art Deco, applied to spectacular effect in the steel-arched tower of the Chrysler Building (1930). With the Empire State Building (1931) and RCA Building (1932), the Chrysler represents the apogee of the first phase of the skyscraper phenomenon.

Further developments were delayed until economic recovery in the late 1940s. A technique was developed in which walls of glass without a weight-bearing function were literally hung on the sides of steel skeletons. Among the first and most enduring realizations of this International Style were Lever House (1952) and the Seagram Building (1958).

More recently, sculptural planes and masses have shaped both small and large buildings, such as the Whitney Museum (1966) and the Waterside Houses (1974). The latest, Post-Modernist trend shows a revival in decorative interest.

Chrysler Building (1930) The world's tallest building until overtaken by the Empire State in 1931.

Whitney Museum (1966) A return to sculptural solidity.

Lever House (1952) One of the earliest glass-and-steel curtain wall constructions.

AT & T Building (1978–82) The Chippendale cornice shows a Post-Modernist trend.

The arts in New York

Creativity found a foothold as soon as the city emerged from the early settlement period. The first theater opened its doors on Maiden Lane in 1732, to be followed by dozens more. But New York was chiefly a commercial center, and artists who achieved prominence – painters Benjamin West and John Singleton Copley, for example – went off to Europe, setting a pattern that was to prevail for nearly two centuries.

Impressionism and other 'isms' that reverberated around Europe in the later 19thC had little influence across the Atlantic. The esthetic ferment did not spill over to the United States until the New York Armory Show of 1913, when Duchamp's *Nude Descending a Staircase* scandalized public opinion. By then, however, most of the men who were to form the first generation of post-World War II Radical Abstractionists were already alive. Encouraged by such artist-teachers as Hans Hofmann, who fled the gathering European tragedy in the 1930s, these artists champed under the restraints of the Depression and War, exploding after 1945 into what seemed to be a movement already mature at the instant of birth.

The controlled 'splash-and-dribble' canvases of Jackson Pollock were no less shocking than the earlier Cubist fantasies which now seemed sedate by comparison. Pollock died young, but compatriots Robert Motherwell, Clyfford Still, Mark Rothko, Willem de Kooning, Philip Guston, James Brooks, Jack Tworkov, Franz Kline and Sam Francis all contributed to the importance of the movement. All were associated with the city, and together they became known as the New York School. They gathered in the same bars, summered on Long Island, and inspired a new row of galleries along E 10th St. It was a zesty era, enhanced not inhibited by its coexistence with the conformist Eisenhower-McCarthy period.

Art, like life, should be free, since both are experimental.
George Santayana

New York, which had long regarded itself as an oasis on the edge of a cultural wasteland, was the natural wellspring of what proved to be a surge to international pre-eminence in the arts. As the only major city to emerge unscathed from the global conflict, it could indulge its artists with almost unlimited support. The Guggenheim Museum, Frank Lloyd Wright's only commission in the city, was intended to serve as a repository for modern painting and sculpture. It was completed in 1959. The Lincoln Center for the Performing Arts was conceived in 1955 to house the Metropolitan Opera, the Philharmonic Orchestra, the City Opera and Ballet companies, a repertory theatre, a concert hall for small classical and popular groups, and the Juilliard School for actors, musicians and dancers. The five principal buildings were finished between 1962 and 1966. Additions to the Metropolitan Museum and the Museum of Modern Art, and the erection of a new home for the Whitney, maintained the pace.

During the last decade, creative endeavour in the visual arts has been highly experimental: Conceptual, Minimal, Neo-Constructivist, Optical – all executed in wildly mixed media: neon, ferro-concrete, forged metal, shaped canvas, boxes and heaps of earth ... The descendants of Pollock are as unrestrained and every bit as provocative.

Culture, history and background

Guide to the galleries

In this vibrant and ever-changing playground of creativity, gallery-hopping is not surprisingly a cherished pastime among culture-conscious New Yorkers. Although the galleries are in the business of selling works of art, browsers are welcome. All galleries are open Tues–Sat, a few on Mon as well, usually from 10am–5 or 6pm. Summer is the slow season, with various closing periods, often July or Aug, or both. The galleries cluster in three distinct areas, 57th St., Madison Ave. and SoHo, and each of these can be explored easily on foot. A walking tour is, in fact, the most practical way to get to know them.

57th St.
Start at Park Ave. and walk w on the s side of 57th St.

Brooks Jackson Gallery Iolas
52 E 57th St. ☎ *755–6778*
Modern European and American paintings and sculpture.

Washburn Gallery
42 E 57th St. ☎ *753–0546*
Eclectic selection of American photographs, paintings, prints, drawings and sculpture of the last 100yr.

Multiples/Marian Goodman Gallery
38 E 57th St. ☎ *755–3520*
Reproductions and unusual contemporary pieces.

Gruenebaum Gallery
38 E 57th St. ☎ *838–8245*
Sculptures, collages, paintings, mostly by living Americans.

Pace Gallery
32 E 57th St. ☎ *421–3292*
Influential representative of luminaries Louise Nevelson, Jim Dine, Piet Mondrian. Non-objective to Photo Realist.

Dorsky Galleries
4 W 57th St. ☎ *489–1020*
Contemporary paintings, graphics, drawings, sculptures.

Gallery Denise Rene
6 W 57th St. ☎ *765–1330*
Closely associated with colorist Constructivist Victor Vasarely. Other Europeans and Latin Americans of that inclination.

Sidney Janis Gallery
6 W 57th St. ☎ *586–0110*
Superstars of American Abstract Expressionism, as well as their Modernist European forefathers.

Brooke Alexander
20 W 57th St. ☎ *757–3721*
American painters since 1960.

Kornblee Gallery
20 W 57th St. ☎ *586–1178*
Living American and British painters and sculptors.

Betty Parsons Gallery
24 W 57th St. ☎ *247–7480*
Potent force in cause of abstract art, international in scope.

Alonzo Gallery
30 W 57th St. ☎ *586–2500*
Contemporary American paintings, sculptures, drawings.

Kennedy Galleries
40 W 57th St. ☎ *541–9600*
American graphics and figurative paintings of last three centuries.

Marlborough Gallery
40 W 57th St. ☎ *541–4900*
19th and 20thC works of many styles and media.

Terry Dintenfass
50 W 57th St. ☎ *581–2268*
Recent representational work.

Allan Frumkin Gallery
50 W 57th St. ☎ *757–6655*
Active New York and California figurative artists.

Kathryn Markel Fine Arts
50 W 57th St. ☎ *581–1909*
Contemporary drawings and graphics.

Getler-Pall Master Prints
50 W 57th St. ☎ *581–2724*
Contemporary American drawings and graphics.

Cross to the N side of 57th St. and walk E.

Arras Gallery
29 W 57th St. ☎ *421–1177*
Multimedia works by Europeans and Americans.

Tibor de Nagy Gallery
29 W 57th St. ☎ 421–3780
Non-objective, representational paintings, sculpture.

Rosa Esman Gallery
29 W 57th St. ☎ 421–9490
Experimental young Americans.

Fischbach Gallery
29 W 57th St. ☎ 759–2345
Primarily American painters of the last 25yr.

Marilyn Pearl Gallery
29 W 57th St. ☎ 838–6310
New salon for avant-gardists.

A.M. Sachs Gallery
29 W 57th St. ☎ 421–8686
Established and lesser-known Americans.

Zabriskie Gallery
29 W 57th St. ☎ 832–9034
Sculpture and photography of postwar period.

Midtown Galleries
11 E 57th St. ☎ 758–1900
Frequent group shows of traditionalist Americans.

Wally Findlay Galleries
17 E 57th St. ☎ 421–5390
One of the chain focussing on French Impressionists, contemporary European and American.

Andre Zarre Gallery
41 E 57th St. ☎ 752–0498
Current Americans, geometric and colorist idioms.

Andrew Crispo
41 E 57th St. ☎ 758–9190
Large-scale paintings and constructions, smaller oils and watercolors, mostly by Americans.

Andre Emmerich Gallery
41 E 57th St. ☎ 752–0124
Early supporter of Abstract Expressionists and those who followed. Large format pieces at SoHo branch.

Marisa del Re Gallery
41 E 57th St. ☎ 688–1843
Abstractionists.

Pierre Matisse Gallery
41 E 57th St. ☎ 355–6269
International artists of 20thC, including Chagall and Giacometti. Owner is the son of Henri.

Witkin Gallery
41 E 57th St. ☎ 355–1461
Historical and contemporary photography.

Hammer Galleries
51 E 57th St. ☎ 644–4400
Impressionists, Post-Impressionists, 19th and 20thC American.

Madison Ave.

Many of these galleries are on cross streets, but near Madison. From 59th St., walk N on the w side of Madison. Return to the Ave. after each short detour, continuing N.

Frank Rehn Gallery
14 E 60th St. ☎ 753–4694
American Realists.

Wildenstein & Company
19 E 64th St. ☎ 879–0500
17th to 20thC paintings, sculpture, antique furniture.

Davis & Long Company
746 Madison Ave. ☎ 861–2811
Three centuries of English and American paintings, drawings.

Christopher Gallery
766 Madison Ave. ☎ 737–3224
Naïve and Realist paintings.

ACA Galleries
21 E 67th St. ☎ 628–2440
Every major American school, from early Realists to Abstract Expressionists.

Babcock Galleries
20 E 67th St. ☎ 535–9353
American paintings of the last 100yr.

Helios Arts
18 E 67th St. ☎ 988–5593
Vintage photography, supplemented by postwar prints.

Hirschl & Adler Galleries
21 E 70th St. ☎ 535–8810
Three centuries of English and American masters.

M. Knoedler & Company
19 E 70th St. ☎ 794–0550
Old masters; vanguardists such as Motherwell.

Monique Knowlton Gallery
19 E 71st St. ☎ 749–9700
Assemblage, painted sculpture.

Culture, history and background

Lerner-Heller
956 Madison Ave. ☎ 861–9010
Contemporary canvasses of marked social comment.

Blum Helman Gallery
13 E 75th St. ☎ 861–7780
Abstract Expressionism onwards.

Cordier & Ekstrom
980 Madison Ave. ☎ 988–8857
On the fifth floor of the former Sotheby Parke Bernet building. International contemporary art.

David Findlay
984 Madison Ave. ☎ 249–2909
American and European works of the last two centuries.

Lee Ault & Company
25 E 77th St. ☎ 861–2317
Includes Latin American works, African sculpture.

Castelli Graphics
4 E 77th St. ☎ 288–3202
Prints by artists represented at SoHo sister gallery.

Aberbach Fine Art
988 Madison Ave. ☎ 988–1100
Paintings with a Surrealist emphasis.

Weintraub Gallery
992 Madison Ave. ☎ 879–1195
Europeans of early Modernist schools.

F. Rolin & Company
1000 Madison Ave.
☎ 879–0077
Primitive art from Asia, Africa and the Americas.

Paul Rosenberg & Company
20 E 79th St. ☎ 472–1134
Primarily painters of the French School.

Acquavella Galleries
18 E 79th St. ☎ 734–6300
Chagall, Braque, Cézanne, Degas. Also Lichtenstein, Motherwell, Frankenthaler.

Graham Gallery
1014 Madison Ave.
☎ 535–5767
American Realists and illustrators prior to 1940.

Perls Galleries
1016 Madison Ave.
☎ 472–3200
Picasso, Rouault, Utrillo and their colleagues.

Grace Borgenicht Gallery
1018 Madison Ave.
☎ 535–8040
Influential in promotion of the New York School and recent movements.

Brewster Gallery
1018 Madison Ave.
☎ 472–9481
Miró, Chagall, Braque, Calder graphics.

Saidenberg Gallery
1018 Madison Ave.
☎ 288–3387
Focus on Picasso, but many examples of important Europeans and Americans of his time.

Gimpel & Weitzenhoffer Gallery
1040 Madison Ave.
☎ 628–1897
Abstract Expressionist paintings and sculpture, current prints.

Carus Gallery
1044 Madison Ave.
☎ 879–4660
Bauhaus, Constructivists, Russian Modernists.

FAR Gallery
22 E 80th St. ☎ 734–7287
Representational American painters and sculptors.

La Boetie
9 E 82nd St. ☎ 535–4865
Expressionists, Dadaists, Surrealists.

Cross Madison Ave.

Coe Kerr Gallery
49 E 82nd St. ☎ 628–1340
American Realists, with examples of Hudson River School.

Return to Madison and turn s on e side.

Robert Elkon Gallery
1063 Madison Ave.
☎ 535–3940
Favors non-objective styles, but not exclusively.

Sid Deutsch Gallery
43 E 80th St. ☎ 861–4429
All manner of quality 20thC work – no discernible preferences.

Serge Sabarsky Gallery
987 Madison Ave. ☎ 628–6281
Scholarly presentations of German and Austrian Expressionism.

Lefebre Gallery
47 E 77th St. ☎ 744–3340
Postwar European paintings and prints, some sculpture.

Staempfli Gallery
47 E 77th St. ☎ 535–1919
Contemporary European, North and South American art.

Xavier Fourcade
36 E 75th St. ☎ 535–3980
Eclectic modern collection.

Ronald Feldman Fine Arts
33 E 74th St. ☎ 249–4050
Experimental works and events that defy classification.

Robert Schoelkopf Gallery
825 Madison Ave. ☎ 879–4638
Abstractionists to Realists.

Marcuse Pfeifer Gallery
825 Madison Ave. ☎ 737–2055
Photography from the Civil War to the present.

SoHo

The artists exhibited here work without ideological labels. Except as noted, anticipate the unimaginable. Walk s on w Broadway from Houston St.

Buecker & Harpsichords
465 W Broadway ☎ 260–3480
Vorpal Gallery
465 W Broadway ☎ 777–3939
Westbroadway Gallery
431 W Broadway ☎ 966–2520
Nancy Hoffman
429 W Broadway ☎ 966–6676
John Weber Gallery
420 W Broadway ☎ 966–6115
Andre Emmerich Gallery
420 W Broadway ☎ 431–4550
Leo Castelli Gallery
420 W Broadway ☎ 431–5160
Mary Boone
420 W Broadway ☎ 966–2114
Sonnabend Gallery
420 W Broadway ☎ 966–6160
Edward Thorp
419 W Broadway ☎ 431–6880
Elise Meyer
410 W Broadway ☎ 925–3527
Heiner Friederich
393 W Broadway ☎ 925–9380
Holly Solomon
392 W Broadway ☎ 925–1900
John Gibson Gallery
392 W Broadway ☎ 966–9808
Susan Caldwell
383 W Broadway ☎ 966–6500
O.K. Harris
383 W Broadway ☎ 431–3600
Cayman Gallery
381 W Broadway ☎ 966–6699
Hispanic films and concerts as well as paintings.
Chuck Levitan Gallery
42 Grand St. ☎ 966–2782

Return to Broome St. and turn E.

Frank Marino Gallery
489 Broome St. ☎ 431–7888
Leslie-Lohman
485 Broome St. ☎ 966–7173
The Kitchen
484 Broome St. ☎ 925–3615
Landmark Gallery
469 Broome St. ☎ 966–1173

Numeroff Gallery
451 Broome St. ☎ 925–2894
Folk art.
Women in the Arts
435 Broome St. ☎ 966–5894

Return to Greene St. and turn N.

Makers Gallery
124 Spring St. (Greene St.)
☎ 966–7224
Crafts in all media.
Pinder Gallery
127 Greene St. ☎ 533–4881
Women's cooperative.
Green Mountain
135 Greene St. ☎ 674–2390
Representational work.
The Drawing Center
137 Greene St. ☎ 892–5266
Max Hutchinson Gallery
138 Greene St. ☎ 966–3066
Sculpture Now
142 Greene St. ☎ 966–3066
Same ownership as Max Hutchinson Gallery (above).
Sperone Westwater Fischer
142 Greene St. ☎ 431–3685

Turn w into Houston St., then s into Wooster St.

Paula Cooper Gallery
155 Wooster St. ☎ 677–4390
Pleiades Gallery
152 Wooster St. ☎ 475–9658

Turn w into Prince St.

Prince Street Gallery
106 Prince St. ☎ 226–9153
Ward-Nasse
131 Prince St. ☎ 475–9125
Jack Gallery
138 Prince St. ☎ 966–4235
Louis K. Meisel
141 Prince St. ☎ 677–1340
Alexander F. Milliken
141 Prince St. ☎ 674–3131

Orientation map

Major places of interest

1 American Museum of Immigration
2 American Museum of Natural History
3 Audubon Terrace
4 Bronx Zoo and New York Botanical Garden
5 Carnegie Hall
6 Cathedral Church of St John the Divine
7 Chrysler Building
8 City Hall
9 Cloisters
10 Cooper-Hewitt Museum
11 Empire State Building
12 Federal Hall National Memorial
13 Flatiron Building
14 Fraunces Tavern Museum
15 Frick Collection
16 Guggenheim Museum
17 Hall of Fame for Great Americans
18 Lincoln Center
19 Madison Square Garden
20 Metropolitan Museum of Art
21 Morris-Jumel Mansion
22 Museum of Modern Art
23 New York Public Library
24 Pan Am Building
25 Pierpont Morgan Library
26 Rockefeller Center
27 St Patrick's Cathedral
28 South Street Seaport Museum
29 Statue of Liberty
30 Trinity Church
31 Union Square
32 United Nations Headquarters
33 Washington Square
34 Whitney Museum of American Art
35 Woolworth Building
36 World Trade Center

US Highway

Interstate Highway

State Highway

Spuyten
Duyvil

ood
Pk.

nwood
9

Ft. Tryon
Pk.

17

ashington
ights

Bronx Park

4

Bronx River Parkway

BRONX

Major Deegan Expressway

Cross Bronx Expressway

Harlem River

Bruckner Expressway

Sound View
Park

Ferry Point
Park

East River

Bronx –
Whitestone Br.

Randalls
Is.

Triborough Br.

ards Is.

Rikers Is.

LaGuardia
Airport

Grand Central Parkway

Astoria Blvd.

Van Wyck Expressway

Northern Blvd.

QUEENS

Queens Blvd.

arry S. Truman Expressway

Interborough Parkway

to J. F. Kennedy
International Airport

1		2		3 miles
1	2	3	4	5 km

Calendar of events

See also *Public holidays* in *Basic information* and *Sports and activities* for further information.

January

Mid-Jan for two weeks. Boat Show. New York Coliseum, Columbus Circle. Same motives and same lavish display as the Auto Show, but the subject is pleasure craft, both power and sail

Between mid-Jan and early Feb. Chinese New Year. Chinatown, lower Manhattan. Ten days of fireworks and celebrations feature silk lions and a fearsome dragon that snakes and dances along Mott St. to frighten evil spirits ☎ 267–5780 for details

Late Jan for one week. Auto Show. New York Coliseum, Columbus Circle. A vast glittery exhibition of foreign and American-made cars: antique, classic, custom and brand new

Late Jan. Winter Antiques Show. 7th Regiment Armory, Park Ave. and E 67th St. This exhibition of superior antiques is also an excuse to see the grand interiors by Stanford White and Louis Comfort Tiffany, usually closed to the public

February

Feb 12–22. Lincoln and Washington Birthday Sales. Department stores. On the days around these national holidays the large stores mount enormous sales

Mid-Feb. Westminster Dog Show. Madison Square Garden, 7th Ave. and 33rd St. Two days of intense competition

Mid-Feb for one week. National Antiques Show. Madison Square Garden, 8th Ave. and 32nd St. Perhaps the largest show of antiques and related objects in the world ☎ 564–4400 for dates

Late Feb. Lantern Day. Chinatown and City Hall, lower Manhattan. On the night of the fifteenth day of the Chinese New Year, children form a parade to present paper lanterns to the Mayor. There are martial arts demonstrations, dancing and singing ☎ 267–5780 for details

March

For Easter events, see *April*

St Patrick's Day, Mar 17. St Patrick's Day Parade. 5th Ave. from 44th St. to 86th St. All New Yorkers are Irishmen on this day. Beer is green, clothing is green, even the line down the middle of 5th Ave. is green. Irish taverns and St Patrick's Cathedral are the centers of activity

Usually around Mar 25. Greek Independence Day Parade. 5th Ave. above 59th St. Less universal than St Patrick's Day, the growing Greek population nevertheless provides a substantial parade each year, with floats and bands

Late Mar for two months. Ringling Brothers and Barnum & Bailey Circus. Madison Square Garden, 7th Ave. and 33rd St. A small parade of elephants and wagons heralds the opening

April

Two weeks preceding Easter. Easter Egg Exhibition. Ukrainian Museum, 2nd Ave. (12th St.). A specially mounted display of hand-painted eggs, a staple of this small museum ☎ 228–0110 for details

Week before Easter. Easter Flower Show. Macy's Department Store, Herald Sq. The nation's largest department store blooms on several floors

Week before Easter. Easter Lilies Display. Channel Gardens, Rockefeller Center

Easter Sunday. Easter Parade. 5th Ave., from 49th St. to 59th St. Not an organized parade at all, but a promenade of celebrants showing off their new spring finery, some of it extraordinary

May

Weekend in mid-May. Ninth Avenue International Festival. 9th Ave. from 36th St. to 59th St. Once known as 'Paddy's Market', this stretch of 9th Ave. specializes in prosaic and exotic foods – an annual gustatory orgy of *kielbasa*, quiche, *falafel*, *knishes*, *tacos*, Belgian waffles, *zeppoli*, *baklava*, *souvlaki* and every fast food conceived by man. Crafts, merchandise and entertainment

May 18. Martin Luther King Jr. Memorial Parade. 5th Ave. above 59th St.

Last weekend in May. Memorial Day Weekend. Official opening of city beaches; antiques show at 7th Regiment Armory; women's 10,000 meter L'Eggs Marathon

Late May–early June. Washington Square Outdoor Art

Exhibition. Washington Sq. and adjacent streets. Artists, amateur and otherwise, fill walls and fences with watercolors (landscapes, tigers on velvet, sedate nudes), metalwork, tooled leather and wire jewelry. Everything is for sale and bargaining is expected. The event is repeated in early Sept

June

Early June–late Aug. Summer Festival. Parks and plazas throughout the city. Leading groups and companies perform outdoors, in Central Park, at the Rockefeller Center, in the Sculpture Garden of the Museum of Modern Art, at the South Street Seaport Museum and at the World Trade Center. Music and other cultural events, many of them free. There is dance, Shakespeare, opera, jazz, pop and folk music ☎ 755–4100 for a daily recorded announcement

Sun in early June. Puerto Rican Day Parade. 5th Ave. above 59th St. Colorful, well-attended, sprightly celebration associated with the patron saint of the Puerto Rican capital, San Juan

Early June for one week. Festival of St Anthony. Little Italy, lower Manhattan. Sullivan St. below Houston St. has lines of booths selling games of chance, sizzling sausages, *calzone*, pizza and flavored ices. Religious observances dominate during the day, secular entertainments take over after dusk. Go hungry, for the aromas are irresistible

Early June. Rose Day Weekend. New York Botanical Garden, The Bronx. Stunning demonstration of the horticulturist's craft, with tours and lectures

Mid-June. Salute to Israel Parade. 5th Ave. above 59th St.

Late June–early July. Kool Jazz Festival. Concert halls and outdoor locations around Manhattan. Jazz in all its permutations, from Dixieland to atonal, takes over from midday to midnight. Some events are free. Check newspapers for details

July

July 4th (Independence Day) *Festivities*
Battery Park, lower Manhattan. Old New York Harbor Festival takes place in the afternoon and evening, with patriotic ceremonies, food, music and performers.
Richmondtown Restoration,

Staten Island. Celebrations matching the Colonial and Federalist ambience.
Riverside Park, West Side Manhattan. This is the best vantage point for the spectacular fireworks over the Hudson River, sponsored by Macy's department store. The display starts around 9:30pm, but check newspapers.
South Street Seaport Museum, lower Manhattan. Tall ships and sailing vessels from other nations and ports often visit. Street festival has music, crafts and food

July–Aug. Summer Festival. Snug Harbor Cultural Center, Staten Island. Music and art exhibitions at weekends throughout the summer

Mid-July through Aug. Mostly Mozart Festival. Lincoln Center, West Side Manhattan. This treasured event commences with a free outdoor concert, then proceeds through the rest of the summer indoors, primarily in Avery Fisher Hall. Ticket prices are unusually low ☎ 874–2424 for details

Jul–Aug. Washington Square Music Festival. Washington Square Park, Greenwich Village. Chamber music by the fountain on Tues evenings ☎ 473–8321

Late July to mid-Aug. New York Philharmonic Parks Concerts. Various park locations in all boroughs. The famed symphony orchestra performs beneath the stars, for free ☎ 755–4100 for details

August

Mid-Aug to early Sept. Lincoln Center Out-of-Doors. Lincoln Center, West Side Manhattan. Free live entertainment on the plaza from noon to sunset ☎ 877–1800 for details

September

Early Sept for two weeks. Washington Square Outdoor Art Exhibition. Washington Sq. and adjacent streets. A duplicate of the spring event (see *May*).
Sun in mid-Sept. 'New York is Book Country' Street Fair. 5th Ave. from 47th St. to 57th St. and adjacent blocks.
Mid-Sept. Steuben Day Parade. 5th Ave. from 59th St. to Yorkville. Exuberant small-scale commemoration of the German officer who aided the Revolutionary cause

Late Sept for 11 nights. *Festa di San Gennaro*. Little Italy, lower

Manhattan. Blocks of gaming and eating booths tempt with the possibility of sudden modest riches and the certainty of excessive calorie consumption. It is becoming an increasingly inter-cultural event, Sicilian sausages being augmented by Cantonese egg rolls

Sun in late Sept. Atlantic Avenue Antic. Southern edge of Brooklyn Heights. This predominantly Syrian neighborhood asserts its individuality with displays of crafts, foods, and Middle Eastern dancing ☎783–4469 for details

Mid-Sept to early Oct. New York Film Festival. Alice Tully Hall, Lincoln Center. Serious film buffs revel in three weeks of afternoon and evening showings, with no need of questionable awards and overheated publicity

October

On or about Oct 5. Pulaski Day Parade. 5th Ave. The Polish community takes its turn

On or about Oct 12. Columbus Day Parade. 5th Ave. Second only to the St Patrick's Day Parade in intensity and numbers, and along the same route

Early Oct for one week. National Arts and Antiquities Festival. 7th Regiment Armory, Park Ave. and 67th St.

3rd Sun in Oct. Old Home Day. Richmondtown Restoration, Staten Island. Crafts demonstrations, dancing and entertainment in this re-created old-time village

Last Sun in Oct. New York City Marathon. From Staten Island to Central Park. Not the oldest, but the biggest marathon, with nearly 16,000 runners following a route from the w end of the Verrazano Narrows Bridge through all five boroughs

Oct 31, late afternoon. Halloween Parade. Greenwich Village, lower Manhattan. Villagers in outlandish costumes wind through the streets of their district, with ghoulish happenings along the route and a party at Washington Sq.

November

Early Nov for six days. National Horse Show. Madison Square Garden. Equestrian competition of jumping and dressage

Last Thurs in Nov. Macy's Thanksgiving Day Parade. Broadway, 77th St. to 34th St.

Traditional 3hr morning event with bands, celebrities and huge helium-filled balloons in the shapes of Kermit the Frog, Snoopy, Superman and Mickey Mouse, among others

Nov 26 – Jan 6. Star of Wonder Show. Hayden Planetarium. The night sky of Bethlehem is vividly reproduced with music and commentary ☎873–8828

Thanksgiving to New Year's Day. Lord & Taylor Christmas Windows. 424 5th Ave. (39th St.). All the big stores vie with each other in Christmas decorations, but this one is the perennial champion, managing to outdo itself every year

December

Late afternoon in early Dec. Rockefeller Center Tree-Lighting Ceremony. 5th Ave. between 50th St. and 51st St. The huge tree rising above the ice-skating rink and the gilded statue of *Prometheus* is illuminated by dignitaries and celebrities to the accompaniment of Christmas carols. Extravagantly decorated trees are also set up in the American Museum of Natural History and the Metropolitan Museum of Art

First Sun in Dec. Christmas in Richmondtown. Richmondtown Restoration, Staten Island. Period Christmas celebration in the restored village, complete with costumed guides ☎351–1611

First night of Chanukah. Lighting of Chanukah Candles. City Hall, lower Manhattan. 92nd St. YM-YWHA, 1395 Lexington Ave.

Dec. Nutcracker Ballet. Lincoln Center. Traditional performance by the New York City Ballet ☎879–5500 for details

The two Suns before Christmas, 11.00–15.00. Fifth Avenue Holiday Mall. 5th Ave., 34th St. to 57th St. The Ave. is closed to traffic, and public entertainments draw shoppers past sublime and gaudy windows

Dec 31. New Year's Eve. All over the city. A 'Big Apple' slides down a flagpole above Times Sq., reaching the bottom at the first second of the New Year to the cheers of thousands of witnesses. Cars sound their horns, boats in the harbor blow their whistles, and celebrants kiss each other in the ballrooms of dozens of hotels. There is also a 5-mile run in Central Park, commencing at midnight, accompanied by fireworks

When and where to go

Before the 1960s, the conventional advice was to avoid New York in its relentlessly humid summer. Probably for that reason, the theater and concert season did not begin until Oct, when most of the new plays opened. That is still one of the best months to visit, when the gathering energy of the city is palpable. But the widespread adoption of air conditioning in the last two decades now makes July bearable, and major new musicals and dramas hold their premieres throughout the year. While affluent New Yorkers still flee to summer cottages by the sea or in the New England hills, there is never that impression of an abandoned city given by, say, Paris in Aug. Some of the de luxe restaurants lock up for two or three weeks, but most remain open for business, as do the museums and landmark buildings. Concerted efforts under the 'New York is a Summer Festival' rubric have brought about a full schedule of established cultural events, as a glance at the *Calendar of events* on the previous pages reveals. Many of these events feature front-rank performing groups at little or no cost – which is decidedly not the case from Oct – May. There is a marked shirt-sleeve looseness among New Yorkers during these hot months, a departure from their inclination towards dressy formality during the rest of the year. Visitors devoted to art should avoid July and Aug, when most galleries are closed.

Apr and May, Sept and Oct are the best months in terms of weather. For that reason, hotels are heavily booked at those times. Demand slackens in Jan and Feb, but although there will be some bone-chilling days, winters are usually not too severe and snowfalls of more than four inches are rare.

Those intent on a shopping holiday will encounter large crowds and frayed tempers in the weeks between Thanksgiving and Christmas. The biggest sales are in Jan and Feb. Sports enthusiasts find that the seasons of the eight major professional teams overlap in early autumn. Allowing for these few caveats, little will be missed no matter what time of year is chosen.

New York is an island city, with four of its five administrative units, called boroughs, separated by water from the North American continent. They are linked with each other and the mainland by 65 bridges and 19 tunnels. Every likely tourist destination is within reach of the extensive public transportation system – by subway, bus, or a combination of the two. Many out-of-town locations can be reached by rail or bus as well, although a car is often preferable.

At the spiritual and geographical center is Manhattan. Even residents of the other boroughs refer to it as "The City," a reality made official by the Postal Service: all addresses in Manhattan are 'New York, NY,' while the others are designated Brooklyn, Queens, The Bronx and Staten Island. Nearly all visitors stay in Manhattan. The major hotels are there, as are about 15,000 restaurants and most of the theaters, concert halls, art galleries, landmarks, corporation headquarters, libraries, universities and best-known churches and department stores.

The outer boroughs, although largely residential and industrial, are by no means bereft, however. The Bronx has its Zoo and Yankee Stadium; Queens has Shea Stadium and the Aqueduct Racetrack; Brooklyn has its beaches and a fine museum; and Staten Island has a Tibetan temple and two complexes of restored architectural treasures.

Area planners

Manhattan

Manhattan is 12 miles along its N–S axis and about 3 miles across at its widest point. The roll of history and fashion flows northward, for development started with a Dutch settlement at the S tip and spread in the only direction available.

Financial District (Map 2U4). This neighborhood long ago assumed the role evident in its present name, and now bristles with concrete and glass monuments to capitalism, among which are a few public buildings surviving from the late Colonial and early Federalist periods. They constitute a captivating history lesson enhanced by vistas of New York's rivers and harbor. Despite the frenetic business activity, however, there is only one hotel of consequence and few first-class restaurants.

Chinatown and Little Italy (Map 2–3S-T4–5). In the Financial District, when space began to run out, corporation rulers transferred their building mania to midtown. In doing so, they leapfrogged a band of small residential communities, former villages that still cling to very specific identities. While neither Chinatown, S of Canal St., nor Little Italy, a block or two to the N, are postcard-pretty, their ethnic vitality persists.

Lower East Side (Map 3R5). This lies to the E, and historically was the first landfall of impoverished immigrants. A dreary area of rubbish-filled streets and sagging tenements – then and now – its only touristic significance is the frenetic Sunday shopping along Orchard St., when startling bargains in high-style apparel can be plucked from heaps of used and poorly made clothing and shoes.

SoHo and TriBeCa (Map 2S4). In the 1960s, the warehouses and lofts of SoHo were 'discovered' by artists seeking larger spaces at lower rents. Inevitably, they drew gallery owners and restaurateurs, until boutiques and stockbrokers began to supplant the painters and sculptors. So the artists moved on to nearby TriBeCa, where a similar transformation is under way.

Greenwich Village (Map 2R4). This area also knows the cycle well. After a time as an upper-middle-class suburb, it too became an artist's enclave. Experimental theaters, art galleries and the new Bohemia flourished here in the early 20thC, and many of the theaters remain. Rows of fine brownstones and carriage-house mews alternate with tacky commercial streets, and the restaurants of SoHo and Greenwich Village blanket the entire field of price and achievement.

Chelsea, Gramercy Park and Murray Hill (Map 4–5P4,Q3–4). North of 14th St., the planned gridwork of streets and avenues takes hold. On the W is Chelsea, at an early stage of gentrification, as growing numbers of antique shops and trendy bars and eateries show. East of Park Ave. and N of 42nd St. are the contiguous neighborhoods of Gramercy Park and Murray Hill, where pockets of 19thC elegance persist. Several quiet and relatively small hotels provide alternatives to the flashy behemoths farther N and the restaurants and nightspots give fair value without sacrifice of elbow room.

The Midtown district, from 42nd St. to 59th St. and Hudson River to East River, and particularly *Midtown East (Map 5)* contains a disproportionate share of the attractions for which New York is known. Most of the major hotels, theaters, shops and world-class restaurants are within its elastic boundaries, as well as the *United Nations Headquarters*, Times Square, *Rockefeller Center, St Patrick's Cathedral*, the *Museum of*

Modern Art, Grand Central Terminal, and dozens of examples of New York's most renowned contribution to architecture, the skyscraper. The pace is swifter here, crowds thicker, rooms and meals more costly, aggravations greater.

By comparison, the Upper *East Side* is relatively tranquil. Along 5th Ave., its western border, are most of the major museums of art and history, dominated by the *Metropolitan Museum of Art*. Mingled with the private townhouses of the side blocks are eclectic galleries and shops; and toward the East River, upwardly mobile young married couples and single people, who favor the postwar highrises, keep the many pubs and discos filled to the walls.

Upper West Side (Map 6J – K2 – 3). This is an area in transition. It is not as sleek as the Upper East Side, and has some concentrations of low income families, but is enjoyed by professionals who find the area and its people less superficial. The *Lincoln Center* for the Performing Arts and the *American Museum of Natural History* are the centerpieces. Between the Upper East and Upper West Side is *Central Park*.

Harlem (Map 8 – 9H3 – 4). The area stretches river to river immediately to the N of these two neighborhoods. Despite its substandard housing, poverty and attendant ills, it boasts a number of important cultural institutions, especially the four specialized museums of *Audubon Terrace*.

The high, narrow neck of land at the NW corner of Manhattan Island has the sanctuary of *Fort Tryon Park* and a remarkable assemblage of medieval chapels and gardens from European monasteries known as *The Cloisters*.

Even in combination, the other four boroughs cannot match this panoply, though each has its charms nevertheless.

The Bronx

The only borough on the mainland. A full day can be profitably spent at the *Bronx Zoo and New York Botanical Garden*, with a side trip to the *Van Cortlandt Mansion and Museum*.

Brooklyn

Had it resisted annexation in 1898, Brooklyn would now be the fourth largest city in the United States. It is still self-contained, with its own civic and cultural centers, concert halls, downtown shopping district, beaches, colleges, and residential neighborhoods both elite and prosaic. Among its inducements are the *Brooklyn Museum*, *New York Aquarium*, *Brooklyn Heights* and the promenade that overlooks an extraordinary panorama of the Manhattan skyline from the *Statue of Liberty* to the *Empire State Building*.

Queens

This borough has both LaGuardia and JFK airports. Sports fans take the subway to the Aqueduct Racetrack for Thoroughbred racing, and to Shea Stadium for Jets football and Mets baseball games. (See *Sports and activities*.)

Staten Island

Despite the 1964 *Verrazano Narrows Bridge*, which connects it with Brooklyn, Staten Island remains somewhat isolated from the other boroughs. Those who take the time to look around, however, will discover pockets of bucolic solitude, notably: *Richmondtown Restoration*, a village of Colonial and 19thC homes and shops; *Snug Harbor Cultural Center*, a living museum of buildings in every 19thC style; the re-created temple that is the *Tibetan Museum*; and the small but remarkable *Staten Island Zoo*.

35

Walks in New York

Many parts of Manhattan, and Brooklyn Heights across the East River, have a surprisingly intimate character, which can be best appreciated on foot. The following walks serve as samples.

Walk 1/An introduction to New York

Tourists and natives alike find themselves passing through the *Rockefeller Center* and its immediate surroundings repeatedly. They come for the shopping along 5th Ave., the views from atop the *RCA Building*, Radio City Music Hall, the city's tallest Christmas tree, and the Easter Parade.

Begin at the **Channel Garden** entrance on the W side of 5th Ave. between 49th St. and 50th St., perhaps after a visit to *St Patrick's Cathedral*, one block N. The Channel Garden, with, appropriately, **La Maison Française** on the S and the **British Empire Building** on the N, has long, raised flower beds, where the plantings are changed with seasons. At the end of this walkway, a golden statue of *Prometheus* hovers above a sunken rectangular plaza that is an outdoor cafe from Apr–Sept and an ice-skating rink from Oct–Mar.

Circle around, glancing up at the narrow limestone slab that is the RCA Building with Art Deco details over and around the high portals. Inside, heroic murals in sepia tones depict muscular workers striding across walls and ceilings. Take the elevator, across the lobby, to the **observation deck** for what many believe is the best viewpoint in Manhattan – more central and less lofty than the *Empire State Building* or *World Trade Center*. Depending on the time of day, a drink in the lounge of the Rainbow Room might then be welcome. Afterward descend to the subterranean concourse, one floor beneath ground level. A village of small shops thrives down there, along arcades that connect buildings from 6th Ave. to 5th Ave., and from 48th St. to 53rd St.

Return to Rockefeller Plaza at the front of the RCA Building and turn right, S, then right again, W, onto 48th St. The amiable mock-Dublin pub **Charlie O's Bar & Grill**, at no. 33, is a good place to stop for a hamburger or a platter of oysters. Continue W to Ave. of the Americas (known to all as 6th Ave.). The wall of intimidating skyscrapers on the opposite side is technically part of the Rockefeller Center, although the buildings were erected in the 1960s. Cross the avenue and walk down one level at the base of the McGraw Hill Building. The fast-paced multi-media production called the *New York Experience* is there, with performances on the hour from late morning to early evening. Return to 6th Ave. and walk N. Sidewalk vendors with food preparation carts line this route in all seasons. If they tempt, take your snack to the marble bench around the fountain in front of the **Time-Life Building** at the corner of 6th Ave. and 50th St. Opposite is the **Radio City Music Hall**. For 50yr it featured big Hollywood 'family' films interspersed with stage shows that focused on the precision dance troupe known as The Rockettes. Business fell off in the 1970s and the hall nearly closed, but was saved by a new policy of special events, rock and pop concerts, and limited-run revues. The ornate vaulted interior must be seen to be believed.

Tickets for guided tours of Rockefeller Center may be purchased at the RCA Building. They leave about every 30min, Mon–Sat 9:30am–5:30pm, and include the observation deck and a backstage look at the Music Hall.

Walk 2/Financial District

From the day the first Dutch settlers crept into hastily constructed bark shelters, the foremost business of New York was commerce. Gradually merchants became financiers, ever more distant from the commodities they bartered, and as ever greater space was needed to contain the people who administered the system, so the present thicket of skyscrapers emerged, a 20thC metropolis built within the limits of a 17thC street plan.

By 1850 few people actually lived below Chambers St. and the *Brooklyn Bridge*, the approximate northern border of what was 'Little Old New York' and is now the *Financial District*. From Mon–Fri 8am–6pm the streets teemed with millions of workers, then at dusk and on weekends the dark canyons heard only the sigh of winds and the rustle of blown refuse. That is less true today, for New Yorkers are starting to move back, and restaurateurs and retailers are following close behind them. So whether a Fri or a Sat is chosen to look around depends on the tastes of the visitor. Most buildings of note are open both days, but most eating places lock up as soon as the last commuter has downed his Martini and headed for home.

A walking tour logically begins with the observation deck of the south tower of the *World Trade Center*, the easiest structure to find in New York City. Exit on to Liberty St. Turn left, to the E, then right, S, on Broadway. Three blocks down is *Trinity Church*. The Gothic Revival third version (1846) of a 1696 original, it stands out from its towering neighbors by virtue of a layer of city grime so black it glistens. After a stroll through the surrounding graveyard, continue S on Broadway to *Bowling Green*. Directly beyond that undistinguished patch of lawn is the **Custom House**, usually cited as one of the city's best examples of the florid Beaux Arts style popular at the turn of the century. The four sculptures in front are by Daniel Chester

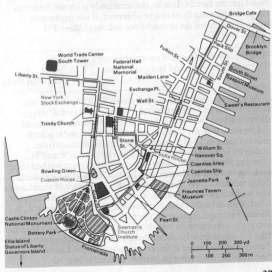

French. They represent the continents of Africa, America, Asia and Europe.

Turn right, SW, into *Battery Park*, following the main path to the semicircular *Castle Clinton National Monument*. An 1807 fortress that never fired on an enemy ship, it served instead as a concert and exposition hall, an immigrant processing center and an aquarium. After a look, walk to the promenade at the water's edge for a panorama that includes *Ellis Island*, the *Statue of Liberty*, **Governors Island** (a military base) and, to the E, *Brooklyn Heights*. Passing the Statue of Liberty ferry dock, turn inland, keeping the park on the left. At the mounted cannon, look across State St. The **Georgian-Federal mansion**, at no. 7, with its inset columned porch, is the last of a row of such homes that once bordered this avenue. Farther along is the **Seaman's Church Institute**, a refuge for retired sailors. The public is welcome to use its cafeteria and tour the collections of nautical memorabilia. Cross over to it, afterward continuing E along bordering Pearl St. In two short blocks, at the corner of Broad St., is the *Fraunces Tavern Museum*, a recreation of a Colonial Georgian residence. It has a museum of Revolutionary War artifacts upstairs, a pleasant restaurant down. Breakfast is the best meal served, but there is also afternoon tea. Proceed along Pearl St. The next corner is Coenties Slip, so named because it was once a docking bay for merchant ships. Long since filled in, it now has Jeanette Park, contributed by the builders of the office building on the N side. Turn left, W, into Coenties Alley, which connects with narrow Stone St., the first paved pathway in the Dutch colony, and ends in Hanover Sq. To the right is the 1854 **India House**, Italian Renaissance in style, built to serve the merchant princes that were its earlier occupants. It is now a private club, but members of the public are welcome to use the restaurant. Turn left, curving N along William St., then left, to the W, into Exchange Pl. Turning right, N, into Broad St., watch for the **New York Stock Exchange**, no. 8, on the left. It's readily identified by the Neo-Grecian facade. Inside, the seemingly inchoate frenzy in the pit of the main floor can be observed, if not necessarily understood, from the second-floor balcony (*Mon – Fri 10am – 4pm* 📷).

Where Jews and Gentiles most are wont
To throng for trade and last quotations.

E.C. Stedman, *Pan in Wall Street*

At the next corner, glance left down Wall St., its concrete canyon framing Trinity Church. The Greek Revival 'temple' directly across the street is *Federal Hall National Memorial*.

Continue E down Wall St., named for the wood stockade erected there in 1653 to protect the Dutch colonists from attack by Indians or the British. Turn left, N, on Water St., crossing Maiden Lane, where young women once washed their laundry in a brook. Continue to Fulton St., and walk E along Schermerhorn Row. Built around 1812 as a block of warehouses and now being rehabilitated, it is essentially Federalist in spirit, albeit with subsequent stylistic overlays. Upstairs, at no. 2, is **Sweet's** seafood restaurant, opened in 1842 and, by some accounts, resting on its laurels since 1900. That doesn't stop the files of customers who dutifully line up for lunch on weekdays. Just round the corner is the entrance to **Sloppy Louie's**, a no-frills spot that treats its patrons as cavalierly as its competitors but produces better fish. Sailing vessels of a more romantic era are moored at the piers of the *South Street Seaport Museum* across the way. When the weather is good, there are concerts, puppet shows, street musicians and chairs in which to sit and admire the view of the Brooklyn Bridge.

Leave along the N side of Fulton St. turning right, N, into Water St. A restored stationer's shop is followed by the **Seaport Gallery** with maritime exhibits and helpful maps of the neighborhood. New shops open (and close) frequently with the ongoing development of the area. At the corner with Peck Slip, look toward the river at the amusing *trompe-l'oeil* painting that covers the entire side wall of a brick building, complete with a reproduction of a bridge tower duplicating the real one just beyond. At the end of Water St. is a forerunner of the sprightly new bar-restaurants beginning to spring up in the district, the **Bridge Cafe**.

Walk 3/Civic Center–Chinatown–Little Italy
Contrasts are endemic to New York, sometimes jarring, sometimes poignant. They tumble over each other, person by person, structure by structure; overweening power and grinding need, harsh modernity and mellowed history, optimism and despair, cosmopolitanism and parochialism. This walk is illustrative.

Start at the juncture of Broadway, Park Row and Vesey St., at *St Paul's Chapel*. Completed in 1766, it is the oldest church and public building in Manhattan. Back on Broadway turn left, to the N. Two blocks up is the *Woolworth Building*, the cathedral-like lobby of which deserves a detour.

Cross Broadway to **City Hall Park**, with the approaches to the *Brooklyn Bridge* in the background. Municipal architecture is more often dreary than inspired, but the 1811 *City Hall*, with a handful of nearby government buildings, is exceptional. Its elegant facade faces S, an evocation of the palaces of the Sun King. Pass City Hall on the right, continuing to the NE corner of the park. Across Chambers St. is the marvelously Baroque **Hall of Records**, and to the right is the towering **Municipal Building**. An agglomeration of styles – the hallmark of the McKim, Mead & White firm – it employs a concave facade, a forest of Corinthian columns before a triumphal arch that pierces the base, and 34 stories of statues, carvings and embellishment that owe debts to every European architectural fancy of the last 600yr. Glimpsed through the arch is a monumental steel sculpture that announces the entrance of the aggressively contemporary **Police Headquarters**.

Cross Chambers St., keeping right of the Hall of Records. The street opens into Foley Sq. On the E is an odd structure that can be said to signal the end of the Classical vogue in Federal architecture. Somber, massive and intimidating, the 1936 **United States Courthouse** mocks the often pleasing 'temples' of a century earlier. Pass in front of this exercise in failed monumentality and its adjacent, marginally more graceful sister, the **New York County Courthouse**, still bearing right, then walk E along Worth St. to the small Columbus Park on the opposite side. Cross over and take Park St., angling off Worth St. and bordering the park.

This, it will be instantly apparent, is *Chinatown*. A Cantonese enclave for more than 100yr, it is home to as many as 100,000 Chinese, and spiritual center for ten times as many relatives who have scattered along the East Coast. Evenings and

39

weekends, they all seem to have returned. The musty sterility of the Civic Center is instantly replaced by a barrage of visual and olfactory stimuli (most of them agreeable or at least intriguing).

Stroll across Mulberry St. and turn right into Mott St. where shades of crimson and yellow flare against the dark backdrop of the upper stories of grimy brick. In just these short blocks, window displays and maddening aromas inspire an irresistible urge to eat, but before snatching up the nearest egg roll, enter the *Chinese Museum (8 Mott St.)*. It's upstairs, past the dancing chicken and above the amusement arcade. At the end of Mott St., turn left, E, onto *The Bowery*. At no.6 is **Olliffee's Pharmacy**, the oldest (1803) pharmacy in America, and at no. 18, an Off-Track Betting Parlor (OTB) in a restored house of the Revolutionary War era.

But Chinatown is not about landmarks. First, to eat. That can be bewildering, for there are over 200 restaurants in these few streets. To surmount the language and gastronomic barrier, try a *dim sum* parlour where you will be served a limitless variety of tasty oddments, each nestling in a small dish. Just look and point and eat, as often as required. At the end, the bill is calculated by the number of empty dishes. **Hee Seung Fung** (*46 Bowery, open 7:30am–5pm daily*) is one such place.

Afterward, double back to Pell St. and turn right, W. Tucked between grocery stores and restaurants are shops offering satin shoes, kites, jade, fans, woks, kimonos, medicinal herbs, paper lanterns, embroidered silks, chopsticks, candles, cricket cages and Buddha figurines; often all together. Narrow staircases lead to clubrooms from which can be heard gongs and drums and the clack of mah-jong tiles. Telephone boxes have pagoda roofs, and banners flutter overhead. In the midst of all this, at Pell St. and Mott St., is the Georgian-Gothic *Church of the Transfiguration*. Turn right, N, into Mott St., shortly passing a Buddhist temple on the right.

At Canal St., turn left, W, one block, crossing over, N, at Mulberry St. For many years, Canal St. was an unofficial *cordon sanitaire* between Chinatown and *Little Italy*, but the former community is expanding N and E, the latter shrinking. Little Italy persists, however, despite the advancing age of its remaining inhabitants, still a Neapolitan-Sicilian bubble of trattorias and cafes and scrupulously fervent allegiances to church and family.

As in Chinatown, uptown and suburban relatives stream back for every native celebration and holiday. There, the big one is Chinese New Year (mid-Jan–early Feb); here, the *Festa di San Gennaro* (Sept). Try to be there, for floats, parades, dancing and miles of sizzling sausage and *calzone*. During the rest of the year the preservation of ethnicity is the draw, largely in the matter of food, although neighborhood *ristoranti* are consistently surpassed by Italian eateries in other parts of the city. Nevertheless, fair value is given by **Puglia** (*corner of Hester St. and Mulberry St.*), **Angelo's** (*146 Mulberry St.*), and **Grotta Azzurra** (*corner of Broome St.*). All are open for lunch and dinner, Tues–Sun. After, or instead, turn right, E, along Grand St. for a *cappuccino* and a pastry at **Ferrara's** at no. 195. It has sidewalk tables in summer. Alternatively, turn left W into Broome St. from Mulberry St. for a similar treat at **Cafe Roma** at no.385. From here, it is only a few blocks w on Broome St. into the creative ferment of SoHo. See *Guide to the galleries* in *Culture, history and background* for a tour that doubles as a walk in this district.

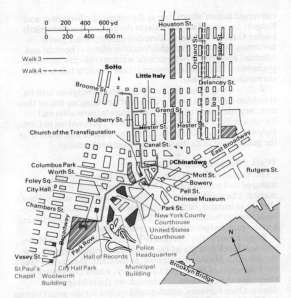

Walk 4/Lower East Side

When the first boatloads of East Europeans squeezed into the Lower East Side in the 1880s, they found choked streets, deprivation and cramped, cold flats. Little has changed, except that Spanish is now more often heard than Yiddish, and there are bathtubs in the kitchens. Two kinds of tourists now stop by – those seeking cultural roots and those seeking bargains. Sun is best; Fri and Sat worst; and on weekdays the absence of crowds leaves the streets less safe and less interesting.

From the subway station at the intersection of Delancey St. and Essex St., walk w on Delancey. Turn right, N on Orchard St. This is the liveliest block on the Lower East Side, so jammed with shoppers, residents and merchants on Sun that cars are banned. Pick your way along the E side, among the sights and sounds of blasting salsa and disco music, clothing hung above like heraldic banners, signs in four languages, people of every hue. Cross back and forth as whim dictates. You may find designer clothes with discounts of 20–50%, if you will accept the inconveniences of communal changing rooms, harried and often brusque sales people and shabby fixtures. Check out **Breakaway Fashions**, at no.125, **Feminique**, no.143½, **JBZ**, no.121, **Fine and Klein**, no.119, **Lace Up**, no.119, **Sosinsky & Son**, no.143 and **Samuel Backenstein**, no.130. The bargains in luggage, fabrics, bathing suits and handbags as well as clothes, continue as far N as Houston St. Turn around and work S, comparing prices. Continue past Hester St., the narrow thoroughfare brought to prominence by a recent film of the same name. Along the way, consider the wares of **Arnie's Place**, no.37, for jeans, **Opium**, no.52 and no.104, for dresses, **P.J. Goodstuff**, no.104, for men's clothing, **Flair's Edge**, no.110, for shoes, and **Alaska**, no.41, for shearling coats.

Turn left, E, on Canal St. All along this route is evidence of the declining Jewish population, in abandoned synagogues and converted tailors' shops, but at the corner of E Broadway and Rutgers St. the old ways persist at the garden-less and strictly kosher **Garden Cafeteria**. Bearded men squabble good-naturedly or lecture their children over plates of borscht and blintzes, and gruffly paternalistic waiters cock disapproving eyebrows at the sight of uneaten scraps of gefilte fish or the surpassing cheesecake.

Walk N along Essex St., past purveyors of religious articles. Hassidim decked in black, ringlets of hair hanging before their ears, negotiate purchases of prayer shawls, *yarmulkes* and Torah scrolls. Turn left W into Grand St., proceeding to *Little Italy* and *SoHo*, where you can end the walk or join *Walk 3* or the gallery tour in *Culture, history and background*.

Walk 5/Greenwich Village

"The Village isn't the same," say those who prospered, matured and moved away. They are correct, but it doesn't matter. The neighborhoods of New York are not static. They shrink, or expand, or divide, or deteriorate, or adjust, or rally. Next year, or tomorrow, The Village will have changed again, but the past and provocative present remain.

Begin a tour at the University Pl. end of Washington Mews, one-half block N of the NE corner of *Washington Square*. To the left is **La Maison Française**, to the right, **Deutsches Haus**. Both are units of *New York University*, which owns much of the property in this area. Proceed down the cobblestoned Mews. Once servants' quarters and stables for the grand houses on Washington Sq. North and 8th St., most of the buildings are now private homes.

Turn left into 5th Ave., towards **Washington Arch**. A wooden version of the monument was first erected in 1886 to commemorate the centennial of George Washington's inauguration. It became an instant landmark, so the architect Stanford White designed this marble rendition, completed in 1892. The statue of *Washington* on the left was carved by A. Stirling Calder, father of Alexander Calder.

Turn left along Washington Sq. North. This block of Greek Revival row houses was built in the 1830s. No. 16 was the site of Henry James's novel, *Washington Square*. Note the bronze lions bracketing the steps of no.6, which now houses university offices and seminar rooms. Painter Edward Hopper maintained a studio at no.3, but the upper floors burned in the early 1970s. Continue along as the street becomes Waverly Pl., turning right into Greene St.

At the foot of Greene St. is **Tisch Hall**, with its flower-and-tree-filled plaza. It is the second of Philip Johnson's commissions for the university. Turn right into W 4th St., which soon becomes Washington Sq. South. On the left is a one-block mall popularly referred to as 'Bobkin Lane,' after the bordering buildings, the **Bobst Library** and **Shimkin Hall**. The controversial library is Johnson's first design for N.Y.U. Step inside to see the 12-story balconied atrium. Outside, turn left, then left again on LaGuardia Pl., and walk S as far as Bleecker St. Turn left, E, to see the three high-rise apartment houses on the right, which are the university-owned **Silver Towers**. In the plaza at their base is a monumental rendering of Picasso's *Silvette*, one of only two exterior sculptures by the influential artist in North America. Return to Bleecker St., now heading W, and continue to Sullivan St. This intersection is the center of the long-established Italian community of the South

Village. Walk N, past poultry stores, dim cafes and unusual shops. Some have been there for almost a century, others change hands and functions with dizzying rapidity.

Turn left on W 3rd St. for a short block, then left again into MacDougal St. The **Cafe Reggio** (*119 MacDougal St.*) is an authentic throwback to the legendary Bohemian and beatnik days of The Village, dark and smoky, with a well-used espresso machine hissing at one side. Continue S and turn right into Bleecker St., crossing 6th Ave. and picking up Bleecker St. again on the other side.

Turn left into Leroy St., which becomes St. Luke's Pl. on the other side of 7th Ave. The houses on the righthand side of this peaceful tree-shaded block date from the 1860s. Turn right into Hudson St., right again into Morton St., to 7th Ave., then left into Bedford St. where Edna St Vincent Millay, the poet and actress, resided for a time, at no.75½. Only 8ft wide, it is the narrowest house in The Village. The oldest is probably no.77, built in 1799.

Just beyond, turn left into Commerce St. At the end of the short block is the **Cherry Lane Theater**, one of several in which the energetic Ms. Millay had a hand. Nearby are the double-gabled houses known as the 'Twin Sisters,' reputedly built by a seafaring father whose daughters would not live under the same roof. Turn right into Barrow St., then left into Bedford St. At the next intersection, take a few paces left into Grove St. to peer through the gate to the courtyard. Among the bordering houses, built in the 1840s, are some of the few surviving wood houses in Manhattan.

Return to Bedford St., continue along Grove St. and turn right into Bleecker St., a commercial artery, dominated by abundant displays of foodstuffs. Turn left into Cornelia St., and left again into W 4th St. for more shops of even greater diversity. Make a right turn at 7th Ave. and continue as far as Charles St., then turn right again and walk to Greenwich Ave. Turn left, window-gazing, then cut across and backtrack down the other side. The triangular garden between 10th St. and 6th

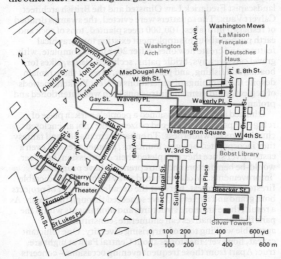

Ave. was made possible by the demolition of the unlamented Women's House of Detention. The adjacent structure with the fanciful brick tower is the **Jefferson Market Courthouse Library**, a mouthful that describes its sequential uses.

Turn right into Christopher St., walking away from 6th Ave., then left into Gay St., which was home (at no.14) to two sisters from Ohio, one of whom wrote *My Sister Eileen*. In a classic case of cultural recycling, her novel begat a play that was transformed into a musical that started the whole thing over again, complete with remakes and a television series. At the end of this crooked street, turn left into Waverly Pl. and follow it to the NW corner of Washington Square. Make one last detour – a half-block to the left. On the right is **MacDougal Alley**, a quaint relic of the privileged past. It is a deceptively ramshackle variation of Washington Mews, its former carriage houses now serving as expensive residences.

Return to the square. Two blocks S, chess and domino players and *kibitzers* form knots around the cement games tables installed there. Back at the central fountain, which is intended more for splashing than beauty and functions on an unpredictable schedule, several musical groups are bound to be performing, at least on fine days. Further E is a statue of *Garibaldi*. Consistent with campus legends everywhere, *Il Signore* is said to unsheath his sword whenever a virgin passes. Finally, stroll over to the *Grey Art Gallery* on the E side, another university facility, featuring exhibitions more lively than the name suggests.

Walk 6/Central Park

An amenity without which life in New York is unimaginable, the park is a product of mid-19thC vision and expediency. At that time, the land N of 59th St. was a place of mosquito-infested swamps, malodorous meat-rendering factories, and the festering hovels of thieves and the homeless. Prompted by poet-journalist William Cullen Bryant and his supporters, the city authorities launched a design competition that was won by landscapist Frederick Law Olmsted and the British architect Calvert Vaux. The squatters were evicted, the swamps drained or reshaped into lakes, 100,000 trees planted, tons of rock and earth pushed about to supplement existing topographical features and create new ones. After 20yr it was complete, with gravel carriageways, bridle paths, secluded glades, lakes for boating and fishing, and playing fields. Most of these remain, despite the trampings of generations of New Yorkers, periods of neglect, vandalism and intrusions both well-intentioned and profane.

Olmsted and Vaux envisioned a people's park, a place of refuge for poor and privileged citizens alike, not an enclosed chunk of ersatz wilderness. To enhance circulation and fantasy, they incorporated bridges, fountains, promenades and even a castle. Ever since they completed their commission, however, would-be benefactors and entrepreneurs have proposed 'improvements.' Most are turned away before the predictable firestorms of protest, but over the decades a number of projects both grand and irrelevant have squeezed through the screen. As a result, there are more structures and monuments within the park than even natives can enumerate, constituting an agreeable walking tour of surprising diversity. One reluctant caveat, however: the stories about Central Park at night are true. Apart from those frequent evening occasions – concerts

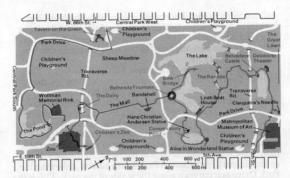

and plays – that provide the security of large crowds, it is statistically unwise to visit after dusk.

Enter the park at 79th St. and 5th Ave., walking W along the path to the N of the Transverse Rd. This hugs the S wing of the *Metropolitan Museum of Art*, continues over a low rise and heads down under an arched stone bridge. Go through, bearing right, N. A few steps farther on is *Cleopatra's Needle*, an Egyptian obelisk given to the city and erected in 1881. Turn about, taking the first footpath to the right. The level green to the N called **The Great Lawn** was once a reservoir, drained and filled in the 1930s and now busy with softball and football players. Above the small lake on the left, S, is **Belvedere Castle**, presently in the later stages of renovation. At the end of the lake is the open-air **Delacorte Theater** (check newspapers for current performances or ☎ 755–1400). Beyond the ticket booth, bear left, S, up the hill to the castle. Paths at the back cross over the Transverse Rd. Take the one to the right, proceeding SW, then SE. Eventually, it winds past the Loeb Boat House. Bicycles, roller skates and rowboats are available for rent. There is a fast-food counter with a patio. Follow the same pathway due E until it soon reaches the concrete oval of **Conservatory Pond**. At its N end is a statue of *Alice in Wonderland*: on the W, one of *Hans Christian Andersen*. Children clamber all over them, especially when stories are told at the Andersen monument on Sat mornings (May–Sept).

Take the walkway that goes W from the S end of the pond, under the Park Drive and along the bank of the lake. **Bethesda Fountain** is just ahead, the most grandiose element of the Vaux contributions. A winged angel surmounts a gaggle of cherubim and, when the plumbing is in order and New York is not having a water crisis, there is pretty splashing in the pool at the base.

Take the exit path leading W along the lake shore to the lovely cast-iron **Bow Bridge**. Another Vaux design, it was restored in 1974, and crosses the lake into **The Ramble**, a cat's cradle of footpaths that curl through low trees, patches of grass and plantings of bush and flower. The section is favored by serious bird watchers. Return across the bridge to the Bethesda Fountain and walk S along The Mall. On the left, E, is a bandshell, site of summer evening concerts.

Continue S on The Mall, passing bronze portraits of *Columbus*, *Shakespeare* and *Robbie Burns* that are less than compelling. Runners, skate-boarders, eaters and musicians compete for space all the way to the end. Once there, bear right to **The Dairy** (open Tues–Sun 10am–4:30pm) from where walking tours depart. Recent restoration of the building was faithful to its Victorian Gothic origins, and the vaulted interior is now an information center with appropriate exhibitions and a slide show. Plans are approved to re-create the loggia that was removed in the 1950s.

Cross over the nearby Transverse Rd., still heading s. The zoo (see *Central Park Zoo*) is within a stone's throw, on the left, E, and it might be time to have a snack in its cafeteria, overlooking the popular sea lion pool. The **Children's Zoo** is 50yd to the N. That can be the end of a tour, but if energy and curiosity remain, leave the zoo through the s gate, bearing right under the drive. Pass the **Wollman Memorial Rink** on your right. At the edge of the pond encountered there, choose the path to the left around the edge of the pond. At the road that enters the park from Central Park South head w, following the Park Drive as it curves N along the w side of the park. This is the final leg of the New York Marathon in Oct, with the finish line at about 66th St. The expanse of lawn to the right, E, is the recently reseeded Sheep Meadow. A road to the left, w, passes the **Tavern On The Green** restaurant – once the barn for the sheep that grazed on the Meadow until the 1930s – and exits on Central Park West.

Children's playgrounds are located at intervals along the E and w borders of the park (see *New York for children*). From May – Oct park roads are closed to vehicular traffic, Mon – Fri 10am – 3pm, Mon – Thurs 7 – 10pm, Fri at 7pm until Mon 6am, holidays 7pm – 6am in the morning of the next working day. From Nov – Apr only the weekend closings apply.

Walk 7/Upper East Side

The wealthy and super-rich made the Upper East Side their habitat in the late 19thC, pushing aside the squatters and farmers then in residence. They erected Italo-Franco-Anglo chateaus and palazzi one after the other, each grander than its neighbor. Those were the last decades before enactment of income tax, however, and even these privileged folk couldn't maintain their 50-room retreats long after that blow. But the rest of us profited, for many of those mansions now serve the public as schools and museums. The result is 'Museum Mile,' along 5th Ave., bordering Central Park, a string of public repositories of arts and antiquities of astonishing diversity stretching from 70th St. to 103rd St. This suggested walk links many of those museums, which are described in detail in *Sights and places of interest*. The walk can be broken off at any point and returned to another day, as interest and energy dictate.

Start at the headquarters of the *Asia Society*, at the NE corner of Park Ave. and 70th St. Opened in 1981, the handsome red granite structure houses galleries of Far Eastern artifacts. Exhibits are changed two or three times yearly.

Cross Park Ave. continuing w on 70th St. Several buildings along the next two blocks are interesting. The **Explorer's Club**, at no.46, reflects the waning Gothic Revival enthusiasm of the pre-World War I years, and no.32 has Florentine detailing of the same period. The prices at **Fraser Morris Fine Foods** at the next corner, Madison Ave., are inhibiting, but glance around if you have an important country picnic in mind.

This district is home to at least a third of the city's important art galleries, and **Knoedler & Co.**, at no.19, dealing in 20thC moderns and some earlier masters, is one of the most influential. Keeping to the N side of the street, watch for the entrance to the *Frick Collection* on the right. Industrialist Henry Clay Frick intended to have his 1914 mansion converted to a museum upon his death, and with that prospect in mind he filled it with paintings of the Renaissance and the French and English 18thC.

From the Frick Collection, turn right, w, into 70th St., then right, N, into 5th Ave., where it forms one of the grand boulevards of the city, the green of *Central Park* to the left and placid residences to the right. At 75th St., turn right, E. On the N side is a Romanesque mansion surrounded by an unusual iron fence, formerly the Harkness House, now a foundation headquarters. Continue to Madison Ave. The striking cantilevered structure on the SE corner is the *Whitney Museum of American Art*, suggesting a fortress, complete with moat and fixed bridge. The leafy cafeteria on the glassed-in sub-street level provides a welcome place to sit down and relax,

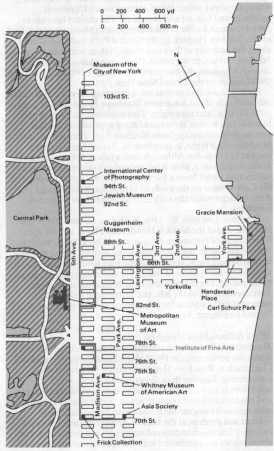

in full view of lyrical Calder mobiles and stabiles.

Walk N on Madison Ave., intimate by contrast with Park Ave. and 5th Ave., with shoulder-to-shoulder art and antiques galleries and compact shops of idiosyncratic mien. Along 76th St. is the exclusive **Carlyle** hotel, choice of John F. Kennedy when he was in town. Military buffs are drawn to **The Soldier Shop** (*1013 Madison Ave.*), with its fascinating collection of painted lead soldiers and assorted paraphernalia of many wars.

Go on to 78th St. and walk W to 5th Ave. to the family home that tobacco heiress Doris Duke bequeathed to New York University. It now houses the highly regarded **Institute of Fine Arts**. At 5th Ave., turn right, N, once again. A cultural annexe of the French Embassy is housed within the building at no.972, designed by the omnipresent McKim, Mead & White (see Stanford White, *Biographies*).

The Gothic Revival house (1899) at the next corner is the **Ukrainian Institute of America** (*open Tues–Fri 2–6pm*), which shelters a collection of contemporary Ukrainian paintings and folk art and costumes. The choices here are to spend the next 2–3hr in the *Metropolitan Museum of Art*, just across 5th Ave.; to pick up the Central Park walk (see *Walk 6*) along the pathway at the S end of the Met; or to continue N along 5th Ave. to visit, in sequence, the *Guggenheim Museum*, the *Jewish Museum*, the *International Center of Photography* and the *Museum of the City of New York*.

Should those alternatives seem daunting, have a coffee at the sidewalk cafe of the **American Stanhope Hotel** (*81st St.*), then go to 82nd St. and turn right. This treelined, unblemished block of row houses serves as a fitting approach to the Met, seen to good advantage from Madison Ave. Turn left, N, into Madison, then right, E, into 86th St. Across Lexington Ave. you are in *Yorkville*. Although once a village of Germans and Slavic immigrants, little is left to lend any middle-European distinction, apart from a *bierstube* or two, with the exception of the **Cafe Geiger** on the S side of 86th St. between 3rd and 2nd Ave., which evokes the authentic atmosphere of a Viennese *konditorei*.

Continue E on 86th St. After York Ave., cross to the N side. Near the end of the block is **Henderson Place**, a mews with little houses of symmetrical lines, rare in New York. Stroll to the end and back, then continue along 86th St. to end the walk in *Carl Schurz Park*, at the lip of the East River. At the N end is *Gracie Mansion*, home of the mayor and unfortunately closed to the public. On the opposite bank is Queens; to the right, Roosevelt Island; to the left, the Triborough Bridge. The nearest subway station for your return journey is back at 86th St. and Lexington Ave.

Walk 8/Brooklyn Heights

Manhattan's first suburb and the first neighborhood to come under the protection (in 1965) of the Landmarks Preservation Commission, Brooklyn Heights is meant for leisurely meandering. Smaller than *Greenwich Village*, which it resembles in part, it is less flawed by commercial shabbiness and modern architectural intrusions. Street after street is lined with restored brownstone houses with hardy plane trees in front and gardens at the back. Lovingly maintained details of cast-iron fences, chandeliered vestibules and flower boxes on the windows are contrasted with the spectacular panorama of harbor and skyline provided by the pedestrian esplanade that hangs above the East River docks.

Start from the BMT or IRT subway stations on Court St., walking s one block to turn right, w, on Remsen St. Prominent among the first buildings encountered are the elegant **Brooklyn Club**, at no.131, and **Brooklyn Bar Association**, no.123. Turn left, s, into Henry St. In the middle of the block, on the left, is **Hunt's Lane**, an alley of carriage houses converted to residences. Continue along Henry St. to Joralemon St., turn right, then right again into Hicks St. After a few steps, wander into **Grace Court Alley** on the right. It is far more handsomely preserved than Hunt's Lane, a true mews with upper-story hay cranes still in place above the stables where horses were once kept. Go N again along Hicks, then left, w, into Remsen, and right, N, into Montague Terrace. Unlike the terrace houses already seen, commissioned individually by their first owners, this grouping of attached residences was designed as a set in 1886 and retains its original look. Author Thomas Wolfe lived a while at no.5. At the end, turn right, E, into Montague St. proper. In the last 10yr, this main shopping and eating street has blossomed with boutiques, craft shops, bookstores and gourmet and health-food emporia. None of the eating places are likely to attract the attention of highbrow Manhattan restaurant critics, but they cover a range of ethnic proclivities and some have sidewalk tables. Consider **Leaf & Bean**, no. 136, **Old Hungary**, no. 142, **Foffe**, no.155 and **Cafe Galleria**, no.174.

After three blocks along Montague St. turn left, N, into Clinton St. then left, w, again into Pierrepont St. **The Long Island Historical Society** building on the corner, erected in 1880, shows the Classical influences in vogue at the time. Exhibits of books, paintings and artifacts related to the heritage of Long Island and New York are open to the public. Continue w along Pierrepont St. The **Unitarian Church** at the corner of

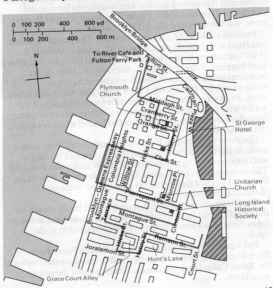

Planning

Monroe Place was designed by the influential early 19thC architect Minard Lafever. Look up to the enchanting turret on no.114. It is hard to believe that the Renaissance Revival pile beneath it was once the duplicate of the Greek Revival mansion at no.108.

Follow Pierrepont St. to the end. Until 1950, it ran downhill to the river's edge. A plan to run the Brooklyn–Queens Expressway through the heart of the Heights was resisted by residents, and the compromise that evolved was to stack the highway in two tiers and divert it along the westerly edge of the neighborhood. As a final fillip it was roofed over, smothering traffic noises and exhaust fumes, and providing a five-block promenade that bestows a glorious, unobstructed vista from the *Statue of Liberty* northward past the spires of lower Manhattan, to the *Brooklyn Bridge* and Manhattan Bridge and all the way to the *Empire State Building*. Take it all in while strolling N, noting the trellised gardens and balconies of the narrow houses that border the promenade. Sunset is a good time, for the heavens blaze behind that famous skyline in a manner that cannot be duplicated on film.

Every river has, moreover, its influence over the people who pass their lives within sight of its waters.

H.S. Merriman, *The Sowers*

Take the next exit right, E, into Clark St., glancing both ways as you cross Columbia Heights and then Willow St., for you might be drawn to explore them further. Beyond Hicks St., pass the old (1885) **St George Hotel**, turning left, N, on Henry St., then left again, W, into Orange St. **Plymouth Church** is in mid-block, a chunky 1847 edifice of little physical distinction. Its importance lies with its founder and first preacher, Henry Ward Beecher. An ardent opponent of slavery, he attracted the attention of Abraham Lincoln, who worshiped here, as did Charles Dickens and Mark Twain. His sister, Harriet Beecher Stow, was the author of *Uncle Tom's Cabin*.

Proceed to Hicks St. and turn right, N. The private wooden residence at the corner of Cranberry St. is one of the oldest (1820) structures in the Heights. At Middagh St., named after a local burgher of the early 18thC, turn left, W. Most of the buildings along this block have been altered beyond recognition, but the splendid 1829 Federalist clapboard house, at no. 24, is an exception; its streetside fence encloses a garden with a willow tree and connects with a former servants' cottage. Step close to examine the carvings and leaded windows around the main door.

Continue to Columbia Heights and turn right, N, as it dips towards the base of the Brooklyn Bridge, framed beneath a walkway connecting two sections of the Watchtower Building. This passage leads into Cadman Plaza W, formerly Fulton St. From 1814–1924 this Fulton St. was linked to the one in Manhattan by ferry.

Turn towards the river. A former fireboat house stands on the site of the old ferry terminal. Now it is a **maritime museum** (*open daily noon–6pm*). Sailing vessels often put in at the dock.

For a grand finale, amble N into the **Fulton Ferry Park**. Ever-improving food and unimprovable views are the staples of the **River Cafe**. Here you can call a taxi to make the return to your hotel.

Sights and places of interest

New York has first-class museums covering a phenomenal range of subjects. Try to squeeze in some of the more specialized ones besides the usual star attractions. Huge collections necessitate frequent rotation of exhibits, and several museums (notably the Metropolitan Museum of Art) are currently undergoing major reorganization. Modern art collections are in a constant state of flux, due to ever-shifting emphases. For all these reasons, detailed cataloguing is impossible and descriptions are intended to convey a general impression. Fortunately, organization is excellent, with clear labeling and helpful floor plans. The sights and places of interest are listed alphabetically, but you can use the comprehensive list of entries below to identify sights by type.

Bridges and tunnels
Brooklyn-Battery Tunnel
Brooklyn Bridge
George Washington Bridge
Holland Tunnel
Lincoln Tunnel
Queensboro Bridge
Queens-Midtown Tunnel
Verrazano Narrows Bridge

Churches and synagogues
Brotherhood Synagogue
Cathedral Church of St John The Divine
Church of the Ascension
Church of the Transfiguration
Grace Church
Judson Memorial Baptist Church
Marble Collegiate Church
Riverside Church
St Bartholomew's Church
St Mark's Church In-The-Bowery
St Patrick's Cathedral
St Paul's Chapel
Temple Emanu-El
Trinity Church

Colleges and universities
Columbia University
Cooper Union
New York University
Yeshiva University

Districts
Bowery, The
Brooklyn Heights
Chelsea
Chinatown
Coney Island
East Side

Financial District
Garment Center
Gramercy Park
Greenwich Village
Harlem
Little Italy
Lower East Side
Midtown East
Murray Hill
SoHo
Theater District
TriBeCa
Upper West Side
Yorkville

Exhibition halls
Burlington House
Guinness World Records Exhibit Hall
New York Coliseum
New York Experience

Historic buildings
Abigail Adams Smith Museum
Castle Clinton Monument
Chelsea Hotel
City Hall
Dakota Apartments
Dyckman House
Ellis Island
Federal Hall National Memorial
Gracie Mansion
Grand Central Terminal
Morris-Jumel Mansion
Old Merchant's House
Richmondtown Restoration
Snug Harbor Cultural Center
Theodore Roosevelt Birthplace
Van Cortlandt Mansion and Museum
Villard Houses

Libraries
Bible House
New York Public Library
Pierpont Morgan Library

Monuments
Cleopatra's Needle
General Grant National Memorial
Hall of Fame for Great Americans
Statue of Liberty

Museums of art
African-American Institute
American Academy and Institute of Arts and Letters
American Craft Museum
Asia Society
Audubon Terrace
Center for Inter-American Relations
Cloisters
Cooper-Hewitt Museum
Downtown Whitney Museum
Frick Collection
Grey Art Gallery
Guggenheim Museum
International Center of Photography
Metropolitan Museum of Art
Museo del Barrio
Museum of American Folk Art
Museum of American Illustration
Museum of Modern Art
Puerto Rican Museum for the Arts
Tibetan Museum
Whitney Museum of American Art

Museums of history and culture
American Museum of Immigration
American Museum of Natural History
American Numismatic Society
Aunt Len's Doll and Toy Museum
Brooklyn Museum
China House
Chinese Museum
Fire Department Museum
Fraunces Tavern Museum
French Institute
Goethe House
Hispanic Society of America
Japan House Gallery
Jewish Museum
Museum of the American Indian
Museum of the City of New York
New York Historical Society
Police Academy Museum
Songwriters' Hall of Fame Museum
South Street Seaport Museum
Ukrainian Museum

Museums of science and technology
Hayden Planetarium
Museum of Broadcasting
Museum of Holography

Music and sports halls
Carnegie Hall
Lincoln Center
Madison Square Garden

Parks and gardens
Battery Park
Bowling Green
Brooklyn Botanic Garden
Bryant Park
Carl Schurz Park
Central Park
Fort Tryon Park
Greenacre Park
New York Botanical Garden
Paley Park
Prospect Park
Riverside Park
Union Square
Washington Square

Skyscrapers and modern architecture
Chrysler Building
Citicorp Center
Empire State Building
Flatiron Building
Ford Foundation Building
Lever House
Pan Am Building
RCA Building
Rockefeller Center
Seagram Building
United Nations Headquarters
Waterside Houses
Woolworth Building
World Trade Center

Zoos and aquarium
Bronx Zoo
Central Park Zoo
New York Aquarium
Staten Island Zoo

Abigail Adams Smith Museum ▥
421 E 61st St. (1st Ave.), NY 10021 ☎*838–6878. Map 5N5*
▨ *✗ Open Mon–Fri 10am–4pm. Closed Sat, Sun.
Discounts for senior citizens; free entry for children under 12.*

An unexpected retreat amid the feverish pace of the East Side, this 1799 carriage house sits on a slope behind stone retaining walls, a fetching remnant of the Federalist era. The estate it served was owned by William Stephens Smiths, but the titular tenant was his wife, the daughter of the eventual second President of the United States. She didn't stay long. After dismemberment of the property, the building became a residence in 1826. It remained in private hands until its purchase in the early 20thC by the Colonial Dames of America. That organization is still headquartered here, and maintains several exhibition rooms. Most of the furnishings are of the early 19thC, although they are not traced to the original owners.

Academy and Institute of Arts and Letters   See
American Academy and Institute of Arts and Letters.

African-American Institute
833 United Nations Plaza (47th St.), NY 10017
☎*949–5666. Map 5O5* ▣ ▤ *Open Mon–Fri 9am–5pm,
Sat 11am–5pm. Closed Sun.*
Appropriately positioned within sight of the *United Nations Headquarters*, this small gallery strives to promote interest in African arts and crafts, both past and present. Frequently changing exhibitions can feature sand paintings, wood carvings, bronze figures, and intricately woven fabrics in unpredictable array.

American Academy and Institute of Arts and Letters
Part of the *Audubon Terrace* museum complex, this is primarily a society of prominent artists and thinkers. Exhibitions of an eclectic nature are laid on at certain times.

American Craft Museum ☆
44 W 53rd St. (6th Ave.), NY 10019, and 77 W 45th St. (6th Ave.), NY 10036 ☎ *397–0630. Map 5N4&O4* 📷 *53rd St. branch open Tues–Sat 10am–6pm, Sun 11am–5pm. Closed Mon. 45th St. branch open Mon–Fri 11am–7pm. Closed Sat, Sun. Half-price entry for senior citizens, students, under-16s.*

Wit, panache, and impeccable workmanship mark the ever-changing one-person and group shows of this two-part museum. Exhibits are generally shared between the two locations. Over the course of a season, works in every material are represented: metal, paper, clay, plastic, fiber, glass, wood. The focus is on American artisans of the 20thC, but other times and cultures are sometimes explored.

A little strip of an island with a row of well-fed folks up and down the middle, and a lot of hungry folks on each side.

Harry Leon Wilson, *The Spenders*

American Museum of Immigration
Liberty Island, NY 10004 ☎ *732–1236. Map 12D3* 📷 ✗ 💺 *Open 9am–5pm. Extended hours in summer. Ferry from Battery Park.*

Housed in the base of the *Statue of Liberty*, this relatively new museum understandably emphasizes the contributions – rather than the travails – of the immigrants who created a nation. Taped reminiscences, slide shows, dioramas, photographs, and displays of clothing, furnishings, and folk art combine to tell the story.

American Museum of Natural History 🏛 ★
Central Park W (79th St.), NY 10024 ☎ *873–4225. Map 6L3* 📷 ✗ 💺 ✳ *Open Mon, Tues, Thurs, Sun 10am–5:45pm, Wed, Fri, Sat 10am–9pm.*

Beloved by generations of schoolchildren for its realistic animal dioramas and models of Indian villages, the museum interprets its mission in the broadest terms. Appealing as the exhibits of mounted Alaskan bears and African lions unquestionably are, adults are drawn to the halls highlighting the crafts, costumes, jewelry, masks, and artifacts of the peoples of Asia, Mexico, and pre-colonial North America. The collections, begun in 1874, include 34 million items, from a 94ft (29m) model of a blue whale to the fabled Star of India.

Calvert Vaux, who shared credit for Central Park, worked with Jacob Wrey Mould on the first building (1877). So many additions were made from then until 1933, however, that only a portion of it is still visible from the rear. Critics cite the southern red granite facade as a superior example of the Romanesque Revival. Perhaps so, if one's notion of romantic architecture derives from ponderous Teutonic fortresses. The main entrance, dominated by a 1939 equestrian statue of *President Theodore Roosevelt*, is even less graceful. Yet in spite of the forbidding exterior, this great museum qualifies as an obligatory stop.

American Museum of Natural History

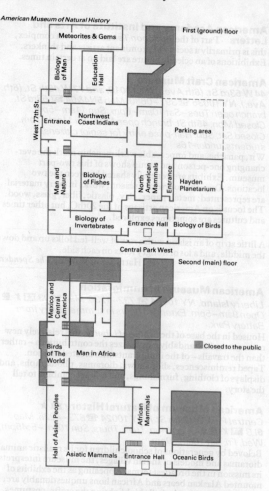

American Museum of Natural History

First (ground) floor

- Meteorites & Gems
- Biology of Man
- Education Hall
- West 77th St.
- Entrance
- Northwest Coast Indians
- Man and Nature
- Biology of Fishes
- Biology of Invertebrates
- North American Mammals
- Parking area
- Hayden Planetarium
- Entrance Hall
- Biology of Birds
- Central Park West

Second (main) floor

- Mexico and Central America
- Birds of The World
- Man in Africa
- Hall of Asian Peoples
- African Mammals
- Asiatic Mammals
- Entrance Hall
- Oceanic Birds

☐ Closed to the public

For maximum impact, choose the W 77th St. entrance rather than the one on Central Park W. Directly beyond the door leading to the first (ground) floor is an impressively scaled ocean-going canoe of a British Columbian tribe. Adjoining rooms are devoted to North American mammals, birds and invertebrates, meteorites and gems.

From the second (main) floor hall, turn left, continuing past animal exhibits to the Gardner D. Stout **Hall of Asian Peoples**, the newest and most ambitious section of the museum. In a masterful mix of scholarship and showmanship, it charts the progress of Eurasian cultures from prehistory to the recent past, employing every imaginable device to delineate evolutionary stages of religion, commerce, language, art and science. A gallery of **Birds of the World** leads on to another incorporating monumental stelae and terra-cotta funeral urns, sculptures, and ornaments from pre-Columbian Mexico and Central America. Close by, **Man in Africa** brings to life the diverse societies of African forest and desert. The rest of this floor and the third floor feature reptiles, primates and birds of several continents. Reassembled **dinosaur skeletons** are the attraction on the fourth floor, especially the awesome Tyrannosaurus Rex that figures in so many Grade B fantasy films.

In addition to the basement cafeteria, there is a cocktail lounge in the lobby, and tables set around hot dog carts on the front steps in summer. Traveling shows, lectures, and music and dance programs augment the permanent exhibitions.

Hayden Planetarium ☆
Central Park W (81st St.), NY 10024 ☎ *873–8828* 🔲 *****
Shows: Mon–Fri 1:30pm, 3:30pm, Sat 11am, 1pm, 2pm, 3pm, 4pm, 5pm, Sun as Sat except 11am, Wed extra show 7:30pm. Fewer shows July–Sept. Admission includes American Museum of Natural History.

Since 1935, the artful technology of the Hayden Planetarium has reproduced on its domed ceiling the movements of constellations, planets, and meteor showers. Seasonal shows focus on the 'Star of Wonder,' nebulae and stellar formations, and the projected end of the world through astronomical accident. Music and commentary supplement the 1hr presentations, and there are 'cosmic laser concerts' (☎ 724–8700 for times and prices). Observing the 2½ -ton projector in action is worth the admission.

American Numismatic Society Housing a large collection of coins and medals, this is part of the *Audubon Terrace* complex.

Aquarium See *New York Aquarium*.

Ascension, Church of the See *Church of the Ascension*.

Asia Society 🏛
725 Park Ave. (E 70th St.), NY 10021 ☎ *288–6400. Map 7M4* 🔲 ✗ *Open Tues–Sat 10am–5pm, Thurs 10am–8:30pm, Sun noon–5pm. Closed Mon.*

A striking addition to a bland stretch of Park Ave., the new 1981 headquarters of the Asia Society echoes imperial palaces of India with its facing of alternately polished and textured red granite. The gallery floors house one of the many benefactions of the Rockefeller family: in this case, the collection of Nepalese and Chinese artifacts assembled by John D. 3rd. That is not the extent of the holdings, however, and there are supplementary loan exhibitions three or four times a year, as well as films, lectures and recitals. As this is not a formal museum operating within the strictures of scholarship, objects on display reflect the tastes of the contributors. Fortunately, those predilections are disciplined and educated. Sculptured metal and polychromed ceramics mingle with ancient many-armed buddhas from Kampuchea and fierce feline temple guardians.

Audubon Terrace 🏛 ☆
Broadway at 155th St. Map 8F2. Subway 1 to 157th St; AA, B to 155th St.

Gathered around a Neoclassical plaza in a NW adjunct to Harlem is a remarkable complex of four museums and associated societies. While they are not all individually of great importance, as a group they rival all but a handful of the city's cultural repositories. Only their location denies them the recognition they deserve.

Ornithologist John James Audubon owned this property at the crest of the slope above the Hudson River and intermittently lived here from 1825 until his death in 1851. It was purchased by a speculator convinced that the steady northward thrust of the city would eventually make him rich. When it became clear that growth had stabilized at a point 5 miles s, the tract changed hands. A master plan was drawn up in 1908, and the present buildings were completed by 1926. They can be characterized as of the Beaux Arts mode, with a typical Greco-Renaissance mix. All the buildings are clustered in the block abutting Broadway between W 155th St. and W 156th St.

Museum of the American Indian ☆
☎283-2420 ⊠ ✳ Open Tues–Sat 10am–5pm, Sun 1–5pm. Closed Mon.

The largest repository of Native American artifacts anywhere, with over four million items on display and in storage, this museum is of particular interest to overseas visitors who plan to go no farther w than Manhattan. Even three large, crammed (if skillfully organized) floors can contain no more than a small portion of the acquisitions. These are rotated from a storage annex in seemingly inexhaustible numbers. 'American' here refers to the entire Western Hemisphere, with Eskimo carvings, Hopi kachina dolls, Chilean silverwork, and tools, funeral urns, tomahawks, jewelry, pottery, beadwork, feather headdresses and costumes, and fetishes from many Indian tribes and empires. The shrunken bodies (not mere heads) of captives of the Ecuadoran Jivaros are a macabre revelation. This museum deserves to be ranked among the best in the city, at least in terms of comprehensiveness.

Hispanic Society of America
☎926-2234 ⊠ Open Tues–Sat 10am–4:30pm, Sun 1–4pm. Closed Mon.

The entrance is marked by an equestrian bronze of *El Cid*, the 11thC Spanish hero – a fitting choice for a museum that concerns itself with Iberian rather than Latin American culture and history. At the very minimum, step into the splendid **main hall** ☆ and savor the rosy blush of terra-cotta Renaissance arches and ornamentation. During certain hours, light through the two-story skylight heightens the play of intricate shadow on carved scrollwork and panels. Of conventional interest are the canvases and drawings of El Greco, Velázquez and Goya. But the Spain of the Catholic kings is upstaged by that of the earlier Moors, with tiled chambers and relics of exquisite workmanship. The Roman and Visigothic occupations are represented as well, and there is a substantial library of pre-1700 books.

American Numismatic Society
☎234-3130 ⊠ Open Tues–Sat 9am–4:30pm, Sun 1–3pm. Closed Mon. Ring bell for entry.

The ground floor is given over to a large display of coins, medals and bank notes, the second floor to a specialist library.

Puerto Rican Museum for the Arts
☎222-2966 ⊠ Visits by appointment only.

What was until recently the home of the American Geographical Society now features permanent and rotating exhibitions of photographs, prints, paintings and sculpture, all with Puerto Rican associations.

American Academy and Institute of Arts and Letters

☎ 368–5900 ⊡ Open Mar–June, Nov–Dec, Tues–Sun 1–4pm. Telephone first to confirm hours and exhibitions.

Primarily an association of celebrated artists and intellectuals, not unlike its French counterpart, this institution mounts periodic exhibitions covering a wide range of subjects, from ancient manuscripts to architectural themes.

Aunt Len's Doll and Toy Museum

6 Hamilton Terrace (141st St.), NY 10031 ☎ 281–4143. Map **8**G3 ▨ X Open Tues–Sun. Closed Mon. Telephone first for an appointment. Subway 1 to 137th St.

An enthusiasm for collecting has a way of getting out of hand – in this case, to the delight of parents and children alike. 'Aunt Len' was a local schoolteacher who gathered over 3,000 dolls, miniature houses with scale furniture, mechanical and clockwork toys, dolls' carriages and accessories. When she saw what she had done, she decided to give everyone else a chance to share it. Every corner and surface is crowded with her acquisitions, and the effect is magical. A visit might be combined with a trip to the several museums of *Audubon Terrace*, some 14 blocks to the N.

Battery Park

Battery Pl. and State St. (foot of Broadway). Map **2**V4.
Named for a rank of cannons that defended the old town from uncertain foes – presumably British – after the Revolution, the present 21 acres occupy the western rim of the extreme southern tip of Manhattan. Financial District workers eat their lunches in view of the *Statue of Liberty* and the now diminished but no less beguiling harbor traffic. Other attractions are the **Verrazano Memorial**, commemorating the Italian explorer who first saw New York Bay in 1524, and the *Castle Clinton National Monument*, once on an islet but later joined by landfill to what is now the park. The ferry to the Statue of Liberty departs from a pier at the edge of the park and the one to Staten Island is nearby.

Bible House

1865 Broadway (61st St.), NY 10023 ☎ 581–7400. Map **4**N3 ⊡ X for groups. Open Mon–Fri 9am–4:30pm. Closed Sat, Sun.

Over 38,000 volumes are on permanent display, including scraps of the Dead Sea Scrolls, pages from the 15thC Gutenberg Bible, and Braille editions once owned by Helen Keller.

The Bowery

Map **3**S5.
A country road from the time of the original Dutch colony, the 'Bouwerie' retained its bucolic status into the 19thC. It went downhill from there – apart from a brief revival in the 1890s as a place for bawdy music halls – and rapidly slid into utter despair. Now it is a grimy concentration of flophouses and bars, the last stop for derelict men and women made homeless by alcoholism, madness and misfortune. There are a handful of discount kitchenware and home furnishing stores, but the persistence of The Bowery as a tourist attraction is a mystery.

Bowling Green
Battery Pl. (foot of Broadway). Map 2U4.
This triangular bit of lawn once hosted early Colonial bowlers
and a statue of *George III*. True to revolutionary tradition, the
monument was pulled down in 1776. The fence that protected
the memorial is all that remains of even minor historical and
visual interest.

Bronx Zoo and New York Botanical Garden
These adjacent and spectacular sights constitute two of the best
reasons for venturing over the Harlem River.

Bronx Zoo ★
Southern Blvd. (185th St.), Bronx, NY 10460
☎ *220–5100. Map 13B–C4* ☒ *Tues–Thurs* ☒ *Fri–Mon in
winter* ☒ *Fri–Mon in summer. Modest extra charges for a
few special sections, also tractor train, aerial tram and
monorail* ✗ *free by appointment* ☎ *220–5141* ▇ ☀ ⬤
*Open Mon–Sat 10am–5pm, Sun and hols 10am–5:30pm.
Most outdoor exhibits closed in winter, roughly Oct–Apr.
Subway 2,5 to Pelham Parkway.*

Many New York attractions are as engaging as ever, others are
in decline, but few have actually improved in recent years. The
Bronx Zoo falls into this last felicitous category. Known
officially as the New York Zoological Park, it was inaugurated
in 1899 and now has over 3,000 animals of 800 species, deployed
in imaginative settings carved out of the hills and meadows of
the original 252 acres. Because such diversity can cause
indecision, the management has provided the means to obtain
overviews and thereby make choices. A tractor train with guide
makes a complete circuit of the grounds, an aerial tram glides
over the African Plains section, and a monorail meanders about
Wild Asia, where tigers and elephants roam free.

To proceed in an orderly manner on foot, begin at the Pelham
Parkway extrance. This leads to the earliest part of the zoo, the
formal Baird Court, centring on the **Seal Pool**, around which
are arranged the **Aquatic Birds**, **Carnivores**, **Monkeys**,
Elephants, and a giant bird enclosure called the **Flying Cage**.
Pause by the 3-acre **Bison Range** for a look at the beasts that
once roamed over thousands of square miles of the Old West.
Beyond that is the **World of Birds**, through which you can pass
in the company of over 500 birds, with no interceding screens.
South of the Elephant House is a popular group of buildings
sheltering the **Reptiles**, **Penguins** and **Gorillas**. Nearby is the
fascinating **World of Darkness**, where a variety of nocturnal
creatures are fooled by artificial lighting into believing that day
is night.

Apart from these necessary structures, animals are at liberty
in much of the park, in simulated habitats. Cleverly
camouflaged moats keep them apart and protect the public.
The Skyfari tramway carries observers above the remarkably
convincing veldt of the **African Plains**, and you can look down
on moving lion prides, antelope and deer.

The park embraces a stretch of the Bronx River, wide enough
here to be called a lake. Most exhibits are to the w, but **Wild
Asia** takes up the E bank. The concept is similar to the African
Plains area, but the Bengali Express monorail follows a looping
route around the perimeter and over the river. Fences
separating clusters of rare animals from the Asian Subcontinent
are the only element detracting from the carefully staged
natural environment.

Bronx Zoo and New York Botanical Garden

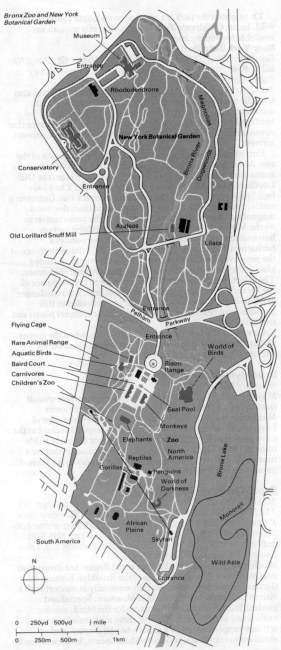

Bronx Zoo and New York Botanical Garden

Museum

Entrance

Rhododendrons

New York Botanical Garden

Magnolias

Bronx River

Dogwoods

Conservatory

Entrance

Azaleas

Lilacs

Old Lorillard Snuff Mill

Entrance

Pelham Parkway

Entrance

Flying Cage

Rare Animal Range

Aquatic Birds

Baird Court

Carnivores

Children's Zoo

World of Birds

Bison Range

Seal Pool

Monkeys

Elephants

Zoo

North America

Reptiles

Gorillas

Penguins

World of Darkness

African Plains

Skyfari

Bronx Lake

Monorail

South America

Wild Asia

Entrance

N

0   250yd   500yd   ½ mile
0   250m   500m   1km

Throughout the park are specimens no longer found in the wild. In the **Children's Zoo**, young and gentle animals are available for petting and feeding.

New York Botanical Garden ☆

Southern Blvd. (200th St.), Bronx, NY 10460 ☎ *220–8700* 🖼 ⒳ 💻 ⚹ *Open 10am–1hr before sunset. Conservatory Tues–Sun. Museum Mon–Fri 9:30am–4pm.*

Adjacent to the zoo on its northern border, these 250 acres also straddle the Bronx River, but here the river is narrow and untamed, tumbling through a deep gorge. Its course is bordered by a 40-acre preserve of virgin hemlock – the trees that covered much of the metropolitan region before the Europeans arrived.

Entry can be made opposite the Pelham Parkway gate of the zoo. At the first main pedestrian intersection, detour W into the azalea glen, then retrace the route E. After the bridge, the **Old Lorillard Snuff Mill** becomes visible on the left. The 1840s building is restored and used as a summer snack bar. Continue E and N, pausing along the way for displays of lilac, dogwood, magnolia and rhododendron. Eventually the paths converge on the **Museum**, which mounts changing exhibitions on horticultural and ecological themes and incorporates a herbarium and botanical library. To the SW is the centerpiece of the preserve, the **Conservatory**. A grand rotunda of leaded glass is the focus of a complex of ten connecting greenhouses. The effect, inside and out, is of an enchanted crystal palace of the Victorian era. After years of deterioration, it was in danger of demolition. Reason and philanthropy prevailed in this glorious rejuvenation, and it contains topiary, desert plants and tropical flora.

Obviously the best time to go is Apr–Aug, when the groves and gardens are ablaze with color, but special events draw visitors at Christmas and Easter.

Brooklyn-Battery Tunnel

Map 2V4 🖼

Master builder Robert Moses intended an overwater span at this site, just S of the *Brooklyn Bridge*, to connect lower Manhattan with the Belt Parkway, which skirts the edge of Long Island on the way to JFK Airport. Despite his clout as the most powerful city planner of his time – from the early 1930s into the 1960s – he bowed to public pressure and settled for a tunnel. At that, it is the longest vehicular tunnel in the United States – nearly 2 miles.

Brooklyn Botanic Garden ☆

1000 Washington Ave. (Eastern Parkway), Brooklyn, NY 11225 ☎ *622–4433. Map 12E3* 🖼 *Tues, Fri* 🖼 *other days* ⒳ *Open Apr–Sept Tues–Fri 8am–6pm, Sat, Sun, public hols 10am–6pm; Oct–Mar Tues–Fri 8am–4:30pm, Sat, Sun, public hols 10am–4:30pm. Closed Mon. Subway 2,3,4 to Eastern Parkway–Brooklyn Museum.*

Much smaller than its big brother in the Bronx (see *Bronx Zoo and New York Botanical Garden*) the Brooklyn Botanic Garden is nonetheless worthwhile, especially in concert with a visit to the neighboring *Brooklyn Museum*. Specialized gardens include one with fragrances for the blind, another exclusively of roses, one of herbs, three authentic Japanese settings supplemented by a superb bonsai display, and an ebullient horticultural tribute to Shakespeare, incorporating 80 plant species mentioned in his plays. The restrained Victorian conservatory was designed by the ubiquitous McKim, Mead & White in 1918, with variously tinted glass panes arching over equatorial fern and fruit trees.

Brooklyn Bridge 🏛 ★
Map *3*U5 ▢ 🔲

Perhaps the most spectacular engineering achievement of its time, the enduring grace of the 1,595ft (486m) span has inspired paeans by painters and poets. John Roebling conceived it in 1857, but construction did not begin until 1869. There was scepticism about its feasibility, the need for a bridge over a river well-served by ferry lines, and the projected expense. In the manner of public projects, those costs routinely multiplied, eventually totaling the then-stunning sum of nearly $16,000,000. Since construction paralleled the reign of one of New York's most corrupt political regimes, undetermined portions of the budgeted funds were diverted to the accounts of the notorious Boss Tweed and his cronies.

Roebling died in the first year of construction, contracting tetanus after his foot was crushed by a docking ferry. His son Washington took over. While rising from an underwater chamber, he suffered an attack of the bends and was permanently disabled. Although confined to a wheelchair, he oversaw the project to its conclusion, employing his wife Emily as a go-between. Thousands of new immigrants, largely Irish and Italian, labored 14yr on the project. Uncounted numbers died, many of them victims of diseases associated with the nascent technology.

Six days after the opening on May 24, 1883, a rumor that the bridge was collapsing raced through the festive crowd of sightseers. There were 12 fatalities in the ensuing panic. Since then, the 133ft (40m) height of the span has proved tempting to the foolhardy and suicidal. At least 34 jumpers have not survived the fall. Despite early doubts about its stability, there is every reason to believe that the grande dame of New York bridges will be there when today's youngest pedestrians bring their grandchildren. There are incomparable **vistas** ☆ of East River traffic and the lower Manhattan skyline from the elevated walkway.

Brooklyn Heights 🏛 ☆
Map *3*U6.

In 1646, a handful of Dutch families decided to give official status to their settlement on the bluffs overlooking the juncture of the Hudson and East rivers and the larger village at the toe of Manhattan Island. They called their new home 'Breuckelen.' The establishment of a regular steam ferry service in 1820 transformed the rural community into a suburb. Shipping magnates and wealthy merchants chose to move in, insulated from the traumas of the troubled city and yet in a position to monitor river traffic. The terraces they lived on competed in harbor vistas and luxury of appointments. A substantial number persisted into the 20thC, but by the 1950s the Heights were in decline.

A plan to ram a highway through the neighborhood was narrowly averted, and the resulting community spirit signaled its renaissance. Now designated an Historic District, it is the most desirable residential enclave in the borough. (See *Walk 8* in *Planning*.)

Brooklyn Museum ☆

*188 Eastern Parkway (Washington Ave.), Brooklyn, NY
11238 ☎ 638–5000. Map 12E3 ▨ ▣ ✷ Open Wed–Sat
10am–5pm, Sun noon–5pm, public hols 1–5pm. Closed
Mon, Tues. Subway 2,3,4 to Eastern Parkway–Brooklyn
Museum.*

Although in constant struggle with fiscal uncertainty, this fine
institution is the keystone of the borough's cultural and
recreational complex that includes the adjacent *Brooklyn
Botanic Garden, Prospect Park* and zoo, and the Brooklyn
Public Library. The museum must be ranked among the most
important in the city and might have challenged even the
nonpareil *Metropolitan Museum of Art* had the initial plans of
the architectural firm of McKim, Mead & White been carried
out. As it is, the scaled-down scheme that was erected at the
turn of the century is an imposing Neoclassical pile, flawed
only by a misguided 1930s modernization that removed the
noble exterior staircase. Some compensation for that
desecration is provided by the two 1916 Daniel Chester French
statues that were moved to pedestals outside in 1963.

Our admiration of the antique is not admiration of the old but of
the natural.

Emerson, *Essays, First Series: History*

Inside are five floors of arts and antiquities spanning
centuries and continents from Egypt to Oceania. Exhibits are
grouped essentially along geographical or societal lines. The
first floor is devoted to the **arts and crafts of the primitive** (or at
least pre-colonial) **peoples of the Americas, Africa and the
South Pacific**. Totem poles of the NW tribes loom over cases of
New Guinean ceremonial masks, Columbian ritual urns, Inca
jewelry, Hopi and Zuni dolls, African fetishes and weapons.
Adjacent rooms house a gallery reserved for art shows drawn
from the Brooklyn community, a cafeteria, and a museum shop
that purveys a remarkable array of crafts from around the world
at reasonable prices.

On the second floor are **arts of Asia and Islam**, spotlighting
ceramics, rugs, textiles, paintings, metal and jade secular and
religious objects from India, China, Persia, Japan, Tibet and
Indochina. A separate print room encompasses European and
American graphic arts from the 14thC to the present.

The pride of the museum is the collection of **relics of
Dynastic and Coptic Egypt** on the third floor, with sarcophagi
mingling with alabaster figurines and an ebony sphinx. Of
particular interest are the **Assyrian reliefs ☆** in the Kevorkian
Gallery, just beyond the elevator vestibule. The wall sculptures,
some from the Palace of Ashurnasirpal II, depict winged deities
and griffin-headed genies. On the right side of the hall is a case
of ceremonial vessels, partly animal-shaped, followed by one
filled with engraved silver bowls. This corridor leads into an
unexpectedly dramatic inner court ringed with shallow cases of
exquisite objects ranging from Egyptian to Cypriot and Greek:
amulets, amphoras, glass bottles as fragile as paper, beakers,
fragments of textiles, busts of monarchs. Additional rooms are
given to still more jewelry, pottery and funerary pieces.

The fourth floor is devoted to **furniture and decorative
arts**, largely of the 17th and 18thC, but also including the early
Colonial period and some Manhattan Art Deco. The Jan
Martense Schenck House, a Dutch two-room dwelling of New

York c.1675, is reconstructed and fully furnished with authentic pieces. There is also a costume institute.

Just inside the fifth floor entrance is a lush **landscape☆** by the 19thC American Albert Bierstadt, startlingly overpowering the viewer with its rolling thunderclouds, shafts of light, alpine cascades and snowy peaks. The smaller canvasses of the Hudson River School that follow are pale by comparison, but are momentarily diverting. The first doorway leads into the East Galleries, reserved for **European painting**. After the glories of the first and third floors, these are disappointingly minor works by important artists. The supposed highlight is *Mlle. Fiorre in the Ballet La Source*, a very early (1866) Degas that looks merely half-finished and gives barely a hint of the off-center composition that was to become his hallmark. Next to it are two minor Corots. The rest of the room holds portraits of modest distinction and some bucolic scenes by Millet. A small room of preliminary studies in pastels and gouache includes an appealing Toulouse-Lautrec, alongside drawings by Manet, Gauguin, Degas and Pissarro. They and their compatriots Renoir, Monet and Cézanne are represented in the last room by larger oils that demand little attention. On the way out of this section, note the 15th and 16thC Italian religious paintings on wood. The rest of the floor is normally used for special exhibitions, often of an Americana theme.

An unusual outdoor court at the rear of the building preserves ornamental fragments scavenged from such lamented buildings as the razed Penn Station. Lectures, films, concerts and gallery talks are a regular part of the museum's program.

Brotherhood Synagogue 🏛

28 Gramercy Park S (3rd Ave.), NY 10003 ☎ *674–5750. Map 5Q4* 🏛 🏛 *No tours Fri, Sat, Jewish hols. Telephone 24hr in advance for appointment.*

From 1859 until 1975, this was a Quaker meeting house, which explains the absence of unessential ornamentation. It is part of the *Gramercy Park* Historic District.

Bryant Park

Ave. of the Americas and 42nd St. Map 5O4

Most midtown blocks have supported disparate functions over the last 150yr of development, but few as profound as this site. In the early 19thC, it was a potter's field. Two decades later, a fortress-like reservoir was completed, and in 1853, an imitation of London's Crystal Palace was erected on an adjacent strip of land. That was destroyed by fire in 1858, and the scorched earth was designated a park, dedicated to poet and journalist William Cullen Bryant (1794–1878). At the turn of the century, the reservoir was drained and filled and the *New York Public Library* and park extension took its place. Office workers drop by to enjoy the sun and concerts of live and recorded music. Lolling among them are a number of drug dealers of placid mien and largely bogus merchandise. They are easily ignored.

Burlington House

1345 Ave. of the Americas (54th St.), NY 10019 ☎ *571–2206. Map 5N4* 🏛 *Open Wed–Sun noon–6pm. Closed Mon, Tues.*

This otherwise undistinguished glass tower in midtown is enlivened by two thistledown fountains in the wide plaza fronting 6th Ave. and by a first-floor gallery that houses

long-term exhibitions of catholic inspiration and execution. In
the recent past, these have included a slick multi-image treatise
on the development of the textile industry and a much-praised
environmental representation of New York called *Ruckus
Manhattan* by the serio-comic Red Grooms. It is possible that
this show will still be in residence when you arrive, but even if it
is not, the sprightly history of this exhibition hall makes a stop
worthwhile.

Carl Schurz Park
Map 7L5.
Schurz was a German-born immigrant who became a US
senator. The park in his name is at the eastern end of 86th St.,
the central artery of the German community known as
Yorkville. The official residence of the mayor, *Gracie Mansion*,
is at the northern edge of the green.

Carnegie Hall
*154 W 57th St. (7th Ave.), NY 10019 ☎ 247–7459. Map
4N3.*
It was feared that the 1891 hall would be demolished along with
the old Metropolitan Opera House after the completion of the
Lincoln Center. Preservationists scored a too-infrequent
victory, however, and funds were raised to renovate the
interior. The acoustics are still superb, and the concert schedule
is full, with artists and groups clamoring for dates.

Castle Clinton National Monument 🏛
*Battery Park (foot of Broadway), NY 10004 ☎ 344–7220.
Map 2V4 ⊙ ✗ ✱ Open 9am–5pm June–Aug daily,
Mar–May, Sept–Dec Mon–Fri. Closed Jan, Feb.*
Concern over a possible second conflict with the English
prompted initial plans for a battery of 28 cannons on the rocky
outcrop 200ft (60m) off the sw tip of Manhattan. The eventual
reality of British impressment of crews of American merchant
ships lent credence to the fear, and additional fortifications
were thrown up. The intention was to discourage hostile ships
attempting to enter the East River, in concert with crossfire
from a similar installation on nearby Governor's Island (still a
military post). Perhaps it worked, for the fort never had a
chance to lose a volley.

When the lingering hatreds of the War of 1812 faded, the
circular sandstone structure was given to New York City. It was
transformed into an entertainment center, hosting concerts and
recitals. By the middle of the century, it had been joined with
Manhattan, and in 1855 it became an immigrant processing
center. By 1892, that function was assumed by *Ellis Island*, and
the fort was converted into a public aquarium, a role it held
until 1941. After World War II, it was restored to its original
status, and is now a Federal landmark administered by the
National Park Service.

Cathedral Church of St John The Divine 🏛 † ☆
*1047 Amsterdam Ave. (112th St.), NY 10025 ☎ 678–6888
Map 8I3 ⊙ ✗ Open 7am–5pm. Occasionally closed for
special events.*
Work on the cathedral started in 1892. By the year 2000, they
hope to have the two towers completed. That will still leave the
transepts and other additions to be undertaken – perhaps
somewhere around 2050? Even now, the interior space is

second only to St Peter's in Rome, and the combined floor space of Chartres and Notre Dame (Paris) would fit within the 146 by 601ft (44 by 183m) area. The measured pace of construction is due to the determination to use methods that reach back to the Middle Ages. English master masons instruct American apprentices in the **stonecutting yard** (*open to the public Mon–Fri 8:45am–3:45pm*). Religious and secular works donated to the cathedral over the last 100yr are offhandedly stored for future display. A recent inventory revealed the surprising scope of the collection, which includes 13th–16thC tapestries and paintings of the Italian Renaissance. They are on view on a circulating basis in the **Museum** ☆ (👁 *Mon–Sat 11am–4pm, Sun noon–5pm; guided tours Mon–Sat 11am, 2pm, Sun 12:30pm.*).

Center for Inter-American Relations
680 Park Ave. (68th St.), NY 10021 ☎ *249–8950.* Map **7M4**
👁 ✗ *by appointment. Open Tues–Sun noon–6pm. Closed Mon.*

The architectural firm of McKim, Mead & White was responsible for many notable buildings of the late 19th and early 20thC in New York, and a substantial number still exist. Perhaps because the third and most famous partner, Stanford White, died at the hands of a jealous husband in 1906, this 1909 structure is a Neo-Georgian departure from the Italianate preferences of their earlier projects. After a period as home for the Russian Delegation to the UN, one of the many Rockefellers bought it and gave it to the Center. Although arts and crafts of every country and age of the Western Hemisphere are exhibited, the emphasis is on Latin America.

Central Park ★
Maps **6&7**.

Throughout its history, pragmatic visionaries have tempered the city's headlong rush to squeeze every penny of profit from the limited available land. In 1844, most of Manhattan N of 50th St. was a wasteland, supporting only squatters. Poet William Cullen Bryant prodded City Hall into acquiring 840 acres between what would be 5th Ave and Central Park West and 59th St. and 110th St. Frederick Law Olmsted and Calvert Vaux submitted the winning landscaping scheme in 1857. Its execution required 20yr, but the results are cherished by every New Yorker – whether cyclist, jogger, stroller, lover, picnicker or baseball player. There are lakes, bridges, ponds, glades, hillocks, meadows, fountains, zoos, boathouses, playgrounds, bandstands, bridle paths, sculptures, terraces, a skating rink and an outdoor theater for summer Shakespeare. In a real sense, it is New York's greatest single achievement. (See *Walk 6* in *Planning.*)

Central Park Zoo
5th Ave. and 64th St., NY 10021 ☎ *360–8213.* Map **7M4**
👁 *Children's Zoo* 🚻 ⬛ ✱ *Open 11am–5pm; Children's Zoo 10am–4:30pm.*

Small, old and crowded, but currently undergoing a much-needed modernization, this is a handy alternative for those without the time or inclination to travel to the far superior *Bronx Zoo and New York Botanical Garden.* Feeding time for the seals (mid-afternoon) is the major draw, but the lions, monkeys, elephants, polar bears, jungle cats and camels are

Chelsea

nearly as diverting, even if they often seem dispirited. An elevated cafeteria provides facilities for creature-watching. Stroll N, crossing the Transverse Rd., to reach the separate **Children's Zoo** where farm animals come forward to be fed and scratched behind the ears. (See *Walk 6* in *Planning*.)

Chelsea
Map 4Q3

The genesis of the neighborhood known as Chelsea is attributed to an unlikely creator. Writer Clement Clark Moore inherited the land and drew up plans for streets and buildings. Many of his blocks of brownstones remain, albeit often scarred by 20thC so-called improvements, but all too frequently they have been displaced by uninspired residential and industrial buildings. There are signs of an intensifying gentrification process, with antique shops, Off-Off Broadway experimental theaters, music pubs, art galleries, and nightclubs sufficiently chic to incite uptowners into long taxi rides. The principal landmark is the *Chelsea Hotel*, one of the first luxury apartment houses. Less well known is the **General Theological Seminary**: enter the door at 175 9th Ave. and emerge in an unexpected square of trees and lawns. Boundaries of the district are 14th St. to 23rd St., 7th Ave. to the Hudson River.

Chelsea Hotel ▥
222 W 23rd St. (8th Ave.), NY 10011 ☎ 243–3700. Map 4Q3.

Constructed in 1884 as one of the first apartment houses, the Chelsea was meant to attract wealthy tenants from a class which until then had nearly always chosen private homes. Inducements were its duplex suites, marble fireplaces, new-fangled elevator, generous proportions, and proximity to what was the main theater and shopping district. In addition, the fireproof construction was so cautiously designed that it exceeds even present-day safety standards.

Unlike the uptown *Dakota Apartments*, completed the same year with similar objectives, the Chelsea slid in reputation as the city rolled northward. In 1905, it was converted to a hotel that has proved irresistible to artists, writers and composers. Thomas Wolfe, Virgil Thompson, O. Henry, Tennessee Williams, Jackson Pollock, and Sarah Bernhardt are but a few of those who lived here. The Bohemian panache they imparted persists, and there are paintings by former and present tenants in the dingy lobby. About half the rooms are available to transients; the rest have permanent tenants.

China House
125 E 65th St. (Park Ave.), NY 10021 ☎ 744–8181. Map 7M4 ▨ Open Mon–Fri 10am–5pm, Sat 11am–5pm, Sun 2–5pm.

Ferocious carved dogs at the entrance, biannual exhibitions of art from the mother country, and cooking and language classes help satisfy (and arouse) the current occidental curiosity about things Chinese. But China House has had a longer life and different sponsorship than might be expected. The parent institute was created in 1926 to aid Chinese-Americans and foster cultural relations with the West. In 1945, a grand East Side house was donated by controversial publisher Henry Luce to serve as headquarters. Luce, co-founder of the Time-Life empire, had been born in China of missionary parents. A full

range of educational and cultural offerings is available to
citizens of Chinese origin and the larger public, including films,
lectures, courses in calligraphy, opera, and vocational training
for newly arrived immigrants. The twice-yearly art exhibitions
are usually held in spring and late autumn.

Chinatown ☆
Map 2T4.
Traditionally defined as eight square blocks between *The
Bowery*, and Mulberry, Worth, and Canal Sts., Chinatown has
spilled over the boundaries in recent years. From 1882, when a
Federal law specifically excluded Chinese immigrants, until the
1960s, when such clearly racial restrictions were raised, the
population of the community was relatively stable. The core of
the neighborhood is gratifyingly exotic, the air heavy with
dialects and enticing aromas. Every other restaurant is hung
with golden ducks and even the telephone booths have pagoda
roofs. (See *Walk 3* in *Planning*.)

Chinese Museum
*8 Mott St. (near Park Row), NY 10013 ☎ 964–1542. Map
3S5 🔄 ✳ Open Mon–Sat 10am–6pm. Closed Sun.*
Dominating the hall is a cousin of the fearsome gilded dragon
that snakes through Chinatown on the shoulders of tireless
young men every New Year's Day (after the first full moon in
Jan). But this small and funky repository – its entrance is off an
arcade of bleeping electronic game machines – also houses
printed materials, fireworks, costumes, coins and musical
instruments. Among the less offbeat exhibits are scores of
labeled wax specimens of Chinese foods, which aid
identification of the real thing in nearby restaurant windows.

Chrysler Building ▥ ☆
*405 Lexington Ave. (42nd St.), NY 10017 ☎ 682–3070.
Map 504 🔄 Open Mon–Fri 9am–5pm. Closed Sat, Sun.*
For a flicker of time after its completion in 1930, this was the
highest structure in the world at 1,048ft (320m), the first to
surpass the Eiffel Tower. But that was a period of intense
speculative competition, and the *Empire State Building* soon
took the title. Over 50yr later, however, the Chrysler is still in
the top ten, and it remains the most satisfying esthetic result of
the skyscraper mania. Art Deco arches of stainless steel
surmount the tower, flaring in the sun, base for a slender spire
that thrusts 123ft (37m) into the clouds. Abstract
representations of automobile parts form friezes and other
decorative details, in deference to the first owner's business.
There is no observation floor, but look at the Cubistic
assemblages of grained marble and chrome in the lobby.

Church of the Ascension ▥ †
*36 5th Ave. (10th St.), NY 10003 ☎ 254–8620. Map 2R4.
Open Mon–Sat noon–2pm, 5–7pm. Closed Sun.*
The first church on lower 5th Ave. (when upper 5th was still
country), this was also the first to be executed in the Gothic
Revival mode then sweeping through Europe. Brownstone was
used for the facing, a material that was to become a favorite of
the well-to-do for their row houses. In 1889, McKim, Mead &
White remodeled parts of the interior and the parish house,
hiring Louis Comfort Tiffany for the design of some of the
stained glass.

Church of the Transfiguration
1 E 29th St. (5th Ave.), NY 10016 ☎ *684–6770. Map* **5***P4*
Open 8am–6pm.

It is said that when an actor asked to be married, he was firmly
dispatched to this 'Little Church Around the Corner,' an
institution presumably not overly concerned about the dubious
professions and social status of its parishioners. The church was
built around 1850 and has a long association with show folk.

Citicorp Center ▥ ☆
153 E 53rd St. (Lexington Ave.), NY 10022 ☎ *559–4259.*
Map **5***N4* ▣ *Open 8am–midnight.*

Posterity has yet to render its verdict on this building. Its
distinctive sloping roof line moves it into the Post-Modernist
category of skyscraper design, away from the rectangular glass
boxes of the Bauhaus school. The roof was intended to house
solar energy collectors, a good intention sacrificed to the gods
of cost accounting. Quibbles aside, the 1978 building brought
life to a dreary block and accommodated into its design the
modest but striking **St Peter's Lutheran Church**. Office
floors begin at 127ft (39m), clearing the church steeple and
providing a public atrium embracing 22 shops and restaurants.
The interior plaza is filled with trees and tables, and live music
is often laid on by the management. Co-operating were Hugh
Stubbins and Emery Roth & Sons – the latter firm was also
partly responsible for such looming local monoliths as the
World Trade Center and *Pan Am Building*.

City Hall ▥
City Hall Park (Broadway and Murray St.), NY 10007
☎ *566–5200. Map* **2***T4* ▣ *Open Mon–Fri 10am–3pm.*
Closed Sat, Sun.

Both dwarfed and enhanced by the taller buildings that enclose
it on three sides, the third and present City Hall (1811) is a
Georgian-Federal-Renaissance gem which even the Sun King
might have accepted (at least as a summer cottage). (See *Walk 3*
in *Planning*.)

Cleopatra's Needle
Central Park. Map **7***L4.*

One of the few obelisks outside Egypt, it was erected in *Central
Park* in 1881, behind the *Metropolitan Museum of Art*. The
red granite spire is covered with hieroglyphics from the time of
Thutmose III (c.1600 BC). Regrettably, the change in climate,
plus air pollution, has worn them down.

The Cloisters ▥ ☆
Fort Tryon Park, NY 10040 ☎ *923–3700 ext 26. Map* **10***B2*
▧ *K* ▬ *Open Tues–Sat 10am–4:45pm, Sun 1–4:45pm.*
*Closed Mon, Sun (Sept–May). Half-price entry for senior
citizens, children. Subway A to 190th St.*

Save The Cloisters for a day when the freneticism of the Big
Apple becomes overbearing. This far-uptown unit of the
Metropolitan Museum of Art is a wondrous oasis in *Fort Tryon
Park*, overlooking the Hudson River from the northern heights
of the island. On the crest of a hill banked by woodland and
meadows, parts of several European monasteries and chapels
have been blended in a unified edifice of blissful serenity. The
collection was founded by George Grey Barnard, who gathered
vast amounts of superb medieval sculpture on his many visits to

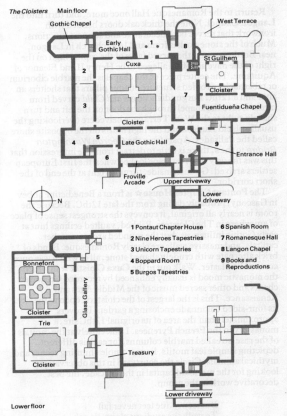

The Cloisters Main floor

Main floor (N and W)

Lower floor

1 Pontaut Chapter House
2 Nine Heroes Tapestries
3 Unicorn Tapestries
4 Boppard Room
5 Burgos Tapestries
6 Spanish Room
7 Romanesque Hall
8 Langon Chapel
9 Books and Reproductions

Europe. It was first opened to the public in 1914 and moved to its present home in 1938, following a donation by the Rockefeller family.

Main floor (N and W) The approach is up a curving road from the bus stop and parking lot, and entry is past nine arches from the **15thC Benedictine monastery of Froville**. Walk through the French 12thC archway into the **Romanesque Hall** and turn right into the **Fuentidueña Chapel**☆ The low black stone baptismal font just inside is from Belgium, the barrel-vaulted apse from Segovia, the fresco above the altar from Catalonia. All are believed to be from the 12thC. On the left is a 16thC painted limestone sculpture from Zamora. The grinning hyena-like creature was meant to be a lion, and is surmounted by a headless Christ figure placing a crown on Mary's head. Return to the Romanesque Hall and turn into the **St Guilhem Cloister**☆ Perhaps because of the delicacy of the ornamentation on the ancient pillars, this is the only indoor cloister. A glass ceiling permits potted plants to grow in winter. Paired capitals and columns feature stylized leaves, flowers and human figures. No two pairs are the same. As in the other rooms, a plan on the wall shows which portions are authentic.

Return to the Romanesque Hall once more, and turn into the
Langon Chapel. Note the thick oak doors banded with
ironwork that serves both decorative and support functions.
Much of the stonework is from an 11thC church in Langon,
near Bordeaux, and the carved faces of the capital high on the
right of the nave are often alleged to be Henry II and Eleanor of
Aquitaine. The centerpiece of the chapel is the marble ciborium
or tabernacle, a roofed structure on four pillars that shelters an
altar and a 12thC Burgundian *Virgin and Child* carved from
birch. Leave the chapel through the door on the left and turn
sharply right to the **West Terrace**, a belvedere overlooking the
usually placid Hudson and the high bluffs on the opposite shore
called the Palisades. Apart from the *George Washington
Bridge* to the S, there is little to detract from the impression that
this was the way the riverscape looked when the first European
settlers arrived. Go back inside, turning right at the end of the
short corridor.

The **Pontaut Chapter House** ☆ is from a Benedictine abbey
in Gascony, probably dating from the late 12thC. Because the
room is nearly all original, it conveys the strongest sense of place
of anywhere in The Cloisters. Ribbed, vaulted ceilings hint at
early Gothic influences, but the rounded arches, somber
capitals, and massive walls are clearly Romanesque. Bands of
brick alternate with crudely shaped stone, all of which was once
covered by plaster. Walk out in the **Cuxa Cloister** ☆ in which
the monastic mood is usually enhanced by recorded Gregorian
chants and other sacred music of the Middle Ages and
Renaissance. This is the largest of the cloisters, open to the sky,
its four-sided colonnade enclosing a garden. It covers
approximately half the area of its original 12thC site, a
monastery in the French Pyrenees. Look closely at the capitals
of the rose-streaked marble columns, for each is different,
depicting simple leaf motifs, lions, complex hunting scenes and
mythical animals. Circle the courtyard in this observation,
looking for the mermaid capital in the E arcade, the best
decorative work in the group.

> But let my due feet never fail
> To walk the studious cloister's pale,
> And love the high embowed roof,
> With antique pillars massy proof
> Milton, *Il Penseroso*

Continue past the Chapter House and enter the **Early Gothic
Hall** to examine the ecclesiastical figures, then move on to the
Gothic Chapel. Differences from the Romanesque style
predominating to this point are evident in the pointed arches
and ribbed vaulting, the 14thC stained glass, and the greater
delicacy of the stonework, especially at the tops of the window
openings. Large effigies and sarcophagi are dotted about. Their
origins are French and Catalan, while most of the glass is
Austrian. Take the stairs down to the lower floor.
Lower floor In the **Glass Gallery**, pause to study the
15th–16thC stained glass from which it takes its name. At the
end is a large section of intricately carved woodwork that once
enclosed the staircase of a house in Abbeville, France. Although
holy figures are duly depicted, the effect is of secular Gothic
exuberance. The room straight ahead houses 37 carved wood
panels, again from Abbeville, but this time they convey a
distinctly religious impression.

Turn left into the **Treasury ☆** which features exquisite chalices of silver and gold, one from the 4thC. This route leads back past the Abbeville woodwork to a door opening into the **Trie Cloister**. Off the main traffic lanes of the museum, this secluded spot encourages the contemplative frame of mind for which it was intended. Each capital varies from the others, the scenes more literal than those so far encountered, and the slender double pillars are of differently colored marble. The plants surrounding the fountain are examples of those found in the Unicorn Tapestries (below). Leave by the doorway at the NW corner, walking along the arcade modeled on the cloister of the abbey at **Bonnefont-en-Comminges**. Here, the attraction is not the architecture but the **garden ☆** that is heady with lemon thyme, marjoram, mace and woodruff. Brick paths separate beds of violets and forget-me-nots, dominated by four quince trees. A low wall affords views of the park to the S, and bird watchers are often surprised by the variety of species attracted to the garden. When ready, re-enter the Glass Gallery and return upstairs.

Main floor (S and E)   From the Gothic Chapel, turn into the **Nine Heroes Tapestries** room. The late-14thC hangings show five of the heroes who featured in this popular theme, among them Alexander the Great, Charlemagne and Julius Caesar. Understandably faded and fragmented, the tapestries provide a foretaste of the splendid 16thC **Unicorn Tapestries ☆** in the next hall. Scholarly consensus ranks this set of seven superb hangings among the finest in existence. That assessment may be restrained, for in concept, detailing and craftsmanship they are peerless. The remarkable petal-by-leaf renderings of plants and flowers make it possible to identify many of the live specimens seen in the Trie Cloister (above). Beyond such surface delights is the telling of a tale with deep symbolic undercurrents. Christ is seen as a Unicorn, Gabriel as a hunter with a horn, Satan as a snake; pagan beliefs mingle with Christian convictions, fruits and blossoms represent purity, lust, fertility. Baronial German furnishings and a flamboyant French Gothic fireplace suggest the surroundings in which the tapestries were for a long time viewed.

The **Boppard Room** is named after the German town where its six 15thC stained-glass panels originated. Go past the late 15thC **Burgos Tapestries**, executed to the glorification of Charles VIII of France, and turn into the **Spanish Room** to see Robert Campin's *Annunciation* triptych (c.1425). The altarpiece is remarkable for the choice of setting: a simple Flemish interior rather than the traditional ecclesiastical or historical environment. The painted Gothic red pine ceiling in this room is also worthy of attention. Leave the museum through the **Late Gothic Hall**, noting the fine 15thC Spanish retable on your way out.

Coliseum   See *New York Coliseum*.

Columbia University ▥
Broadway (116th St.), NY 10027 ☎ *280–1754. Map 8I2* ▣
Open 24hr. Subway 1 to 116th St. – Columbia University.
Established in 1754 as King's College, and fueled by over two centuries of alumni bequests and gifts, Columbia is now one of the wealthiest universities in the US. As a member of the prestigious group known as the Ivy League, which includes Harvard, Yale and Princeton, it is also one of the most

distinguished. With the end of the Revolution, 'King's' College
became 'Columbia,' and after an intermediate move to Madison
Ave. and 49th St., settled here at Morningside Heights in 1897.
Over the years, the original men's college has joined with a
teacher's college and Barnard College for women, and courses
now include business administration, law, medicine, dentistry,
librarianship, journalism, social work and public health.
Founding father Alexander Hamilton graduated from here, and
Dwight Eisenhower was the university's president after World
War II before moving on to higher office.

The original layout of the campus and two of the first
buildings were products of McKim, Mead & White.
Fortunately, their design was opened up to permit larger
pedestrian plazas which in turn lent greater drama to the most
prominent building, **Low Library**. Its style is Neoclassical,
with a surmounting dome and a portico with ten columns and a
coffered ceiling. The elevated site makes the most of the
building's monumentality. Halfway up the wide front steps is a
statue of *Alma Mater* by Daniel Chester French, best known for
his sculptures of Abraham Lincoln. Low Library is essentially an
administration building. **Butler Library**, to the S, is the main
repository of the university's 5-million-volume collection.

The Terrace Restaurant on the top floor is open to the public.
Given its auspices, the food and service are quite good, and it
affords excellent views of Manhattan.

Coney Island

*Brooklyn. Map **12**F3. Subway B, D, F, M, N, QB to Stillwell
Ave. – Coney Island.*
For generations of working-class New Yorkers, Coney Island
was Riviera-on-the-Subway, a wide strip of powdery sand that
gave surcease from the steaming streets and tenements of the
city. It has fallen on hard times, the shattered and burned-out
housing inland occupied by only pensioners and the poor, the
Steeplechase Park amusement center a wasteland. Still, the
beach has been cleaned up, the boardwalk repaired, the original
Nathan's Famous grills hundreds of incomparable hot dogs
daily, teenagers squeal through roller-coaster dips at Astroland,
and families gape at the sharks and dolphins of the *New York
Aquarium*. The district is on the Atlantic Ocean in S Brooklyn,
along Surf Ave. between W 37th St. and Ocean Parkway.

Cooper-Hewitt Museum 🏛 ☆

*2 E 91st St. (5th Ave.) ☎ 860–6868. Map **7**K4 🖼 ✗ Open
Tues 10am–9pm, Wed–Sat 10am–5pm, Sun noon–5pm.
Closed Mon.*
In this pricey venue at the top of the 5th Ave. 'Museum Mile,'
even millionaires built their mansions flush with their property
boundaries, forgoing lawns and gardens. But in that lamented
time before the imposition of income taxes, Scottish-born
Andrew Carnegie was more than simply rich. He had just sold
his steel company (1901) for over $250 million. When he built
this 64-room house in the same year, he left himself a green
buffer all around and transplanted mature trees from upstate.
Only a friend and business associate like Henry C. Frick could
indulge himself in a similar fashion (see the *Frick Collection*).

If pressed, an art historian might describe the Carnegie house
as Georgian, but the design was carried out with such an
elephantine hand that this label is hardly appropriate. Despite
the unfortunate facade, there is a pleasant garden behind the

cast-iron fence and a marvelous stained-glass canopy over the entrance. Within are the decorative art acquisitions of Peter Cooper (founder of *Cooper Union*) and his granddaughters Eleanor and Sarah Hewitt. The only New York branch of the Smithsonian Institution, its subtitle is the National Museum of Design. That objective is broadly defined, to incorporate wallpapers, furniture, glassware, metalwork, lace and ceramics, with superb examples of each. The dual strengths of the museum are its textiles and over 30,000 drawings. The drawings include many works by Dürer, Rembrandt and Winslow Homer. Fabrics and embroidery come from as far afield as Persia, Spain, France, India, Egypt and Italy, and span 14 centuries.

Cooper Union ▥
Cooper Sq., NY 10003 ☎ *254–6300. Map 2R4. Open 8am–10pm.*

Peter Cooper became a millionaire through participation in the key 19thC industries of railways and iron-making. In the benevolent if paternalistic manner of his fellows, he founded this college for the training of artists and engineers and built the somber pile (1859) that still houses part of the institution. The Foundation Building rather resembles a railway station of the time – dark, brooding, ponderous – with supposedly Italianate portico and arcades.

Still, Cooper made provision for a free-tuition curriculum for talented persons of any race, sex, creed or economic status at a time when such notions were deemed dangerous to the natural order of things. That policy persists and has profited tens of thousands of Americans who might not otherwise have had the chance of higher education. The Great Hall within hosted many celebrated speakers of the last century, among them suffragette Susan B. Anthony, abolitionist Henry Ward Beecher, Mark Twain and, in a rare New York appearance, Abraham Lincoln.

Craft Museum   See *American Craft Museum.*

Dakota Apartments ▥
1 W 72nd St., NY 10023. Map 6M3.

Until 1884, members of New York's establishment would not consider living in anything but a private house. This luxury 10-story apartment building changed their minds, even though it was so far uptown that wags said it was in Dakota Indian territory. Its capacious rooms, high ceilings, thick-walled quiet, and offbeat Bavarian fortress exterior ensure its continued cachet with celebrities and other privileged folk. *Rosemary's Baby* was filmed here. John Lennon was murdered outside the entrance in 1980.

Downtown Whitney Museum
26 Wall St. (Nassau St.), NY 10005 ☎ *431–1621. Map 2U4* ▣ *Open Mon–Fri 11am–3pm. Closed Sat, Sun.*

A child of the uptown *Whitney Museum of American Art*, born in 1975, this branch caters for the largely non-residential population of the *Financial District*, as demonstrated by its limited hours. After migrations around lower Manhattan, it seems to have found a home on the mezzanine level of the *Federal Hall National Memorial*. Rotating shows from the permanent collection and other sources are augmented by art appreciation and studio classes.

Dyckman House 🏛

4881 Broadway (204th St.), NY 10543 ☎ *923–8008
(Morris-Jumel Mansion) for information. Map* **10B2** 🅿 *Open
Tues–Sun 11am–5pm. Closed Mon. Subway 1 to 217th St.*

The original owner of the property was Jan Dyckman. He came
to New Amsterdam in 1661 and swiftly assembled the
substantial estate he was to pass on to his descendants. For no
recorded tactical reason, the house built here in 1748 was
burned to the ground by British troops near the end of the
Revolutionary War. The existing replacement was erected in
1783, before they left Manhattan. The estate was once thick
with fruit trees and was tilled by frugal farmers well into the
19thC. Parts of the orchard still bloomed past 1900. Brick and
flagstone form portions of the lower sections of the house, with
weatherboarding rising to a low gambrel roof. The effect is
appropriately Dutch Colonial, and some of the furnishings are
authentic not only to the period but to the original family.

Although it is a long subway ride N to the Inwood district, the
tranquil setting and park-like grounds smooth nerve ends
frayed by the clamor of midtown.

East Side ☆

Map **7L4.**

From 5th Ave. to the East River and 59th St. to 92nd St., this
chic precinct (also known as Upper East Side) harbors most of
the city's major museums, upscale single people, and resident
millionaires, foreign and domestic. Tree-shaded cross streets
near 5th Ave. are lined with attractive brownstones, the owners
of which have succeeded in fending off the blandishments of
developers. Commercial interlopers tend to be low-profile
boutiques and art and antique galleries. Near the river are the
luxury enclaves of **Beekman Place** and **Sutton Place**. Along the
avenues, beautiful people swirl in a fickle flow from this
month's bistro to today's bar and meet each other standing in
line for the latest film. (See *Walk 7* in *Planning* .)

Ellis Island

New York Harbor, NY 10004 ☎ *732–1236/1286. Map*
12D3 🅿 ✗ *Open May–Nov 9:30am–6pm. Ferry from
Battery Park 9:30am, 11:45am, 2pm, 4:15pm.*

The echoing, gloomy halls must have seemed forbidding to the
12 million immigrants who passed through this bureaucratic
purgatory between 1892–1954. Some were held for weeks and
months before being permitted entry to the tantalizing city in
sight across the bay. Planning is under way for the restoration of
the island's 30-odd buildings.

Empire State Building 🏛 ★

350 5th Ave. (34th St.), NY 10001 ☎ *736–3100. Map* **5P4**
🅿 ✗ 🚻 ♿ *Open 9:30am–midnight. Check visibility notice
before buying tickets.*

From its inception, the Empire State Building attracted
superlatives – in achievement and in tragedy. Now only the
third highest building in the world, after the Sears Building in
Chicago and the downtown *World Trade Center*, it
nevertheless remains the foremost symbol of New York. And it
does, after all, stand 1,472ft (448m) high, including TV mast.
By comparison, the Eiffel Tower is 984ft (300m).

King Kong swatted at biplanes from his perch in the 1931

classic, a plane crashed into the 79th floor in 1945, and at least
17 people have flung themselves to their deaths off parapets and
down elevator shafts. The distinctive stepped cap was sketched
in during one of the later design stages. It was to have been a
mooring mast for airships. One attempt to bring that fanciful
notion to reality resulted in some celebrated citizens nearly
being blown away, and the idea was discarded. Without the
rounded cap, the original 86 stories were only 2ft (61cm) higher
than the *Chrysler Building*. With it, another 200ft (61m) and a
second public observatory were added. Perhaps as remarkable
as its height was the fact that the Empire State came in under
schedule and under budget.

Twice a month, 6,500 windows must be washed. There are
60 miles of water pipes within the walls and 60,000 tons of
structural steel. For reasons best known to the participants, an
annual foot race is run *up* the 1,575 steps to the 86th floor. The
facing is limestone, fashioned in modified Art Deco. The
observatory on the 86th floor is wide open, the one on the 102nd
floor enclosed with glass. Go during the day or at night, saving
the other time for another of Manhattan's aeries.

Federal Hall National Memorial ⛫
26 Wall St. (Nassau St.), NY 10005 ☎ *264–8711. Map 2U4*
◎ *K by appointment. Open Mon–Fri 9am–5pm. Closed
Sat, Sun.*

Paradigm of the early 19thC enthusiasm for the Greeks, Federal
Hall is not the building in which Washington took his oath of
office in 1789, as is inferred by many. The **statue of George
Washington** outside stands where the first President did indeed
make those vows, but the building behind was not completed
until 1842. It housed government offices from then until 1955,
when it was converted to its present use as a museum. The main
floor has artifacts of the Revolutionary War period – such as
railings from the porch on which Washington repeated the
famous words – while the *Downtown Whitney Museum* of
contemporary art takes up most of the mezzanine level.

Architects Town & Davis resisted the impulse to slap on
sculptured friezes and ornate capitals, opting for fluted Doric
columns and an unadorned pediment, all of marble quarried a
few miles N of the city. Their only major deviation from their
Greek inspiration was the interior rotunda, but the dramatic
space works, which is ample justification. All in all, it is a
trimlined Parthenon of disciplined stolidity and the finest
example of Greek Revival in Manhattan.

Financial District ☆
Map 2U4.

Bits and scraps of Little Old New York remain, but the
southern end of Manhattan has long shuddered beneath the
thrusting monoliths of international commerce and the
machinations taking place within. The world eavesdrops on
every whisper at the Stock Exchange, and conglomerates eye
each other from their steel and concrete aeries.

Not long ago, the restaurants closed in this district in the
evenings and at weekends, and Sun afternoons drew only a few
strollers down ghostly windswept canyons. Now a trickle of
people are moving back to live in rehabilitated warehouses and
middle-aged skyscrapers, and visitors come for sun and nautical
history to the *South Street Seaport Museum*. (See *Walk 2* in
Planning.)

Fire Department Museum

104 Duane St. (Broadway), NY 10007 ☎ *570–4230. Map*
2T4 🔄 *ƙ ✳ Open Mon–Fri 9am–4pm, Sat, Sun 9am–2pm.*
New York bristles with quirky and beguiling specialized
museums tucked into out-of-the-way corners. They take little
time to explore and often enchant in unexpected ways. This is
one. Three floors of antique firefighting equipment are
currently housed in a 1909 fire station, although a move to
a new location seems likely. A lovingly polished silver-plated
steam engine highlights the collection of hand- and horse-
drawn vehicles that dates back to the early 19thC. Insatiable
buffs might also check out the **Firefighting Museum**, a 15min
walk away on the 15th floor of the Home Insurance Company
building (*59 Maiden Lane*).

Flatiron Building 🏛 ☆

175 5th Ave. (23rd St.), NY 10010. Map 5Q4.
The reasons to visit are its status as the first true skyscraper (a
disputed claim) and its odd triangular shape (dictated by its plot
at the confluence of 5th Ave. and Broadway). In the earliest tall
buildings, made possible by the invention of the electric
elevator, metal cages supported floors while masonry facings
bore their own weight. In the decade before the Flatiron, new
techniques allowed riveted steel frames to bear both floors *and*
facing. That sort of steel skeleton was employed here, 286ft
(87m) high and only 6ft (2m) wide at its narrow end. To calm
the conservative citizenry, a rusticated limestone facade
imitated a stacked Italianate palace. Nevertheless, many were
convinced that the building would collapse in the high winds
characteristic of the area. It didn't. You can enter the lobby
during business hours, but there is no compelling reason to do
so.

Ford Foundation Building 🏛

320 E 43rd St. (2nd Ave.), NY 10016 ☎ *573–5000. Map*
5O5 🔄 *Open Mon–Fri 9am–5pm. Closed Sat, Sun.*
Atriums are in danger of becoming a cliché as pervasive as
sunken plazas in contemporary New York commercial
architecture – a sop to planning boards and environmental
groups dismayed by the loss of landmarks and the addition of
thousands of new commuters straining public services.
Resulting spaces are often bleak and inhuman. The Ford
Foundation presented a gift to the city, however, not a burden,
with this 1967 headquarters. Its interior is enclosed within a
glass shell hung between four granite columns and contains a
third of an acre of mature trees and shrubs. A brook, hushed
and clear, curls through the garden. Passersby are welcome to
step inside for a moment's respite.

Striking as it is, the exterior is in harmony with the scale of
the block, contributing rather than intruding. The offices
above the greenery are for the staff of the Foundation, which
was created by Henry and Edsel Ford. It is the largest
philanthropic trust in the world, concerning itself with a broad
spectrum of human welfare issues, although best known for its
contributions to education and the arts.

Fort Tryon Park

Map 10C2 💷 ✳ 🚌 *Subway A to 190th St.*
While *The Cloisters* museum is the prime motive for a subway
ride to this pastoral far-north Manhattan sanctuary, also

tendered are hills, woodlands, meadows, a small but fascinating botanical garden, a children's playground with wading pool, and staggering Hudson River vistas from the site of the namesake fortification. During the week, only an occasional cyclist or jogger interrupts the solitude.

Fraunces Tavern Museum
54 Pearl St. (Broad St.), NY 10004 ☎ *425–1778. Map 2U4* ▣ *X̷ by appointment* ▣ *Open Mon–Fri 10am–4pm. Closed Sat, Sun.*

Tourist literature routinely implies that this is the tavern where George Washington bade farewell to his troops. It isn't. Rather, it is a 20thC approximation of debatable accuracy, constructed on the site of the original and incorporating parts of the remaining walls. The first building was a three-story mansion, converted into a tavern in 1762 by Samuel Fraunces. A West Indian, he became steward to Washington when the English took New York in 1776. The General returned on December 4, 1783 for lunch with his officers and delivered the famous address. Downstairs is now a restaurant; upstairs and in adjacent buildings there is a collection of Revolutionary musketry and mementoes and two period rooms.

French Institute
22 E 60th St. (Madison Ave.), NY 10022 ☎ *355–6100. Map 5N4* ▣ *Open Mon–Thurs 10am–8pm, Fri 10am–5:30pm, Sat (Sept–June) 10am–1:30pm. Closed Sun.*

In a spectrum of activities to gladden the heart of every Francophile, the institute offers language and cooking classes, recent and venerable films, concerts, recitals, lectures – all relating to the mother country. Students and homesick expatriates can find French magazines and newspapers and perhaps a new friend in the small gallery and library.

Frick Collection ☆
1 E 70th St. (5th Ave.), NY 10021 ☎ *288–0700. Map 7M4* ▣ *x̷⁂ Open Sept–May Tues–Sat 10am–6pm, Sun 1–6pm; closed Mon. June–Aug Wed–Sat 10am–6pm, Sun 1–6pm; closed Mon, Tues, July 1. Children under 10 not admitted, 10–16 only with adult.*

From the 1890s onward the part of 5th Ave. facing lower Central Park has been a millionaires' row. Now the privileged live in duplex penthouses, for not even the very wealthy can afford to maintain the palatial residences built by their antecedents. Most of those mansions have been demolished, a few converted to institutional uses. The Andrew Carnegie residence, for example, is now the *Cooper-Hewitt Museum*. All this makes the Frick Collection even more special, for the house is much the way it was left by the first and only owner – filled with paintings, furniture, clocks and Persian carpets.

Carnegie and industrialist Henry C. Frick were business associates who parted company over policy disputes. Frick chose to build his house (in 1914) only 20 blocks s of his former friend's 64-room residence. Although bearing allegiance to no particular style, its low roofline and front lawn are a welcome visual break in the prevailing wall of high-rises. And there is no more gracious oasis in the city than the interior court with its splashing fountain and flowering plants. After Frick's death, a harmonious addition doubled the floor space. The house was opened to the public in 1935.

Frick Collection

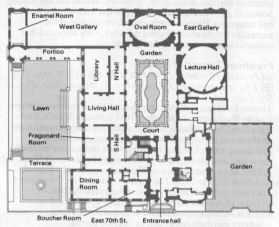

Entrance is made from E 70th St. The first important room
on your left is the **Boucher Room**, with eight panels
representing the *Arts and Sciences* that François Boucher
painted for one of Madame de Pompadour's legendary Rococo
bedrooms. Next is the corner **Dining Room** ✿ which is perhaps
the most striking room in the mansion, with its French
furniture and 18thC paintings by Hogarth, Gainsborough and
Reynolds. To the N is the **Fragonard Room** ✿ where four
paintings known as *The Progress of Love*, once owned by
Madame du Barry, celebrate the different stages of love. The
other seven panels were also executed by Jean-Honoré
Fragonard, a disciple of Boucher and a favorite at the court of
Louis XV. Furnishings in the room are consistent with the
period. The high point of the **Living Hall** is the El Greco
portrait of *St Jerome* over the fireplace. It is flanked by two
Hans Holbein paintings, and there are also works by Titian and
Bellini. On the center table is a bronze by Pollaiuolo. Leading
off from this room are the **South Hall**, notable for Vermeer's
Officer and Laughing Girl, and **North Hall**, which has Ingres'
portrait of *La Comtesse d'Hausonville*. The **Library**
concentrates once again on English painting, with a George Romney portrait
of *Lady Hamilton* and a luminous early Turner. Priceless
Chinese vases add to the authentic appeal of this paneled room.

Largest of the chambers is the **West Gallery** ✿ with its
imposing chilliness offset by the splendor of the masterpieces.
They deserve a methodical clockwise examination. (On the
way, turn into the small **Enamel Room** for a look at Limoges
painted enamels of the 15th–17thC.) Among the treasures of
this trove are a trio of Rembrandts, two works by Van Dyck, a
Velazquez, a Goya and an El Greco. Turner was a progenitor of
the Impressionist revolution that followed his death in 1851,
and his vivid cityscape of Dieppe is particularly significant in
this respect.

Pass through the **Oval Room** with its Whistlers and terra-
cotta *Diana* into the **East Gallery** where Goya, Gainsborough
and Van Dyck are featured. Finally, there is the **Garden
Court** ✿ with its glass roof and fountain. Chamber music

concerts take place on occasional Suns. Inquire at the entrance desk for detailed information.

Garment Center
Map 4P3.

Neither steel nor automobiles nor their ilk are fabricated in New York so, by default, people in suits conjuring advertising jingles and peddling stocks describe themselves as 'industries.' As that word is commonly understood, however, the primary manufacturing enterprise of the city is clothing. Somewhere between 80,000 and 300,000 citizens are employed in the rag trade, depending upon how a statistician tots up the cutters, shippers, salesmen, suppliers, designers, messengers, models, packers, deliverymen, buyers, union organizers and sewing machine operators. Between breakfast and dinner, all of them seem to pour through the streets of this scruffy district along 7th Ave. between 34th and 40th Sts., dodging handcarts, gulping coffee from paper containers, grabbing lapels, scuttling to appointments, making deals. The fashions they produce often rival the best of Paris and Milan.

General Grant National Memorial ⌷
Riverside Drive (122nd St.), NY 10027 ☎ 666–1640. Map 8H2 ⌷ ✗ Open Wed–Sun 9am–5pm. Closed Oct–May, Mon, Tues.

Popularly known as Grant's Tomb, it is no accident that the official designation honors the Civil War service of Ulysses S. Grant rather than his scandal-ridden tenure as the eighteenth President. The mausoleum is fashioned after a 4thC Greek tomb and was financed by private contributions rather than by Congress. After its completion in 1897, both Grant and his wife were interred within, behind impressive bronze doors. A gallery shows photographs and memorabilia from both careers. The Gaudi-esque mosaic benches around the plaza outside are more interesting.

George Washington Bridge ⌷
Map 10D1 ⌷

Dreamers of the 19thC insisted that the broad Hudson River could be spanned, but it took the capitalistic euphoria of the late 1920s to bring together the necessary funds and determination. The bridge was completed in 1931, within months of the *Empire State, Chrysler* and *RCA Buildings* and, like them, was defiant of the economic desolation of the Great Depression. For a time, the 3,500ft (1,067m) between its main towers made it the longest suspension bridge in the world. Budgetary considerations and public opinion fortunately prevented plans to sheath the open steel framework in concrete and granite, as envisioned by architect Cass Gilbert. A second deck for trams and trains was planned by engineer Othmar H. Ammann, but was not added until 1962, when it was given over to general road traffic. There are eight lanes on the upper deck, six below.

Goethe House
1014 5th Ave. (82nd St.), NY 10028 ☎ 744–8310. Map 7L4 ⌷ Open Wed, Fri, Sat noon–5pm, Tues, Thurs 11am–7pm. Closed Sun, Mon.

Films, lectures, art exhibitions and research materials fill this cultural repository, one of dozens sponsored by the Federal Republic of Germany around the world.

Grace Church ▥ †

*802 Broadway (10th St.), NY 10003 ☎ 254–2000. Map
2R4. Open Mon–Fri 9am–5pm, Sat, Sun for services only.*

Although a practicing engineer, James Renwick took advantage
of the mid-19thC tolerance for professional generalism to
design this fine Episcopal church. Its success led to
commissions for *St Patrick's Cathedral* and the Smithsonian
Institution in Washington, all in the Gothic Revival style then
in favor. The wealthy congregation already had a church
downtown, but opened a competition in 1843 for a new one
closer to their homes. Renwick won, although he was only 25,
and construction began in the same year. The marble steeple
with its delicate filigrees and curls replaced the wooden original
in 1884. There is a lovely **English garden☆** to the N, in front of
the rectory, a later Renwick accomplishment. Although the
parishioners were largely from fashionable society, propriety
was briefly rent when circus promoter P.T. Barnum wangled a
wedding of his stellar attraction, Tom Thumb, to a lady midget
also in his employment.

A style of Architecture (the Gothic) which, to me at least, is, in
comparison with all others, the most beautiful of all, and by far
the most in harmony with all the mysteries of religion.

John Keble, *Lectures on Poetry*

Gracie Mansion ▥

*East End Ave. (E 88th St.), NY 10028. Map 7K5 ▨ ▮ Visit
by appointment only Apr–Oct, Wed 10am–4pm. Write to:
Mayor's Office of Special Events, 42 Broadway, New York,
NY 10004.*

Now the residence of the mayor, the mansion is named after the
merchant who built it in 1799. Prominent details are the
encompassing veranda and lattice railings at porch and roof
levels. It is hard to believe that the house once served as a public
rest room in *Carl Schurz Park*, in which it is still located. The
wealth that permitted Archibald Gracie to erect this stately
Federalist house evaporated when two of his ships were seized
by the French in 1807. His family was forced to sell in 1823, and
it went neglected for a century, even though the city purchased
it in 1887. Popular Fiorello LaGuardia was the first mayor to
move in, during World War II. Tours are difficult to arrange,
and tourists are fenced off at some distance, so the best way to
view it is from the deck of a Circle Line tour boat (see *Addresses
and telephone numbers in Basic information*).

Gramercy Park ▥ ☆

Map 5Q4.

A small community forever battling against the dreary
commercial encroachments nibbling at its edges, these few
square blocks evoke 19thC residential elegance as no other area
in Manhattan can. The focal point is the rectangular park from
which the district takes its name. The park is protected by a
high fence, and only people living in the surrounding houses
have keys to the gate. Edwin Booth is represented by a statue
inside; by all accounts, he was a better actor than his brother
John Wilkes Booth, the assassin of Lincoln. Another president,
Theodore Roosevelt, lived nearby. Gramercy Park is part of an
official Historic District, a designation awarded to many areas
of the five boroughs by the city's Landmarks Preservation

Commission. Although the agency's powers are tenuous, it has prevented the demolition or defacement of many worthwhile examples of the architectural heritage.

Grand Central Terminal

Park Ave. and 42nd St., NY 10017. Map **5O4** 💷 ⓡ 𝒴 *Open 6am–2am.*

An attempt to level the terminal to make way for yet another speculative office tower was thwarted in the late 1970s. Grand Central was therefore saved from the fate of Penn Station, over on the West Side. The conservationist effort was worthwhile. Straddling Park Ave., the main facade looks s, toward what was in 1913 the center of population and commerce. Its Beaux Arts adornment includes a heroic sculpture group comprising of Mercury, Athena and Hercules draped around a clock, but this is masked from street level by the second-story ramps that encircle the terminal and join lower and upper Park Ave.

Inside, a vast vaulted space 125ft (38m) wide, and more than twice as long, arcs over rush-hour throngs of 120,000 daily commuters. Despite their headlong rush, not even those who have accumulated 20yr of workday arrivals and departures are unaware of the grandeur of this main concourse. Line paintings depict the celestial constellations against the pale blue ceiling, and light streams through high arched windows. It can still awe, despite the intrusion of an Off-Track Betting Office and the distraction of the giant Kodak picture-of-the-month on the N wall. Take it all in from the new bar inside the Vanderbilt Ave. entrance or wend down to the **Oyster Bar and Restaurant** (see *Restaurants*) between the main and lower levels. Despite the inauspicious location, this is one of the top seafood restaurants in town.

Grant's Tomb   See *General Grant National Memorial*.

Greenacre Park

51st St. (2nd Ave.). Map **5N5**.

An admirable trend has private benefactors contributing public 'vest-pocket' parks that bestow touches of grace and greenery in otherwise congested neighborhoods. This is a somewhat ostentatious example, its open space cluttered up with banks of lights, a slatted pavilion and a semi-sculptural arrangement of rough-hewn sentinels, but it is nevertheless an agreeable retreat from exhaust fumes and noise.

Greenwich Village �🏛 ☆

Map **2R3**.

Those who could afford it fled the disease, fires and squalor of the city in the s to build homes in this rural village of the late 18thC. Pastoral serenity was shortlived, for the northward sprawl of the metropolis soon swamped it. The rich moved farther uptown, and artists took their places, turning row houses into flats and studios. Henry James, Winslow Homer, Edgar Allen Poe and, later, Edna St Vincent Millay and Edward Hopper lived here, and 'The Village' became America's Left Bank. Although present-day rents are beyond the means of most poets and painters, laissez-faire lifestyles pertain, and eccentricity remains in evidence. *Washington Square* is the focal point of an area that is usually delineated by Houston St., 14th St., 4th Ave. and the Hudson River. (See *Walk 5* in *Planning*.)

Grey Art Gallery
33 Washington Pl. (Washington Sq. E), NY 10003
☎598–7603. Map *2*R4 ⌦ *✗ by appointment. Open
Sept–June, Tues, Thurs 10am–6:30pm, Wed
10am–8:30pm, Fri 10am–5pm, Sat 1–5pm; closed Sun,
Mon. Open July–Aug Mon–Fri 11am–7pm; closed Sat, Sun.*

A farsighted chairman of the New York University art
department spearheaded the effort to collect examples of the
New York School of Abstract Expressionism before popular
acceptance caused their prices to skyrocket. For 20yr, the
collection was stored or parceled out for display in
administrative offices. This gallery was created to make it
available to the community. That mission has been expanded to
include frequently rotated exhibitions of art and photography
that combine scholarship and inventive juxtaposition. (See
Walk 5 in *Planning*.)

Guggenheim Museum 🏛 ☆
1071 5th Ave. (89th St.), NY 10028 ☎860–1313. Map *7*K4
⌦ *✗* 🅿 Open Wed–Sun 11am–5pm, Tues 11am–8pm.
Closed Mon.*

Curmudgeonly genius Frank Lloyd Wright detested New York
– he suggested that it be razed and begun again – and the
Solomon R. Guggenheim Museum was his only completed
commission in the city. To say that the result was controversial
falls some way short of the truth. Along a boulevard
characterized by conservative apartment houses and
Neoclassical public buildings, the exterior of the Guggenheim
resembles a flower pot teetering on the edge of a coffee table.
The circular central gallery with its spiral stripe of glass is
smaller at the base than at the top and squats off-center on a
floating horizontal slab. Wright wanted a marble facing, but the
concrete used instead had an unfortunate yellow cast. Reaction
was predictably divided, even before the 1959 opening.
Scornful perplexity was perhaps the most common response,
not unlike that accorded the non-objective and abstract works
of art displayed inside. By then, however, Wright was unable to
counter-attack as he was dead.

However one feels about the exterior, there can be little
argument over the effectiveness of the interior design, at least in
the core structure. Simple logic insists that the best way to view
a museum's exhibits is to begin at the top and work down, not
exhausting yourself with thoughts of missing rooms and finding
elevators. That's how it is here. Take the elevator to the top and
descend along the spiral ramp, past bays of paintings and
sculptures. Illumination comes from the glass dome and
continuous window band, supplemented when necessary by
artificial lighting.

The collections and loan exhibitions tread a line between the
modern art establishment – represented by Picasso, Mondrian,
Braque, Klee, Chagall and Kandinsky – and exponents of the
New York School of Abstract Expressionism and their
successors. Younger experimental artists provide spice. The
adjacent horizontal gallery is given to the Thannhauser
collection of Impressionists and *their* descendants – Manet,
Pissarro, Gauguin, Van Gogh, Cézanne. Once out of the door,
the question persists as to whether the architecture serves to
enhance or overwhelm the art it is intended to set off. Whatever
you decide in the end, it certainly sharpens the experience on a
first visit.

Guinness World Records Exhibit Hall

Empire State Building (350 5th Ave. – 34th St.)
☎947–2335. Map **5**P4 ▨ ❋ *Open 9:30am–6:30pm.*

Trafficking in predictable astonishments presented through video, film and replicas, the hall is an understandable favorite with those suffering a surfeit of profundity from other exhibitions. Compare yourself with lifesize photographs of the tallest, fattest, fastest humans, all under the rubric of the famous encyclopedia of trivia published by the Anglo-Irish brewer. It's fun, for a quick circuit.

Hall of Fame for Great Americans 血

Bronx Community College, 181st St., Bronx, NY 10453
☎220–6187. Map **10**B3 ▣ *Open 10am–4pm.*

This neglected national monument was dedicated in 1901, when the land it stood on was part of the new uptown campus of *New York University*. Stanford White designed the first three buildings for academic use – a domed library flanked by two classroom buildings devoted to the study of philosophy and languages. They are above-par representations of his work, but were built at the crest of a steep incline leading toward the Harlem River, and their high foundations lacked any visual interest.

To mask the foundations and simultaneously attract the prestige coveted by its administration, the university decided to invent a memorial to Americans who had made substantial contributions to the arts, sciences, statesmanship and pedagogy. White conceived a semicircular Neoclassical loggia, with busts of such national heroes as Lincoln, Benjamin Franklin, Edison, Thomas Paine and Alexander Graham Bell. To be considered for inclusion, candidates must have been dead for at least 25yr. The offbeat vista takes in northern Manhattan and *The Cloisters*, as well as a section of the Hudson River and the New Jersey Palisades on the far shore. The campus is now Bronx Community College, part of the City University of New York.

Harlem

*Map **8**H3.*

At the turn of the century, Harlem was still a semi-rural district of shrinking farms alternating with summer homes of the city to the S. Blocks of tenements were spreading out from the main streets, however, and shortly before World War I, they began to fill with American blacks migrating from the harshly segregated South. Their lot improved little, but despite unspeakable poverty, there existed a number of lively music halls and nightclubs. During the 1920s and early 1930s, whites from downtown engaged in the social ritual of dancing to jazz and drinking bathtub gin at such places as the Cotton Club (in which blacks worked and entertained but could not be patrons). Many foreigners still cherish that romantic image, which is no more real today than that of cowboys driving cattle herds through downtown Dallas.

It is necessary to stress, therefore, that Harlem is an uninviting area, its addicts and desperate unemployed posing a constant threat to residents and outsiders alike. With admitted exceptions, it is emblematic of the failures of American society, and of interest chiefly to visiting sociologists. That said, there are isolated streets and institutions deserving the attention even of casual tourists. Among these are the museums of the

Audubon Terrace complex, the *Museo del Barrio*, *Aunt Len's Doll and Toy Museum*, the **Schomburg Center for Research in Black Culture** (*515 Lenox Ave. near 135th St.* ☎*862–4000*) and the **Studio Museum** (*2033 5th Ave. at 125th St.* ☎*427–5959*). Architectural restorations of note include the Victorian cottage row of **Sylvan Terrace** near the *Morris-Jumel Mansion* and the 1890s **St Nicholas Historic District**, popularly known as Strivers' Row. The safest way to see these is by chauffeured car, while the most informative is, without doubt, by the Penny Sightseeing Co. (☎*247–2860*), which specializes in tours of Harlem.

The district is bounded, roughly, by 96th St., 165th St., Broadway and the East and Harlem rivers. Spanish Harlem, called El Barrio by its largely Puerto Rican residents, is the subdivision from 5th Ave. to the East River and N to 125th St. Remnants of Italian Harlem are found in the vicinity of the intersection of 116th St. and 2nd Ave.

Hayden Planetarium   Part of the *American Museum of Natural History* complex, the Planetarium features 'cosmic laser concerts,' as well as the more usual heavenly explorations.

Hispanic Society of America   Part of the complex known as *Audubon Terrace*, a splendid museum that focuses on the culture and history of the Iberian Peninsula rather than the Spanish and Portuguese colonies of America.

Historical Society   See *New York Historical Society*.

Holland Tunnel
Map *2S2* ▨
The first road tunnel (1927) under the Hudson River, and therefore something of a technological feat, it links Jersey City and Canal St. in Manhattan. The longer, westbound tube is over 1½ miles in length. Even though the air is changed by giant fans every 1½ min, few drivers envy the guards who take it in turns to be stationed inside. The tunnel is named after the chief engineer.

International Center of Photography
1130 5th Ave. (94th St.), NY 10028 ☎*860–1777. Map **7**K4* ▨ *⚭ Open Tues–Fri noon–8pm, Sat, Sun noon–6pm.*
One of New York's latest museums (1974) is housed in a 1914 Georgian-Federal row house, its bricks and shutters made more attractive by contrast with the grandiose mansions that are customary along this stretch of 5th Ave. The expanding collection focuses on 20thC luminaries Ernst Haas, E. Eugene Smith, Henri Cartier-Bresson, Weegee, and Robert Capa, supplemented by special theme and one-person shows twice a year. Lectures, audiovisual presentations, workshops and a book-and-print shop contribute to the generally lively atmosphere.

Jacques Marchais Center of Tibetan Art   Until recently, this was the official designation of the *Tibetan Museum* on Staten Island. Jacques Marchais, the founder, was in fact a female (and American) art dealer, but in the 1940s a male (and French) name was still a business asset.

Japan House Gallery
333 E 47th St. (1st Ave.), NY 10017 ☎*832–1155. Map 5O5*
▧ *✗ by appointment. Open 11am–5pm, Fri during
exhibitions 11am–7:30pm.*

The contemplative and ordered *shibui* tradition flourishes in
this otherwise electric neighborhood, with frequent loan
exhibitions of such delicacies as Noh masks, decorated paper
screens, scrolls, and diverse Shinto and Buddhist objects.
Founded in 1907 to promote understanding between the two
countries, the parent Japan Society has grown even more
relevant with the influx of Japanese businessmen and their
families and attendant adjustment problems. While
symposiums, lectures and counseling programs are major
features of the society's agenda, the gallery is of greater interest
to tourists. Frequently changed shows focus on everything
from ceremonial swords and kimonos to contemporary
photography and art films.

It was three years before we saw New York again. As the ship
glided up the river, the city burst thunderously upon us in the
early dusk – the white glacier of lower New York swooping
down like a strand of a bridge to rise into uptown New York, a
miracle of foamy light suspended by the stars. A band started to
play on deck, but the majesty of the city made the march trivial
and tinkling. From that moment I knew that New York,
however often I might leave it, was home.

F. Scott Fitzgerald, *My Lost City*

Jewish Museum
1109 5th Ave. (92nd St.), NY 10028 ☎*860-1888. Map 7K4*
▧ *✗ Open Mon–Thurs noon–5pm, Sun 11am–6pm.
Closed Fri, Sat.*

Within this conventional 1908 'chateau,' with its bland 1963
wing, is an important collection of Judaica of interest to people
of all faiths. Special exhibitions of contemporary painting and
sculpture are mounted on the first floor beyond a vestibule that
reproduces a section of a Persian synagogue, with lighted niches
for Torah containers.

The second floor is devoted to ceremonial objects, both
intricately wrought and stunningly simple: wedding rings,
Torah headpieces and crowns, circumcision instruments,
eight-candle menorahs, prayer-holding mezuzahs, spice boxes,
holiday ritual pieces and amulets.

The third floor is a mixture of folk arts, coins, medals, Torah
arks, and artifacts of the Jewish experience in Colonial
America, and the Middle East. Especially poignant are
reminders of the poverty of Lower East Side immigrants and
the incomprehensible tragedy of the Holocaust.

The fourth floor exhibit, a diorama of Israel executed by
schoolchildren, is unexpectedly charming and enlightening.

Judson Memorial Baptist Church ▥ †
55 Washington Sq. S (Sullivan St.), NY 10012
☎*477–0351. Map 2R4 Open Mon–Fri 9am–5pm. Closed
Sat, Sun except for Sun service 11am; July–Aug closed
Mon.*

More than merely supportive of the cultural and political
concerns of its *Greenwich Village* constituency, Judson
initiates. Parishioners and ministers carry forth energetic

85

Lever House

programs in the arts and community affairs. Architects
McKim, Mead & White elected a Venetian variation on their
customary predilection for the Romanesque, and the 1892
facade continues to brighten the hodgepodge of Washington
Sq. South. The adjacent campanile is now part of a *New York
University* residence hall.

Lever House 🏛 ☆

390 Park Ave. (53rd St.), NY 10022. Map 5N4.
In its way as difficult to miss as *St Bartholomew's Church* two
blocks s, Lever House was in the forefront of the Bauhaus-
influenced third phase of skyscraper fever that seized the
imagination of developers in the post-World War II years. The
builders embraced the new glass-and-steel curtain wall
technology, but with important variations. For one, they broke
the unvarying high-rise canyon of Park Ave. by the astonishing
decision not to use every bit of available air space. The wide side
of the unadorned slab tower is turned s, at a right angle to the
avenue, permitting air and sun to circulate. For another, the
color is an unusual blue-emerald. In its totality, Lever House is
the promise of the International Style that was to be denied by
its descendants. Even architects Skidmore, Owings & Merrill
infrequently matched their achievement in subsequent efforts.

Liberty Island See *Statue of Liberty.*

Lincoln Center 🏛 ☆

*140 W 65th St. (Columbus Ave.), NY 10023 ☎877–1800.
Map 6M3 ⬛ 𝄡 inexpensive ▣ ℝ ⵊ Open 10am–5pm;
theaters various times.*
An ambitious conglomeration of six concert halls and theaters,
the Lincoln Center for the Performing Arts is the home of the
Metropolitan Opera Company, New York Philharmonic
Orchestra and New York City Opera and Ballet. It also hosts a
variety of visiting ballet and repertory companies, symphony
orchestras, and popular and classical musical artists and events.
No project of such magnitude, especially one concerned with
the arts, could hope to sail from conception to realization
without conflict. The Lincoln Center provoked dismay,
outrage, and a chain reaction of second-guessing that persists to
this day, all on a scale consistent with its monumentality.
  It happened that in the post-World War II years, several of
the city's premier performing arts organizations were seeking
new premises. This need coincided with planners casting about
for ways to arrest the decline of various Manhattan
neighborhoods. The new United Nations Headquarters
accomplished that on the *East Side*, helping to establish New
York as a world capital of statesmanship. It seemed that the
proposed Lincoln Center might do the same for the arts. On
balance it has, allowing for quibbles over decor and acoustics.
Admittedly, the architectural whole is more impressive than its
parts, despite the participation of Eero Saarinen and Philip
Johnson.
  Approach is customarily made from Columbus Ave., up
long, low steps into the main plaza. Most impressive at night
when the center fountain and facades are lit, the **New York
State Theater** is on the left, **Avery Fisher Hall** on the right,
and the rounded arches of the **Metropolitan Opera House**
directly ahead. To reach the **Vivian Beaumont Theater**, cut
between the Opera House and Avery Fisher Hall. The larger

structure to the N is the **Juilliard School**, a prestigious arts college. The Beaumont building incorporates the research library and Museum of the Performing Arts, a branch of the public library system. To the S of the Opera House is a treelined park with a bandstand. In warmer months, the pedestrian spaces are enlivened by outdoor cafés, ice cream kiosks and wandering street musicians.

To greater or lesser degree, the buildings reveal classical inspiration informed by modernist sensibilities, austere to romantic in interpretation according to the predilections of their designers. Each enjoys the presence of large-scale artworks by notable painters and sculptors. Avery Fisher Hall, with the New York Philharmonic in residence, has Richard Lippold's *Orpheus and Apollo*; the Opera House, two Marc Chagall murals; the New York State Theater, a Lee Bontecou and a Jasper Johns, among others.

Restaurants are the Allegro Café (*noon–8pm*) and Fountain Café (*noon–midnight*) in Avery Fisher Hall, and the Grand Tier (*open 2hr before performances to ticketholders*) in the Opera House. Guided tours of the Center are approximately 1hr in length (☎ 877–1800 ext 516). Backstage tours of the Opera House are also available (☎ 582–7500). Box office telephones are listed by theater under *Nightlife*.

Lincoln Tunnel
Map 4O1 🚇 *only when crossing W–E.*
The three tubes of the tunnel were completed in 1937, 1945 and 1957, and the one in the middle is the longest at over $1\frac{1}{2}$ miles. They connect the city of Weehawken in New Jersey with W 38th St. in Manhattan, providing an additional Hudson River crossing. Construction of the approaches entailed the demolition of a large slum area.

Little Italy
Map 3S5.
Sicilian and Neapolitan immigrants made this their urban hamlet during the same period (1880–1925) that European Jews were establishing their Lower East Side community on the other side of *The Bowery*. Bounded on the W by Lafayette St., and by Houston St. and Canal St. to the N and S, the neighborhood is shrinking, but still vibrant. The quarter was always small, for arriving Italians and their children dispersed quickly throughout the five boroughs. But this warren of narrow streets and stunted tenements became symbolic of the Old Country and retains that flavor. Gray-haired women in black clutch string bags as they move from fish shop to bakery while their menfolk play *bocce* (Italian bowls) or sip espresso at coffee houses around the corner. The *Festa di San Gennaro* in Sept booms with brass bands and sizzles with booth after booth of sausage and *calzone*. (See *Walk 3* in *Planning*.)

Lower East Side
Map 3R5.
Although immigrants of every race and nationality have made this shabby tenement district E of *The Bowery* and N of Canal St. their first stopover, its identity is East European Jewish. That image persists, although blacks and Hispanics dominate now. Millions of indigent Slavs, Poles, Russians and Lithuanians poured into these mean streets from 1870 until harsh new laws stemmed the flow in the 1920s. They lived in

five-story buildings without plumbing, two or three families to an apartment. For decades, the population density surpassed that of Calcutta. The lucky ones were streetcart sellers, the others labored in the sweatshops of the garment trade. Yiddish was the prevailing tongue, and at one time there were 500 synagogues. A taste of that era – and some remarkable shopping bargains – can be had on Sun along Orchard St. (See *Walk 4* in *Planning*.)

Madison Square Garden
8th Ave. (33rd St.), NY 10001 ☎ *564–4400. Map 4P3* ▆▆
▆ *Opening times vary according to events scheduled.*
Although the present complex is the fourth version on the third site, only the first two were even in the vicinity of Madison Square. Nor did any of them have plants or flowers in sufficient quantities to justify the 'Garden' label. In all its manifestations, from 1871 to the present, Madison Square Garden has been concerned with sports and popular entertainment. It stages circuses, ice shows, hockey, basketball, horse and dog competitions, rodeo, prizefighting, rock concerts; it also has 48 bowling lanes. For no good reason, the architecturally imposing Penn Station was razed to street level in 1968 to permit the construction of this insipid building. That desecration aside, this is where many major events take place.

Marble Collegiate Church ▥ †
272 5th Ave. (29th St.), NY 10001 ☎ *686–2770. Map 5P4. Open Mon–Fri 9am–5pm. Closed Sat, Sun except for Sun services.*
An 1854 edifice by Samuel A. Warner, it was commissioned by a congregation of the Dutch Reformed faith, which had its roots in the earliest settlement. The official landmark designation is due as much to age as to architectural worth. Consistent with its time, both Gothic and Romanesque motifs were used in a satisfactory (if not especially striking) blend. One of the pastors is Dr Norman Vincent Peale, author of the Eisenhower-era best-selling guide to the good life, *The Power of Positive Thinking*.

Metropolitan Museum of Art ▥ ★
5th Ave. (82nd St.), NY 10028 ☎ *879–5500 (office), 535–7710 (recorded information), 570–3949 (concerts, lectures). Map 7L4* ▆▆ *⟋ on rented tapes* ▣ ▆ ✦ ⚊ *entrance on 5th Ave. (80th St.). Open Tues 10am–8:45pm, Wed–Sat 10am–4:45pm, Sun and hols 11am–4.45pm. Closed Mon. Free entry for children under 12 accompanied by adult. Photography without flash permitted, except at special temporary exhibitions.*
Grand in concept and numbing in scope, this is the largest repository of art and antiquities in the Western Hemisphere. There are 18 departments and 248 galleries with well over one million prints, paintings, sculptures, furnishings, costumes, ceramics, musical instruments, armor and reassembled sections of ancient temples and palaces. Barely 25% of the collection is on view at any one time. There are, in addition, three libraries, two auditoriums, an art and book shop, a gift shop, a cafeteria, a restaurant with table service, a snack shop, and a variety of concerts, films and lectures.

It might all be intimidating, were it not for an imaginative administration determined to enhance accessibility. Huge,

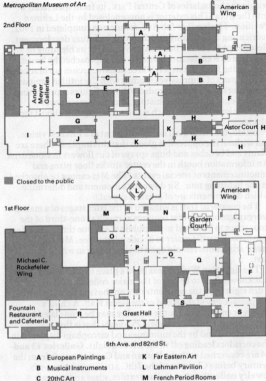

Metropolitan Museum of Art

2nd Floor

André Meyer Galleries

American Wing

Astor Court

■ Closed to the public

1st Floor

American Wing

Garden Court

Michael C. Rockefeller Wing

Fountain Restaurant and Cafeteria

Great Hall

5th Ave. and 82nd St.

A European Paintings	K Far Eastern Art
B Musical Instruments	L Lehman Pavilion
C 20thC Art	M French Period Rooms
D Drawings and Prints	N English Period Rooms
E Recent Acquisitions	O European Sculpture and Decorative Arts
F Sackler Wing	
G Greek and Roman Art	P Medieval Art
H Special Exhibition Area	Q Arms and Armor
I Islamic Art	R Greek, Cypriot and Roman Art
J Ancient Near Eastern Art	S Egyptian Wing

colorful banners billow from the 5th Ave. facade, touting the two or three special exhibitions always on view. These nearly always tie in with popular enthusiasms of the moment – Chinese costumes, the treasures of Tutankhamun, Viking artifacts – the better to draw infrequent museumgoers who are unfamiliar with the permanent exhibits. Galleries are laid out in an orderly manner, attendants are gracious and often bilingual, there are special programs for children, and ready access for older or disabled people. There is an air of authority flushed with innovation and a desire to relate past to present. The philosophy works: nearly four million people visit every year.

The building itself is of interest, an amalgamation of the architectural styles dominant at the time of each addition. Its core is the unassuming Ruskinian Gothic structure that was the first home of the museum in 1880. The only major edifice

89

within the boundaries of Central Park, its front then faced W
into the trees. This exterior is now enclosed by the Lehman
Pavilion. The familiar 5th Ave. facade was completed in 1902,
reorienting the building and dictating its future development.
Best defined as of the Beaux Arts School for its blending of
Roman and Renaissance conceits, it is approached by broad
steps rising from the street. Three massive arches are bracketed
by four pairs of impressive columns with Corinthian capitals.
Resulting niches were intended to house figures representing
the four epochs of human history, but these were never
commissioned. Wings reach N and S to a length of almost three
blocks.

Inside, the Great Hall is the fulfilment of a Piranesi vision,
but without the oppressive gloom that this implies. There are
plants and benches and huge sprays of cut flowers in stone urns.
An information booth in the center stocks floor plans and
announcements of special events. The Met cannot be absorbed
in one lightning tour. Sit down for a moment and determine
which departments are of greatest appeal.

The curatorial staff is engaged in the later stages of a master
reorganization plan that requires as much as one-third of the
floor space to be closed to the public at any one time. The effect
is to make it a trifle easier to decide what to see. Most of the
major attractions remain open to view either in whole or in
part.

The **Egyptian Wing** ☆ is as good a place to start as any, for it
is acknowledged to be one of the major collections of its kind.
Turn right from the main entrance on the first floor, following
the passageway at the N end of the Great Hall. A child's
innocent enthusiasm for the macabre may be stimulated by the
sepulchre of *Lord Chamberlain Per-nedbi* that is first
encountered and by the mummies and sarcophagi displayed in
the corridors leading off to the left and right. **Galleries 13 and
14** are concerned with the Roman and Coptic periods from the
century before Christ until the 7thC AD. There is a superb
jewelry collection ☆ as well as textiles, glass and ceramic
objects of ceremonial and household use. **Gallery 10** is a long
room of meticulous paintings, facsimiles of those found in
temples and burial places. Next are artifacts of the Ptolemaic
period, including numerous funerary figures, sculptures and
reliefs. Papyri from the *Book of the Dead*, a compilation of
medicinal formulas and religious rituals, date from around the
5thC BC.

While the galleries encompassing the 1st to 18th dynasties
are closed, you have to view the next series of rooms in reverse
order – from the 30th to the 19th dynasties. Their delicately
crafted reliefs, facsimiles of tomb paintings and funerary relics
finally lead up to the **Sackler Wing**. This handsome two-story
pavilion encloses (and somewhat overwhelms) the **Temple of
Dendur** ☆ A gift of the Egyptian government, it was
painstakingly dismantled, pieces numbered and charted, and
sent here for reassembly. Light through a vast bank of glass in
the N wall bathes the temple and reflects on the water of the
U-shaped pool that frames it. Reorganization continues in
adjacent galleries, currently scheduled for reopening some time
in 1983.

To maintain historical sequence, return to the Great Hall and
cross to **gallery 11**, where a portion of the **Greek, Cypriot and
Roman collection of statuary and ceramics** ☆ is on view.
Many of these pieces were contributed by the first director of

the museum, Luigi Palma di Cesnola, who was responsible for their discovery and excavation. Just beyond is the Fountain Restaurant and Cafeteria (*open Tues 11am–8:15pm, Wed–Fri 11am–4:45pm, Sat–Sun noon–4:15pm*).

The adjoining **Michael C. Rockefeller Wing**☆ opened in Feb 1982, with 42,000sq. ft (3,900sq. m) of the arts of Africa, Oceania, and pre-Columbian and native America. Among over 1,500 objects on display are Papuan masks of barkcloth and cane, Olmec jade and ceramic figurines, Mayan reliefs, wood carvings of Benin and the Ivory Coast, and Eskimo sculptures. The collection was donated by Nelson A. Rockefeller and named after his son, who disappeared on an anthropological expedition in 1961.

Return again to the Great Hall and go down the corridor to the right of the central staircase. This leads into the section devoted to **medieval art**. After a clockwise circuit of the tapestries and ecclesiastical objects, make your way to the **arms and armor gallery**, which is dominated by a mounted troop of knights and augmented by heraldic banners, crossbows and other armaments.

A door in the W wall leads into the enclosed garden court of the **American Wing**☆ Trees, 19thC statues and a reflecting pool provide a quiet resting place beneath a glass roof. At the N end is the 1824 Greek Revival facade of a former Wall St. bank. Enter the door at the right to view portions of the most extraordinary collection of **American furniture and decorative arts** in existence. Three floors of 18 period rooms and 12 galleries proceed from Colonial times (1630) into the Federal period, ending about 1825. Installations still in progress will carry the story forward to the early 20thC. Splendid Chippendale bureaus and paintings of the **Hudson River School** are joined with comprehensive assortments of silver, pewterware, antique glass, ceramics and textiles. For a chronological view, begin on the third floor of the wing and walk down.

Afterwards, leave the garden court by the doorway at the S corner. Pass through a large **gallery of European sculpture and decorative arts**, covering essentially the same time period as the American Wing. Bear right, then left, through the **English period rooms**. Just beyond is the entrance to the **Lehman Pavilion**, where Robert Lehman's collection of early Italian and 19th and 20thC French art is displayed in modern galleries and somber period rooms, the latter reconstructed from his house on W 54th St. Among the Italian works are drawings by Leonardo da Vinci and Botticelli. Of the later period, Ingres' *Portrait of the Princess of Broglie* is characteristic of his uncanny aptitude for naturalistic reproduction. The Fauvists, an Expressionist offshoot of Post-Impressionism, are represented by Vlaminck and Derain. A quick circuit of the wing is sufficient. Leave by the door through which you entered, noting in passing the 1880 facade of the original museum building. Turn right into the **French period rooms**, which include a reconstructed 18thC Parisian storefront and boudoir furnishings commissioned by Marie-Antoinette. An adjoining room has additional **European sculpture and decorative arts**. Return to the Great Hall. This is a good interval at which to break off the visit, saving the rest for another day.

On that occasion, mount the central staircase to the W of the Great Hall. Remarkable riches are confronted on the second floor, and the layout does not lend itself to a programmed tour.

Straight ahead are the enormously popular **galleries of European paintings** ☆ They commence with large Baroque canvases of debatable content but undeniable drama. Continuing W, a maze of smaller galleries reveals the gems of the **Dutch collection**. Rembrandt's *Aristotle Contemplating A Bust of Homer* ☆ is the work of the artist's mature years, less theatrical than some of his earlier masterpieces. The concern with light remains, but it is a subtle mist, not a blinding shaft through clouds or portal. An oddity was Rembrandt's decision to clothe Aristotle in contemporary dress. The *1660 Self Portrait* ★ is an unsparing examination of his late middle age, the face pallid and corpulent, but with dignity intact. Vermeer was also intrigued by the properties of light, but in a narrow optical sense. The flesh of his *Young Woman with a Water Jug* ★ has the luminosity of an eggshell lighted from within by a candle flame. Any emotional impact is vitiated by the serenity of his subject matter and compositions, but he inspires admiration for his flawless technique.

For powerful imagery, move on to the **Spanish section** and El Greco's *View of Toledo*, his only landscape and one of his greatest works: a big, somber canvas that conveys an uneasy sense of foreboding through its lowering storm clouds. The portrait of *Juan de Pareja* ★ by Velázquez was acquired in 1970, the most costly single purchase the museum has ever made. Velázquez was perhaps unequalled in his sensitive portrayal of character, and in this painting he focuses all his skill on bringing the humanity of a friend to eternal life.

The connecting **French galleries** include fine examples of Claude and Watteau as well as Poussin's celebrated *Rape of the Sabine Women*.

Complete your tour of the European galleries with a wander through the **English rooms**, where portraits by Reynolds and Gainsborough hang alongside Turner's visionary cityscape, *The Grand Canal*.

To the N of these rooms is an enchanting accumulation of lutes, sitars, gongs, temple bells, nose flutes, sarindas and other exotic **musical instruments** ☆ To the S side of the entrance to the European galleries are select examples of **20thC art**, including works by Modigliani, Georgia O'Keeffe, Stuart Davis, Jackson Pollock, and such instantly recognizable paintings as Picasso's portrait of *Gertrude Stein* and Ivan Albright's *Fleeting Time Has Left Me Old*. Return to the top of the central staircase and turn right into a corridor given to **recent acquisitions** and **drawings and prints**.

This empties into the **André Meyer galleries**, an important, recently installed collection of 19thC European art. Turn left into a room of drawings by Degas, Renoir and Manet. In the center are Degas bronzes of dancers ☆ – his favourite subject. Only one piece of Degas sculpture was exhibited in his lifetime, yet here alone are 12. In the second room is the charming miniature oil on wood, *The Dancing Class*, and a dozen more sculptures, all by Degas. The instinctive grace of his dancers is only made more profound by the odd angularity or awkward position, or the implied sheen of sweat brought on by endless repetition of exercises. Further confirmation of his mastery is found in the third room, dominated by a large bronze figure (1922) with a tutu of real muslin.

Bearing right, you enter a large hall filled with heroic sculptures by Rodin and Maillol. Especially arresting is the former's tormented study of *Adam*. The rest of the Meyer galleries are devoted to paintings, a cornucopia of 19thC artistic fecundity. The transition away from both Classicism and Romanticism towards as yet unimagined frontiers is illustrated here in the manifold works of Corot and Courbet. The 'Establishment' these artists competed with is also represented by the polished Neoclassicism of Ingres. Despite Courbet's own strivings towards greater realism, he is said to have been dismayed by Manet's rejection of principles of perspective. In the 21 canvases by this younger artist, you can see striking concessions towards the two-dimensionality of the picture-plane. His flat, poster-ish portraits are almost devoid of shadow and simulated depth. Manet is often classified erroneously as an Impressionist, but his real kinship lies with such Post-Impressionists as Cézanne and Van Gogh, both equally well represented here. The scope and complexity of these works–most of them mounted in a large central room that does them full justice – is nothing less than breathtaking.

Eventually, these galleries lead into the **Islamic art collection**, the highlight of which is the **Syrian Nur Ad-Din House☆** (1707). The wall panels of the room produced here are modelled out of gesso, with ornate floral patterns and inscriptions in Arabic. Adjacent galleries show ceremonial vessels, chess pieces and silk carpets and hangings. Beyond the halls containing **Greek and Roman art** and **Ancient Near Eastern art**, you reach the open balcony square above the Great Hall.

Continuing N past **Far Eastern art**, go through the special exhibition areas until you arrive at the **Astor Court☆** Yet another recent addition, it is a reconstruction of a Chinese garden of the Ming dynasty (1368–1644), based on an authentic example that still exists in Soochow. It is a pleasantly tranquil spot in which to pause for a while and reflect upon all that has been experienced so far within the walls of this vast treasure house.

Complete your tour by traveling two escalator flights down to the **Costume Institute☆** Its biannual exhibitions have featured ancient Chinese garments, Parisian haute couture, and theatrical wardrobes.

Also down in the basement is the **Junior Museum**, created to introduce children and teenagers to the mysteries of art and history manifest in the floors above. There are frequent lectures and films intended to be shared with parents, as well as displays drawn from the larger collections.

Recorded cassette tours are available at moderate rentals, covering 21 subjects and galleries, some of them in languages other than English. Lectures, films and concerts range from discussions of painting techniques to cinematic explorations of biblical and esthetic inter-relationships to recitals by the Juilliard Quartet.

Midtown East
Map 5.

This concentration of corporate headquarters, foreign consulates, publishing houses and advertising firms brings to it streams of business people and diplomats, and shoppers are inexorably drawn towards the fabled luxury emporia of 5th Ave. Coping with this elitist influx are many of Manhattan's most exclusive hotels (Palace, Waldorf-Astoria, Grand Hyatt) and restaurants (Four Seasons, Lutèce, Le Cygne). It's also a residential area, but only for people who needn't concern themselves with the price of a second Mercedes. Penthouses with roof terraces, gardens and even swimming pools perch above the East River, their foliage visible from the streets. Principal sights are *St Patrick's Cathedral*, the *United Nations Headquarters*, *Grand Central Terminal*, and those exemplars of the International Style in architecture, *Lever House* and the *Seagram Building*.

Morris-Jumel Mansion ⬧

Edgecombe Ave. (W 160th St.), NY 10032 ☎ 923–8008. Map 10E3 ▨ ✕ Open Tues – Sun 10am – 4pm. Closed Mon. Subway 1 to 157th St.; AA, B to 163rd St. – Amsterdam Ave.

Given its age (1768), Georgian core, and Federal overlay (1810), the mansion warrants attention for its architecture alone. But great historical figures lived and loved and dined here, and as is only fitting, ghosts are reported to have materialized. Roger Morris was the builder. Although a friend of George Washington, he was a loyal subject of the King and left the country at the outbreak of the Revolution. Both Washington and the British general Henry Clinton made the house their headquarters during the War. After a period of service as a tavern, it was bought by French wine merchant Stephen Jumel for his wife Eliza. They renovated the house in Federal style and filled it with Empire furniture, much of which is still here.

The Jumels laid on lavish parties and banquets, which encouraged New York Society to overlook the rumor that Eliza was the illegitimate child of a prostitute. She reportedly commenced an affair with Aaron Burr before Stephen died in 1832, surprising only in part because the former Vice President was then in his seventies. Scheming Eliza and the brilliantly devious Burr kept house for a while after Stephen's death, but it was not a happy match and he soon moved out. Burr's room is at the top of the stairs, and there is a portrait of Eliza in her 80th year. The ghosts? A Hessian soldier and Eliza herself. Perhaps they are aided by the secret passageways.

Murray Hill ☆

Map 5P4.

A low-key residential quarter with indistinct boundaries, Murray Hill lacks the kind of attractions that capture the attention of developers and tourists. No doubt that suits the residents, who make no effort to grab the spotlight. Following the usual pattern from Colonial farmland to Federalist village to elegant suburb to bypassed backwater, Murray Hill managed to avoid the usually inevitable decay. Compressed by commercial development along the central N – S avenues, it is delineated, roughly, by Park Ave. and 3rd Ave. from 33rd St. to 42nd St. Strips of 19thC terraces and mews such as Sniffen Court (36th St., between Lexington and 3rd Aves.) have been transformed into quietly handsome private apartments and houses. Several good hotels trade tranquillity for the slightly out-of-the-way location, and a number of competent restaurants have opened in recent years.

Museo del Barrio

1230 5th Ave. (104th St.), NY 10029 ☎ 831–7272. Map 7J4 ▨ ✕ Open Tues – Fri 10:30am – 4:30pm, Sat, Sun 11am – 4pm. Closed Mon.

The vitality of Puerto Rican culture is repeatedly validated by the changing exhibitions of photographs, paintings and crafts in this gallery of El Barrio (Spanish Harlem). Pre-Columbian figures and works by other contemporary Latin Americans broaden the appeal.

Museum of American Folk Art
49 W 53rd St. (6th Ave.), NY 10019 ☎ *581–2474. Map* **5***N4*
☒ *Tues evening* ☒ *𝑋 for the blind* ✹ *Open Tues*
10:30am–8pm, Wed–Sun 10.30am–5.30pm. Closed Mon.
In the beginning (1961), this small museum concerned itself with *early* American folk art. That policy has been modified to cover any work produced by unschooled but talented American craftsmen. The permanent collection and frequently changed shows include enchanting assortments of weather vanes, carved and painted saints, Colonial toys, ceramics, kitchen implements, and clean-lined furniture that predates Danish Modern by a century.

Museum of American Illustration
128 E 63rd St. (Park Ave.), NY 10021 ☎ *838–2560. Map*
7*M4* ☒ *Open Mon–Fri 10am–5pm. Closed Aug and Sat, Sun.*
Rotating exhibitions of commercial art for books, magazines and print advertising are mounted under the sponsorship of the Society of Illustrators. The permanent collection is augmented by theme shows and the eagerly anticipated annual exhibition of award-winning works.

Museum of the American Indian
Part of the *Audubon Terrace* complex, this has the largest collection of Native American artifacts in the United States.

Museum of Broadcasting
1 E 53rd St. (5th Ave.), NY 10022 ☎ *752–7684. Map* **5***N4*
☒ *𝑋 by appointment* ✹ *Open Tues, Wed, Fri, Sat noon–5pm, Thurs 12:30–7:30pm. Closed Sun, Mon. Mornings reserved for groups by appointment.*
Over 7,000 recorded radio and television programs from the 1920s to the present are available for transmission in 23 individual listening/viewing booths. Selected TV shows, changed daily, are presented on giant screens, usually illustrating a sociological, journalistic or dramaturgical point. Although the emphasis is on television, with particular attention to the years prior to the introduction of tape technology around 1960, there are recorded broadcasts by President Warren Harding and Lord Haw Haw as well as a lengthy catalog of commercials. While it might be wise to inquire about the availability of specific programs, no advance booking is required.

Museum of the City of New York ☆
5th Ave. (103rd St.), NY 10029 ☎ *534–1672. Map* **7***J4*
☒ *𝑋 ✹ Open Tues–Sat 10am–5pm, Sun 1–5pm. Closed Mon.*
A museum as lively as the city it celebrates, the five floors of this Neo-Georgian building are crammed with historical dioramas, antique playthings, model ships and decorative arts. Take the elevator to the top and work down.
  On the fifth floor are two rooms from the first Rockefeller mansion, done up in High Victorian manner and featuring furnishings by English designer Charles Eastlake. On the third

floor are the dolls' houses and tiny trams, model farms and penny banks, miniature table settings and hobby horses. On the way out, linger over the Duncan Phyfe furniture, characterized by graceful curves, restrained inlays and stylized swags and lyres. Phyfe worked in Albany, NY, and New York City from around 1783–1854 and borrowed from Hepplewhite, Sheraton, and French Empire examples to formulate his own style.

The second floor has still more period rooms, ranging from the Colonial to the Theodore Roosevelt era. Model ships and displays trace maritime development from New Amsterdam onwards, and spill over to the first floor. Space is left for a dazzling multimedia presentation that spins through four centuries of local history in barely 20min, employing light, sound, and 24 synchronized projectors. Concerts and walking tours of the city are presented some Suns during warm weather.

Museum of Holography ☆

11 Mercer St. (Canal St.), NY 10013 ☎ *925–0526. Map 2S4* 🏠 ✱ *Open Wed, Fri–Sun noon–6pm, Thurs noon–9pm. Closed Mon, Tues.*

In its present state, holography may be only the first tentative flicker of a 21stC mass communication technique – film-in-the-round in your living room. Or it might be a technological trick that never develops beyond the level of a sideshow curiosity. At this unique museum, it is treated as an art form. Film is exposed to laser beams and mounted within a plastic cylinder. With illumination, the photographic image appears to be in three dimensions, changing as the observer walks around it. The effect is otherworldly and fascinating. Special exhibitions are mounted on a quarterly basis, with evening lectures.

Museum of Immigration See *American Museum of Immigration.*

Museum of Modern Art ★

11 W 53rd St. (6th Ave.), NY 10019 ☎ *956–7070. Map 5N4* 🏠 ✗ 🅿 *Open Mon, Tues, Fri, Sat 11am–6pm, Thurs 11am–9pm, Sun noon–6pm. Closed Wed.*

Known with ironic affection by its acronym – MOMA – this daring and innovative museum first lobbied for the validity of modern art at a time when that belief was by no means conceded, then in later years assumed the role of arbiter. An artist represented in its collection is among the anointed, assured of at least a sliver of immortality. It is alleged by some that the museum has retreated from the forward edge of the avant-garde, that it has grown conservative and protective of its stature. Evidence can be cited in support of that conclusion but, given the uncertain directions of contemporary art over the last decade, caution is understandable. In any event, controversy is the blood and breath of an institution like MOMA.

Modern art is here defined as commencing with the Impressionists in the 1880s and, although the history of the many movements that have since evolved favors abstract and non-objective modes, figurative options are also shown. Magic Realist Andrew Wyeth's *Christina's World*, for example, is one of the most popular canvases on view. The scope of the founders' intentions is demonstrated by the extensive film library and samples of superior design in such otherwise mundane objects as chairs, toasters, typewriters and tableware (**Goodwin Gallery**).

A far-reaching expansion program is underway, involving the construction of a new West Wing that will more than double gallery and storage space. Once it is completed, works on display in the older wing will be moved so that further renovation can proceed. The first temporary casualty of all this has been the outdoor **sculpture garden**☆ – a leafy retreat of pools and fountains dominated by Rodin's majestic *Balzac* and Gaston Lachaise's equally heroic *Standing Woman*. The garden has been closed and excavated as the first stage in redevelopment, but is due to be restored by mid-1983. Even if everything is finished according to the perhaps optimistic schedule, the museum's vigorous acquisitions policy and rapid turnover of exhibits make a room-by-room guide of the building impossible. The following outline is intended to give only a general idea of the scope of the collection.

The bookshop is to the right of the main entry hall, and large temporary shows are customarily mounted on the first floor. To view the permanent exhibitions, take the elevator (or new escalator) to the second floor. Approximate chronological order of the development of modern art commences with the large Impressionist canvas of a lily pond by Monet, and continues with examples of work by those following in his wake. Van Gogh's tortured vision is manifest in *The Starry Night*☆ while Cézanne anticipates the Cubist preoccupation with form in *Still Life with Apples*☆ Outside mainstream developments, Rousseau's informed naivety is perfectly expressed in his *Sleeping Gypsy*, featuring a robed man and a lion in the desert, and *The Dream*, in which a female nude reclines on a couch in a jungle populated by benign creatures.

The Cubist experiments of Picasso and Braque are well represented, the figures and inanimate objects reduced to mere starting points in complicated explorations of planes and form. Colors are somber and clearly secondary, except in the large Picasso, *Les Demoiselles d'Avignon*★ (1907). Vivid hues return with the work of Léger, Chagall, the mostly German Fauvists, and the explosive Futurists. Matisse's equally vibrant tones inspire *The Red Studio*☆ with a delightful intimacy. Less interesting, but probably better known, is his *Dance* – five nudes cavorting in an awkward circle.

The third floor carries on with samplings of Dadaism, in the once-shocking work of the French-born American Marcel Duchamp, and Surrealism, in the startling juxtapositions of René Magritte. Here also are works executed by Picasso after 1930. His renowned anti-war mural *Guernica*, installed in the museum for over 40yr, has now been returned to Spain, in deference to the artist's wishes, but there is ample testimony to his genius in the works that remain. First among the ensuing generation of Abstract Expressionists was 'Action Painter' Jackson Pollock, appropriately represented here by a canvas entitled *One*. Pollock's technique of applying paint in balletic swoops and traceries was, for him, a critical part of the creative process. Moving on from other major mid-20thC artists such as Willem de Kooning and Hans Hofmann, we come to Post-Abstract Expressionists Jasper Johns and Robert Rauschenberg. A chaotic but arresting 'combine-painting' by the latter incorporates painted surfaces with three-dimensional objects such as a car tire. Even more provocative is the totally black canvas by Ad Reinhardt, which has yet to persuade most viewers of its validity as a work of art.

Films are shown almost daily in the basement theater, which

is to be supplemented by another, larger auditorium.
Programs are as likely to be composed of Hollywood classics
as the obscure or experimental films that might be expected.
Tickets are available in the lobby, and are included in the cost of
admission to the museum.

Museum of Natural History   See *American Museum of Natural History*.

New York Aquarium
Boardwalk (W 8th St.), Coney Island, Brooklyn, NY 11224
☎ *266–8500. Map* **12F3** 🖼 🅿 ✱ *Open 10am–5pm.*
From 1892 until 1941, the aquarium was in Castle Clinton (see
Castle Clinton National Monument) in lower Manhattan. That
monument was threatened by proposed highway construction,
so the fish were transported to this new aquarium at *Coney
Island*, on the southern rim of Brooklyn. It is a schizophrenic
operation, part amusement center, part marine science
laboratory. That does not diminish its appeal. Predictably,
popular exhibits are the sharks, two-ton beluga whales,
performing porpoises, and electric eels that light up bulbs.
Some of them are flown to Florida for the winter, so the best
time to go is between May and Oct.

New York Botanical Garden   Incorporating a river and
specialized gardens and ponds of astonishing diversity, these
250 acres constitute the northern half of the *Bronx Zoo and
New York Botanical Garden* complex.

New York Coliseum
Columbus Circle (59th St.), NY 10019 ☎ *757–5000. Map*
4N3. *Opening times and entrance fees vary according to
current exposition.*
A bland, undistinguished building with cavernous spaces for
trade expositions. The annual auto and boat shows are among
those of interest to the general public.

New York Experience
1221 Ave. of the Americas (48th St.), NY 10036
☎ *869–0345 Map* **5O4** 🖼 ✱ *Open Mon–Thurs
11am–7pm, Fri, Sat 11am–8pm, Sun noon–8pm.*
A glossy, fast-paced multiscreen sound-and-light zip through
the life and times of the city, and a good way to start off a first
visit. Most of the senses are brought into play, dense fog billows
over your feet, and the swivel chairs are necessary to keep up
with the action. The show takes less than an hour, so expect
only a breezy skim over the surface, not any degree of
profundity.

New York Historical Society ☆
170 Central Park W (77th St.), NY 10024 ☎ *873–3400.
Map* **6L3** 🖼 *Open Tues–Fri 11am–5pm, Sat 10am–5pm,
Sun 1–5pm. Closed Mon.*
The name is misleading, for although the orientation is America
as viewed from a New York perspective, the net is widely cast.
Founded in 1804, the society moved to its present home in
1908. While it lives in the shadow of the *American Museum of
Natural History*, just across the street, the five floors of galleries
are well worth perusal. In most cities, this would be regarded as
a major museum.

There are examples of folk art, period rooms, carriages, drawings and watercolors by John James Audubon, works in silver, Colonial maps and prints, early American toys and carvings, farm and household implements, even fire engines. The fourth floor is devoted primarily to portraits and landscapes, mostly by American painters, the third floor concentrates on such primitive art as weathervanes and cigarstore Indians (large, eye-catching wooden figures used in the 18th and 19thC to advertise the sale of tobacco).

In addition to the research library on the second floor, there is an entrancing collection of **antique toys**☆, mechanical and carved, highlighted by a Noah's Ark crowded with paired beasts. On the ground floor, prints, maps and drawings illustrate the growth of the city from the days of Dutch rule, and in the basement is an array of horse-drawn coaches and carriages.

New York Public Library
5th Ave. (42nd St.), NY 10018 ☎ *790–6161. Map* **5**O4 *X Open Mon–Wed 10am–9pm, Fri, Sat 10am–6pm. Closed Thurs, Sun.*

The city-wide library system has over six million volumes and three times as many related materials – much of it in this, the main branch. They are housed in what many regard as *the* paradigm of the Beaux Arts style that was in vogue at the beginning of the 20thC. Certainly its 5th Ave. facade is more subdued than that of the flamboyant *Metropolitan Museum of Art*. Beyond the famous pair of reclining lions (sometimes called Patience and Fortitude), long steps and a terrace lead up to the Roman portico.

The library is for reference, not for lending, but there are frequent exhibitions of books and prints. *Bryant Park* is on the other half of the block.

New York University
Washington Sq., NY 10003 ☎ *598–3127. Map* **2**R4. *Open Mon–Sat 8am–10pm. Closed Sun.*

With over 44,000 registered students, most of them postgraduate or involved in adult education programs, New York University claims to be the largest private university in the country. Founded in 1831, its first permanent home was a Gothic Revival pile at the NE corner of *Washington Square* in Greenwich Village (see *Walk 5* in *Planning*). That was replaced by the present unremarkable structure in 1894.

Over the last century, expansion has been unremitting, with a post-graduate School of Business Administration in the *Financial District*, a medical-dental complex on the *East Side*, a respected Institute of Fine Arts on 5th Ave., and a second campus in The Bronx. Fiscal retrenchment in the 1970s forced the sale of the Bronx campus and other smaller units, but the university retains ownership of most of the buildings on the E and S sides of Washington Sq., and these are only the most visible of substantial properties in the area.

The schools of law and medicine are ranked among the best in the nation. Distinguished teachers and graduates have included Samuel Morse, Thomas Wolfe, Jonas Salk, Joseph Heller, Albert Sabin, Lillian Hellman and Edward Koch.

Numismatic Society   See *American Numismatic Society*.

Old Merchant's House

29 E 4th St. (Broadway), NY 10543 ☎ *777–1089. Map* **2***R4*
📷 *Open Sun 1–4pm, other times by appointment.*
No one seems to be certain, but the house is attributed to
Minard Lafever, pre-eminent architect of the early 19thC. The
design falls between Federal and Greek Revival, and was
completed as a speculation in 1832. Merchant Seabury
Tredwell bought it in 1835. His family lived here until 1933,
and since then it has been restored and preserved by the
Historic Landmark Society. The original furnishings and floor
coverings are still in place, and there is an intriguing secret
passage.

Paley Park

3 E 53rd St. (5th Ave.). Map **5***N4. Open Mon–Sat May–Oct
8am–7pm, Nov, Dec, Mar, Apr 8am–6pm. Closed Jan, Feb
and Sun.*
A chunk of valuable midtown real estate was here employed,
not as a multistory parking lot or apartment block, but as an
enclosed 'vest-pocket' park. The combination of trees, chairs
and simulated waterfall was underwritten by the chairman of
the board of the Columbia Broadcasting System and presented
as a gift to the people of New York City. A gift which turned out
to be just what they wanted; it is so popular that there is often a
line.

Pan Am Building 🏛

200 Park Ave. (45th St.), NY 10017. Map **5***O4* 📷 ⍟ *Open
6am–2am.*
Praise has not been the Pan Am's lot, even before its completion
in 1963. In effect, forming a visual octagonal wall across Park
Ave., it does almost nothing right. The fact that Bauhaus doyen
Walter Gropius had a hand in it is little compensation. But it is
unavoidable, so enjoy the cocktail lounge at the top, which has
decent views toward Wall Street and the *United Nations
Headquarters*. A fatal accident in 1977 ended its rooftop
heliport function.

Pierpont Morgan Library 🏛

29 E 36th St. (5th Ave.), NY 10016 ☎ *685–0008. Map* **5***P4*
📷 *Open Tues–Sat 10:30am–5pm, Sun 1–5pm. Closed
Aug, Mon, and Sun in Jul.*
One of the quiet pleasures of subdued *Murray Hill*, the library
was constructed for financier J. Pierpont Morgan in 1902 by the
omnipresent firm of McKim, Mead & White. The Neoclassical
design reflects Pierpont Morgan's passion for the Italian
Renaissance. An unobtrusive 1928 addition was finished 15yr
after his death.

   Consistent with its name, the building is primarily a
repository of rare books, illuminated manuscripts, and other
documents of the Middle Ages and Renaissance, but there is
also a great deal more that warrants attention: stained glass,
sculpture, enamel- and metal-work, and a number of somber
Italian and Flemish paintings.

   The **West Room**, with its carved, painted ceiling and red
damask curtains, has been kept exactly as it was during
Pierpont Morgan's lifetime.

Planetarium, Hayden   See *American Museum of
Natural History*.

Police Academy Museum

235 E 20th St. (2nd Ave.), NY 10003 ☎ *477–9753. Map 5Q5* ⊡ ✳ *Open Mon–Fri 1–5pm. Closed Sat, Sun.*

Not recommended for those of nervous disposition, the museum makes a forthright depiction of crime prevention and punishment in New York. Displays of the improvised weapons of teenage street gangs are mixed with semi-historical lethal artifacts of the gangster era.

Prospect Park

w of Flatbush Ave., Brooklyn. Map 12E3 ✳ *Subway D, M, QB to Prospect Park.*

Frederick Law Olmsted and Calvert Vaux collaborated on this landscape design (1866–74), as they had on the larger *Central Park* in Manhattan. Many think this is the better of the two, with fewer roads and a more imaginative composition of wooded glades, water, and pathways. A small *zoo* established in 1935 along Flatbush Ave. contains elephants, zebras, monkeys and bears (☎ *965–6560; open Apr–Nov 8am–5pm, Dec–Mar 8am–4:30pm*). Nearby is the **Lefferts Homestead**, built in 1783 in the Dutch Colonial style, and fitted out with period furnishings (☎ *as above; open Wed–Sun 1–5pm, closed Mon, Tues, second Sat of each month in winter*).

In gentler times, this bucolic setting adjacent to the *Brooklyn Museum* and *Brooklyn Botanic Garden* would constitute a rare urban retreat. Sad to say, it is subject to severe acts of vandalism and lack of funds. Go only during daylight.

Puerto Rican Museum for the Arts

When the American Geographical Society moved out of town, this collection took its place in the *Audubon Terrace* complex.

Queensboro Bridge

Map 5N5 ⊡

Once it was possible to drive halfway along this bridge over the East River and turn right into an elevator that lowered to **Roosevelt Island** (formerly Welfare Island). For safety and security reasons, that service was ended in the mid-1970s when the island became home to an ambitious new residential community, called Southtown, an attempt to integrate all economic classes in new housing financed by both public and private funds. No cars are allowed and travel to and from the island is now by cable car. The bridge, symbolic of *East Side* glamor, appears in dozens of old movies.

Queens-Midtown Tunnel

Map 5O5 ▨

This two-tube, four-lane East River tunnel is of note only because it is likely to be the one used by arrivals from LaGuardia and JFK airports. It emerges between 36th and 37th Sts. in Manhattan.

RCA Building ▥ ☆

30 Rockefeller Plaza (5th Ave. and Ave. of the Americas, 49th and 50th Sts.), NY 10017 ☎ *489–2947 (observation roof). Map 5O4* ▨ ✳ *Open Apr–Oct 10am–8:45pm, Nov–Mar 10:30am–7pm.*

Centerpiece of the 19-building *Rockefeller Center* development, the RCA stands highest at 850ft (259m) and 70 stories. Completed in the Depression years, its ground-floor murals are in the heroic Social Realist mode. The observation roof proffers panoramic vistas of Manhattan that many natives feel surpass those of taller buildings to the s. (See *Walk 1* in *Planning*.)

Richmondtown Restoration ▥ ☆
441 Clarke Ave., Staten Island, NY 10306 ☎ *351–9414. Map 12F2* ▣ ✗ *by appointment* ▣ ✿ *Open July–Aug Tues–Sat 10am–5pm; closed Sun, Mon. Sept–June, Sat 10am–5pm, Sun noon–5pm; closed Mon–Fri. Ferry from Battery Park. Take a taxi or S113 bus from the Staten Island Ferry terminal.*

Eventually this is to be a museum village of over 30 buildings – restored, reconstructed, reassembled, re-created – ranging from the early Colonial period to the 19thC. The Staten Island Historical Society has been working on this project for 40yr, and while progress is painstakingly slow, the rewards are evident. Several buildings are fully furnished and open to the public, among them a colorful **general store** ☆ and a 1696 elementary school. Costumed artisans give demonstrations in pottery, leatherwork, weaving and printing. The grounds include a mill pond, and picnicking is encouraged.

Riverside Church ▥ †
490 Riverside Dr. (122nd St.), NY 10027 ☎ *222–5900. Map 8I2. Open 8am–10pm.*

Despite the 74-bell carillon and 20-ton bell at its top (both the largest of their kind anywhere in the world), the 392ft (120m) tower of this inter-denominational church looks vaguely like a Gothic 1930s office building – and is, in part. There is an **observation deck** ☆ which affords a sweeping panorama of the Hudson River from Wall St. to the *George Washington Bridge (open Mon–Sat 11am–3pm, Sun noon–4pm* ☎ *749–7000 for times of carillon performances).*

Riverside Park
Maps 8 & 10E–F2.

New Yorkers owe an eternal debt to Frederick Law Olmsted and Calvert Vaux, the 19thC landscape architects who created *Central Park, Prospect Park* in Brooklyn, and this sylvan strip of trees and hills bordering the Hudson River. It runs from W 72nd St. to W 125th St., banked by the E by a wall of handsome apartment houses and blemished only by the Henry Hudson Parkway, which was built along its length in the 1930s. The **Soldiers and Sailors Monument** (*W 89th St.*) and *General Grant National Memorial* (*W 122nd St.*) are within its boundaries.

Rockefeller Center ▥ ☆
Map 5O4

John D. Rockefeller Jr. put together the grand scheme for this 22-acre compound of office towers – a 'city within the city'. The heart of the complex is between 5th and 6th Aves. and 49th and 50th Sts. Here are found the sights familiar from tourist literature, most of them completed in the 1930s. Dominating is the *RCA Building*, facing E. While it does not compare in scale or inventiveness with the contemporary *Chrysler Building*, it bears a mantle of restrained elegance. At the NW corner of its base is the Art Deco **Radio City Music Hall**, with a

breathtaking vaulted interior in which rock concerts and
elaborate revues are staged. To the E, directly in front of the
entrance, is a sunken plaza that is an ice-skating rink in winter
and outdoor cafe in summer. A gold statue of *Prometheus* floats
above. At the approach of Christmas, a tree over 70ft (21m)
high is placed behind him. Still further E, banks of plants and
flowers take up the center of a pedestrian precinct that ends at
5th Ave. (See *Walk 1* in *Planning*.)

St Bartholomew's Church 🏛 † ☆
*109 E 50th St. (Park Ave.), NY 10022 ☎ 751–1616. Map
5O4 ⊚ Open 8am–6pm. Closes 3pm during major hols.*
Providing a welcome antidote to the slab-sided canyon of
midtown Park Ave., this pinkish pile of glorious Byzantine-
Romanesque excess features Stanford White's **triple portals**
(1903)☆ salvaged from an earlier church by James Renwick,
located downtown on 24th St. The present church opened in
1919, and the prominent dome was finished in 1930. See it
quickly, for the Episcopalian church has financial problems and
developers are casting covetous eyes.

St John The Divine   See *Cathedral Church of St John The Divine*.

St Mark's Church-In-The-Bowery 🏛 †
*2nd Ave. (10th St.), NY 10003 ☎ 674–6377. Map 3R5.
Parish hall open 9am–5pm. Main building closed indefinitely
for repairs.*
One of the oldest houses of worship in Manhattan, this church
was built on farmland in 1799. The basic structure is Federal,
with a Greek Revival steeple added in 1828. Dutch Director-
General Peter Stuyvesant is buried here, in ground he once
owned. A fire in 1978 destroyed much of the roof and interior,
and costly restoration is still underway. In the meantime,
poetry readings and dance recitals take place in the parish hall.

St Patrick's Cathedral 🏛 † ☆
*5th Ave. (51st St.), NY 10022 ☎ 753–2261. Map 5N4 🕮
except by prior approval. Open 7am–8pm.*
When James Renwick submitted his drawings in 1850, the
fashion for Gothic Revival was on the wane. By the time the
cathedral was completed in 1888, it must have seemed dated.
No matter, for the style returned to favor soon afterwards, and
by then St Patrick's was already in the ranks of the timeless.
Echoing great cathedrals of Europe (for Renwick formulated
his ideas after intense study of European examples), it is part
lacy stonework, part soaring caprice, part massive pretence.
Authenticity might have demanded flying buttresses, but the
site would not accommodate them and they were not required
structurally, for the roof was lighter than in the earlier Gothic
prototypes.
 The siting of the cathedral was to cause consternation in some
quarters. At the time, Irish immigration had reached sufficient
proportions to be threatening to the Protestant majority. The
latter found it distasteful in the extreme to endure such a blatant
monument to the Roman faith, especially in the midst of a
neighborhood chosen by the monied classes as refuge from the
teeming masses downtown. In time, both groups came to
uneasy union in the face of succeeding waves of even less
familiar creeds.

St Paul's Chapel 血 † ☆
Broadway (Fulton St.), NY 10002 ☎ *285–0874. Map 2U4.
Open 8am–3:45pm.*

The only existing non-residential building in New York that
predates the Revolution (1766), it holds its own against the
silvery glass curtain walls of the *World Trade Center*, at least
when viewed from street level. Made of Manhattan schist
quarried at the site, the exterior facing is brownstone. Apart
from the steeple, added in 1794, it is authentic Georgian, inside
and out, although the blue and pink paint was perhaps not
always so vivid. Architect Thomas McBean is believed to have
been a pupil of James Gibbs, who designed St Martin-in-the-
Fields in London.

Chandeliers of Waterford crystal dominate the interior, and
the altar screen (1787) is by Pierre L'Enfant, the Frenchman
who later planned Washington DC. George Washington put in
frequent appearances during his first presidential term. His
pew is marked. The graveyard is a shaded resting place for
footsore souls still living, and there are lunchtime concerts of
classical music on Mon, Tues and Thurs.

Seagram Building 血
375 Park Ave. (52nd St.), NY 10022. Map 5N4.
First came *Lever House*, just across Park Ave., then the
Seagram (1958). After them, the glass-and-metal box
International Style went downhill, swallowed up in greed and
misinterpretation of its deceptive simplicity. (For confirmation
of that conclusion, simply look s to the *Pan Am Building*.) The
plaza in front of the Seagram may appear banal but, considering
the almost unbelievable cost of midtown property, even this
much walking space seems generous. The narrow slab looming
above is the color of well-aged bourbon, consistent with the
preoccupation of the client, a prominent distiller. Ludwig Mies
van der Rohe was the architect, Philip Johnson his assistant.

Snug Harbor Cultural Center 血 ☆
914 Richmond Terrace, Staten Island, NY 10301
☎ *448–2500. Map 12E2* ▨ *Entrance to grounds and most
exhibitions* ▨ *Guided tour and some exhibitions and
performances. Grounds open 10am–dusk; exhibitions
Wed–Sun 1–5pm. Ferry from Battery Park. Take a taxi or S1
bus from the Staten Island Ferry terminal.*
Sailor's Snug Harbor, a wealthy charitable foundation
providing shelter for retired merchant seamen, purchased these
80 waterfront acres in 1831. The organizers proceeded to build,
in a grand manner that might seem inconsistent with their
mission. Their dedication left a trove of over 20 contiguous
buildings representative of the Greek Revival, Italianate,
Victorian and Beaux Arts modes. One of the architects was
Minard Lefever, as prominent in the early 19thC as Stanford
White was to be 75yr later.

Now renamed and anointed a National Historic Landmark
District, Snug Harbor is still in the process of often tentative
conversion to an arts center. Should all the acquired buildings
be utilized eventually for that purpose, it would be an
unprecedented complex. As it is, only a few galleries are
presently in use, and on a limited schedule. Fiscal concerns and
public indifference appear to be frustrating the great plans of
the trustees. In the meantime, the complex is a compressed
lesson in 19thC architecture.

SoHo ▥ ☆
Map 2S4.

Whoever coined the name no doubt had the famous London quarter in mind, but the two places have little in common. This 'SoHo' is a contraction of 'SOuth of HOuston St.' (Incidentally, that street is pronounced 'HOWston,' not 'HEWston.') Less than two decades ago, SoHo was a dreary industrial district with broken concrete pavements piled high with boxes of refuse and pot-holed streets of worn Belgian blocks. Trucks backed into loading bays, rows of sewing and die-cutting machines clattered and thumped behind grimy windows, crates of fabrics and plastics were trundled about by forklifts and bowed backs. At night, everyone left.

It will not be reassuring to learn that this description still applies – but only in part. In the early 1960s, artists of the New York School, no longer content with easel painting in conventional studios, sought ever-larger work space. The problem was cost. They discovered the lofts of what was then called 'The Valley' – five- to ten-floor buildings with vast unpartitioned rooms designed for warehouses, shipping firms and labor-intensive light industries. Marginal businesses were closing up, and artists moved in. This was illegal, according to zoning laws. Yet they doubled their transgression by adding living spaces to their new studios, installing bathrooms and kitchens. Hanging plants and curtains were glimpsed from the streets. Other artists with similar needs – filmmakers, dancers, sculptors – followed the leaders.

By 1970, the trickle became a torrent. Since the municipal authorities could no longer ignore the fact that their ordinances were being violated, they simply changed them. Bona fide artists could now live in the converted lofts. SoHo went from cultural work place to artistic community to general free-for-all in just a few years. Bars, restaurants, food and craft shops catering to artists were supplemented by branches of established uptown galleries. Stockbrokers and lawyers bought up the lofts and fitted them out with saunas, billiard tables, luxury bathrooms and eight-track hi-fi equipment. Rents skyrocketed and many artists left. But SoHo remains a vital, passionate community, despite pretentious boutiques and eating places with breathtaking prices.

Saturday is the time to go, for the art-lover's ritual gallery tour and a drink at an engaging pub. (See *Guide to the galleries* in *Culture, history and background*.) Along the way, observe the **cast-iron facades** for which the district is also known. After a brief mid-19thC period during which SoHo was the fashionable center of town, hotels and stores were displaced by factory buildings. To dress them up, cast-iron motifs taken from European palaces were prefabricated in sections and assembled on the site, apparently an American innovation. Entire buildings were erected in four or five months by this method. Although they proved not to be fireproof and the technique was abandoned in the early 20thC, over 200 examples survive. They are notable for their gargoyles, Corinthian columns, and ornamentation and sculptural detail taken from Venetian, Romanesque and French Second Empire examples. Most of them are within an official landmark district created by the city to ensure their preservation.

SoHo is bounded by Houston St., Canal St., Sullivan St. and Broadway. The main street is West Broadway, and the oldest house (1806) is at 107 Spring St.

Songwriters' Hall of Fame Museum 🏛 ☆
1 Times Sq. (Broadway and 42nd St.), NY 10036
☎221–1252. Map **4**O3 ⌷ ♣ *Open Mon–Sat 11am–3pm.*
Closed Sun.

An aural art form doesn't lend itself readily to visual
presentation, but this modest museum makes the effort.
Memorabilia on display include Gershwin manuscripts and
Fats Waller's piano, as well as old-time jukeboxes and theater
posters. Some musical instruments can be played by visitors.

South Street Seaport Museum 🏛 ☆
16 Fulton St. (South St.), NY 10038 ☎ 766–9020. Map
3U5 ⌷ ✗ ♣ *Open 11am–6pm.*

A living museum-in-progress, the Seaport contributes mightily
to the resurrection of lower Manhattan as a place to stroll and
live and cherish. Centered around Piers 15, 16, 17 and 18, just s
of the Brooklyn Bridge and what remains of the Fulton Fish
Market, it makes nine antique sailing vessels available for
viewing. All are in a seemingly endless process of renovation,
but manage to convey a sense of the romantic epoch of early
steam and clipper ships that made the city the busiest port in the
New World. Six can be boarded. The four-masted, metal-
hulled *Peking* is the present pride of the fleet, soon to be
usurped by the classic 1885 square-rigged *Wavertree*. Among
the others are the 1908 lightship *Ambrose* and an 1893 schooner,
the *Lettie G. Howard*. During the warmer months, concerts of
sea shanties and folk rock are held.

Seafarers required land-based support services, and the
museum has taken them into account. It has spent over $5
million on quayside rows of Greek Revival, Georgian, Federal
and Victorian warehouses and ship chandleries. Schermerhorn
Row and Front St. are in advanced stages of restoration. The
official historic district takes in the blocks from the East River
to Water St. and from Fulton St. to Beekman St. A
development corporation credited with successful shop and
restaurant complexes in other East Coast cities is to undertake
further renovation. In the meantime, smaller entrepreneurs are
moving in and sprucing up the area. (See *Walk 2 in Planning*.)

Staten Island Zoo
613 Broadway (Forrest Ave.), Staten Island, NY 10310
☎442–3100. Map **12**E2 ▨ ⌷ on Wed ♣ *Open*
10am–4:45pm. Ferry from Battery Park. Take a taxi or S107
bus from the Staten Island Ferry terminal.

Specialization can make otherwise modest institutions rival
grander establishments blessed with better resources. Although
this zoo is of principal interest to residents of Staten Island, its
reptile collection rivals any in North America. Typical of this
comprehensiveness are specimens of every known type of
rattlesnake. There is also an aquarium and a well-regarded
collection of birds.

Statue of Liberty ☆
Liberty Island, New York Harbor, NY 10004 ☎732–1236.
Map **12**D3 ▨ ▣ ♣ *Open 9am–6pm. Ferry from Battery*
Park.

A description of 'Miss Liberty' is as enlightening as one of a
telephone. Everyone knows what she looks like, although the
first sight of her is undiminished by déjà vu. French sculptor
Auguste Bartholdi created her out of thin, beaten copper

panels, with the engineering counsel of Gustave Eiffel, a man of recognized expertise in such matters. At 151ft (46m), the statue dwarfs that wonder of the ancient world, the Colossus of Rhodes.

While the cost of the statue itself was underwritten by French contributions, the American public was slow to come up with the requisite matching funds to build the pedestal. It was nearly 20yr from conception to unveiling, in 1885. The statue weighs 225 tons, each eye is 2ft 6in (75cm) wide, and the tip of the up-raised torch is 395ft (120m) above sea level. Inside, an elevator carries visitors halfway up and 168 steps lead to the perforated crown. This gives a remarkable view of the bay, from the *Verrazano Narrows Bridge* to Manhattan. A staircase up the arm has been closed for years. The *American Museum of Immigration* is housed in the points of the star-shaped base.

Temple Emanu-El
5th Ave. (65th St.), NY 10021 ☎ 744–1400. Map 7M4.
Open 10am–5pm, services Sun–Thurs 5:30pm, Fri 5:15pm,
Sat 10:30am. (For services, enter by 5th Ave. door; at other
times, by E 65th St. door.)
The largest Reform Jewish synagogue in North America, it can accommodate 2,500 worshipers. Limestone is the primary material, buttressed by steel. Its size is the principal attraction for sightseers, given the ambiguity of its half-Turkish, half-Italianate make-up.

Theater District
Map 4O3.
Depending upon context, Broadway is either the city's longest avenue or a synonym for the theatrical district through which it passes on its diagonal slash through midtown. **Times Square** is essentially the intersection of that famous street and 7th Ave. Within the area bounded by 40th St., 55th St., 6th Ave. and 8th Ave. are many large movie theaters and most major legitimate theaters. The huge electrified signs and marquees that gave Times Square the sobriquet 'Great White Way' are still there, although they now advertise Japanese cameras as well as coming attractions. Crowds of gawkers, New Jersey teenagers, matinee ladies from the suburbs, French sailors, winos, disco dancers, hustlers, and tourists from everywhere fill the streets. On New Year's Eve, they are wall-to-wall, over 100,000 strong (but watch it on television).

Despite repeated efforts to clean it up, 42nd St. between 7th and 8th Aves. is a sludge of pornographic cinemas, prostitutes, addicts and troublemakers. Avoid it, and the northerly stretch of 8th Ave. it joins, but don't let it deter you from seeing a show on the streets nearby. Restaurants in the area cater to every taste and budget. Few are more than middling-good, most are noisy, but they specialize in pre and posttheater meals.

Theodore Roosevelt Birthplace
28 E 20th St. (5th Ave.), NY 10003 ☎ 260–1616. Map 5Q4
▨ ⚔ Open Wed–Sun 9am–5pm. Closed Mon, Tues.
The twenty-sixth President (1901–09) was born in this house in 1858 and lived here until 1873. The Roosevelts were a large and wealthy family even then, and this Greek Revival house, rebuilt to original specifications, reflects that prosperity. In the five period rooms open to the public, careful attention has been paid

to authenticity. The parlor is agleam with crystal chandeliers and gilt-framed mirrors. Plump horsehair sofas and chairs are arranged in inviting groups and fringed satin curtains frame the tall windows. No oddities here, but an impression of elegant solidity consistent with the time and social class.

Trophies reflect Roosevelt's roles as rancher, big-game hunter, explorer and soldier. Tiger and bear skins cover the floor of one room, and there are branding irons, a stuffed lion, uniforms and cavalry bugles. Yet this complex man – a progressive republican at home, an imperialist abroad – was above all a dedicated public servant. One glass case after another, filled with campaign buttons, public documents, family records and letters, and newspaper cartoons, attests to the energy he applied to that calling. (See also *Gramercy Park*).

Tibetan Museum 🏛

338 Lighthouse Ave., Staten Island, NY 10306
☎ *987–3478. Map 12F2* 🖭 *✗ by appointment. Open Apr–Nov, Sat, Sun 1–5pm; closed Mon–Fri. Telephone for Dec–Mar opening times. Ferry from Battery Park. Take a taxi or S113 bus from the Staten Island Ferry terminal. Near Richmondtown Restoration.*

The Staten Island Ferry is worth taking just for the breathtaking views it affords. But if an additional excuse is required, this museum should head the list. Within the relatively accurate replica of a Buddhist temple (1947) are exquisite bronzes, scrolls, painted silks and religious books. Many are Tibetan in origin, but China, Nepal and adjacent regions are also represented. Linger afterwards in the terraced gardens dotted with Oriental deities and animal sculptures.

Transfiguration, Church of the   See *Church of the Transfiguration*.

TriBeCa
Map 2T4.
When the artists who resurrected *SoHo* were forced out by landlords and speculators who saw the profits to be realized in sales to non-artists with regular incomes, many simply moved a few blocks s and w. They called their new homestead TriBeCa, for 'TRIangle BElow CAnal St.' Inevitably, the SoHo phenomenon is asserting itself, with galleries, bars, restaurants, a funky disco or two. Down here, where streets have names instead of numbers and the straightforward grid of uptown does not apply, the approximate boundaries are West St. to Church St. and Barclay St. to Canal St.

Trinity Church 🏛 ✝
Broadway (Wall St.), NY 10006 ☎ *285–0872. Map 2U4 ✗ Open 7am–6pm. Museum* 🖭 *open Mon–Fri 10:30am–noon, 12:30–3:30pm, Sat 10:30am–3:30pm, Sun 12:30–3:30pm.*
The first Trinity Church was erected here in 1698, entirely of wood. That burned down in 1776, in the first of the two great fires that decimated old New York. The second version was razed in 1839, and the present Gothic Revival manifestation (by Richard Upjohn) went up in 1846. No one has seriously considered washing the outside since, and the red sandstone is now so black it nearly shines. Over the intervening years, additions have included a chapel (1913) and bronze entry doors

(1894) modeled on those of the Baptistry in Florence. A small museum displays photographs and artifacts relating to the history of the church. Pause in the graveyard for a glance at the memorials to statesman Alexander Hamilton and steamboat inventor Robert Fulton.

Ukrainian Museum

203 2nd Ave. (12th St.), NY 10003 ☎ *228–0110. Map* **3***R5* ▨ *Open Wed–Sun 1–5pm. Closed Mon, Tues.*

Embroidery is the specialty – on garments, textiles and ritual panels – but the intricately decorated Easter eggs are equally entrancing. There are two galleries, also featuring folk carvings and metalwork.

Union Square

Map **5***Q4.*

When 14th St. was the primary shopping and theatrical boulevard of the late 19thC, Union Square enjoyed a prominence that lasted, in altered stages, into the 1930s. By then, it was a vigorous if shabby version of Speakers' Corner in London's Hyde Park. Anarchists, trade unionists, radicals and simple eccentrics mounted soapboxes and endured hecklers. It no longer boasts even that distinction, and there is little to detain the tourist.

United Nations Headquarters 🏛

1st Ave. (45th St.), NY 10017 ☎ *754–1234. Map* **5***O5* 🖭 𝕏 ⓡ ▨ *Open 9am–5:20pm.*

John D. Rockefeller Jr. donated the East River site, and the first three buildings were ready for occupation in 1952. Despite the presence of several significant works of art by Marc Chagnall and Barbara Hepworth, the overall visual effect of the complex is somewhat vapid, in the manner of quasi-governmental edifices.

Most offices and rooms are closed to the public, but are of little general interest. The library is open to scholars and journalists. One-hour tours with multilingual guides leave about every 10min from the Main Lobby of the **General Assembly Building**. That is the low structure with the concave roofline to the N of the simple slab of the **Secretariat Building**. The latter is probably the more familiar from photographs.

Tickets to sessions of the General Assembly, the Security Council and certain other meetings can be obtained at the Information Desk shortly beforehand. (*Admission is free, but on a first-come basis; starting times are usually 10:30am and 3pm.*) The opening of the General Assembly, usually Mon of the third week in Sept, is the most intriguing time to go, but also the most popular.

Outsiders can lunch at the Delegates' Dining Room on the top floor of the **Conference Building**, which sits astride the FDR Drive at the edge of the river. They are seated in order of arrival; no reservations are accepted. (*Lunch only, Mon–Fri.*) A coffee shop in the concourse is open daily (*9:30am–5pm*). Nearby shops sell souvenirs, books, UN postage stamps, and handicrafts of many nations.

Upper West Side ☆

Map **6***J2.*

Of all the recently resurgent neighborhoods – *SoHo*, *TriBeCa*, *Chelsea*, Park Slope in Brooklyn – the Upper West Side most

resists easy classification. It is too large, for one thing – from
Central Park W to the Hudson River, and from 59th St. to as far
N as 120th St., according to some definitions. Secondly, it lacks
the handy ethnic, social or cultural identity of other districts.
Well-to-do refugees from the more fashionable *East
Side* have long lived here, in such still desirable apartment
houses as the gabled *Dakota Apartments*. But they
understandably chose the narrow strips along *Central Park* and
Riverside Drive, and the blocks in the middle were allowed to
fester.

Many people mark the renaissance of the Upper West Side
from the completion of the *Lincoln Center* (1966) and this
event was no doubt influential. Another factor was the
escalating rents of Greenwich Village, which drove out writers
and other professionals associated with publishing and
communications. The newcomers spruced up their apartments,
their buildings, even whole blocks. They opened gourmet and
book shops and brought new life to those already there. Pubs of
sufficient atmosphere attracted customers whose conversation
was of royalty contracts and writer's block. Dim, woody bistros
featuring allegedly Provençal cuisine proliferated at such a rate
that natives refer to one stretch as 'Quiche Alley.' Ratification
of the area's new-found panache was the arrival of Eastsiders,
who not long ago were insisting that only the imminent demise
of a close relative would cause them to cross Central Park.

Diversity continues, with smart boutiques beside seedy but
colorful bodegas, workingmen's bars adjoining glittery singles'
hangouts, upper-crust Bohemians jostling with welfare
mothers in corner delis. Important sights and institutions
include the *American Museum of Natural History*, the *New
York Historical Society*, the *Cathedral Church of St John The
Divine*, *Columbia University*, *General Grant National
Memorial* and the city's grandest boulevard, Riverside Drive.

Van Cortlandt Mansion and Museum 🏛

*Van Cortlandt Park (242nd St. and Broadway), Bronx, NY
10471* ☎543–3344. *Map* **13B4** 🔲 ✗ *Open Tues–Sat
10am–4:45pm, Sun noon–4:45pm. Closed Mon. Subway 1
to 242nd St. – Van Cortlandt Park.*

George Washington spent a lot of time in and around New
York, usually with British troops hot on his heels. This country
house (1748) with its deceptively modest stone exterior served
as one of his headquarters, as did the *Morris-Jumel Mansion* in
Manhattan. It has elements of the Dutch Colonial style, but is
essentially Georgian. Note the carved faces in the window
keystones. Unlike most of the city's historic houses, it remains
in a preserved rural setting, although the nearby meadows are
now playing fields. Nine rooms are open to the public,
including a cellar kitchen with a Dutch oven, and a parlor with a
spinet and excellent Chippendale pieces. Note the Delftware
and English china, crewelwork, cooking implements, doll house
and unusual cupboard bed.

Verrazano Narrows Bridge

Map **12E2–3** 🔲 *only when crossing w–e.*

When opened in 1964, it became the longest suspension bridge
in the world, a position it held until 1981 when overtaken by the
Humber Bridge in Britain. Two decks and 12 lanes link Staten
Island and points w with the Belt Parkway in Brooklyn.
Giovanni da Verrazano was an Italian explorer in French

employment, who is believed to have been the first European to sail into the bay. The New York Marathon starts at the W end of the bridge on the last Sun in Oct.

Villard Houses (Palace Hotel) ⏛

451 Madison Ave. (51st St.), NY 10022. Map 5N4.
This U-shaped Italian Renaissance palace, commissioned by German-born financier Henry Villard, was a departure for the firm of McKim, Mead & White. As the most popular architects of the late 19thC, they had dabbled in most revivalist styles except this one. In effect, these are six connected brownstone houses unified by a Roman esthetic. After changes in ownership that included the Random House publishing firm and the Roman Catholic Archdiocese of New York, they were purchased by Harry Helmsley. He intended to tear them down, but was prevailed upon to restore them instead and erect his Palace Hotel to the E. The houses were incorporated into the overall design and became part of the hotel. The cost was substantial, but the result is a triumph of enlightened development.

Washington Square ⏛

Map 2R4.
Now it is the heart of *Greenwich Village* – playground, meeting place, open-air venue for street musicians, *de facto* campus of *New York University*. Over the centuries, it has been hunting preserve, potter's field, public execution place, military parade ground. Brick Greek Revival row houses of the 1830s survive along the N side. Stanford White's **Washington Arch** (1892) marks the S end of 5th Ave., while Philip Johnson's **Bobst Library** is dominant in the SE corner. (See *Walk 5* in *Planning*.)

Waterside Houses ⏛

FDR Drive (25th and 30th St.), NY 10016. Map 5P5.
These arresting brown monoliths repudiated the notion that subsidized public housing was inevitably banal while simultaneously proving a harbinger of the Post-Modernist reaction to glass Bauhaus boxes. Completed in 1974, the four towers at the shore of the East River have beveled, faceted corners and channeled planes, massed with pleasing irregularity.

Whitney Museum of American Art ⏛ ☆

Madison Ave. (75th St.), NY 10021 ☎*570–3676 (general information), 288–9601 (film information). Map 7M4* 🎦
Tues 5–8pm and at all times for senior citizens and students 🎦 *at all other times* ● *Open Tues 11:30am–8pm, Wed–Sat 11am–6pm, Sun noon–6pm. Closed Mon.*
Depending upon whose interests are promoted – or ignored – the show called the Whitney Biennial is predictably cited as presumptuous, bland, stunning, inept and seminal. The ambitious survey of contemporary American art rarely fails to outrage or dismay the creative community, which may be fairly taken as evidence that the museum is doing something right. As befits the basic premise, the exhibition ranges from such luminaries as James Rosenquist and Wayne Thiebaud to fresh unheralded talents, from the arrestingly experimental to polyresin sculpture so life-like it all but breathes. There are, in addition, avant-garde films, slide and video presentations of

'site works' by conceptual artists, and dance programs and events that push conventions beyond their limits. The Biennial is normally held from late Jan to mid-Apr.

At other times, works of particular schools and trends are grouped for varying lengths of time. They are supplemented by rotated selections from the permanent collection. Virtually every major American talent of the last 50yr is represented, with an ample showing of their predecessors in the first 30yr of this century. Among the later artists are Willem de Kooning, Louise Nevelson, David Smith, Andy Warhol and Hans Hofmann; the earlier ones include Stuart Davis, Edward Hopper, George Bellows and Reginald Marsh. But the strength of the Whitney lies in its refusal to settle back and wait for artists to establish themselves. The trustees take chances, from acquiring kapok-and-vinyl 'soft' sculptures to rooms of randomly tuned radios to heaps of fabric and timber. In the process, they make curious choices, but their nerve is refreshing.

All this came about through the energy and commitment of Gertrude Vanderbilt Whitney, a sculptress who happened to be rich. She began by expanding her studio in *Greenwich Village* into exhibition space and purchasing the work of unacknowledged young artists. Periodic moves to larger premises led from 8th St. to 54th St. to the present location. As is often true of New York museums, the Whitney building (1966) is as provocative as the creations it houses. Marcel Breuer met the requirements of his clients with the sort of unconventional solution for which he was noted. The building is sheer on three sides, but the facade rises in three cantilevered tiers from the moated patio below street level, the top floor looming over the pavement and the suspended bridge connecting pavement with lobby. The granite sheathing is pierced by assymetrically placed trapezoidal windows. Interior walls are in part raw concrete bearing the impressions of the grains of the forming planks.

Some 50 Alexander Calder mobiles and stabiles are positioned around the courtyard and inside the tall plate glass of the basement floor.

A small airy cafeteria edged with potted trees serves lunch, snacks and cocktails (*Wed – Sat 11:30am – 4:30pm, Sun noon – 5pm, Tues 11:30am – 7:30pm including dinner*).

Woolworth Building ▥ ☆

233 Broadway (Barclay St.), NY 10007. Map 2T4 ▣ *Open Mon – Fri 9am – 5pm. Closed Sat, Sun.*

Although best known as the consulting architect for the *George Washington Bridge*, Cass Gilbert was a favorite of tycoons and Federal bureaucrats, largely on account of his unabashed enthusiasm for the Neoclassicism in vogue during the 50yr bracketing the turn of the century. His 1907 Beaux Arts **US Customs House** (next to *Bowling Green*) bows only to the *Metropolitan Museum of Art* in effusive grandeur. It is said that he drew inspiration for that design from the Paris Opera House, and there is little question that the British Houses of Parliament played a role in his Woolworth commission. Replete with Gothic traceries and gargoyles carved primarily from terra-cotta, a blend of modern technology and stylistic nostalgia that so often fails, this 'Cathedral of Commerce' is one of the most successful of the first generation of skyscrapers.

From its completion in 1913 until the opening of the *Chrysler Building* in 1930, Woolworth's monument to himself and his empire of five-and-dime stores was the tallest in the world. The observation floor has long been closed to the public, but you can step into the lobby to admire the terra-cotta and marble walls, bronze ornamentation, and vaulted ceiling.

World Trade Center ▥ ☆
Church St. (Liberty St.), NY 10007 ☎ *466–7377. Map 2U4* ▨ ▣ ▣ ☀ *Open 9:30am–9:30pm.*

Long before their completion in 1974, the twin towers of the World Trade Center encountered censure, on both esthetic and environmental grounds. They were visually banal, displaced a thriving market district of little charm but much vitality, threw the lower Manhattan skyline out of balance, and placed unnecessary strain on public transport and services. Those complaints are now irrelevant. Rentable space was leased, shops and restaurants were installed, and there are no more stunning vistas in the urban world. At 1,350ft (411m) they are eight stories taller than the *Empire State Building*, but were surmounted within months by the Sears Building in Chicago.

The **observation decks** are in 2 World Trade Center. There is an **enclosed deck**☆ on the 107th floor, and an open rooftop promenade on the 110th. The latter is not for the vertiginous, nor is it open in blustery or otherwise inclement weather. On a clear day, you can see 75 to 100 miles. Most of the 40 shops and 22 restaurants are at ground level or below, but the **Windows on the World** restaurant in 1 World Trade Center takes advantage of the views from the 107th floor. The Vista International Hotel between the towers opened in early 1981, the first important downtown hotel to be built in over a century.

Yeshiva University ▥
187th St. (Amsterdam Ave.), NY 10033 ☎ *960–5400. Map 10C3. Subway 1 to 181 or 191 Sts.*

The largest and oldest Jewish university in the Western Hemisphere, it began in 1886 as a seminary called Yeshiva Eitz Chaim. Now a full-fledged university with over 7,000 students engaged in both undergraduate and post-graduate studies, it maintains reverence for its origins while drawing wide respect for its courses in medicine and the mathematical sciences. The main building is a Moorish-Byzantine extravaganza of tiles, cupolas, minarets, domes and arches, completed in 1928.

Yeshiva University Museum ☆
Yeshiva University Library, 2520 Amsterdam Ave., NY 10033 ☎ *960–5390* ▨ *Open Tues–Thurs 11am–5pm, Sun noon–6pm. Closed Mon, Fri, Sat.*

A rich collection focuses on the Jewish experience through photography, religious objects, paintings, and scale models of ten famous synagogues of the ancient world.

Yorkville
Map 7L5.

Germans were among the earliest large immigrant groups of the 19thC. Many of them settled in this Upper East Side district centring on 86th St., but they were speedily assimilated and had largely dispersed by the 1930s. Traces of their occupation remain, with a *bierstube* or two, several bakery-coffee houses, and some dark-paneled restaurants specializing in *wienerschnitzel* and *sauerbraten*. Prodigals return for the Steuben Day parade in mid-Sept.

Where to stay

An unprecedented surge in hotel construction and renovation signaled the emergence of the city from the miasma of the 1970s. Harry Helmsley, a pragmatic visionary with the financial clout to realize his fantasies, burst into the local consciousness with the purchase or erection of no fewer than six hotels. Western International is restoring the venerable **Plaza** to a semblance of its former glory. Air France introduced Gallic panache with the **Parker Meridien**. And Hilton International created the **Vista International** in the *Financial District*, curiously deprived of transient lodgings.

These thousands of new rooms are all of the grand and super deluxe category, however, and there's the rub. Budget accommodations are invariably mean and soulless, and there are few enough even of those. Nothing is available that might be compared in cost and homeliness to family-run Italian *pensioni* or British bed-and-breakfast houses. The best that can be expected in this category is a reasonably clean room with minimal amenities: no more than a private shower, daily sheet changes and a TV set, and none of those are certain. At the other end of the scale, full baths, ankle-deep carpets, and meticulous housekeeping are the rule, and such additional touches as refrigerators, fresh-cut flowers, closed-circuit movies, and mints at bedside are common. Even in these establishments, however, 24hr room service is increasingly rare.

Whatever their classification, a majority of the worthiest choices are found in midtown Manhattan, in an area bounded by 3rd Ave. and 7th Ave. from 38th St. to 60th St. There is a scattering through the Upper *East Side*, a handful w of Times Sq. and a half-dozen motels near the airports. Rates are moderated somewhat by location, season, and duration of stay. To make up for the absence of businessmen, for example, hotels devise weekend package plans to attract suburbanites and tourists with such extras as theater tickets or brunches and up to 40% off standard room rates. Availability of discounts fluctuates with occupancy levels, obviously, and finding a room at any price can be a chore between Apr and Oct, especially at short notice. On those occasions, it is wise to inquire at hotels outside the immediate midtown area, particularly those in the *Gramercy Park* and *Murray Hill* districts. Ideally, reservations should be made at least a month in advance.

Children under 14 often may stay in their parents' room at little or no extra charge. Ask when booking. Several hotels have swimming pools and other recreational facilities to keep teenagers occupied, and lists of babysitters are customarily available. Dogs and other pets are usually prohibited or discouraged. Garage parking is often free to guests, but most levy an in-and-out charge when cars are used.

An 8% city sales tax is added to room bills, but the most unpleasant surprise at checkout time might be the hefty surcharge added for telephone calls. Not all hotels do this, but it is a good idea to inquire on arrival. Tipping is expected, and is not especially complicated. The bellman expects to be tipped according to the number of bags carried, and to get something extra if they are heavy. A doorman expects something small for merely opening a car door, and more if he devotes some time to hailing a taxi. Add 15% to the bill for room service waiters.

When hotels, restaurants and clubs are described elsewhere, they are shown in individual entries in **bold** type.

114

Hotels classified by area

Lower Manhattan (below 14th St.)
Vista International ▮▮▮□ 🏨

Chelsea (W 14th St. – W 23rd St.)
Chelsea ▮▮□

Gramercy Park/Murray Hill (E 14th St. – E 42nd St.)
Bedford ▮▮▮▮
Doral Park Avenue ▮▮▮□ ✿
Gramercy Park ▮▮□
Kitano ▮▮□
Sheraton-Russell ▮▮▮▮
Tuscany ▮▮▮▮

Midtown East (E 42nd St. – E 59th St.)
Algonquin ▮▮□
Beekman Tower ▮▮▮▮
Berkshire Place ▮▮▮▮
Beverly ▮▮□ ✿
Doral Inn ▮▮□ ✿
Elysee ▮▮▮
Gotham ▮▮▮
Grand Hyatt ▮▮▮▮ 🏨
Halloran House ▮▮□
Harley ▮▮▮▮
Inter-Continental ▮▮▮▮
Lexington ▮▮□
Loew's Drake ▮▮▮▮
Loew's Summit ▮▮▮▮
Lombardy ▮▮▮▮
Middletowne ▮▮□ ✿
Palace ▮▮▮▮ 🏨 🏛
Plaza ▮▮▮▮ 🏨
Roosevelt ▮▮▮
St Regis-Sheraton ▮▮▮▮ 🏨
San Carlos ▮▮□ ✿
Sherry-Netherland ▮▮▮▮ 🏨

United Nations Plaza ▮▮▮▮ 🏨
Waldorf-Astoria ▮▮▮▮ 🏨

Midtown West (W 42nd St. – W 59th St.)
Barbizon Plaza ▮▮▮▮
Best Western Skyline ▮▮□ ✿
Dorset ▮▮▮▮
Holiday Inn-Coliseum ▮▮□ ✿
Howard Johnson's ▮▮□ ✿
Marriott's Essex House ▮▮▮▮ 🏨
Milford Plaza ▮□
New York Hilton ▮▮▮▮
New York Sheraton ▮▮▮▮
Park Lane ▮▮▮▮
Parker Meridien ▮▮▮▮ 🏨
Ramada Inn-Midtown ▮▮□ ✿
Ritz-Carlton ▮▮▮▮
St Moritz ▮▮▮▮
Salisbury ▮▮□ ✿
Sheraton Center ▮▮▮▮
Sheraton City Squire ▮▮▮▮
Warwick ▮▮□
Windsor ▮▮□
Wyndham ▮▮□ ✿

Upper East Side (E 60th St. – E 95th St.)
American Stanhope ▮▮▮▮
Carlyle ▮▮▮▮ 🏨
Mayfair Regent ▮▮▮▮ 🏨
Pierre ▮▮▮▮ 🏨
Regency ▮▮▮▮ 🏨
Westbury ▮▮▮▮ 🏨

Upper West Side (W 60th St. – W 96th St.)
Excelsior ▮▮□ ✿ 🏢
Mayflower ▮▮▮▮

Queens (JFK Airport)
Hilton Inn at JFK ▮▮▮
Howard Johnson's at JFK ▮▮□

Algonquin
59 W 44th St. (near 5th Ave.), NY 10036 ☎ 840–6800. Map 5 O4 ▮▮□ 🛎 200 🛏 200 ▦ 🅿
🍴 AE CB 🍷 🄾 VISA
Location: Near Grand Central Terminal. Dorothy Parker, George Kaufman, Robert Benchley and others once traded japes and aphorisms around the famous Round Table here. That is history, but this turn-of-the-century hotel is still the clubby choice of many literary and theater folk. But be sure to check your room before accepting it, because some are dated or even shabby. The lobby, crowded with sofas, wing chairs and ill-matched tables, has the feel of a well-used country inn. Afternoon tea and cocktails can be taken there. Although the late-night buffet garners little culinary kudos, it is nevertheless popular after final curtains. The Algonquin's checkout time of 3pm

is unusually generous.
✦ □ ↗

American Stanhope
995 5th Ave. (81st St.), NY 10028 ☎ 288–5800. Cable: HOPESTAND. Map 7 L4 ▮▮▮▮
🛎 600 🛏 600 ▦ 🅿 🍴 AE CB 🍷 🄾 VISA
Location: Opposite Metropolitan Museum of Art. With a gracious style that reflects its Upper East Side environs, this medium-size stopping place boasts commodious lodgings, blessed serenity, a limousine shuttle to midtown and, during warm months, an engaging sidewalk cafe. It is perfectly situated for those intending to spend many daylight hours along museum row from the *Frick Collection* to the *Cooper-Hewitt Museum*. Weekend discount packages include breakfast and museum passes.
🍴 ✦ □ ↗ 🏢

115

Barbizon Plaza

*106 Central Park S (6th Ave.),
NY 10019* ☎ *247–7000.*
☎ *424442. Cable: BARBPLAZA.
Map 5N4* ▮▮▮ ⟲ *805* ▭ *805* ▤▤
⇌ ▭ AE CB ⊕ ⓒ VISA

*Location: Midtown, near shops and
theaters.* The lobby manages to be
both glittery and dowdy at the
same time, and the rooms are often
gloomy. But the hotel enjoys a fine
central location, an unintimidating
if rather sedate disco called the
Library, and the moderate Inn on
the Park restaurant. Owned by the
Best Western motel chain, it offers
family and weekend discounts.
⇕ ▭ ⤢ ☀ ▲ ☂ ⓨ ⊙

Bedford

*118 E 40th St. (near 5th Ave.),
NY 10016* ☎ *697–4800.* Map
5O4 ▮▮▮ ⟲ *135* ▭ *135* ▤▤
⇌ AE CB ⊕ ⓒ VISA

*Location: Near Grand Central
Terminal and United Nations.*
Frequent visitors often prefer the
relative tranquillity of Murray Hill
to the thumping heart of midtown.
Prices are usually lower, hotels
smaller, package tours fewer, and
there are bonuses in facilities and
personal attention to compensate
for the few extra blocks of distance.
The Bedford offers family rates
and kitchenettes with every room,
and mother, father and children
can stay for the price of a single in
more glamorous locations.
▱ ⇕ ▭ ⤢ ☀ ▲

Beekman Tower

*3 Mitchell Pl. (1st Ave. and 49th
St.), NY 10017* ☎ *355–7300.*
Map *5O5* ▮▮▮ ⟲ *160* ▭ *160* ▤▤
⇌ AE CB ⊕ ⓒ VISA

*Location: Near the East River and
United Nations.* The term
'apartment hotel' implies studios
and suites with kitchen facilities.
Such hotels appeal to executives
who must entertain small groups or
to families on extended visits,
assuming they are willing to
eschew a few customary hotel
amenities. This is one of them,
although there is in addition a
cocktail lounge with piano music
and an agreeable vista of midtown
towers and the busy river.
▱ ⇕ ▭ ⤢ ◁ ⓨ ♫

Berkshire Place

*21 E 52nd St. (Madison Ave.),
NY 10022* ☎ *753–5800.* Map
5N4 ▮▮▮ ⟲ *420* ▭ *420* ▤▤
⇌ AE CB ⊕ ⓒ VISA

*Location: Near Rockefeller Center,
St Patrick's Cathedral.* Formerly a
no-nonsense executive stopover,
but now spruced up under new
ownership and aggressively
promoted with advertising and
generous weekend packages.
Suburban couples escaping the
kids find themselves treated to
breakfast in bed, chocolates at
bedside and bowls of fresh flowers,
all at almost half the price of the
same rooms Mon–Thurs.
Harmonious tints of green, peach
and beige accompany tasteful
seating arrangements and
decorative accessories. The
handsome lobby soothes with print
fabrics, potted palms and ivy,
amidst which you can take an
above-par afternoon tea. With
these allurements, and the best 5th
Ave. shops just outside the door, it
is hardly surprising that the many
guests now have no more pressing
business than enjoying themselves.
⇕ ⴵ ▭ ⤢ ☀ ▲

Best Western Skyline ✿

*725 10th Ave. (near 49th St.),
NY 10019* ☎ *586–3400.* Map
4O2 ▮▮▮ ⟲ *230* ▭ *230* ▤▤ ▭
⇌ AE CB ⊕ ⓒ VISA

*Location: w of Times Sq. Theater
District.* On the one hand, this
motel allows easy entrance and exit
from the city by car; prices are
reasonable, especially for family
groups, and there is an indoor
swimming pool. On the other, it is
at some distance from major
attractions and in a barren setting
of parking lots and marginal
commercial enterprises. If it were
better situated, its upper-middle
level of accommodation would
make it difficult to rival.
⇕ ▭ ⤢ ☀ ≈ ▲

Beverly

*125 E 50th St. (Lexington Ave.),
NY 10022* ☎ *753–2700.* Map
5O4 ▮▮▮ ⟲ *200* ▭ *200* ▤▤
⇌ AE CB ⊕ ⓒ VISA

*Location: Midtown East, near
Grand Central Terminal.* Moderate
cost and a midtown situation
usually suggest shabbiness. But
although no one is likely to regard
the Beverly as an undiscovered
treasure, it is certainly above that
category. The cramped reception
area does not calm suspicions and
the corridors are gloomy, but many
rooms have serving pantries and
terraces and all are recently
decorated in soothing tones. Room
waiters are on call past midnight.
There is a 24hr pharmacy on the
premises, a bar and restaurant.
⇕ ▭ ⤢ ☀ ▲ ⓨ

Carlyle ▥

*35 E 76th St. (Madison Ave.),
NY 10021* ☎ *744 – 1600. Map
7L4* ▥ ♋ *500* 🛏 *500* 🍴 ⇌
AE CB ⓓ ⓒ

*Location: Upper East Side, one block
from the Whitney Museum.* Many
hotels pretend to offer Continental
standards of hospitality, but here
the grand traditions of Europe
really are emulated. Over-sized
rooms pamper with bathroom
phones and custom toiletries. Most
have serving pantries and well-
stocked refrigerators. There is
24hr room service, and the cashier
exchanges currency until
midnight. Pets are permitted at an
extra charge, and dog walkers are
on hand. Afternoon tea is an event,
as is an hour spent with stylish
singer-pianist Bobby Short or the
great jazz musician George
Shearing in the Cafe Carlyle.
Limousines stand ready to shuttle
guests to midtown shops and
theaters. A few steps away, in
Madison Ave., is a large
concentration of dealers in rare
antiques and works of art, where
browsers are generally welcome.

⌂ ‡ ☐ ⬚ 🏊 ☕ 🍷 🎵

Chelsea

*222 W 23rd St. (8th Ave.), NY
10011* ☎ *243 – 3700. Map4Q3*
▥ ♋ *400* 🛏 *370* AE ⓓ ⓒ
VISA

*Location: In Chelsea, near Madison
Sq.* Definitely not for everyone;
neither the immediate
neighborhood nor the reception is
beguiling. And yet there is a certain
rough-hewn Bohemian appeal
about this 100yr-old pile. Artists of
every esthetic persuasion have
passed through, leaving behind the
samples of their work that cover
the walls. Don't expect special
attention, and examine your
assigned room before accepting it.
Some are large and quite
comfortable, others are dreadful.
Permanent residents occupy about
half the rooms.

‡

Doral Inn ✿

*541 Lexington Ave. (49th St.),
NY 10022* ☎ *755 – 1200* ♋
236641. Map 5O4 ▥ ♋ *700* 🛏
700 🍴 ⇌ AE CB ⓓ ⓒ VISA
Open all year.

*Location: Midtown East, near
United Nations and Grand Central
Terminal.* Big brother to the **Doral
Park Avenue**, it is neither an inn
nor as appealing as its sibling. Like
so many of the city's commercial

hotels, it is clean, brisk, bustling
and largely unremarkable. The
airline crews and salesmen who
frequent it can squeeze in some
racquetball and a sauna between
flights. The suites on the top two
floors have terraces, kitchens and
bars, but at a stiff increase in price.

‡ ☐ ⬚ 🏊 ☕ 🍷

Doral Park Avenue ✿

*70 Park Ave. (38th St.), NY
10016* ☎ *687 – 7050. Cable:
DORALPARK NY. Map5O4* ▥
♋ *200* 🛏 *200* 🍽 ⇌ AE CB
ⓓ ⓒ VISA

*Location: Near Grand Central
Terminal.* Murray Hill doesn't
have the gloss and hum of the
midtown core around Rockefeller
Center, but that is its virtue. This
serene stopping place, small by Big
Apple standards, makes the most
of its setting. Reasonable needs are
skillfully met, without fuss or
show, although the restaurant and
room service close down before
10pm. All bedrooms have
refrigerators; some have serving
pantries. There is a sidewalk cafe in
summer, and most central office
buildings and tourist sights are
within walking distance.

⌂ ‡ ☐ ⬚ ☕ 🍷

Dorset

*30 W 54th St. (near 6th Ave.),
NY 10019* ☎ *247 – 7300. Cable:
DORSETOTEL. Map4N3* ▥
♋ *400* 🛏 *400* 🍽 🍴 nearby
⇌ AE CB ⓓ

*Location: Near Rockefeller Center,
Museum of Modern Art, and 5th
Ave. shops.* The fact that over half
its rooms are under permanent
lease is testimony to the desirability
of this underpublicized hostelry.
The paneled lobby is a welcoming
retreat from the midtown bustle,
the front desk staff uncommonly
amiable. Personalities from the
nearby ABC television network
headquarters frequent the
streetside bar-cafe at lunchtime.
Some rooms have pantries and
balconies. There is no charge for
children under 14 sharing their
parents' rooms. A complimentary
New York Times arrives with
breakfast.

⌂ ‡ ☐ ⬚ ☕ 🍷

Elysee

*60 E 54th St. (near Park Ave.),
NY 10022* ☎ *753 – 1066*
♋ *220373. Map5N4* ▥ ♋ *110*
🛏 *110* 🍽 ⇌ ⓓ ⓒ VISA

*Location: Midtown between 5th Ave.
and Park Ave.* In refreshing

contrast with its larger competitors, the Elysee celebrates its diminutiveness with distinctive decorative schemes and such whimsies as names instead of numbers for its rooms. With only 110 of these this is only eccentric, not impractical, but don't be surprised at motifs Moorish, Colonial, oriental. Even the **Monkey Bar** downstairs chooses to entertain with comedians rather than innocuous piano music. There are scheduled coaches to the airport.

⌂ ‡ □ ⌐ ⚲ ⅄

Excelsior ⌂ ✿

45 W 81st St. (near Central Park W), NY 10024 ☎ *362–9200. Map* **6***L3* ▯ ⌖ 300 ⌷ 300 ▤ ⇌ ⟨AE⟩ ⟨CB⟩ ⓘ ⟨⟩ ⟨VISA⟩

Location: *Near American Museum of Natural History.* Nothing memorable, but it is clean, quiet and the price is unusually reasonable. It is also one of the few options for those who wish to stay in the Upper West Side.

⌂ ‡ □ ⌐ ⚲

Gotham

700 5th Ave. (55th St.), NY 10022 ☎ *247–2200* ⓣ *238190. Map* **5***N4* ▯▯▯ ⌖ 350 ⌷ 350 ▤ ⇌ ⟨AE⟩ ⟨CB⟩ ⓘ ⟨⟩ ⟨VISA⟩

Location: *Near Rockefeller Center and 5th Ave. shops.* Given its unbeatable situation and undisputed elegance, it is surprising that the Gotham is not better known. Perhaps that lack of awareness accounts for rates at least 25% lower than those of the **St Regis-Sheraton**, directly across the street, although they are in many ways comparable. The Gotham was in fact planned as a sister establishment and completed one year later (1905). It has enjoyed a costly rejuvenation in recent years.

⌂ ‡ □ ⌐ ☫ ◍

Gramercy Park

2 Lexington Ave. (21st St.), NY 10010 ☎ *475–4320. Map* **5***Q4* ▯▯▯ ⌖ 500 ⌷ 500 ▤ ⇌ ⟨AE⟩ ⟨CB⟩ ⓘ ⟨⟩ ⟨VISA⟩

Location: *Near Gramercy Park, away from main traffic arteries.* The relatively quiet situation is the primary attraction for its predominantly European clientele, which has included second-string rock groups and film actors. There are other reasons too: among them access to the attractive private park a half-block away, the clusters of

historic houses within range of a morning stroll, and non-confiscatory tariffs. Apart from the unfortunate color schemes in many of the rooms, there is an amiable warmth that finds its glamour in its guests rather than in its fixtures.

⌂ ‡ □ ⌐ ☫ ⅄

Grand Hyatt ⌂

42nd St. and Park Ave., NY 10017 ☎ *883–1234. Map* **5***O4* ▯▯▯▯ ⌖ *1,407* ⌷ *1,407* ▤ ▤ ⇌ ⟨AE⟩ ⟨CB⟩ ⓘ ⟨⟩ ⟨VISA⟩

Location: *Next to Grand Central Terminal.* A leader in the city's hotel boom, this 1980 addition to the Hyatt holdings also takes a giant share of the credit for the continuing rehabilitation of E 42nd St. The effect of the place is sleek, showy, and quintessentially New York, although by the standards of others in the chain, this Hyatt is downright sedate. Nevertheless, there is drama in abundance in its exuberant architecture. The effect of the four-story atrium is horizontal rather than vertical, one side knuckling out over the street. There is a tiered waterfall beneath a vast spidery wire sculpture, rows of greenery, great columns cloaked in brass and steel. All rooms have color and cable TV, there is a health club with sauna, squash and tennis, and Trumpet's is one of the city's better hotel restaurants.

‡ ⅋ □ ⌐ ⌘ ☫ ⅄

Halloran House

525 Lexington Ave. (near 48th St.), NY 10017 ☎ *755–4000* ⓣ *668844. Map* **5***O4* ▯▯▯ ⌖ 650 ⌷ 650 ▤ ⇌ ⟨AE⟩ ⟨CB⟩ ⓘ ⟨⟩ ⟨VISA⟩

Location: *Midtown East, near Grand Central Terminal and United Nations.* Livelier than most of the rather anonymous commercial hotels that stretch along Lexington Ave., Halloran House offers a health club, swimming pool, two restaurants and a bar named after the owner – Biff's Place – that swings to jazz or pop from 5pm until whenever. The bedrooms satisfy basic needs, with the welcome addition of small personal safes in the closets.

‡ ⅋ □ ⌐ ⚲ ⇌ ☫ ⅄

Harley

212 E 42nd St. (3rd Ave.), NY 10017 ☎ *888–1624. Map* **5***O5* ▯▯▯ ⌖ 793 ⌷ 793 ▤ ▤ ⇌ ⟨AE⟩ ⟨CB⟩ ⓘ ⟨⟩ ⟨VISA⟩

Location: *Near Grand Central*

Terminal and United Nations. One of the chain assembled or built by Harry Helmsley, the Harley is geared to the expense account crowd, and on the assumption that traveling executives have little time for ceremony, it is forthright rather than frisky, though all comforts are provided. Multi-lingual stenographers are available. Breakfast trays arrive with the *Wall Street Journal*. Rooms are crisply conservative. When business people go home for the weekend, sharply discounted rates draw the suburbanites for museum-hopping and Broadway shows.

‡ ⑃ □ ⬚ ⧸ ⇌ ☗

Hilton Inn at JFK
318–10 135th Ave., Jamaica, NY 11430 ☎ *322–8700. Map 13E5* ▥▮ ⇗ *351* ▭ *351* ▦ ☐ ⇛
AE CB ⑩ ⑩ VISA
Location: Next to Kennedy Airport. This is an alternative for those with early-morning flights or less than a day in town. A conventional vertical motel with the usual facilities, it provides swift and regular transport to the terminals.

‡ ⑃ □ ⬚ ☗

Holiday Inn-Coliseum ✿
440 W 57th St. (9th Ave.), NY 10019 ☎ *581–8100. Map 4N3* ▥▮ ⇗ *600* ▭ *600* ▦ ⬚ ⇛
AE CB ⑩ ⑩ VISA
Location: Midtown West, near Columbus Circle. A conventional motel representative of the mother chain, it doesn't mean to surprise, and succeeds. The immediate neighborhood is grim but unthreatening, with the Lincoln Center, major theaters and Central Park all within walking distance. Businessmen and families on tight budgets find it satisfactory, and children enjoy the rooftop swimming pool.

‡ ⑃ □ ⬚ ⇌ ☗ ☗ ⟐

Inter-Continental
111 E 48th St. (Lexington Ave.), NY 10017 ☎ *755–5900* ⑩ *7105816535. Cable: BARCLOTEL. Map 5O4* ▥▮ ⇗ *777* ▭ *777* ▦ ⬚ ⇛ AE
CB ⑩ ⑩ VISA
Location: Near Grand Central Terminal and United Nations. Several changes in management, the last three treading on each other's heels, have not altered the courtly European flavor. An aviary with live songbirds is still the lobby trademark. The spacious public

areas and halls suggest bedrooms of larger dimensions. Thick walls and double windows ensure quiet, while TV, AM-FM radio, free closed-circuit movies, and 24hr room service remove the need to brave the streets for food and diversion. The Theater District is only a few blocks w and several celebrated restaurants are even closer. Within the building is the oldest pharmacy in New York, **Caswell Massey**, featuring colognes, soaps, and hairbrushes that have their origins in Colonial times.

⌂ ‡ ⑃ □ ⬚ ⧸ ☗

Howard Johnson's ✿
851 8th Ave. (near 51st St.), NY 10019. Map 4N3 ⑩ *147183.* ⇗ *300* ▭ *300* ▦ ⬚
▦ ⬚ AE CB ⑩ ⑩ VISA
Location: w of the midtown Theater District. One of a trio of relatively new midtown motels, it shares the virtues and the liabilities of the others – ready access by car, walking distance from the major theaters and moderate tariffs; but charmless rooms and a bleak neighborhood.

‡ □ ⬚ ⧸

Howard Johnson's at JFK
135–9 145th St., Jamaica, NY 11436 ☎ *659–6000. Map 13E5* ▥▮ ⇗ *390* ▭ *390* ▦ ⇛ AE
CB ⑩ ⑩ VISA
Location: Next to Kennedy Airport. The reason for being here is proximity to the airport, although you will find adequate comfort and service.

‡ ⑃ □ ⬚

Kitano
66 Park Ave. (38th St.), NY 10016 ☎ *685–0022* ⑩ *424429. Cable: AMEKITANO. Map 5O4* ▥▮ ⇗ *91* ▭ *91* ▦ ⬚ ⇛
CB ⑩ VISA
Location: Near Grand Central Terminal. The Japanese-owned and operated Kitano offers an intriguing blend of Colonial American order and *shibui* serenity. About half the bedrooms are done up in chintz, the others with Oriental understatement. There are several authentic *tatami* suites featuring hot tubs and bedrolls. Avoid the cheapest rooms, for they are excessively small. More efficient than sybaritic, the hotel provides no room service and the noon checkout is early.

⌂ ‡ □ ⬚

Lexington

511 Lexington Ave. (E 48th St.), NY 10017 ☎ *755–6963. Map* 5O4 ▮▮ ☎ 800 ▭ 800 ▤ ▭ ▭ ▭ 🄰🄴 🄳 🄲🄳 𝚅𝙸𝚂𝙰

Location: Near Grand Central Terminal and United Nations. The immediate neighborhood is noisy and commercial, and the hotel itself is an ageing edifice of no distinction. But the management keeps the average-size bedrooms perked up, endlessly painting, papering and upgrading. Services are comparable to those of more expensive competitors, except for the languid check-in. Chateau Madrid is the long-running restaurant-nightclub with a pronounced Latin flavor on the ground floor, its performances tangy enough for adults, tame enough for kids.

✦ ☐ 🗷 🖉 🏄 🏖 🍴

Loew's Drake

440 Park Ave. (56th St.), NY 10022 ☎ *421–0900. Map* 5N4 ▮▮ ☎ 650 ▭ 650 ▤ ▭ 🄰🄴 🄳 🄲🄳 𝚅𝙸𝚂𝙰

Location: Midtown East. During extensive recent renovation, a lounge was carved from the already small lobby, further constricting the crowds that eddy around the reception desk and elevators. Still, the people-watching is great, over breakfast, high tea, or substantial highballs. Upstairs, the rooms off the canary-bright twisting halls reveal luxury touches – hideaway refrigerators, AM-FM radios, digital clocks, same-day laundry service, first-run films, four-poster beds (in some rooms), and serving pantries (in the suites). The prime East Side venue is the best reason to stay here.

✦ 🖒 ☐ 🗷 🏖 🖉

Loew's Summit

569 Lexington Ave. (51st St.), NY 10022 ☎ *752–7000* ☎ *147181. Map* 5N4 ☎ 770 ▭ 770 ▤ ▭ ▭ 🄰🄴 🄲🄳 🄳 🄲 𝚅𝙸𝚂𝙰

Location: Near midtown shopping and United Nations. All the comforts are to be found in this large hotel of the international breed – once inside, you might be in any of its counterparts in Lisbon, London or Rio, right down to the concierge. There are few surprises, good or bad. Refrigerators, bathroom telephones, in-room films and radios are standard. For additional indulgences, ask for a room on the

ESP (Extra Special Patron) plan. For this, there is, of course, a surcharge.

✦ ☐ 🗷 🖉 🏄 🏖 🍴 🍸

Lombardy

111 E 56th St. (near Park Ave.), NY 10022 ☎ *753–8600. Map* 5N4 ▮▮ ☎ 160 ▭ 160 ▤ ▭

Location: Near smart shops and Rockefeller Center. This is a 'co-op' hotel, meaning that the individual rooms and suites are privately managed. Its virtue is that the uniformity of most hotel lodgings is evident only in the floor plans. Rooms are decorated according to the tastes of their owners. Given the Park Ave. location, the standards and resources of those owners are high, and this is reflected in the furnishings, fabrics and accessories. Serving pantries with refrigerators are the rule, and in keeping with the European ambience a continental breakfast is included in the remarkably reasonable rate. The clubbily masculine bar on ground level is so traditional it requires coats and ties. As hotel restaurants go, the Lombardy Laurent is high caliber.

▭ ✦ ☐ 🗷 🖉 🏄 🍸

Marriott's Essex House 🏨

160 Central Park S (near 6th Ave.), NY 10019 ☎ *247–0300* ☎ *125205. Map* 5N4 ☎ 810 ▭ 810 ▤ ▭ ▭ 🄰🄴 🄲🄳 🄳 🄲 𝚅𝙸𝚂𝙰

Location: On Central Park, near Lincoln Center and shopping areas. Although it aspires to rank with the cream of Manhattan hotels, the Essex House falls short. Participants in large conferences and formal dinners mill about the paneled and chandeliered lobby at all hours. And the King's Wharf restaurant is out of place in this precinct. That said, however, the hotel nevertheless qualifies as a strong runner-up to the best. Its location is excellent, the staff speak 18 languages, the bedrooms are spacious. There are scales in the bathrooms for weight-watchers; and when the maid turns down the bed at night she leaves a chocolate mint. Bills can be paid in foreign currency.

✦ ☐ 🗷 🏖

Mayfair Regent 🏨

610 Park Ave. (65th St.), NY 10021 ☎ *288–0800* ☎ *236257. Map* 5M4 ☎ 500 ▭ 500 ▤ ▭ ▭ 🄰🄴 🄲🄳 🄳 🄲 𝚅𝙸𝚂𝙰

Location: Upper East Side, in art

and antiques country. The Mayfair Regent earns a respect approaching reverence. In part, that assessment reflects the personal attention that is only possible when the number of guests is carefully limited. No one seems to know exactly how many rooms there are, for most are privately owned, but the total available to transients is probably no more than 125 at any one time. Most of them are suites, sumptuously appointed. The presence on the premises of the redoubtable **Le Cirque** restaurant lends stature, although it is independently operated. Ceilings soar, carpets cover ankles, wood and metal surfaces glow. There are even working fireplaces in some suites. Smooth functioning is assured by a succession of managers from the likes of London's Connaught and Venice's Gritti Palace. High tea in the lounge offers cucumber sandwich slivers and brews of loose leaves kept warm with a cozy.

🛏 ‡ ☐ ⬚

Mayflower
Central Park W (61st St.), NY 10023 ☎ *265–0060. Map 4N3*
▥▥ ☏ 400 ▭ 400 ▦ ⬚
AE CB ⊙ ⓘ VISA
Location: Near Lincoln Center and New York Coliseum. The otherwise resurgent Upper West Side is woefully short of decent hotels. By default, top slot goes to the Mayflower. Although it is not in the same league as the East Side leaders, recent refurbishment of already spacious rooms makes it a reliable choice. The parkside Conservatory restaurant has live entertainment and an above-par Sunday brunch. Suites with pantries cost no more than a standard double at many expensive crosstown competitors. There is an airport limousine.

🛏 ‡ ☐ ⬚ ♫

Middletowne ♣
148 E 48th St. (near Lexington Ave.), NY 10017 ☎ *755–3000. Map 5O4* ▥▥ ☏ 192 ▭ 192 ▦
⬚ AE CB ⊙ ⓘ VISA
Location: Midtown East, near Grand Central Terminal. Visitors settling in for a week or more sometimes wish it were possible to trim the overheads implicit in full hotel services in exchange for more home-like quarters. They can do precisely that here, trading waiters and elaborate lobbies for comfortable rooms that are all

equipped with full kitchens, including stoves, refrigerators and, if desired, silverware and crockery. Some suites have fireplaces and/or terraces. Rates might be negotiable for longer stays. There is neither bar nor restaurant, but both are abundant in this neighborhood.

🛏 ‡ ☐ ⬚ ⚑

Milford Plaza
270 W 45th St. (8th Ave.), NY 10036 ☎ *869–3600* 📺 *147193. Cable: MILPAZ NY. Map 4O3* ▥
▥▥ ☏ 1,310 ▭ 1,310 ▦
AE CB ⊙ ⓘ VISA
Location: Heart of the Theater District. This used to be the Royal Manhattan, a commercial hotel of little distinction. It is no more sumptuous under its new name and management, nor is the neighborhood less seedy, the rooms less cramped. They are cheerier, however, newly furnished and equipped with television and radios. Security arrangements are reassuring. For those who feel that a New York holiday means seeing a different show each night, there is no more convenient situation, and the reasonable rates leave enough dollars for an extra matinee.

‡ ☐ ⬚ ⚒

New York Hilton
1335 6th Ave. (53rd St.), NY 10019 ☎ *586–7000* 📺 *238492. Cable: NYHILTH. Map 5N4* ▥▥ ☏ 2,131 ▭ 2,131 ▦
⬚ ⥥ AE CB ⊙ ⓘ VISA
Location: Midtown, at Rockefeller Center. Big, brassy and bustling, this vertical town within the city makes it unnecessary to brave the weather. Everything is here, from shops to secretarial services to a week's worth of bars and restaurants and live entertainment. Of the many types of room, only the claustrophobic singles are to be avoided. Comforting features include closed-circuit films and heated bathroom floors. Half-day rates are available for lie-downs and wash-ups between energetic shopping excursions and theater matinees.

‡ ♿ ☐ ⬚ ⚒ ♈ ♫

New York Sheraton
870 7th Ave. (56th St.), NY 10019 ☎ *247–8000* 📺 *126452. Map 4N3* ▥▥ ☏ 1,295 ▭ 1,295
▦ ⬚ ⥥ AE CB ⊙ ⓘ VISA
Location: Midtown, near Carnegie Hall, Theater District. Predictability is, for many

travelers, a virtue, which helps explain the unending expansion of the world-girdling Sheraton empire. This is one of the better realizations of the formula. The vast warren of cozy cubicles is efficiently serviced, convenient for everything and brimming with restaurants, bars and shops.

🛉 ♿ ☐ ☎ ⬚ 🍴 ♟ 🅨 ⊙

Palace 🏨 🏨

455 Madison Ave. (50th St.), NY 10022 ☎ *888–7000. Map 5N4*
▥▥▥ 🕿 773 ☐ 773 ▤▤ ⟷ ⟷
Ⓐ Ⓔ Ⓒ Ⓑ ⓓ ⓓ Ⓥ ⓢ ⓐ

Location: Midtown, near shopping.
Preservation of worthwhile buildings has a checkered history in New York. More often than not, commerce has triumphed over heritage. Not so The Palace. Bent upon erecting a princely flagship for his ever-growing real estate empire, Harry Helmsley was persuaded not only to spare the proud Villard Houses from demolition, but to restore them to their 1886 opulence. His efforts were rewarded by a fat dossier of enthusiastic press notices and bookings that stretch months in advance. The Franco-Italianate interiors were lovingly scrubbed and mended, revealing marble inlays, Tiffany glass, frescoes, rich panelling, gold-leaf ceilings, and intricately carved wood friezes. In the adjoining modern tower, guest rooms are unusually spacious and continue the theme with huge Baroque headboards, soft velvets, and tasteful Louis XV reproductions. With all this visual pampering, service sometimes falters by comparison, but not for lack of trying. The concierge, for example, can arrange for translators of nearly 40 languages. There aren't five other hotels in town that can match this experience.

🛉 ♿ ☐ ☎ 🦅 🍴 ♟ 🅨

Park Lane 🏨

36 Central Park S (near 5th Ave.), NY 10019 ☎ *371–4000*
🕿 *668613. Map 5N4* ▥▥▥ 🕿 640
☐ 640 ▤▤ ⟷ ⟷ Ⓐ Ⓔ Ⓒ Ⓑ ⓓ ⓓ
Ⓥ ⓢ ⓐ

Location: Across from Central Park, near shops and Lincoln Center.
Much is made of the fact that Harry Helmsley, owner of half a dozen New York hotels, chose to live in this one. The in-house management sets high standards, for though this modern highrise cannot achieve the grace of the

older luxury hotels, it certainly tries. Lavish applications of brocade and suede dress the corridors and public rooms. There is a concierge to secure theater tickets and limousines. Try afternoon tea in the Park Room and you won't be disappointed. The higher the room on the park side of the hotel, the better the views will be.

🛉 ♿ ☐ ☎ 🦅 ⟨⟨ 🍴 🅨

Parker Meridien 🏨

118 W 57th St. (6th Ave.), NY 10019 ☎ *245–5000. Map 4N3*
▥▥▥ 🕿 600 ☐ 600 ▤▤ ⟷ ⟷
Ⓐ Ⓔ Ⓒ Ⓑ ⓓ ⓓ Ⓥ ⓢ ⓐ

Location: Near Central Park, Rockefeller Center and Carnegie Hall. Air France is the parent company, and the Gallic touch is evident, although not as pervasive as its advertisements insist. Aubusson tapestries adorn the walls, a multilingual concierge attends to arrangements for booking theater tickets and limousines, and the bars and restaurants smack of the Champs-Élysées. The jogging track, the squash and racquetball courts, and the whirlpool and sauna cater to the fitness mania of the contemporary international business-person; the 100 lavishly appointed 'executive apartments' also offer luxury. Breakfast in bed includes croissants and is usually accompanied by a copy of the *International Herald Tribune*. All rooms have stocked minibars and closed-circuit movies. There are weekend package plans and corporate discounts are available.

🛉 ♿ ☐ ☎ ⟷ 🍴 🅨

Pierre 🏨

5th Ave. and 61st St., NY 10021 ☎ *838–8000* ⓣ *127426. Map 5N4* ▥▥▥ 🕿 700 ☐ 700 ▤▤ ⟷
⟷ Ⓐ Ⓔ Ⓒ Ⓑ ⓓ ⓓ Ⓥ ⓢ ⓐ

Location: Across from Central Park, near museums and shops. Monarchs and presidents select the Pierre. Long limousines line the curb outside and studiedly inconspicuous men stand about whispering into micro-transmitters. There isn't a safer address in town. Marble baths and floral-painted basins are happy touches, as are magnifying shaving mirrors and electrically operated window draperies. The staff makes notes of preferences in flowers and other idiosyncracies and try to remember names. Barely half the rooms are available to temporary visitors, but they are given no hint of second-class status. Book as far in advance as possible.

☎ ‡ ᵬ □ ⊡ ⋙ ◁ ☙

Plaza ▦
5th Ave. and 59th St., NY 10019
☎ *759–3000* ☏ *236938. Cable:*
PLAZA NEW YORK. Map 5N4 ▐▐▐▐
☎ *900* ⊡ *900* ▤▤ ⫤ ⫼ AE
CB ⊕ ⊙ VISA

Location: Corner of 5th Ave. and Central Park. Seemingly endless renovations are nearly finished in this long-time favorite of celebrities. Brass window and door frames gleam, carpeting is new, statuary and capitals sparkle. Viennese strings accompany tea in the Palm Court, and there is music for dancing in the Edwardian Room. Hallways and rooms are lavishly proportioned. Many rooms overlook Central Park; many have refrigerators, radios, alarm clocks and antique furnishings.

‡ □ ⊡ ◁ ☙ ♈ ♬ ⩗

Ramada Inn-Midtown ❀
790 8th Ave. (near 48th St.), NY 10019 ☎ *581–7000* ☏ *147182.*
Map 403 ▐▐▐ ☎ *365* ⊡ *365*
☎ ⫤ AE ⊕ ⊙ VISA

Location: Midtown, Theater District. Parents appreciate the relatively modest family rates, and their children like the swimming pool, a rare facility in the city. Inside, fair value is given, with crisp decor and exemplary maintenance. Outside, exceptionally tawdry 8th Ave. gives pause even to hardened New Yorkers.

‡ □ ⊡ ≈ ☙

Regency ▦
Park Ave. and 61st St., NY 10021 ☎ *759–4100* ☏ *147180.*
Map 5N4 ▐▐▐ ☎ *500* ⊡ *500* ▤▤
☎ ⫤ AE CB ⊕ ⊙ VISA

Location: Upper East Side, amid exclusive shops and galleries. Moneyed Europeans and their counterparts in the American elite choose the Regency at least partly for its low profile. The keynote of the style is Louis XVI, naturally updated by such niceties as bathroom telephones and scales. The rooms luxuriate in extravagant applications of marble and brocade, and an alert staff is ready to satisfy the merest whim. Book far in advance.

☎ ‡ ᬀ □ ⊡ ⋙ ☙ ♬

Ritz-Carlton
112 Central Park S (near 6th Ave.), NY 10019 ☎ *757–1900.*
Map 5N4 ☎ *300* ⊡ *300* ▤▤
☎ ⫤ AE CB ⊕ ⊙ VISA

Location: On Central Park, near Lincoln Center. The renovation that seems to have been going on forever is nearly complete, and the former Navarro has even chosen a new and grander name to mark the transformation. European show-business celebrities choose this hotel over others of perhaps greater panache simply because it is quieter and equally well situated. The upper floors offer glorious views of the park.

☎ ‡ □ ⊡ ⋙ ◁

Roosevelt
45th St. and Madison Ave., NY 10017 ☎ *661–9600* ☏ *645629.*
Cable: THE ROOSEVELT NYC.
Map 504 ▐▐▐ ☎ *1,050* ⊡ *1,050*
▤▤ ⫤ AE CB ⊕ ⊙ VISA

Location: Grand Central Terminal area: Given its size, no-nonsense atmosphere, and midtown situation, the Roosevelt identity is that of a businessman's stopover. Its public rooms and most of the bedchambers have been primped up in recent years, and telex and photocopying machines are made available to visiting workaholics. Consistent with their guests' occupations and early rising habits, the house restaurants and services tend to close down by 11pm. Sturdily comfortable it is, glamorous it is not.

‡ □ ⊡ ☙ ♈

St Moritz
50 Central Park S (6th Ave.), NY 10019 ☎ *755–5800* ☏ *668840.*
Map 5N4 ▐▐▐ ☎ *800* ⊡ *800* ▤▤
☎ ⫤ AE CB ⊕ ⊙ VISA

Location: Overlooking Central Park, near theaters and shopping. Decades of advertisements in *The New Yorker* magazine proclaimed it the 'Biggest Little Hotel' in town, but most citizens know it for its sidewalk cafe. Rooms are compact, and those high in front seem larger by virtue of the expansive views of the park. The entry to the street-level Rumplemayers restaurant is, improbably, lined with stuffed animals; ice cream concoctions are the big item. Harry's Bar doesn't match its namesake in Venice, but is an amiable retreat in which to pass pre-dinner hours. Book ahead.

☎ ‡ □ ⊡ ⋙ ◁ ☙ ♈

St Regis-Sheraton 🎖️
2 E 55th St. (5th Ave.), NY 10022
☎ *753–4500. Map 5N4* ▥
🕿 *520* 🛏️ *520* ▦ 🅰🅴
🆑🅱 ⓘ ⓒ 🆅🅸🆂🅰

Location: Midtown, near Rockefeller Center. Unlike most of its contemporaries of the turn of the century – decayed, demolished or converted to other uses – the 1904 St Regis has not only prevailed but taken on added luster at the grand-luxe pinnacle. Even back then, it cost financier John Jacob Astor nearly six million dollars to build and furnish what was to be the tallest hotel in the city. In opulent detail, it rivaled the **Waldorf-Astoria**, its principal competitor for the carriage trade. Astor went down with the *Titanic*, but the St Regis rolls on. She carries her age well, from the buffed brass doorman's booth at the entrance to commodious bedchambers, intricately carved moldings and a Maxfield Parrish mural in the **King Cole Room**. The aristocracy still stays here, including now the princes of film and pop music. Book well in advance.
🖾 ‡ 🗆 🗗 ⚓ ⚑ 💐

Salisbury ♣
123 W 57th St. (near 6th Ave.), NY 10019 ☎ *246–1300*
Ⓣ*668366. Map 5N4* ▥ 🕿 *320*
🛏️ *320* ▦ 🖾 ⇌ 🅰🅴 🆑🅱 ⓘ ⓒ 🆅🅸🆂🅰

Location: Across from Carnegie Hall. A family of four can have a suite here for the cost of a double in one of the posh hotels nearby. More than half the rooms have kitchenettes, most have at least a refrigerator, so there can be economies in eating out. Major shopping streets, the Lincoln Center, theaters and Rockefeller Center are all within blocks. Even conceding its lack of elegance or of such facilities as bars, the Salisbury is good value.
🖾 ‡ 🗆 🗗 💐 ⚓

San Carlos ♣
150 E 50th St. (near Lexington Ave.), NY 10022 ☎ *755–1800.*
Map 5O4 ▥ 🕿 *144* 🛏️ *144* ▦
⇌ 🅰🅴 🆑🅱 ⓘ ⓒ 🆅🅸🆂🅰

Location: Midtown East, near Grand Central Terminal. Like its neighbor, the **Beverly**, this small and unassuming place trades value for pretension. Many rooms have serving pantries, an incentive for budgeteers who can't bring themselves to lunch on

hamburgers. There is no restaurant, bar or room service, but this is a lively district with many cafes and take-out food shops willing to make deliveries. Transportation to the airports can be arranged.
🖾 ‡ 🗆 🗗 💐

Sheraton Center
811 7th Ave. (52nd St.), NY 10019 ☎ *581–1000. Map 4N3*
▥ 🕿 *1,842* 🛏️ *1,842* ▦ 🖾
⇌ 🅰🅴 🆑🅱 ⓘ ⓒ 🆅🅸🆂🅰

Location: Near Rockefeller Center and Theater District. When it opened as the Americana, the jibe was that it was "a little far from the beach," implying its style was more suited to Miami than New York. This was not unfair, but things have improved somewhat under the Sheraton aegis. Tranquillity cannot be claimed an asset, yet the rooms are comfortable, if uninspired, the in-room movies are diverting, and every midtown tourist attraction is within walking distance.

Major upgrading was reserved for the luxury section known as the Sheraton Towers, which has a separate reception area on the 46th floor with its own express elevator and lobby bar-restaurant. The rooms are not usually larger than those below, but come with extra touches – electric blankets and shoe-polishers, nightly turndown service, bathrobes, and complimentary continental breakfasts. Rates are about 20% higher.
‡ ♿ 🗆 🗗 ⚓ ⚑

Sheraton City Squire
790 7th Ave. (near 51st St.), NY 10019 ☎ *581–3300* Ⓣ*421130.*
Map 4N3 ▥ 🕿 *720* 🛏️ *720* ▦
🖾 ⇌ 🅰🅴 🆑🅱 ⓘ ⓒ 🆅🅸🆂🅰

Location: N edge of Times Sq. Theater District. Of all Manhattan's motels, this achieves the happiest compromise between cost and convenience. Parking is free, lodgings are routinely comfortable, there is a swimming pool and its situation is as touristically central as it can possibly be.
‡ 🗆 🗗 💐 ≈ ⚓

Sheraton-Russell
45 Park Ave. (37th St.), NY 10016 ☎ *685–7676* Ⓣ*421308.*
Map 5P4 ▥ 🕿 *175* 🛏️ *175* ▦
🖾 ⇌ 🅰🅴 🆑🅱 ⓘ ⓒ 🆅🅸🆂🅰

Location: Murray Hill, s of Grand Central Terminal. The oak-lined lobby and its library set the cultivated tone. Fireplaces in some rooms and the prevailing calm of corridors and public spaces buttress that impression. Similar rooms and accouterments a few blocks to the N cost 20% more, simply because they are somewhat closer to the freneticism of midtown.

◠ ‡ ▢ ◪ ▨ ⛪ ☥

Sherry-Netherland 🏨
751 5th Ave. (59th St.), NY 10022 ☎ 355–2800. Map **5N4**
▥▥▥ ☎ 372 ▭ 372 ▦▦

Location: SE corner of Central Park.
Less than a third of the Sherry-Netherland's space is available to short-term visitors, the rest being on permanent lease, and the management understandably feels no compulsion to sell itself to travelers. The fact that they accept no credit cards is emblematic. Residents of the upper-floor suites expect tranquillity and unobtrusive attendance to their needs. The rooms that are available lean to handsome evocations of 19thC European styles, but are equipped with refrigerators and the usual gadgets. The location couldn't be better – at the foot of 'Museum Mile' and at the top of the 5th Ave. shopping district, with the park directly across the street.

◠ ‡ ♿ ▢ ◪ ▨ ◁€ ☥ ♫

Tuscany ♣
120 E 29th St. (near Park Ave.), NY 10016 ☎ 686–1600
☏ 640243. Cable: TUSCOTEL.
Map **5P4** ▥▥▥ ☎ 143 ▭ 143 ▦▦
▱▱ ▰ AE CB ◑ ◉ VISA

Location: Near Grand Central Terminal and United Nations.
Perhaps the best dollar-for-dollar value in its class, it charms in many small details – at the entrance, a large thermometer-barometer; on the desk, an arrangement of flowers; in the bedroom, a serving pantry with refrigerator; in the bathroom, a telephone and three-nozzle massaging showerhead; in the closet, an electric shoe-polisher; outside the window, another thermometer. It is quieter by many decibels than its larger cousins deeper in the midtown district, yet is only a few blocks farther from the action. The capable staff treats guests with an avuncularity that is at once amusing and reassuring. Conventioneers and tour groups are never in evidence. The hotel is

also less likely to be booked up at short notice, and checkout time is a civilized 2pm.

‡ ▢ ◪

United Nations Plaza 🏨
1 United Nations Plaza (44th St.), NY 10017 ☎ 355–3400
☏ 128603. Cable: UNPLAZATEL.
Map **5O5** ▥▥▥ ☎ 289 ▭ 289 ▦▦
▱▱ ▰ AE CB ◑ ◉

Location: Near United Nations Headquarters. The hotel's International Style of architecture is appropriate to its ownership by the eponymous world organization. The ground floor Grill dazzles with alcoved, faceted mirrors. Guest rooms begin on the 27th floor. The views are arresting, and they can also be enjoyed from the huge indoor swimming pool. On the 39th floor is a tennis court, exercise room and sauna. Felicitous touches include made-to-order breakfast doughnuts, baskets of fruit on arrival, jogging maps, and limousine service to Wall St. The experience of staying at this hotel is often flawed by an energetic young staff that speaks a total of 27 languages but can be disorganized and inattentive.

‡ ♿ ▢ ◪ ◁€ ≋ ♪ ⛪

Vista International 🏨
3 World Trade Center, NY 10048 ☎ 938–9100 ☏ 661130
VISTANY. Map **2U3** ▥▥▥ ☎ 825
▭ 825 ▦▦ ▱▱ ▰ AE CB ◑ ◉
VISA

Location: World Trade Center.
Since 1836 no one has built a major hotel in lower Manhattan, despite the thousands of out-of-town businessmen who swarm through the district every week. Until 1981 visitors found it necessary to commute from midtown. Apart from filling that glaring need, the Vista has enhanced a neighborhood: its dining rooms are several cuts above those in most of its competitors, and add such weekend features as a sumptuous seafood buffet and a 'Country and Western Fair' with barbecued ribs, *enchiladas, chorizo* and appropriate live music. Rooms are conventionally comfortable, with such amenities as alarm clocks, AM-FM radios and closed-circuit movies. 'Vista Club' rooms on the 20th and 21st floors enjoy complimentary breakfasts with morning newspapers, a private lounge with free drinks and hors d'oeuvres, and a special concierge. All guests have access to the

jogging track, racquetball courts, sauna and swimming pool on the top floor. Several discount weekend packages heap the extras still farther and even include such delights as: free bicycles and ferry tickets, tours of SoHo and the 'Heritage' trail, theater tickets and limousine service to midtown.

⌂ ‡ ‖ ▢ ▱ « ⇌ ♨ ⅄ ♫

Waldorf-Astoria 🏨
301 Park Ave. (49th St.), NY 10022 ☎ *355–3000* ☜ *666747. Map 5O4* ‖‖‖ ☜ *1,400* ▭ *1,400*
▤ ▱ ▭ ⇌ AE CB ⊙ ⊙ VISA

Location: Midtown East, near Grand Central Terminal. The original Waldorf, a name long synonymous with luxury, gave way to the Empire State Building. This replacement threw open its doors in 1931, but it is really too large to measure up on all counts to the reputation of the original. Nevertheless, all the amenities you might expect are in place, and the rooms and suites of the 'Towers' section are superior or equal to comparable accommodations elsewhere. The lower floors are crowded with a remarkable variety of shops, restaurants and bars, among them the famous Peacock Alley, a kind of indoor sidewalk cafe. There are several top restaurants within walking distance of the hotel, although every meal for a week could be taken within the building without repetition.

‡ ‖ ▢ ▱ ♨ ♨ ⅄

Warwick
65 W 54th St. (6th Ave.), NY 10019 ☎ *247–2700* ☜ *147179. Map 5N4* ‖‖‖ ☜ *500* ▭ *500* ▤
▱ ▭ ⇌ AE CB ⊙ ⊙ VISA

Location: Midtown, near TV network headquarters and Museum of Modern Art. Overshadowed by the mammoth **New York Hilton** across the street, this medium-size hotel attracts a clientele of communications executives and TV luminaries. It surpasses its assertive neighbor in dignity and reassuringly traditional refinements. Recent refurbishment didn't stop with the lobby: spacious bedrooms were primped and refitted, too. Some have serving pantries or refrigerators. An exercise room is available, as are closed-circuit films.

‡ ▢ ▱ ♨ ♨

Westbury 🏨
15 E 69th St. (Madison Ave.), NY 10021 ☎ *535–2000*
☜ *125388. Map 7M4* ‖‖‖ ☜ *325*
▭ *325* ▤ ▱ ⇌ AE CB ⊙ ⊙
VISA

Location: Upper East Side, amid smart boutiques and art galleries. The Trust House Forte chain does not always impress in Europe, but its incursions here are of the highest order – particularly evidenced by the Westbury. Converted from a 1920s apartment house, this fashionable and luxurious retreat endeavors to retain a residential quality – that is, if one is accustomed to crystal chandeliers, sprays of dewy-fresh flowers and 17thC tapestries in the vestibule. Most bedrooms do not stint in space or detail, although some baths are rather on the dainty side. The streetside Polo Lounge has considerable *éclat*.

⌂ ‡ ‖ ▢ ▱ ♨ ♨

Windsor
100 W 58th St. (6th Ave.), NY 10019 ☎ *265–2100. Map 5N4* ‖‖‖ ☜ *295* ▭ *295* ▤ ▱ ▭
AE CB ⊙ ⊙ VISA

Location: Near Central Park, 5th Ave. shops, Carnegie Hall. Noted for comfortable, if uninspired, lodgings and efficient security arrangements, the Windsor is yet another holding of the ubiquitous Harry Helmsley. There is no room service, but there is a dining room open for all meals, and the bar has unobtrusive piano music most evenings. All the suites are equipped with pantries or kitchenettes.

⌂ ‡ ▢ ▱ ⅄ ♫

Wyndham ✿
42 W 58th St. (near 5th Ave.), NY 10019 ☎ *753–3500. Map 5N4* ‖‖‖ ☜ *202* ▭ *202* ▤ ▱
⇌ AE CB ⊙ ⊙ VISA

Location: Near corner of Central Park and 5th Ave. The owner-managers live on the premises and cater to theater folk settling in for long runs on Broadway. Diana Rigg, Peter Falk, Tom Conti, Stacy Keach, and Jane Seymour are only a distinguished few of the once and future guests. No two rooms are alike, and suites on the higher floors feature some interesting antique furnishings. There is a reasonable bar and the restaurant is good but you will have to make do without room service.

⌂ ‡ ▢ ▱ ⅄

Where to eat

In New York, eating is a basic need elevated to an event, a debating issue, an investment opportunity, conversation topic, even reason for existence. There are 28,000 eating places in the five boroughs, over half of them in Manhattan alone.

Distinctive regional American styles – Creole-Cajun, Tex-Mex, Pennsylvania Dutch – can be found but they are inadequately represented here. New York does share the American passion for steak, however. If you ask any American who has spent time away from home what he or she most missed, it will be that two-inch thick slab of steak seared a charred mahogany outside, rosy-pink within, captured juices flowing at the stroke of the knife. The cut varies – strip sirloin, porterhouse, filet mignon – as do the accompaniments – baked potato, cottage fries, onion rings – but the basic image is almost universal.

In recent years, seafood has become almost as popular. With the rapid increase in the price of beef in the 1970s, tatty waterside haunts long favored by an avid minority suddenly found themselves having to turn customers away. Slick new fish-houses opened, and traditional restaurants expanded their menus beyond crabmeat cocktails and breaded flounder. In a twinkling, however, a pound of shrimps cost more than a pound of sirloin, and a new kind of eatery inevitably appeared: the fish-and-steak house. If anything can be described as an American cuisine, this is it. Beef and seafood, simply prepared, in hefty portions. These twin yearnings are easily satisfied in New York, at tariffs ranging from the almost reasonable to the heartstopping.

This type of cooking is essentially straightforward, however, and novelty and wonderment must be sought elsewhere. In this city of immigrants, exponents of every major cuisine that the inhabited continents have fostered compete for attention. The classic modes are purveyed in abundance: French, inevitably, with admirable exponents of *nouvelle* and *haute cuisines*, but also Russian, Czech, Polish, Swiss, German, Danish and Hungarian; Chinese, of course, in most of its variations, but also Korean, Indian, Japanese, Thai, Filipino, Indonesian and Pakistani; Italian, in all its manifestations, but also Greek, Portuguese, Turkish and Spanish; Mexican, but also Brazilian, Cuban and West Indian. In all, more than 30 national gastronomies are represented, supplemented by such hybrids and subspecies as Kosher Chinese, Soul, Puerto Rican, Polynesian, Jewish and Cuban Cantonese. And, there is the catchall 'continental' category, harboring all manner of predilections, but usually with a Gallic rallying point.

Happily for the gourmand, ethnic groups cling more tenaciously to their food preferences than to their creeds and ikons, though they have had to adapt available ingredients to the recipes of their former homelands. Availability and quality of produce, along with dietetic need, have always influenced culinary invention, and it is best to approach the restaurants of New York with an understanding of this gustatorial heterogeneity. Chunks of Maine lobster and Long Island littleneck clams may be substituted for the cuttlefish and sheep innards in the *paella* of Valencia, but it will be no less tasty for that. American caviar does not yet match the lofty Caspian standard, but it is half the price, and vastly superior to the inky lumpfish roe masquerading in the supermarkets. A few transplanted chef-proprietors still air-freight Dover sole and

127

Brittany turbot, out of chauvinistic myopia or simple snobbery, but their bay scallops and bass were harvested within 100 miles. And while Americans have little interest in larks and pigeons, unlike the French, the local duckling and quail are unsurpassed.

These efforts to duplicate the fare once set before them by parents and mentors inevitably attract audiences from the larger community. The evolution is unending, and it has brought New York the widest selection of good to superior restaurants in its history. Although restaurants of French, Italian and Chinese cuisine dominate every listing of the city's top-drawer establishments, no matter how immutably classic they pretend to be, they too continue to change and diversify. Sauces are lighter, vegetables are lifted from the pot while their flavor remains, ingredients retain their separate identities. Even the once stodgy Cantonese, Neapolitan, and Provençal kitchens have aired out moldering recipe books and applied new techniques.

None of this is to assert that every meal is sublime. As everywhere, mediocrity and ineptitude prevail. Bringing together the elements that make up an agreeable dining experience proves elusive. Several of the prettiest restaurants feature grumpy personnel and truly appalling food. On the other hand, above-average viands are often set before customers in garish or dreary quarters so cramped it is difficult to raise a fork.

The selection that follows is but a wisp of a hint of available choices. As far as possible, it reflects a consensus of the best restaurants in the city – numerous others of all prices and styles can be found throughout New York, and for a guide to the most likely locations see *Area planners* in *Planning*. Although the price range is necessarily skewed toward the high end, there are many suggestions of places where wholesome and/or exotic meals may be sampled at what are, for New York, budget levels. Included are a number of newer restaurants that appear to have sufficient strength to beat the odds. The usual caveats still apply: even the hardiest performers stumble, through changes in management, departures of key personnel, last-minute substitutions and shortages, or simple off days. Loyalists will continue to exchange blows over the relative virtues of **Christ Cella** and **The Palm**, **Lutèce** and **La Grenouille**, all recommended here. No amount of arbitration will resolve the disputes, and anyway they're fun.

What to expect

In the luxury category – achieved or pretended – four discernible strata of staff are nearly always present. The *maître* (or *maîtresse*) *d'hôtel* greets customers in calibrated degrees of warmth or *hauteur* at the entrance to the dining area. He (or she) checks reservations, assigns seating, and often escorts guests to their tables. The captain then takes over. Assigned responsibility for a specific section of the room, he brings menus, advises on unlisted dishes, points out specialities of the house. He might never return, concentrating on directing his minions. Or he might take orders for cocktails and meals, supervise or perform tableside preparations, even pour water and fill wine glasses. Waiters are the workhorses, identified by less formal attire. Depending upon the organizational structure, they may absorb some or all of the captain's duties, as well as bringing food, drinks, and wine. The busboy, younger and in still another costume, and often an apprentice, clears dishes, replenishes bread baskets and empties ashtrays.

One other post is rapidly disappearing – that of the *sommelier* or wine steward. Where he exists, his sole function is to aid in selection of bottles, to open them and to pour. Those who find the tasting ritual silly or intimidating might think of it as a harmless ceremony, no more meaningful than a man opening a door for a woman. Others will appreciate the *sommelier*'s knowledge of his cellar and willingness to discuss alternatives.

New York waiters – and New Yorkers in general – have an undeserved reputation for churlishness. Service can be lackadaisical, and individuals are sometimes sullen or arrogant, but in roughly the same proportion as in any large city. More frequently, complaints are of benign ineptitude, for there is a shortage of formally trained employees. The slack is taken up by recent arrivals to the city, by students and the legions of young actors, dancers and artists drawn to the area every year. As often as not, their spriteliness compensates for their lack of experience, especially in those trendy bistros in which food is less than the main event.

There are agreeable surprises as well as lapses. Year-round availability of usually seasonal commodities often delights, as with oysters in non-'R' months and fresh fruit in Feb. This convenience is expensive, however, and winter tomatoes can be as hard as croquet balls and April apples often taste like potatoes. The prodigious portions of food can dismay – for instance, prime rib hanging over the rim of the plate, leaving little room for the heap of cottage fries. Travelers accustomed to spicy-hot seasonings may be disappointed by the mildness of Indian and Mexican dishes, but insistence on authentically fiery food usually produces results.

Cocktails, wines and other drinks

The specifically American custom of a pre-dinner cocktail or two persists in New York as elsewhere. As will hardly need explaining, cocktails are diverse but always potent. The best-known is the martini, which is two to three ounces of gin or vodka with a splash of dry vermouth, usually taken over ice. Garnished with pickled onions rather than the conventional green olive or strip of lemon peel, it becomes a Gibson. Some people still order a Manhattan, a sweetish mix of two ounces of rye whiskey with red vermouth swirled with bitters and topped with a cherry. Combinations and variations are endless. Even at a conservative count, there are no fewer than 1,000 recognized cocktails and related concoctions. Some are favored for particular meals or foods – the Bloody Mary for brunch and the Margarita before Mexican or Latin meals. But in recent years, a glass of white wine, perhaps with a dash of cassis (kir), or soda water (spritzer), or mineral water with lime is increasingly preferred to the harder spirits, and such dark liquors as bourbon and scotch have suffered declines in sales. The practices of smoking cigarettes and drinking cocktails throughout a meal are still seen, but are regarded as gauche, at least in more sophisticated places. While still wines are appropriate for most cuisines, beer is thought satisfactory for Middle-European, Chinese, Mexican and Indian meals.

New Yorkers were long reluctant to embrace the wines of California. This attitude was part pretension and part pragmatism. Seaports tend to face across the water rather than inland, and European bottlings were substantially cheaper than the Cabernets and Zinfandels of the West. Currency

fluctuations changed that, and blind tastings in Paris and
elsewhere proved that the vintages of the Gironde and Napa
valleys bore separate but equal virtues. The French and Italians
still dominate the city's wine cards, but the California challenge
mounts as more labels of the select wineries are introduced.
Labels to look for are Robert Mondavi, Sterling, Heitz Cellars,
David Bruce, Stag's Leap, Charles Krug, Beaulieu, Burgess,
Caymus and Mayacammas, among many, many others.
Popular-priced wines are blends of several varieties of grapes
and typically carry names suggestive of type – 'Chablis,'
'Burgundy,' 'Chianti' – or such fanciful appellations as
'Emerald Dry' or 'Rhine Garten.' The better pressings are
composed primarily (at least 51% or more) of a single varietal
grape and bear that name, without adornment. Some would be
known to European wine buffs, others are native strains or
hybrids. Among the prominent reds are Cabernet Sauvignon,
Petite Sirah, Pinot Noir and Zinfandel; favored whites are
Chardonnay, Chenin Blanc, Johannisberg Riesling and
Sauvignon Blanc. While weather is a factor in California wines,
its influence is less pronounced than in Europe. Estimable red
vintages of recent years are those of 1968, 1970, 1974 and 1977.
Least successful were the years 1971, 1972 and 1973. Whites
have stayed on a fairly even keel. Few pre-1970 bottles are
available.

New York State is a distant second in production, accounting
for only 10% of domestic consumption. Its Finger Lakes and
Hudson Valley vineyards are best known for sparkling wines,
but a number of vintners create worthy blends of offbeat
varietals. Try Konstantin Frank, Benmarl and Bully Hill.

Refrigerated beers, both domestic and imported, are sold
everywhere, in greatest profusion at pub-style restaurants. Tap
water is excellent.

Restaurants classified by area

Shezan ▮▮▯ ✿
21 Club ▮▮▮▮
Un Deux Trois ▮▮▮
Upper East Side (*E 60th St. – E 96th St.*)
Chez Pascal ▮▮▮ ◠
Cirque, Le ▮▮▮▮ ◠
Claude's ▮▮▮▮ ◠
Côte Basque, La ▮▮▮▮ ◠
Czechoslovak Praha ▮▮▮
Elaine's ▮▮▮▮
Folie, La ▮▮▮▮
Hoexter's Market ▮▮▮
Lavandou, Le ▮▮▮ ◠
Maxwell's Plum ▮▮▮
Monello, Il ▮▮▮
Mortimer's ▮▮▮
Parioli Romanissimo ▮▮▮▮
Plaisir, Le ▮▮▮ ◠

Relais, Le ▮▮▯
Uzie's ▮▮▮
Veau d'Or, Le ▮▮▮
Vienna '79 ▮▯ ◠
Upper West Side (*W 60th St. – W 96th St.*)
Café des Artistes ▮▮▯
Caravelle, La ▮▮▮ ◠
Copenhagen ▮▮▮
Ginger Man, The ▮▮▯
Saloon, The ▮▮▯
Shun Lee West ▮▮▮▮
Tavern On The Green ▮▮▮▮
The Bronx
Anna's Harbor ▮▮▯ ✿
Thwaite's Inn ▮▮▯
Brooklyn
Gage and Tollner ▮▮▯ 🏛
River Cafe ▮▮▮▮

Restaurants classified by type of cuisine

American
Anna's Harbor ▮▮▯ ✿
Bridge Cafe, The ▮▯ ◠ ✿
Christ Cella ▮▮▮▮
Gage and Tollner ▮▮▯ 🏛
Ginger Man, The ▮▮▯
Hoexter's Market ▮▮▮
Jane Street Seafood Cafe ▮▮▯
Louisiana ▮▮▮
Oyster Bar and Restaurant ▮▮▯
Palm, The ▮▮▮▮
Sloppy Louie's ▯ ◠
Sparks ▮▮▮▮
Thwaite's Inn ▮▮▯
Chinese
Shun Lee Dynasty ▮▮▮
Shun Lee West ▮▮▮▮
Sichuan Pavilion ▮▮▯
Continental/International
Box Tree ▮▮▮▮
Bread Shop Cafe, The ▮▯ ✿
Café des Artistes ▮▮▯
Claude's ▮▮▮▮ ◠
Coach House, The ▮▮▮▮
Elaine's ▮▮▮▮
Four Seasons ▮▮▮▮
Greene Street ▮▮▯
Joanna ▮▮▮
Maxwell's Plum ▮▮▮
Mortimer's ▮▮▮
One Fifth ▮▮▮
Raoul's ▮▮▮
River Cafe ▮▮▮▮
Saloon, The ▮▮▯
SoHo Charcuterie ▮▮▮
Spring Street Restaurant ▮▯
Tavern On The Green ▮▮▮▮
21 Club ▮▮▮▮
Windows On The World ▮▮▯ ▮▮▮ ▮▮▮
Czech
Czechoslovak Praha ▮▮▮
Danish
Copenhagen ▮▮▮
French
Caravelle, La ▮▮▮ ◠
Chanterelle ▮▮▮▮
Chantilly, Le ▮▮▮ ◠

Chez Pascal ▮▮▮ ◠
Cirque, Le ▮▮▮▮ ◠
Côte Basque, La ▮▮▮▮ ◠
Cygne, Le ▮▮▮▮
Folie, La ▮▮▮▮
Grenouille, La ▮▮▮▮ ◠
Lavandou, Le ▮▮▮ ◠
Lutèce ▮▮▮▮ ◠
Odeon ▮▮▮
Plaisir, Le ▮▮▮ ◠
Quilted Giraffe, The ▮▮▮ ◠
Relais, Le ▮▮▯
Restaurant Leslie ▮▮▮
Un Deux Trois ▮▮▮
Veau d'Or, Le ▮▮▮
German/Austrian
Vienna '79 ▮▯ ◠
Greek/Middle Eastern
Dardanelles ▮▮▯
Sea Fare of the Aegean ▮▮▯ ✿
Indian
Gaylord ▮▮▮
Madras Woodlands ▮▯
Raga ▮▮▮ ✿
Shezan ▮▮▯ ✿
Italian
Barbetta ▮▮▮
Girafe ▮▮▮▮
Monello, Il ▮▮▮
Orsini's ▮▮▮▮
Parioli Romanissimo ▮▮▮▮
Salta in Bocca ▮▮▮ ✿
Sardi's ▮▮▮
Trattoria da Alfredo ▮▯
Uzie's ▮▮▮
Japanese
Hatsuhana ▮▮▯
Korean
Arirang House ▮▮▯
Latin American
Cabana Carioca ▮▯ ✿
Parador, El ▮▮▯
Russian
Russian Tea Room, The ▮▮▮
Spanish
Rincón de España, El ▮▮▯
Thai
Thailand ▮▯

131

Anna's Harbor ✿
565 City Island Ave., City Island, NY 10464 ☎ *885–1373. Map 13C5* ▮▮▯ ☐ ◁≣ *Open Mon–Thurs 11:30am–midnight, Fri–Sat 11:30am–1am, Sun noon–midnight.*

City Island packs at least 20 seafood eateries into a few short blocks, but this is one of the few open all year. It is a vast barn of a place that can seat 600 patrons at a time; food nevertheless comes quickly, in prodigious quantities and of high quality. There are chewy nut-sweet fried clams, slabs of broiled sea trout, and the *combination marinara* with lobster, king crab, mussels, shrimp and clams. Heavy-handed colored plastics cover nearly every surface of the interior, but food, view and prices, which are markedly lower than for similar fare in Manhattan, compensate. A special low-price luncheon, for example, includes clam chowder or fruit juice, a main course of flounder, tilefish, Boston scrod, fried clams, chips, green salad, dessert and coffee. *Specialties: King crab fra diavolo, seafood combination Newburg, bouillabaisse.*

Arirang House
28 W 56th St. (near 5th Ave.), NY 10020 ☎ *581–9698. Map 5N4* ▮▮▯ ☐ ▭ AE CB ① ① VISA *Open Mon–Sat noon–2:30pm, 5–10:30pm (11pm Sat).*

Korean cuisine hovers, as might be expected, between Chinese and Japanese, but carves out its own identity. Blisteringly hot sauces are mostly optional – dips rather than intrinsic to the dish. The waitresses here have been described as butterflies, and they are undeniably enchanting in their *han pok* ensembles. Tables are close. Try a ginseng cocktail before, *jung jong* (rice wine) during, and plum wine after. *Specialties: Pul koki (fire beef), yauk hae (steak tartare), sam hapco (shrimp, abalone, sirloin tip, vegetables).*

Barbetta
321 W 46th St. (near 8th Ave.), NY 10036 ☎ *246–9171. Map 4O3* ▮▮▮ ☐ ▭ AE CB ① ① VISA *Open Mon–Sat noon–2pm, 5–11pm.*

The entry rooms have the look of Tuscan *palazzi*, hinting of an ancient patina buffed and scoured and buffed again. Beyond the large main room, a summer garden beckons, with a pool and stone cherubim beneath shimmering ornamental trees. The food usually does justice to the surroundings, but concentrate on the pasta and veal. There are pre-theater dinners, and patrons may return after the show for their desserts. *Specialties: Cold bass, veal scaloppina, vitello tonnato.*

Box Tree ⌂
242 E 50th St. (near 2nd Ave.), NY 10022 ☎ *758–8320. Map 5N5* ▮▮▮ ▭ *Open Mon–Fri noon–2pm, 6:30–10:30pm, Sat–Sun 6:30–10:30pm.*

An eatery of such *haute* aspirations and *très haute* prices inevitably draws mixed responses. Most patrons find the meticulous assemblage of antiques and reproductions very pretty, brightened as it is by tiny wall sconces and Tiffany chandeliers, pewter objects and floral displays. Others feel it verges on the precious, a conviction reinforced by the theatrical demeanor of waiters and such gestures as the rose that introduces the bill. For them, the snug arrangement of eight tables is not cozy, but crowded. Few quibble over the food, however, for it rarely disappoints. Witness the triumphant *vacherin*, a wizardry marrying hazelnut meringue, raspberries and froth of cream. Reservations must be weeks in advance; there are two seatings nightly. Wine is the only liquor. *Specialties: Terrine of duck liver, trout mousse, carré d'agneau.*

The Bread Shop Cafe ✿
157 Duane St. (near W Broadway), NY 10013 ☎ *964–0524. Map 2T4* ▮☐ ☐ *Open Sun–Fri noon–3pm, daily 6pm–midnight.*

TriBeCa, the new neighborhoods of SoHo and N of Wall St., has spawned many bistros in the few years since it was given a name. Many are venturesome, some banal, most misguided. This one is likely to survive till the next full moon – which seems faint praise only to those unfamiliar with the volatility of the district. It is part bakery, part eatery, with both lunch counter and tables. At night it is dark, with illumination only by small guttering candles on each table. Take a very good friend for uncomplicated food cooked with precision. Reservations are a good idea. *Specialties: Fish of the day, any dessert.*

The Bridge Cafe 🍴 ✿
16½ Dover St. (Water St.), NY
10038 ☎ 227–3344. Map **3**T5
◫ ▭ ➤ ♁ Open daily
noon–3pm, 6pm–midnight,
late lunch Sat, Sun, to 4pm.
Wavy floors, a stamped tin ceiling,
and a well-used bar-counter attest
to the age of this venerable
seamen's watering hole. It is
believed that the core structure
went up in 1801, though there have
inevitably been remodelings.
Since the recapture of the cafe from
incipient disintegration 2yr ago, an
imaginative menu at uncommonly
fair tariffs has drawn a growing
clientele of politicians from the
nearby Civic Center and aware
New Yorkers from the burgeoning
lower Manhattan and Brooklyn
communities. The owner's
boast is that there is no freezer
on the premises. Everything is
at its freshest – fish, vegetables,
fowl. The blackboard of the day's
fare changes daily, according to
market availability. Among the
seasonal staples the chili, calamari,
tortellini and omelets are
remarkable. Wines are priced at
only slightly above retail, and there
are several imported beers on tap.
Mulled cider and Irish coffee with
real whipped cream are sufficient
reason to stop by after a chilly day
at the nearby South Street Seaport
Museum. They accept neither
reservations nor credit cards.
*Specialties: Black bean soup, boned
roast duck with green peppercorns,
fish stew, pecan pie.*

Cabana Carioca ✿
123 W 45th St. (near 6th Ave.),
NY 10036 ☎ 581–8088. Map
5O4 ◫ ▭ ▦ ⊙ 𝘝𝘐𝘚𝘈 ♁
Open daily noon–11pm.
When the tariffs of the city's best-
known restaurants seem too
dizzying, consider the ethnic
restaurants. The Cabana Carioca,
serving Brazilian food, is in a
midtown block handy for the
Broadway theaters but constituting
a veritable Little Rio. Brazilian
food has not caught the attention of
the larger populace, so a full dinner
for two here is still very reasonable.
The street entrance and flight of
stairs to the Cabana Carioca do not
look promising, but press on. On
the second floor, if it were not for
the bar, you might think you had
blundered into an animated private
party. Try to arrive on Wed or Sat,
when the national dish, *feijoada*, is
on hand. Otherwise, venture into
the mysteries of the stew the

Portuguese call *cozido* or take the
safer route of shrimp *paulista*.
The best soup is *caldo verde*.
Desserts are the bland Latin norm.
Specialty: Feijoada.

Café des Artistes
1 W 67th St. (Central Park W),
NY 10023 ☎ 877–3500. Map
4M3 ◫ ▭ ▦ ⊙ 𝐀𝐄 ⊙
⊙ 𝘝𝘐𝘚𝘈 Open Mon–Sat noon–3pm,
6–10:30pm, Sun 11am–3pm,
5–9pm. Closed Christmas,
Jan 1.
George Lang has transformed this
long dreary dining room into one of
the liveliest bistros on the West
Side. Praise for the rejuvenation
lies more with the menu than the
decor, if only because the decor
needed less effort – with touch-
ups, a nostalgic 1920s glow was
wrested from the former
dowdiness. Murals by Howard
Chandler Christy featuring
chastely voluptuous nudes are set
off by banks of plants and ornate
mirrors. Vaguely familiar faces
lean over hurricane lamps and
snowy napery. The already
ambitious *carte* is supplemented by
up to a score of daily specials in all
categories. Standards are gazpacho
with unexpected chunks of
shrimp, oysters in two or three
guises, duckling more tender than
crispy. There can be
disappointments, but at these
reasonable prices grousing is
inappropriate. *Specialties:
Gravlax in dill marinade, pork
cassoulet, bourride with aioli.*

La Caravelle △
33 W 55th St. (near 5th Ave.),
NY 10019 ☎ 586–4252. Map
5N4 ⊙ 𝘝𝘐𝘚𝘈 Open Mon–Sat
noon–2:30pm, 6–10:30pm.
Closed Sun, Aug.
Perhaps a shade too traditional to
be awarded a place at the very tip of
the gastronomic pyramid, La
Caravelle is nonetheless striving to
avoid slipping from that pinnacle.
For those not inclined to expend
their treasure on cuisines *nouvelle*
and *minceur*, it is among the
happiest of choices for the
commemoration of events. There
is almost always a celebrity or two
to lend credence to the selection,
although they are of the
established, rather than chic,
stripe. Stab a finger at the menu –
there will be no disappointments,
and several delights. *Specialties:
Poularde à l'estragon, quenelles,
Caneton smitane, veal Calvados.*

Chanterelle
89 Grand St. (Greene St.), NY 10013 ☎ *966–6960. Map 2S4*
▥▥▥ ⌷ ▭ ▭ AE ◉ VISA *Open Tues–Sat 6:30–11pm. Closed Sun, Mon, July.*

Anti-establishmentarians develop their own rituals, uniforms and convictions. For a while, it seemed that every bar and restaurant in the new Bohemia of SoHo was to be a garage or loft stripped to bare brick walls, hung with green industrial lamps and filled with potted ferns. Chanterelle has only its lofty space in common with its neighbors. It is of a spare serenity, with brass chandeliers above, gray carpeting below and antiseptic white everywhere else. The young chef-owner pursues his trade with not a trace of frivolity, which may be counted among his few failings. His productions demonstrate respect for *nouvelle cuisine*, but none of the extremes to which some of his colleagues have gone. Furthermore, measured growth is evident. If the meal there last year was good, the one tonight will be better. The menu changes constantly. Reserve ahead.
Specialties: *Fish soup, squab mousse, duck and endive salad, salmon, the cheese board.*

Le Chantilly ⌂
106 E 57th St. (near Park Ave.), NY 10022 ☎ *751–2931. Map 5N4* ▥▥▥ ⌷ ▭ ▭ AE ◉ VISA *Open Mon–Sat noon–2:30pm, 6–10:30pm.*

Although a relative newcomer (1978), Le Chantilly is a seamless facsimile of the second generation of grand luxe restaurants that trod the heels of Le Pavillon and **La Côte Basque** in the early 1960s. All the design elements are *comme il faut* – banquettes, conical glass chandeliers, closely spaced tables, flowers in brandy snifters, mirrored walls, an indifferent mural of the eponymous Loire chateau, and even a celebrity row along the entry corridor. But the fact that Le Chantilly is interchangeable with a dozen others of the classical Gallic family (subspecies Manhattan) hardly demeans it. All is thoroughgoing professionalism – formal and intolerant of novelty or unsettling surprises. Ties and jackets and reservations are required.
Specialties: *Mousse of two fish, sweetbreads with morels, terrine of eel, petite marmite, pheasant with truffle sauce.*

Chez Pascal ⌂
151 E 82nd St. (near 3rd Ave.), NY 10028 ☎ *294–1334. Map 5L5* ▥▥▥ ⌷ ▭ ▭ AE ◉ VISA
Open Mon–Sat 6:30–11pm.

There are people who have no need to agonize over which Manhattan restaurant to select for the big splash. They simply rotate – **Lutèce** on Tues, **La Grenouille** on Wed, **La Côte Basque** on Thurs and Chez Pascal on Fri. At least they *look* like the same crowd – immaculately coiffed, bespoke suits, Halston frocks, tasteful flares of gold at wrist and throat. The space doesn't permit grandeur, just burnished wood, mellowed brick and gray upholstery. Tables are relatively large, set with balloon goblets that permit the proper savoring of a Chateau Lafite. It will take a wine of that caliber to do justice to the food. Mediocrity is not permitted.
Specialties: *Bouillabaisse, cassolette d'huîtres, ocean bass en croûte, rack of lamb, salmon steak.*

Christ Cella
160 E 46th St. (7th Ave.), NY 10017 ☎ *697–2479. Map 4O3* ▥▥▥ ⌷ AE CB ◉ ▭ VISA *Open Mon–Fri noon–10:30pm, Sat 5–10:45pm. Closed Sat, hols.*

Call it 'Krisella' or 'Kreechella.' Either way, it is a place for people who like their food simple – and are willing to pay for it. The two floors of this 1926 landmark steak house are assertively plain, with bare floors, indifferent seascapes on the walls, uncushioned chairs and waiters in aprons. There isn't even a written menu, but the recited selections do not tax the memory. Basic appetizers are shrimp or crabmeat cocktails, Caesar salad; entrées are roast beef, sirloin steak, veal or lamb chops, broiled fish, scallops; desserts are cheesecake, ice cream. Obviously, people who prefer drama or elegance or intricacy of preparation should go elsewhere. Those who have business to conduct, without distraction, find it suits their purposes exactly. Men must wear jackets and ties. ***Specialties:*** *Sirloin, filet mignon, fish of the day, hashed brown potatoes.*

Le Cirque ⌂
58 E 65th St. (near Madison Ave.), NY 10021 ☎ *794–9292. Map 5M4* ▥▥▥ ⌷ ▭ ▭ AE CB ◉ *Open Mon–Sat noon–3pm, 6–10:30pm.*

Nancy and Ronald Reagan dine

here when in the city, and, however one might feel about their ideology, their taste in restaurants (on this evidence) cannot be faulted. The First Lady reportedly lunches on *pasta primavera* – vegetables tossed with noodles, butter and cream – a concoction not listed on the menu but available whenever the appropriate ingredients are on hand. The pâtés are notable, as are *carpaccio* (marinated uncooked beef), game birds, *quenelles de brochet* with two sauces, and pastries. If the dishes named seem schizophrenic, there is the handy explanation that the owner is Italian, the chef French and the pastry-chef German. Yet that combination is nirvana for those gourmets who admire the specialties of all three countries. Should there be disappointments, they will be in the occasional imperiousness of the captains and in the frequently high noise levels of the dining room. *Specialties: Fish terrine, fettuccine with white truffles, escalope de veau, lotte with saffron, aiguillettes of duck, noisettes of venison.*

Claude's △
205 E 81st St. (near 3rd Ave.), NY 10028 ☎472–0487. Map 5L5 ▥ ▭ AE CB ◐ ⓒ VISA Open Mon–Sat 6–10:30pm.
In New York there are a number of restaurants that are set up primarily with the convenience of the chef-owner in mind. These places frequently attract a masochistic clientele willing to suffer at the altar of gastronomy under the strict supervision of the resident guru. Should you wish to dine at Claude's, for example, you must be a party of four and must tender advance notice of 48hr. Permission to ingest its delicacies is granted during only 4½hr of each 24, excluding Sun. Large sums of currency are given in return. The trouble is, Claude's is nearly as good as it thinks it is, and the faithful bridle at any suggestion that it falls short of perfection. *Specialties: Striped bass, filet of beef, bouillabaisse, game in season.*

The Coach House
110 Waverly Pl. (near Washington Sq. W), NY 10011 ☎777–0303. Map 2R4 ▥ ▭ ▦ AE CB ◐ ⓒ VISA Open Tues–Sun 5:30–10:30pm. Closed Mon, Aug.
Having been long and consistently ranked among the best in the city

(or state, or country), The Coach House may have faded from that stature, but still warrants attention. What might startle is the fact that the food served is not of the Gallic variety that dominates such lists, but is essentially American. It has certain international accents, to be sure, but the staples are prime ribs of beef, baby lobster tails, lump crabmeat and chicken pie. These are revelatory versions of a native cooking style usually given short shrift. Reservations are essential. *Specialties: Black bean soup Madeira, loin lamb chop, rack of lamb, pecan pie.*

Copenhagen
68 W 58th St. (near 6th Ave.), NY 10019 ☎688–3690. Map 5N4 ▥ ▭ ▦ AE CB ◐ ⓒ VISA Open Mon–Sat noon– 3pm (Sat 4pm), 5–11pm.
It's best to arrive early, to get first crack at the *smorgasbord*. The uninitiated swoop at the oblong center table, heaping fish bits and melon balls on their plates. But in the only authentic Danish restaurant in town, certain rituals should first be observed. A glass of Akvavit, poured to the rim from a bottle encased in ice. Then the buffet, approaching with firm grip on plate and restraint on the impulse to take something of everything at once. Start with herring, smoked salmon, a few plump shrimps. Return to table. Eat. Another Akvavit, perhaps. The empty plate is removed while you are filling another with cold roast beef, duck and salads. And so on. Make the round trip as often as desired, saving room for fruit and cheese, but not necessarily the indifferent hot items at the end. Desserts are selected from a trolley. There is a conventional menu as well, including open sandwiches. *Specialties: Herring in several preparations, duck, cod.*

La Côte Basque △
5 E 55th St. (near 5th Ave.), NY 10022 ☎688–6525. Map 5N4 ▥ ▭ ▦ AE Open Mon–Sat noon–3pm, 6–11pm.
Henri Soulé is credited both with the introduction of serious *haute cuisine* to New York and with its propagation, by nurturing the ambitions of the talented young chefs in his employ. Soulé clones sprouted on every fashionable block. Some persist, more than 20yr later. His own fabled

restaurants went into decline or closed. That seemed the ultimate fate, until recently, of La Côte Basque, but miraculously it has been resuscitated, its theatrical spaces primped and its performances both in the kitchen and out front restored to their former integrity. The original Lamotte murals of the Basque coast and harbors are still there, models to be emulated by the proprietors of otherwise equally ambitious places who consistently choose vapid pastel depictions of chateaus and meadows. Reception is gracious, the staff once again informative and anticipatory. The fixed-price lunch is 30% cheaper than dinner. *Specialties: Billy-bi, pâtés, ragoût de homard aux morilles, quail with foie gras, cassolette of morels with lobster and snails.*

Le Cygne ⌂
55 E 54th St. (Madison Ave.), NY 10022 ☎ *759–5941. Map 5N4* [symbols] *Open Mon–Fri noon–3pm, 6–11pm, Sat 6–11pm. Closed Sun, Aug.*

You may very well have your best meal in New York at 'The Swan.' The host treats with equal favor patrons old and new, celebrities and unknowns, and he harbors no lofty notions of his station. He makes menu suggestions, clears dishes, and fills glasses with grace and warmth. The new facility (next door to the original) is cool grays and slate blue, severely modernist outside and faintly nautical (as in QE II) within. The upstairs room is as soothing as the main floor, a touch less frenetic at peak hours. Bouquets of flowers are everywhere. Fixed-price lunches and dinners are not inexpensive, and with supplemental charges and injudicious wine selections, dinner for two can rocket into the stratosphere . . . and higher. *Specialties: Kidneys in mustard sauce, paupiette of salmon with mousse of sole, chicken in champagne sauce, sweetbreads served with chanterelles.*

Czechoslovak Praha
1358 1st Ave. (73rd St.), NY 10021 ☎ *988–3505. Map 5M5* [symbols] *Open daily noon–11pm.*

Early German and East European immigrants established a beachhead on the Upper East Side, founding a number of restaurants and coffee houses before moving on to the suburbs. The best of these have prevailed, long after the ethno-social composition of the neighborhood has changed. Refugees from Middle Europe return here repeatedly, however. No effort is made to replicate a cafe in downtown Prague, but the room is comfortable enough and candlelight makes it almost handsome. Consider headcheese (brawn), goulash, rabbit, chased by the appropriate imported lager. *Specialties: Soup of the day, duck, stuffed cabbage.*

Dardanelles
86 University Pl. (near 12th St.), NY 10003 ☎ *242–8990. Map 2R4* [symbols] *Open Mon–Fri noon–3pm, 4:30pm–10pm, Sat–Sun 6–10pm.*

Armenian food rarely provokes ecstasy, even when it reaches out to gather in Greek, Lebanese and Moroccan variations. Attractively set up, if a trifle gloomy, this Greenwich Village stand-by survives in part because it doesn't take itself too seriously. It is rarely crowded, and is therefore a good last-minute choice when one is casually dressed on a stroll through the neighborhood. It is also good value and has a leisurely pace. Occasionally, there is an *oud* player. *Specialties: Fassoula poulaki, yoghurt soup, enguinar, moussaka, patlijan karni yarik.*

Elaine's
1703 2nd Ave. (near E 88th St.), NY 10028 ☎ *534–8114. Map 7K5* [symbols] *Open Mon–Fri noon–3pm, 6pm–2am, Sat–Sun 6pm–2am.*

Luminaries of the literary world and, by mutual attraction, also from show business and politics make this saloon-restaurant their own. The proprietress takes care of them, saving their favorite tables and shooing away *paparazzi* and gawkers. There is no reason to believe they come for the essentially Italian food, for it is only serviceable, and may account for the fact that no one shows up before 10pm. *Specialties: Seafood salad, fettuccine Alfredo.*

La Folie
21 E 61st St. (Madison Ave.), NY 10021 ☎ *765–1400. Map 5N4* [symbols] *Open Mon–Thurs 6pm–midnight, Fri 6pm–1am, Sat 6pm–3am.*

Don't go to this restaurant merely

to eat. Food preparation here is frequently slapdash and occasionally coarse, and the dining-room staff is easily distracted. But La Folie is spangled with mirrors, its space divided into tiers, its walls and upholstery clothed in emerald fabrics, and patrons come with other things on their minds than *mousseline of lobster* (bland) and *escargots Bourguignonne* (unwieldy). There is, in particular, a 'soft' disco on Sat night after 11pm with an audio level that permits conversation. Three-course pre-theater (6–8pm) and post-theater dinners are available. Given amiable companions, the anticipation or savoring of a Broadway play, and an inclination to dance the rest of the night away, the kitchen's shortcomings seem less grievous. Avoid ordering *à la carte*, however. *Specialties: Tournedos, mignons de veau, lobster thermidor.*

Four Seasons
99 E 52nd St. (Park Ave.), NY 10022 ☎ 754–9494. Map **5**N4 ▥ ▭ ▭ AE CB ◑ VISA Open Mon–Sat noon–3pm, 5–11:30pm.
Lunch is the main event here, and the Grill Room is the arena. Publishers stroke brand-name authors and their agents in a daily ritual in which every change of table or occupant is duly charted. The dinner *locus* shifts to the Pool Room, with its floral bounty and marble-bound pool. It is a vaulted space three stories high at the base of the Seagram Building. Some find it visually chilly, but the tables are comfortably spaced, and much of the artwork is rotated four times a year, as are menu selections. The food, usually of the highest caliber, is almost worth the prices. The scope is broad enough to qualify for the catchall 'continental' label, with chocolate cake the preferred topper. The superior cellar highlights American vintages. Fixed-price pre-theater dinners are a way to sample at lower cost, available Mon–Fri 5–7pm. *Specialties: Shellfish, lamb, game fowl.*

Gage and Tollner ▥▥
372 Fulton St. (near Borough Hall), Brooklyn, NY 11201 ☎875–5181. Map **3**V7 ▥ ▭ AE ◑ ⊞ VISA Open Mon–Fri 11:30am–9pm, Sat 4–11pm.
This is an officially designated landmark, handy for Brooklyn Heights. The gaslit Gay Nineties atmosphere is authentic, because it opened in 1879. It hasn't changed much since, and some of the staff look as if they might also have been around as long. They wear emblems attesting to their years of employment. A seafood restaurant in a port city oddly lacking in this respect, the bisques and soles and snappers are all good, in some cases surpassingly so. Mutton chops are also available, and the fried chicken is good. *Specialties: Clam broil, bay scallops, oysters.*

Gaylord
50 E 58th St. (near Madison Ave.), NY 10022 ☎ 759–1710. Map **5**N4 ▥ ▭ ▭ AE CB ◑ ⊞ VISA Open Mon–Fri 11:30am–3pm, 5:30–11pm, Sat–Sun 5:30–11:30pm.
Purveyors of Third World cuisines are inclined toward cramped spaces, fluorescent lighting and wall-to-wall Formica. Gaylord broke the mold. It is cushily appointed, especially in the front room, with squashy seating and subdued illumination. The bias is northern Indian, with a tandoori emphasis. Clay-lined ovens in a glass booth are attended by cooks who fashion crimson chickens and several types of flat bread. Purists protest at the mild seasonings, but most Westerners are grateful. For a special treat, ask for the resident palmist to visit your table. He delivers forecasts in a marvelously Baroque sing-song. *Specialties: Tandoori chicken, thali, mixed grill.*

The Ginger Man
51 W 64th St. (near Broadway), NY 10023 ☎ 399–2358. Map **6**M3 ▥ ▭ ⊞ AE CB ◑ VISA Open Mon–Sat 11:30am–4pm, 5pm–midnight, Sun 11:30am–10pm.
Sustenance, not wonderment, is the function of the hamburgers and full dinners in this turn-of-the-century tavern-restaurant directly across Broadway from the Lincoln Center. The patrons, after all, are either anticipating or savouring the ballet or opera or concert they will attend or have just attended. In that frame of mind, a profound culinary experience would be wasted, even if it were available. Serviceability is therefore the keynote and simplicity the greater virtue. Choose from the menu accordingly. From 6–8pm and 10pm until closing it is jammed,

from the glass-enclosed sidewalk room all the way to the back. On weekends there is live jazz. *Specialties: Hamburgers, omelets, sole.*

Girafe ⌂
208 E 58th St. (3rd Ave.), NY 10022 ☎752–3054. Map **5**N5
▥▥ ⬚ 🖃 AE ⓓ CB VISA *Open Mon–Fri 12–3pm, 5:30pm–1:30am, Sat 5:30pm–1:30am. Closed Sun, hols, first three weeks in July.*
Despite the name and the pictures of African beasts, this is a prototypal Northern Italian eatery in the Upper East Side style. Costly it is, but very good, too. Regulars seem to prefer the close proximity of the ground floor, where sculptured hair and black suits predominate. Strangers are led up the spiral staircase to the more spacious second-floor room, where they are no less skillfully attended, by captains who take their responsibilities seriously. Off-menu specials are suggested and preparations are carefully described. The soups and antipasti are unremarkable, but the half-portions of pasta are an excellent starter choice. If it is autumn (the white truffle season), and money is no object, they will grate a shower of the precious pungent fungus over the top. Main courses of veal, poultry and fish are fresh and copious. *Specialties: Vermicelli alle vongole, fettucine verdi al sugo, spigola al brodetto, pollo al scarpariello.*

Greene Street
101 Greene St. (near Prince St.), NY 10012 ☎925–2415. Map **2**S4 ▥▥ ⬚ 🖃 ⓨ 🜲 AE ⓓ CB VISA
Open Sat–Sun noon–3pm, daily 6pm–midnight.
This dazzling new eatery functions as an all-inclusive drinking-dining-entertainment center. The interior expands beyond the SoHo standard with walls of brick and groves of greenery within a towering cube of space modified by balconies and staircases. The young, courteous and uniformly attractive waiters are capable of reeling off numbingly long lists of daily specials. *Nouvelle* departures from classical French assumptions are the inclination of the dedicated executive chef, with deviations toward larger portions and slightly richer sauces. Most preparations are well above par, and prices are surprisingly fair. It is easy to start

with cocktails in the busy front bar and stay past midnight. Piano or chamber music usually accompanies dinner (allowing for the latest enthusiasm of the owner); there is jazz most nights at 11pm (for which there is a cover charge and a two-drink minimum for non-diners). Reservations are essential.

La Grenouille ⌂
3 E 52nd St. (near 5th Ave.), NY 10022 ☎752–1495. Map **5**N4
▥▥ ⬚ 🖃 AE ⓓ *Open Mon–Sat noon–3pm, 6–11pm.*
The leadership in classical French cookery in New York is held by a bare handful of restaurants, whose relative position is a subject warmly debated by those who can afford frequent comparisons. **Lutèce** is surely one, La Grenouille another. La Grenouille has infelicities, to be sure. One *maître d'* is a relic from the Prussian school of hospitality, although it must be conceded that certain customers tend to demand their rights more vociferously than is necessary in a place like this, simply to show they will not be intimidated. Divert your attention from the lot of them by scanning the array of appetizers and pastries set by the entrance. This table underscores the primary reason you have come, and when you are ushered into the main dining room with its tiny lamps and bowls and vases and pots of variegated blooms, momentary irritations at the door peel away. Ask questions, even if they reveal ignorance. Preparations and options will be patiently explained by captains who apparently have unlimited time just for you. They always seem to know when to go away, too. Choose from the menu without fear, for the simplest dishes are likely to surpass the best versions previously enjoyed, and the complicated ones are those you will recall 5yr hence. The list here is hopelessly inadequate to the task. Reserve far in advance and avoid weekends. *Specialties: Billy-bi, little neck clams Corsini, Dover sole, rognon de veau moûtardier, crêpes soufflées.*

Hatsuhana
17 E 48th St. (5th Ave.), NY 10017 ☎335–3345. Map **5**O4
▥▥ ⬚ 🖃 AE CB ⓓ CB VISA *Open Mon–Fri noon–2:30pm, 5:30–9:30pm, Sat 5–9:30pm.*
The idea of ingesting raw fish can

be daunting, even for those to whom oysters on the half-shell are routine. Make the first attempt here: it is authentic, the close quarters make it easy to strike up a conversation, dieters can save calories, the cost is low, and a full meal is light enough to precede 2hr in a theater seat. Young Japanese adroitly slice quiveringly fresh tuna and shrimp, wrap them in sheets of kelp, top with salmon eggs, arrange them artistically on lacquered trays of vinegared rice, all within inches of the diners at the two long narrow pine counters. Most customers eat at the *sushi-sashimi* bars where they can see their food prepared, but there are tables, too. Expect to wait for a seat. *Specialties: Chirashi (assorted sashimi), kushi-yaki (raw seafood skewered with vegetables), mirugai no ichimi-yaki (spicy broiled clams), oshitashi (spinach in sesame and soy sauce).*

Hoexter's Market

1442 3rd Ave. (83rd St.), NY 10028 ☎*472-9322. Map 7L5* |||| ☿ ◎ AE CB ◎ ◎ VISA *Open Mon–Fri 6pm–midnight, Sat–Sun noon–4pm.*

Strikingly attractive people fill the large front bar and rear dining room. Even the waiters are handsome, as well as facile at their trade. The eating space is stripped brick and bare wood, relieved by panels of beige carpeting. *Carpaccio* (thin leaves of raw beef) is a superlative starter, for all the beef here is of prime grade. Moist smoked chicken with fresh horseradish sauce, mussels, oysters raw or in a breaded preparation called 'Unger,' and the twin pâtés are as good. Steak and up to four daily fish comprise most of the entrees. They are precisely cooked, with sauces that enhance rather than cloak. The chocolate fudge cake is a stunner. By 10pm, the bar is belly-to-back with even more seekers and strivers. Around midnight, the tables are pushed aside and it becomes a disco, so it is entirely possible to spend an agreeable 10hr within these walls. Reservations are a necessity. *Specialties: Fish of the day, bias-cut steak, veal chop.*

Jane Street Seafood Cafe

31 8th Ave. (Jane St.), NY 10014 ☎*243-9237. Map 2R3* |||| ☐ ☿ AE VISA *Open Tues–Thurs 6–11pm, Fri–Sat 6pm–midnight, Sun 6–10pm.*

This is a hint of spare and salty New England in the NW corner of Greenwich Village. The ceiling is low and of molded tin, the walls exposed brick, tables are bare wood and there is even a fireplace – with a fire, when weather dictates. Wear your most comfortable clothes, bring your own wine and settle in to a meal composed of produce fresh from the market. Everyone raves about the bread, the coleslaw, the chowder, but those are merely starters. Little that follows will disappoint. As no advance reservations are accepted, there will be a wait. The bar in front is convivial. *Specialties: Manhattan clam chowder, fish of the day, fried oysters, Key lime pie.*

Joanna

18 E 18th St. (Broadway), NY 10003 ☎*675-7900. Map 5Q4* |||| ☐ AE *Open daily 11:30am–2am. Closed Christmas, July 4.*

Almost monthly, there is a new entrant in the bistro-of-the-moment sweepstakes. Votes are cast by feet and the relative lengths of lines of supplicants. The winner is decreed by acclamation. Decor must be fresh and frisky, the patrons likewise, the food at least palatable and the hours late. With luck, the taker of the laurel, and perhaps a contender or two, survive the critical first year on sheer momentum. The others close or decide to be something else. Joanna persists, vaguely Belle Epoque with exaggerated blowups of floral stamens and pistils, frequented by pop-eyed suburbanites, punky disco babies and athletic-chic hipsters and Upper East Siders in tight leather trousers. It only closes long enough to re-provision and sweep out. Weekend brunch is an event. *Specialties: Fried squid, oysters, paillard of chicken, gravlax, baked potato with caviar.*

Le Lavandou ⌂

134 E 61st St. (near Park Ave.), NY 10021 ☎*838-7987. Map 5N4* |||| ☐ AE *Open Mon–Sat noon–3pm, 6–10pm.*

A wave of intimate, sprightly French restaurants broke upon these shores in the mid-1970s. They were owned and operated by dedicated young careerists who had no wish to be cogs in conglomerate feeding stations. Chefs of their tender years could be expected to make mistakes, often in capitalization and administration, but a number of them rode out the rough waters and prospered. Jean Jacques Rachou, for example, created Le Lavandou and went on to revive **La Côte Basque**. It has been argued that his first baby has suffered slightly in the process, but if so, it is barely perceptible. A gracious establishment it remains, unforbiddingly elegant, a place to acquire insight into the mysteries of the French kitchen without any sense of rigorous instruction. *Specialties: Paupiette de sole, casserole de petits gris, salade de crabe et homard, croustade de pèlerines aux poireaux.*

La Louisiana

132 Lexington Ave. (near 29th St.), NY 10016 ☎ *686–3959. Map 5P4* ▯▯▯ ▭ *Open Mon–Sat 6–11pm.*
Cooking of the American South is too often dismissed as merely fried chicken and grits (a cereal substance unworthy of description). Yet in the hands of able practitioners of appropriate heritage, it is the most distinctive of the American regional cuisines. Unfortunately, it is infrequently represented this far N, and less still in a form likely to draw converts. The advent of this charming little spot therefore filled a gap in New York's otherwise comprehensive culinary library. Only a quick flight to New Orleans could surpass its renditions of a cooking that can best be described as Soul-Cajun-Creole. To a substantial degree, it is the creation of poor people compelled to make the best of ingredients once shunned by the middle and upper classes – vegetable greens, leftover organs and extremities of pigs, shellfish free for the gathering. What those years of deprivation has wrought is wondrous, and while purists will quibble, La Louisiana is the place to learn about it. *Specialties: Gumbo, crudité de boeuf, scallops Rockefeller, catfish, garlic shrimp.*

Lutèce △

249 E 50th St. (near 2nd Ave.), NY 10022 ☎ *752–2225. Map 5O5* ▯▯▯ ▭ ▭ AE CB ⓪ *Open noon–3pm, 6–11pm. Closed Sun, Mon lunchtime, Aug.*
Lutèce is the standard against which any American restaurant that presumes to purvey *haute cuisine* must be measured. Hardly a half-dozen establishments in New

York approach its mark, and probably not that many in the rest of the country. While to dine here is an event and very nearly an honor – reservations must be secured at least two weeks in advance – no one is made to feel less than an eagerly anticipated guest. Rank, class, prominence and frequency of visit have no discernible bearing on treatment at the hands of the staff. That is the way it should always be, of course – especially at these prices – but too rarely is. The captains contrive to be attentive but not unctuous, friendly but not familiar, helpful but never patronizing, and their young minions carry through without a clatter or pretense. This exquisite balance, which carries from reception to appetizer to entree to coffee, is orchestrated by chef-proprietor Andre Soltner and his wife, who functions as *maîtresse d'*. Mr Soltner has been here more than 20yr, and is perhaps the only man in America that the great chefs of France acknowledge as their equal. He emerges from the cramped narrow kitchen periodically, circulating among his patrons, his whites so unsoiled as to suggest that he now administers rather than stirs – but the dishes that follow his appearances are still as good. Human endeavor can only aspire to perfection, however, and there are quibbles. The famous Garden Room might be a hangar for a scaled-down Zeppelin, its vaulted severity softened by white latticework and ferns in brass pots. And the Soltners persist in an untranslated menu with prices noted only in the copy handed to the presumed host, ignoring the fact that the woman might be the one who is paying. Those grumps aside, simply stab at the card. Everything on it is a specialty. The cellar is a library of the great vintages of Bordeaux and Burgundy, usually at breathtaking prices. A secondary list of serviceable wines offers rational substitutes.

Madras Woodlands

310 E 44th St. (near 2nd Ave.), NY 10017 ☎ *986–0620. Map 5O5* ▯▯▯ ▭ ▭ AE CB ⓪ ⓒ VISA *Open Mon, Wed–Fri noon–2:30pm, 5:30–10pm, Sat–Sun 1–10pm.*
To describe a restaurant as vegetarian to one of the unconverted majority is to convey images of pseudo-meatloaf and

imitation eggs, bean curd and soya bean derivatives. The problem lies in attempting substitutions for familiar recipes. Here, the food is itself, pretending to be nothing else, and it is astonishingly good. Combinations of exotic spices and textures dance on the tongue, obviating the need for meat, fish and eggs. The decor contributes, by avoiding the queasily garish colors that too often typify Indian eateries in New York. Much of the clientele is drawn from the nearby United Nations and the local Indian community. **Specialties:** *Dosai, melakai podi, vegetable curry, medhu vadai.*

Maxwell's Plum

1181 1st Ave. (64th St.), NY 10021 ☎ *628-2100. Map* **7M5**
▥ ▭ ⓨ AE CB ⊕ ⊙ VISA
Open daily 11:30am–1am.

From its inception, astonishment was expressed that a high-volume emporium of such multipurpose exuberance could actually produce dishes deserving serious gastronomic attention. Out front, there is a glass-enclosed café, its ceiling and upper walls bristling with scores of plaster animal heads. Short-order burger-and-chili cookery prevails here, spiced with seasonal boar and venison options. Up a step or two, a large U-shaped bar caters to a rapacious singles crowd. Beyond that, a (relatively) formal dining room beneath panels of glorious stained glass attempts to forge its own version of upper-middle-brow culture. Often it succeeds with beef, pastas and duck. Almost as often it falls short, usually in pursuit of novelty. But joyous flamboyance is all too rarely encountered, and many can forgive the Plum its trespasses. **Specialties:** *Black bean soup, roast wild boar, sweetbreads.*

Il Monello

1460 2nd Ave. (near 76th St.), NY 10021 ☎ *535–9310. Map* **7L5** ▥ ▭ AE CB ⊕ ⊙ VISA
Open Mon–Sat noon–3pm, 5pm–midnight.

This sort of Upper East Side Italian eatery tends to attract men in black silk suits, faintly silvery white-on-white shirts, diamond rings and sculptured hair. They probably have nothing to do with the profession you imagine, and in this case they have chosen an Upper East Side Italian eatery that also serves commendable food – a rare species. Try to ignore the heavy-handed decor and concentrate on mussels, clams, fish stews, veal and ambrosial tortellini. Try to ignore the captains, too, functionaries who are impatient with your lack of knowledge of what is, and what is not, available in the kitchen. **Specialties:** *Pastas, veal.*

Mortimer's

1057 Lexington Ave. (75th St.), NY 10021 ☎ *861–2481. Map* **7L4** ▥ ▭ ⓨ AE ⊕ ⊙ VISA
Open Mon–Sat 6pm–2:30am, Sun 6pm–midnight.

The ingredients of success cannot be isolated, otherwise everyone would do it. What wizardry transforms a restaurant with OK food at middling-high prices in unremarkable surroundings into a white-hot center of attention for trendsetters and their eager followers? Probably even the owners of Mortimer's don't know. They are simply grateful, and no doubt utter small prayers that they don't unwittingly jar the composition out of balance. To witness the phenomenon at flood stage, drop in after 11pm – always assuming that the lemmings have not pressed on to still another *boîte*. A parade of costumed lovelies and their attendants fill the arenas of a big bar and a modest dining room. If they choose to eat, it is from a fairly direct continental menu, mostly in English, featuring such fashionable items as *gravlax* and *paillard of chicken*. Considering the floor show, prices are reasonable. **Specialties:** *Mushrooms fines herbes, calf's liver, entrecôte Bordelaise.*

Odeon

145 W Broadway (Thomas St.), NY 10013 ☎ *233–0507. Map* **2T4** ▥ ▭ AE ⊙ VISA
Open Sun–Fri noon–3pm, 7pm–2:30am, Sat 7pm–2:30am.

This is an 'Art Moderne' cafeteria of World War II vintage left pretty much as it was, with a speckled-marble floor and chrome-tubular chairs with leatherette upholstery. Tapes of Betty Hutton and the Andrew Sisters are background music, and the staff wear pencil-thin ties and wraparound aprons in imitation of an era none of them remember. Some customers show up in New Wave green cropped hair or pleated pegged trousers or jackets with Joan Crawford shoulders. Most, however, are simply jeans and tweed sorts of the

141

TriBeCa-SoHo art community. They come for semi-*nouvelle cuisine* concoctions of leeks and truffles and lobster out-of-the-shell with *crème fraîche*. Most of the food is imaginative and some of it splendid. Full dinners are served until 12:30am, light suppers until 2:30am; the clientele grows more entertainingly bizarre as the night wears on. *Specialties: Lobster à la Nage, civet of duck, smoked Norwegian salmon, rack of lamb.*

One Fifth

1 5th Ave. (8th St.), NY 10003 ☎ *260–3434. Map 2R4* ▥ ▯
▬ 𝄞 *AE* *CB* *⊙* *⊙* *VISA* *Open Mon–Fri noon–3pm, 6pm–12:30am, Sat–Sun noon–4pm, 6pm–12:30am.*

As the name suggests, One Fifth is at the base of 5th Ave., a half-block from Washington Square Park. Salvaged artifacts from a ship called the *Caronia* set the nautical tone. The clam and oyster bar at the front, the live duo that plays at night, and the wine list are the best reasons to go. Weekend brunch is popular. *Specialties: Cassoulet, pepper steak.*

Orsini's

41 W 56th St. (near 5th Ave.), NY 10019 ☎ *757–1698. Map 5N4* ▥ ▯ *AE* *CB* *⊙* *⊙*
VISA *Open Mon–Sat noon–3pm, 5:30pm–1am. Closed Sat lunch in summer and Sun.*

The chi-chi crowd has a warm spot in its heart for Orsini's, but no longer besieges it, so there is room for mortals possessed merely of discretionary income. Romantics head for the dim downstairs room, but for lunch and being seen, the airy upstairs chamber is preferred. Clients unknown to the management are treated as well as glamorous old friends. The kitchen is competent, and tableside preparations are brisk, not showy. *Specialties: Osso buco, scampi, veal chops.*

Oyster Bar and Restaurant

Grand Central Terminal (42nd St. and Vanderbilt Ave.), NY 10017 ☎ *532–3888. Map 5O4* ▥ ▯ ▬ *AE* *CB* *⊙* *⊙* *VISA*
Open Mon–Fri 11:30am–midnight. Closed Sat, Sun.

Reclaimed from oblivion a few years back, this venerable (1913) fish house is better than ever. The cavernous vaulted space is sheathed in beige tiles, its high

arches echoed by pinlight traceries. When seasons and shipments overlap, the menu is crammed with more than 120 items, changed daily according to availability. The day's catch can include such rarities as *loup de mer*, shark, sea urchin, sand dab and ray. Five to ten types of oysters are usually on hand, along with chowders, pan roasts, stews, lobsters and crabs. Lake sturgeon, salmon and trout are smoked on the premises. Everything is super-fresh, and the simplest preparations are best. Service is speedy, without flourishes. There is an unexcelled list of California white wines. Since they do not close between lunch and dinner, unhurried pre-theater meals are possible. *Specialties: Broiled fish, bouillabaisse, waterzooi, shellfish.*

The Palm

837 2nd Ave. (near E 45th St.), NY 10017 ☎ *687–2953. Map 5O5* ▥ ▯ *AE* *CB* *⊙* *⊙* *VISA*
Open Mon–Fri noon–10:45pm, Sat 5–11pm.

Steak is the reason for The Palm, and for its annex across the street, Palm Too. Admirers of precisely seared slabs of unadorned prime beef are a manly lot, it would appear, impatient with the fancy rituals of those swishy French places. Beef is what they want, and they get it, along with loaves of hashed brown potatoes, preceded by shrimp and followed by cheesecake, all in stupefying portions. Sawdust is on the floor, faded cartoons line the walls and ceiling, and women are mostly decoration, preferably silent. The bored waiter recites the menu, for none is written, and there isn't all that much to remember. Those inclined to stoking up in such places insist that this is one of the three best steak houses in New York and are willing to pay for the privilege. Reservations for lunch, none for dinner.

El Parador

325 E 34th St. (near 1st Ave.), NY 10016 ☎ *679–6812. Map 5P5* ▥ ▯ ▬ *Open Mon–Sat 5–11pm.*

Of all the world's cuisines, Mexican seems the least amenable to transplantation. At least this is true on the evidence of New York's proponents of that not-always-fiery cookery. None of them do more than approximate, and enthusiasts must take what they can get. Settle in over a margarita – tequila and lime juice with a salted glass rim – while perusing the menu. *Seviche* (a marinated raw fish cocktail) is the best starter, but from there you are on your own. The decor simulates Old Mexico rather more engagingly than most of the competition and lights are kept low, so those who associate *guacamole* and *tostadas* with romance will be content. Expect a wait, for they don't accept reservations. *Specialties: Shrimp en salsa verde, chicken El Parador.*

Parioli Romanissimo
1466 1st Ave. (near 76th St.), NY 10021 ☎288–2391. *Map* **7**L5
▥ ▭ AE CB ① ▣ *Open Tues–Sat 6–11pm.*

No satisfactory explanation is advanced for the practice – primarily of Chinese and Italian restaurants – of not listing on the menu dishes nonetheless nearly always available. They do that here, but the food, hidden or not, is so good and the ambience so seamlessly amiable that quibbling is small-minded. Be sure to reserve ahead, for they cannot serve more than 50 or 60 at a time. Among your fellow diners are certain to be an actor or two, a fashion designer, a recognizable power broker. They come here to eat, not to ogle their peers, which is a refreshing change to other celebrity hangouts. Although the starters and main courses are estimable, you can do worse than to hand the menu unread back to the captain and inquire about delights they might be concealing in the kitchen tonight. He will not be evasive, and if he mentions game, have it. *Specialties: Vitello tonnato, any pasta, filet of beef alla Romana.*

Le Plaisir ⌂
969 Lexington Ave. (near 70th St.), NY 10021 ☎734–9430. *Map* **7**M4 ▥ AE CB ① ▣ *Open Mon–Sat 7– 10:30pm.*

Fashion is fleeting, of course, and there is no way to tell if Le Plaisir will still be packing in the fireflies that lead the swarm by the time you get there. In the meantime, the management continues to shift tables a few inches nearer and snug the chairs just a hair closer to accommodate the throngs. Let it be said that it has aroused this interest by merit. Someone in the kitchen understands that it isn't enough (at these prices) for food to simply taste good (indeed superb,

most of the time). It must enrapture the eye on presentation, too. This is done with such finesse that the diner will want a photograph of the plate before he disturbs its composition. *Specialties: Shellfish sausage, mousse of quail liver with quail eggs, duck with peaches, sweetbreads with crayfish.*

The Quilted Giraffe ⌂
955 2nd Ave. (near 50th St.), NY 10022 ☎753–5355. *Map* **5**O5
▥ ▭ ▤ AE CB ① ▣ VISA *Open Mon–Fri 6–10pm. Closed Sat, Sun.*

Jaded? Weary of snails in their shells, salmon in pastry envelopes, sole sprinkled with almond slivers, and similar conventionalities? Owner-chef Wine (his real name) fabricates antidotes . . . or scares timid venturers back to the traditionalists. Innovation is primary, provender is from the top of the bin, and almost everything emerges from the kitchen raw, quickly warmed, or barely seared. Combinations can be outrageous – shellfish and raspberries, ravioli stuffed with chocolate – and perversely bland. But most of it works, the reward for experimentation. *Specialties: Scallop and crabmeat strudel, poached bass with ginger, caviar and crème fraîche in a crêpe.*

Raga ♣
57 W 48th St. (near 5th Ave.), NY 10036 ☎757–3450. *Map* **5**O4 ▥ ▭ ♪ AE CB ① ▣ VISA *Open Mon–Fri noon–3pm, 5–11pm, Sat–Sun 5–11pm.*

The Indian restaurant that deviates from the stereotype is no longer a novelty in the City. But Raga achieves a blend of formality and engaging exotica that is less chilly than others of the genre while preserving an unpatronizing authenticity in its dishes. There is tandoori, if you must, although the popularity of simple broiled chicken is a puzzlement in the presence of eggplant, *bhurta*, *nargisi kofta* and *jingha chat*. Many nights, there is live flute or sitar music. *Specialties: Seekh kebab, lobster malabar, oysters Bombay, murgh mumtaz.*

Raoul's
180 Prince St. (near Sullivan St.), NY 10012 ☎966–3518. *Map* **2**S4 ▥ ▭ AE ⑩ VISA *Open daily 6:30pm–midnight.*

This enormously popular SoHo

bistro doesn't look like much – just an old saloon of a sort found all over Manhattan. Sanguine anticipation of the superior meal promised by friends and guidebooks is not enhanced by the sight of busboys stripping sheets of paper off a roll to cover the tabletops. Think of it as a remembrance of student days on the Left Bank, for that is the intent (along with economy). The blackboard menu is equally pragmatic, for the dishes fashioned each night are dependent upon ingredients on hand at the market that morning. Vegetables are fashionably crunchy, chops are tender and thick, snails are a revelation, fish balances between fresh and undercooked with magical precision. Look, too, for *couscous*, calf's brains, sweetbreads, unusual game birds. ***Specialties:*** *Fish of the day, pâté, steaks, cakes.*

Le Relais

712 Madison Ave. (64th St.), NY 10021 ☎ *751–5108. Map **7**M4* ▥ ▭ ▨ 🚗 AE *Open daily noon–3pm, 5:30–11pm.*

London pubs and Rive Gauche bistros are institutions that resist transplantation. Perhaps it is the alien language, the customers, the ambient sound. Nevertheless, this immensely popular cafe evokes half-remembered afternoons in the shadow of the Sorbonne, with hints of Gauloises in the air. Inside are velvet banquettes, walls crowded with framed mirrors and etchings, gaggles of East Siders seated haunch to denimed haunch, and aproned waiters who remain calm and cogent despite the clamor. The short menu is adjusted to seasonal availabilities, but might include sorrel soup, bass cloaked in seaweed, tender soft-shelled crabs and rosy-centered lamb. ***Specialties:*** *Saddle of lamb, artichoke stuffed with seafood.*

Restaurant Leslie

18 Cornelia St. (near 6th Ave.), NY 10014 ☎ *675–1255. Map **2**R3* ▥ ▭ *Open Mon–Sat 6–10:30pm.*

The eponymous co-owner is one of the first women in the city to break into the upper kitchen hierarchies. Her *métier* is *nouvelle cuisine*, although her allegiance to its much-debated revisionism is less than slavish. Among her whimseys are fish simmered in claret, pheasant with plums, sweetbreads sprinkled with American sturgeon

roe. Some efforts fall short, most do not, but part of the allure is in watching her move across the high wire without a net. The tiny dining room is cool without sterility, occupied most nights by uptowners who can afford to dine wherever they wish. As there is no liquor license, the bill can be kept within reason by bringing along a liter or two of wine. Reservations are necessary. ***Specialties:*** *Twin breasts of chicken in mustards, terrine, roast lamb.*

El Rincón de España

226 Thompson St. (near Bleecker St.), NY 10012 ☎ *475–9891. Map **2**R4* ▥ ▯ ▭ ▨ AE CB ◉ VISA *Open daily, 6pm–midnight.*

Some restaurants flare like meteors and burn out as quickly; others quietly appear and hum along at an unwavering tempo, immune to fashion. Spanish food does not dazzle, and that might be another reason for the longevity of El Rincón de España. Lost in the seedy flash of the most abused quarter of Greenwich Village, its *paellas* and shellfish concoctions have attracted a steady patronage for decades. Prominent flavorings are garlic and that most costly of spices, saffron. Aficionados are advised that the northwestern region of Galicia is the primary influence, a fact as relevant as the distinction between Bologna and Naples in Italian cookery. Shun the sangria and overlook the vulgar decorative approximations of a Torremolinos tourist trap. Usually, there is a guitar player. ***Specialties:*** *Gazpacho, caldo Gallego, mussels.*

River Cafe

1 Water St., Brooklyn, NY 10001 ☎ *522–5200. Map **3**T6* ▥ ▭ ◁€ ⬚ ⟡ 🚗 AE CB ◉ *Open daily noon–2:30pm, 6:30–11:30pm.*

The breathtaking views of the Manhattan skyline from this remodelled barge beneath the Brooklyn Bridge more than compensate for occasional lapses in the cooking – and these deficiencies are infrequent, the result of daring rather than indifference. The culinary mix is one part classic Gallic conceit, one part chauvinistic produce. Ingredients are Key West shrimp, Smithfield ham, California snails, New Jersey pheasants – resolutely American – but the twin sauces, aspics and terrines cry out their Old World origins. Furnishings here are agreeable – bamboo, bentwood and the requisite portholes – but the decor is the vista, which reaches from the Statue of Liberty to the Empire State Building. The best time to be there is at dusk, when interior illumination is kept low. A piano is played, and tables are set out on the terrace in summer. Sunday brunch is popular, and reservations are essential at all times. *Specialties: Breast of duck, supremes of pheasant, cold Maine lobster with caviar, game terrine, oysters and sea urchins.*

The Russian Tea Room
150 W 57th St. (near 7th Ave.), NY 10019 ☎ *265-0947. Map 4N3* 🍴 ▭ AE CB ⊕ ⊚ VISA *Open daily 11:30am – 1am, (Sat 2am).*

Restaurants where celebrities gather are notorious for indifferent food, but here is an exception. A number of eccentricities endear the Tea Room to clients as diverse as Woody Allen, Jackie Onassis, the Aga Khan, Diana Rigg, Rudolf Nureyev, Liza Minnelli, Joseph Heller and Max von Sydow (to drop the names of some regular customers). There is the fact that it really does serve superb Russian food, a cuisine not in great favor in these parts. Also Christmas decorations wreathe the light fixtures – all year. And none of the many clocks have the same time. Perhaps most of all, as violinist Isaac Stern said, it is "a private-professional club where the public is allowed." Non-celebrated folk with the wherewithal to afford attendance are *not*, however, permitted to approach the stars, which helps assure their frequent return. While gazing upon each other, they dip into borscht, dine on salmon *kulebiaka* or *shashlik* or *luli kebab*, and rhapsodize over the finest grades of caviar. Surely the Tea Room will sail majestically into the next century, its slogan intact – 'Slightly to the left of Carnegie Hall.' *Specialties: Blinis with red caviar and sour cream, lamb dishes.*

The Saloon
1920 Broadway (64th St.), NY 10023 ☎ *874-1500. Map 6M3* 🍴 ▭ AE CB ⊕ ⊚ VISA *Open daily noon – midnight.*

The waiters no longer navigate on roller skates as they did when this shiny new Lincoln Center eatery first opened, thereby reducing the number of times coffee ends up in the saucer rather than the cup. On the other hand, the never more than high-average food has perceptibly slipped into unevenness. This is the result, no doubt, of the over-ambitious menu and the crush of music devotees who like the proximity to their concert seats. Still, a satisfying meal can be had at fair prices.

Salta in Bocca ♣
179 Madison Ave. (near 33rd St.), NY 10016 ☎ *684-1757. Map 5P4* ▭ AE CB ⊕ ⊚ VISA *Open Mon – Sat noon – 3pm, 5 – 10:30pm.*

It is an inexplicable truism that the most sublime of dishes in Northern Italian restaurants are often not listed on the menu. Patrons must ask, or hope, that the captain will volunteer the information. At Salta in Bocca, the fried cornmeal known as *polenta* falls into this secretive category. It arrives with a variety of garnishes, all tasty. The Italians are the only Europeans who regard maize to be edible in any form, but that is to the profit of Bolognese and Manhattanites. Pasta dishes can be shared as an appetizer, and the management doesn't mind if a couple does the same with mussels or clams. This reasonableness is carried through to the prices. Although Salta in Bocca rivals the best in town, the final accounting is within the grasp of almost any budget. Simply ignore the dreadful paintings and arrive for dinner, not lunch. *Specialties: Zuppa di vongole, chicken viareggina, osso buco, saltimbocca, veal Genovese.*

Sardi's
234 W 44th St. (near Broadway), NY 10036 ☎ *221-8440. Map 4O3* 🍴 ▭ AE CB ⊕ ⊚ VISA *Open daily 11:30am – 12:30am.*

Food is nearly an irrelevance in a place that achieved the status of a theatrical institution decades ago. Probably it is a trick of memory, or youthful naivety, but the *fettuccine* and 'devilled roast beef bones' seemed pretty good back then. But who cares? This is a repository of showbiz caricatures – hundreds of them – and was the meeting place of table-hopping stars and gossip columnists in the heyday of Helen Hayes, the Lunts and Walter Winchell. Celebrities still drop in after their curtain calls and enjoy patters of applause from the other diners even if their current plays were demolished by the critics. Identifying the persons depicted in those drawings that line the walls also distracts attention from the plate. *Specialties: Pasta, chicken.*

Sea Fare of the Aegean ♣
25 W 56th St. (between 5th Ave. and 6th Ave.), NY 10019 ☎ *581–0540. Map 5N4* ▮▯ ▭ ▬ *AE* *CB* ⓓ ⓞ *VISA* *Open Mon–Sat noon–11pm, Sun 1–11pm. Closed Christmas, Thanksgiving, Jan 1.*

On a celebrated block of restaurants, there is no better dollar-for-dollar value than this 38yr-old institution. The faded facade does not impress, nor do the seascapes and harbor scenes inside, nor the inconsistent and rather dour service. But the fish is just off the boat, and the high turnover ensures that it spends not one unnecessary moment under refrigeration. Despite the implication of the 'Aegean' label, most dishes are without precise ethnic orientation, although Greek, Indian and Creole variations make appearances. Never entirely empty, the pace does slacken in late afternoon and early evening. *Specialties: Bouillabaisse, poached red snapper, brook trout stuffed with crabmeat.*

Shezan ♣
8 W 58th St. (5th Ave.), NY 10019 ☎ *371–1414. Map 5N4* ▮▯ ▭ *AE* ⓒ ⓓ ⓞ *VISA* *Open Mon–Fri noon–2:30pm, 6–11pm, Sat 6–11pm.*

The sub-street setting might have been gloomy, but the management chose soft gray wall carpeting, reflective ceilings and diffused illumination that expanded space and muffled noise. Those who wish them can request authentically fiery seasonings for the Pakistani-northern Indian food; otherwise, Occidentals will be brought dishes that do not sear the roof of the mouth. Given the slightest encouragement, the captains dispense continuous avuncular advice about selections and preparations – not always correct, but often amusing. A request to split individual choices among the patrons at a table is always honored – a good idea for the uninitiated. Napkins are spread upon laps, crumbs are brushed away, plates are always hot. *Specialties: Murgh tikka lahori, bhuna gosht, chingiri jhol.*

Shun Lee Dynasty
900 2nd Ave. (48th St.), NY 10017 ☎ *755–3900. Map 5O5* ▮▯ ▭ *Open daily noon–2:30pm, 5:30pm–11pm.*

When it opened back in the mid-1960s, the Dynasty demolished the widely held beliefs that all Chinese food was Cantonese, invariably served in grungy fly-specked warrens of little charm. The decorator filled the space with softly clacking windchimes and strings of tinkling opalescent seashells, panels and drapes of glass and glittery fabric. The frenzy for the spicy Hunan and Szechuan cuisines was developed, if not actually launched, here. There are equally successful branches but with slightly different names at 155 E 55th St. and 43 W 65th St. (see **Shun Lee West** below). *Specialties: Shark-fin soup, hacked chicken, calf's liver.*

Shun Lee West
43 W 65th St. (near Broadway), NY 10023 ☎ *595–8895. Map 6M3* ▮▯ ▭ *AE* *Open daily noon–3pm, 5pm–midnight.*

The newest in a chain that introduced high style in Chinese restaurants – **Shun Lee Dynasty**, Shun Lee Palace – this one serves Lincoln Center. It is a happy diversion from, and improvement upon, the quiche-and-burger emporia that dominate the neighborhood. One might even go there simply to eat, rather than to fuel up for a session of Puccini or Bach. The decor is essentially what was left behind by an unlamented French *boîte* – sedate, just a bit frayed, but preferable to the pervasive plastics of Chinatown. The proprietors introduced New Yorkers to the spicy Szechuan and Hunan cuisines, and the chili oil is shaken with a generous hand, if requested. A particularly agreeable notion is the after-concert *dim sum* supper (from 10pm), when a full meal might rest too heavily in the stomach. *Specialties: Hot-and-sour soup, moo shu pork, sea bass Hunan, hacked chicken.*

Sichuan Pavilion
322 E 44th St. (near 2nd Ave.), NY 10017 ☎ *986–3775. Map 5O5* ▮▯ ▭ *AE* *CB* ⓓ *VISA* *Open daily noon–11pm.*

Authenticity is overrated, as can be attested by anyone who has braved some of the cherished peasant stews of the Mediterranean. Yet the infatuation with Sichuan (*née* Szechuan*)* preparations doubtless produced travesties, and who could complain of the importation of ten chefs from the People's Republic to bring enlightenment? Many of the recipes presented are unique to this restaurant. One could only wish that the management had also brought over an authentic decorator as well. *Specialties: Steamed bass, smoked duck, lobster, rabbit.*

Sloppy Louie's ⚓
92 South St. (near Fulton St.), NY 10038 ☎ *952–9657, Map 3U5* □ □ *Open Mon–Fri 11am–10pm. Closed Sat, Sun.*
The conventionalities of the two-fisted fish-house are carried to extremes here – no liquor, no reservations, no romance, no credit cards, no decor, avuncular waiters, tables shared with strangers, and it closes before most New Yorkers are even thinking about dinner. Seafood buffs are undeterred. Molluscs, crustaceans and flat fish, however they are prepared, are nearly always flawless. Side dishes of coleslaw and fried potatoes are as unremarkable as the desserts. Expect to wait for a seat.
Specialties: Fried oysters, shad roe, broiled halibut and lemon sole.

SoHo Charcuterie
195 Spring St. (Sullivan St.), NY 10012 ☎ *226–3545. Map 2S4* ▥ □ □ □ *AE* ⓓ ⓒⓑ *VISA Open Mon–Wed noon–3pm, 6–11pm, Thurs–Fri noon–3pm, 6–11:30pm, Sat 11am–4pm, 6–11:30pm, Sun 11am–4:30pm. Closed July (two weeks), Aug.*
At the front is a Frenchified delicatessen, deep in sausages and imported smoked salmon and imaginatively shaped breads. In the back, self-consciously stringent decor prevails, a meld of high-tech and bentwood and bare polished floors. The fabrications brought to the table slide from the extravagantly simplistic (strips of raw red beef) to compilations of divers ingredients in which color, shape, line and texture are paramount. Some of each work, but at prices that rival those of uptown eateries in which dash and discipline are in more predictable balance. Under the circumstances, weekend brunch is the best bet, but book well in advance.
Specialties: Duck livers, truffled pasta, loin of veal.

Sparks
210 E 46th St. (near 3rd Ave.), NY 10017 ☎ *687–4855. Map 5O5* ▥ □ □ □ *AE* *CB* ⓓ ⓒ *VISA Open Mon–Fri noon–11pm, Sat 6–11:30pm.*
Despite its aggressive advertising to the contrary, Sparks doesn't quite measure up to the steakhouses of glossier reputation. On one important count, however, it surpasses all of them. Indeed, few restaurants of any category can match its inventory of fine wines. European wine buffs can here test the remarkable vintages of California, from Robert Mondavi and Sterling, to Mirassou and dozens of other estimable products. There are French, Spanish and Italian bottles, too. Between sips, stick to the simplest of beef preparations.

Spring Street Restaurant
149 Spring St. (near W Broadway), NY 10012 ☎ *966–0290. Map 2S4* ▥ □ *AE* ⓓ ⓒ *VISA Open daily 11:30am–4am.*
SoHo has a number of pub-restaurants of this bubbling, lively sort, in which it is possible to drop in for a beer and stay until the small hours. Its predominantly young clients don't dress up to come here: mountaineer-casual is the mode, but pressed and polished, for this is an important meeting place. Perhaps because they are young and have other things on their minds, they don't seem to object to the lack of delicacy in the food preparation. They might have a point: what appears from the clangorous kitchen is usually satisfying, sometimes imaginative and – in a city where dinner can empty pockets fast – relatively cheap. *Specialties: Fresh fish.*

Tavern On The Green
Central Park W (67th St.), NY 10023 ☎ *873–3200. Map 6M3* ▥ □ ▬ *AE* *CB* ⓓ ⓒ *VISA Open Mon–Fri noon–4pm, 5:30pm–1am, Sat 11am–1am, Sun 10am–1am.*
Tavern On The Green is something that must be mentioned simply because it is there and everybody knows about it. Once a barn for the sheep that wandered in the adjacent meadow, it has been a restaurant for much of this century. Successive managements have consistently fallen short in matching the dining experience to the promise of the building and the

park surroundings. The latest to try is a Mr Leroy, of the flamboyant East Side **Maxwell's Plum**, an apostle of the 'eat-with-the-eyes' theory of restaurateurship. It is visually provocative, crammed with carved plaster, etched mirrors and brass, crystal and copper ornamentation in copious profusion. It is also noisy, disorganized, and pretentiously cute. The food can be good, but it is impossible to predict which dishes at what hours. The service is erratic.

Thailand
106 Bayard St. (Mulberry St.), NY 10013 ☎ *349–3132. Map 2T4* ▯▯ ▭ ▭ *Open Tues–Sun 11am–11pm.*

It might seem sacrilegious to venture into Thai food while in Chinatown, for a year of uninterrupted consumption would not exhaust the Szechuan, Mandarin, Cantonese and Hunan cuisines to be sampled in its perhaps 200 restaurants. But this admittedly seedy little place across from Columbus Park deserves consideration, and its prices are as low as any in the neighborhood. The menu is bewilderingly comprehensive, with nearly 100 listed items. A party of four can take advantage of the variety.
Specialties: Squid salad, mee krob, yum salads, beef curry.

Thwaite's Inn
536 City Island Ave., City Island, NY 10464 ☎ *885–1023. Map 13C5* ▯▯ ▭ ▭ *AE* *CB* ⊕ ▭ *VISA* *Open Mon–Thurs noon–10pm, Fri–Sat noon–11pm, Sun 1–9pm.*

There has been a Thwaite's in City Island – New York's own fishing village in The Bronx – since 1870. Unlike most of the neighboring seafood eateries, it stays open all year, with fresh fish at fair tariffs. Stick to uncomplicated dishes and prepare for hefty portions.

Trattoria da Alfredo
90 Bank St. (Hudson St.), NY 10014 ☎ *929–4400. Map 2R3* ▯▯ ▭ *Open Wed–Mon noon–2pm, 6–10pm. Closed Tues and for three to four weeks in June/July.*

There are several good reasons why it is necessary to make reservations a week or more in advance for Trattoria da Alfredo. It can seat no more than 32 people at a time, has a loyal following, eschews fussiness

in preparation, sends forth some of the best pasta dishes in town, and is so inexpensive that the management finds it necessary to impose a minimum tariff at dinner. Part of the explanation for this last uncommon circumstance is that it serves no wines or spirits. You bring your own, thereby saving the 100–150% markup imposed by fully licensed restaurants.
Specialties: Funghi farciti, zucchini, all pastas.

21 (Twenty-one) Club
21 W 52nd St. (near 5th Ave.), NY 10019 ☎ *582–7200. Map 5N4* ▥▥▥▥ ▭ ▭ *AE* *CB* ⊕ ▭ *VISA* *Open Mon–Sat noon–midnight. Closed Sat in summer and Sun.*

Once a Prohibition-era speakeasy, '21' went on to become a sanctuary for the power elite. Celebrities are on view, but the carefully tonsured and garbed regulars that frequent the place are more often senior partners in important law firms, executives of multi-national corporations, or the men who decide who will be permitted to run for political office. It is not a club in the sense that the general public is excluded, but strangers are granted no more than distant courtesy.
Specialties: Shellfish, brook trout, petite marmite, pheasant.

Un Deux Trois (One Two Three)
123 W 44th St. (near Times Sq.), NY 10020 ☎ *354–4148. Map 4O3* ▥▥▥▥ ▭ ▭ *AE* *Open Mon–Fri 11:30am–2:30pm, 5:30–11:30pm, Sat–Sun 6–11:30pm.*

Its allegiance to the brasserie archetype is not slavish, but with purple handwritten menus, paper tablecloths and hearty rather than delicate victuals, the point is made. At lunch, its clients run to executive sorts, but at nightfall, a disco-theater crowd prone to spiky hair and violet cheekbones mingles with specimens of the Concorde Set. Contrary to local pattern, selections from the regular *carte* are usually preferable to the daily specials. Crayons are provided for doodling. Reservations not accepted. *Specialties: Onion soup, mussels, steak au poivre, rabbit stew.*

Uzie's
1444 3rd Ave. (82nd St.), NY 10028 ☎ *744–8020. Map 7L5* ▥▥▥▥ ▭ *AE* *CB* ⊕ ▭ *VISA* *Open Sat–Sun noon–4pm, Mon–Fri 6pm–midnight.*

With the same ownership, kitchen

and basic menu as **Hoexter's Market**, it draws the same upscale clientele and is really quite good, if less than memorable. Service is often inconsistent. Weekend brunches are special. **Specialties:** *Fish of the day, bias-cut steak, veal chop.*

Le Veau d'Or

129 E 60th St. (near Park Ave.), NY 10022 ☎838–8133. Map **5N4** 🍴 🖵 AE Open Mon–Sat noon–2:30pm, 6–10:15pm.

If there has ever been a moment when this place was not packed with ravenous humanity, it has escaped the memory of its habitués. Staff and patrons are a congenial lot though, patient with each other in the presentation and consumption of consistently good food. Something more than a bistro but less than a *temple de cuisine*, it manifests none of the frequent hyper-trendiness of the former nor the often plodding solemnity of the latter. Walls are chock-a-block with travel posters, Parisian street signs, inconsequential paintings and objects of vague or specific Gallic origin. Seating is fairly comfortable, although it is necessary to guard against dipping your elbow in your neighbor's *vichyssoise*. Go in an attitude of cheerful anticipation and you will be rewarded. **Specialties:** *Pâté du chef, poussin en cocotte, frogs' legs.*

Vienna '79 ⌂

320 E 79th St. (2nd Ave.), NY 10021 ☎734–4700. Map **7L5** 🍴 🖵 AE CB ◐ VISA
Open daily 5:30–11:30pm. Closed last week Aug, first week Sept, also Sun June–Sept.

One influential critic rates this among the best restaurants in town, another deems it merely adequate. Reality lies somewhere between. The room is small – only 70 seats – and despite acoustic ceiling tiles and carpeting, somewhat noisy. But the colors are warm grays, mirrors along one wall expand space, and flowers in painted ceramic pots brighten the tables. Host-owners Peter and Karl are amiable professionals with impressive credentials who have chosen to purvey Austro-Germanic dishes of a lightness not usually associated with that form of cookery. *Nouvelle cuisine* it isn't, but neither is it leaden. Sauces are reduced, not artificially thickened. Provender is snappingly fresh and treated gently. Every ingredient of

every dish is arranged with an almost Oriental regard for complementary hues and textures. Constituent parts are never less than satisfactory, and frequently sublime. Austrian wines are the best buys from the carefully chosen cellar. **Specialties:** *Schnecken Wachauer art, rindfleischsalat, rostbraten Esterhazy, kalbsleber auf Berliner art.*

Windows On The World

1 World Trade Center, NY 10048 ☎938–1111. Map **2** U4. Three restaurants, all 🖵 🍴 ⬛ AE CB ◐ ◑ VISA
The Cellar in the Sky 🍴 Open Mon–Sat 7:30pm (one seating). *The Hors d'Oeuvrerie* 🍴 ⟨⟨ 🎵 Open Mon–Fri 3pm–1am, Sat noon–1am, Sun noon–3pm, 4pm–midnight.
The Restaurant 🍴 ⟨⟨ Open Mon–Fri 5–10pm, Sat noon–3pm, Sun noon–7:30pm.

There are three distinct eating places under the **Windows On The World** umbrella, all of them in the N tower on the 107th floor. Getting past the demigod at the reception desk of **The Restaurant** can be a chore, but persevere, for it justifies the temporary aggravation. Surely there is no more stunning vista anywhere – sparkling spires, bands of winking sapphires, silvered waters and webs of bridges. All is made available to view from tiered tables in a muted spaceship environment. As is usual in rooftop restaurants, perfection on the plate proves elusive. The simplest offerings are the safest – terrines, liver ragoût, rack of lamb, roast duckling. The premise of **The Hors d'Oeuvrerie** is to make entire meals of appetizers, a gimmick that was overdue. The starter dishes of different countries – Chinese *dim sum*, Spanish *tapas* – are featured on a rotating monthly basis. Jazz performers are on duty from 4:30pm until closing. Reservations are unnecessary. **The Cellar in the Sky** has no views, but attempts to compensate with ambitious seven-course meals enhanced by five different wines. It has only a single sitting each evening for a maximum of 36 diners. Reservations are essential for **The Cellar** and **The Restaurant**, often two or more weeks in advance. Avoid the hectic Sunday buffet and brunch. Available wines at the complex are often of superb quality, and at remarkably rational prices.

Nightlife

On the evidence of what is available, it might be inferred that half the population of New York never sees the light of day. Following cocktails and dinner, there can be opera, ballet, a symphony concert, a Broadway musical. After that, they can choose the late show at a cabaret or supper club, or drop in at a disco or jazz loft. Many places stay open until 4am, and most revelers find that enough. But the hardy and knowledgeable move on to after-hours bars, essentially illegal and with the lifespan of a fruit fly, but thriving. Finally, perhaps, they decompress with croissants or bagels at a 24hr Art Deco diner.

The rest of us, however, must make choices – but before we do so, some considerations. Apart from opening nights, theaters impose no dress codes. Many restaurants, nightclubs and discos do, however, if only to prohibit denim clothing. That being the case, it is advisable to plan an evening with an eye on compatible districts and events. For instance, don your dressiest outfit and combine a deluxe restaurant with the trendiest of discos or cabarets, all on the East Side. For an evening in SoHo-Greenwich Village, jeans and a sweater will do for a pub crawl, dinner, and a jazz or rock club. Something in between is suitable for opera or ballet at the Lincoln Center, a post-theater supper and intimate conversation at a piano bar, all on the West Side.

Liquor laws are liberal. Establishments serving alcoholic beverages are required to close between 4am and 8am (4am and noon on Sun), although most do not open before 11am and lock up whenever business is slow. Anyone aged 18 and over can purchase liquor, although some bars and clubs set a higher age limit and require two items of positive identification.

Bars and clubs offering live entertainment often fix a 'cover' charge that is, in effect, an admission fee; and the range can be considerable, depending on the standard or elaborateness of the show. In discos it tends to rise with the chicness of the place. It might be collected at the door or simply added to the bill. Typically, in such places, there is also a 'minimum' charge for consumption of beverages and/or food, per person.

Fine food and music are rarely found in combination. Getting something to eat – a hamburger, a bowl of chili – is nearly always possible, but in general expect no more than alleviation of hunger pangs. Exceptions are such establishments as **Hoexter's Market**, which divides its functions by first serving its meals and then transforming itself into a disco, and **Greene Street**, where the owner is determined to create an all-inclusive dining-and-entertainment complex (for these two see *Restaurants*).

To learn who is appearing where, consult the entertainment listings of the Fri and Sun editions of *The New York Times*, the weekly magazines *New York* and *The New Yorker*, and, for more off-beat diversions, the weekly newspaper *The Village Voice*. Even then, call ahead for reservations and to inquire about last-minute changes in hours and performers.

There has been no attempt here to locate sexually-oriented clubs, theaters, massage parlors or cinemas. They soon make themselves apparent, and in any case are too ephemeral for print. It is sufficient to note that all predilections are accommodated. For guidance, check *The Village Voice* and that tasteful journal, *Screw*. Prostitution is illegal, although that does not dissuade its practitioners. While street-walkers are flamboyantly visible around Times Sq., their sisters who work hotel bars are cautious and less readily identifiable.

Ballet

Surely no other city enjoys ballet in such abundance and variety. In addition to a dozen or more locally based companies, the troupes of other cities and nations are regular visitors. There are four principal venues.

Brooklyn Academy of Music
30 Lafayette Ave. (downtown Brooklyn), NY 11217 ☎ *636–4100. Map 12D2.*
Known for the biennial seasons of the Pennsylvania Dance Company, among others.

City Center
131 W 55th St., NY 10019 ☎ *246–8989. Map 4N3.*
The Joffrey Ballet, the Alvin Ailey Dance Theater, and the Paul Taylor Dance Company.

Metropolitan Opera House
Lincoln Center, NY 10023 ☎ *580–9830. Map 6M3.*
Host for the American Ballet Theater, of which Mikhail Baryshnikov is the artistic director.

New York State Theater
Lincoln Center, NY 10023 ☎ *870–5570. Map 6M3.*
Home of the New York City Ballet.

Bars

Passing the night in a bar (or several) is a common diversion and, except when it becomes an addiction, not as decadent as it sounds. Certainly there are hundreds of bars devoted to nothing more elevating than the diligent consumption of alcohol. But the owners know that success lies in distractions. These may be no more than the preservation of antique trappings – stamped tin ceiling, potbellied stove, stained-glass window – but can escalate into exciting meals, collections of imported beers and wines, live music and entertainments of every description, or disco dancing. Alternatively, it may be simply a matter of creating the kind of environment that attracts crowds of likeminded seekers-after-companionship. The roster that follows merely indicates the possibilities. Unless otherwise noted, all bars are open seven days a week, usually from 11am or noon until at least 2am, and serve food.

Fake Tiffany lamps and dark-stained plywood too often substitute for atmosphere in American bars, along with inept imitations of that untransplantable institution, the British pub. Exceptions exist, however. **Fanelli's** (*94 Prince St. in SoHo* ☎ *226–9412, closed Sat, Sun*) predates the Civil War, and looks it. Neighborhood workingmen share it with recent artistic immigrants. **McSorley's Old Ale House** (*15 E 7th St.* ☎ *473–8800*) is even older, and did not miss a working day during the 13yr experiment called Prohibition. About a decade ago, it grudgingly allowed women inside the door. There still isn't a sign to mark **Chumley's** (*86 Bedford St. in Greenwich Village* ☎ *243–9729*), and it retains the Bohemian aura of Edna St Vincent Millay and Eugene O'Neill. Yellowing book jackets of former clients line the walls, and there is a working fireplace in winter. Good burgers, too. O. Henry was a regular patron of **Pete's Tavern** (*129 E 18th St.* ☎ *473–7676*), which opened in 1864. It has an open garden for warm-weather dining, with mostly Italian food. **McFeely's** (*565 W 23rd St.* ☎*929–4432*) breathes its Victorian origins and adds fairly ambitious fare supplemented by live piano. The venerable **P. J. Clarke's** (*915 3rd Ave. at 55th St.* ☎*759–1650*) remains dark and cobwebby in the corners, with sawdust beneath the feet, an archetypal Irish saloon; but the clientele wears three-piece suits now, and chatters of media campaigns and TV audience shares. **Charlie's** (*263 W 45th St.* ☎*354–2911*) mirrors Clarke's, but with less obviously upmarket custom. **The White Horse Tavern** (*W Hudson St. and 11th St.* ☎*243–9260*) was established in Greenwich Village in 1880. Dylan Thomas, Norman Mailer, poet Delmore Schwartz and Brendan Behan gathered there. British pub grub – shepherd's pie, steak and mushroom pie – is on the menu of the 1868 **Landmark Tavern** (*626 11th Ave. at 46th St.* ☎*757–8595*). Drop in after the theater, but before midnight, or for Sunday brunch.

Bars with shorter histories but nearly equivalent atmosphere include:

Blue Mill Tavern   50 Commerce St. (in Greenwich Village) ☎243–7114. A former Prohibition speakeasy
Broome Street Bar   363 W Broadway (in SoHo) ☎925–2086
Harvey's Chelsea   108 W 18th St. ☎243–5644. Tavern restaurant
The Lion's Head   59 Christopher St. (in Greenwich Village) ☎929–0670
Molly Malone's   287 3rd Ave. (in Gramercy Park) ☎725–8375

Wine bars, in which the titular tipple is the only one available, have not received widespread acceptance. Among the few are the appropriately designated **Claret's** (*33 E 60th St.* ☎*758–1051*) and the **Wine Bar** (*422 W Broadway, in SoHo* ☎*431–4790*).

Desperate loneliness pervades hotel bars, and the occupants seem to exude their disinclination to venture more than 100ft from their bedrooms. Among the dozen exceptions, so engaging that even New Yorkers stop in, are **Bemelman's Bar** in the plush **Carlyle** (*Madison Ave. and 76th St.* ☎*744–1600*). Jazz piano is the backdrop, and the justification for the cover charge. The **Blue Bar** at the **Algonquin Hotel** (*59 W 44th St. near 5th Ave.* ☎*840–6800*) is a snuggery that burbles with talk of book packages and theatrical contretemps. Bankers' pin-stripes dominate at the handsome **Oak Room** of the **Plaza** (*5th Ave. and 59th St.* ☎*759–3000*) where the principal diversion is eavesdropping on the collision of egos.

The hope of human contact, of conversation, however brief, is a primary motive for barhopping. When it became clear that increasing numbers of unmarried people were choosing to retain that status, the 'singles bar' became an explicit entity. Few unencumbered folk admit to visiting such places, which leaves open the question of why they flourish nevertheless. And, of course, they fall into categories, subject to unpredictable change and fashion. Most are for practicing heterosexuals, but some are for those of minority persuasions. Allegiances shift, but for the majority interest try:

Boodles   1478 1st Ave. (near 77th St.) ☎628–0900
Friday's   1152 1st Ave. at 63rd St. ☎832–8512
Grass   1445 1st Ave. at 75th St. ☎737–3328
The Greenery   1340 1st Ave. (near 72nd St.) ☎570–0060
Jim McMullen's   1341 3rd Ave. at 77th St. ☎861–4700

It will be noted that these are all within an extended crawl of each other, which is, of course, what most habitués (or habituées) plan. Other places of a similar kind will be encountered along the way.

Cabarets and supper clubs

Gorgeous chorines (as chorus-girls were known), over-plumed and under-dressed, once descended sweeping silvery staircases to the strains of Cole Porter, attended by top-hatted tap-dancing young men. Those days are gone, except in Las Vegas, but leaner versions persist, with contemporary variations. Expect cover charges and indifferent food at unjustified prices.

Cachaca

403 E 62nd St. (1st Ave.), NY 10021 ☎ *688 – 8501. Map 5N5*
◎ ♩ ♫ ♥ ⚏ AE CB ⓘ CO VISA
Open Tues – Sun 8pm – 4am. Closed Mon.
Brazilian *bossa nova*, live and infectious, begins at 11pm. During dining hours, not-too-loud disco music encourages dancing, and entertainers perform the *capuera*, a martial arts dance from the Amazonian jungles. All this and an occasional famous patron divert from the food.

La Chansonnette

890 2nd Ave. (near 47th St.), NY 10017 ☎ *752 – 7320. Map 5O5*
♩ ♫ ♥ ⚏ AE CB ⓘ CO *Open Mon – Sat 6pm – 2am. Closed Sun.*
Some far-sighted entertainers, weary of the constant travels usually dictated by their profession, buy their own showcase restaurants and settle down. Rita Dimitri did. She is of the Jacques Brel-Edith Piaf school of world-weary angst. Between her shows there is cheek-to-cheek dancing to a live trio.

Chateau Madrid

Lexington Ave. and 48th St., NY 10017 ☎ *752 – 8080. Map 5O4*
♩ ♫ ♥ ≋ AE CB ⓘ CO VISA
Open Tues – Sun 6pm – 2:30am. Closed Mon.
In what is just about the last refuge of the showgirl revue, five to eight shapely women strut and preen through their routines with admirable enthusiasm. While they are no doubt immune to the common cold, their scanty costumes are not so much erotic as mildly naughty. Children will see nothing that they haven't already seen on afternoon television. Authentic flamenco dancing and guitar playing are performed in the adjacent Flamenco Suite. To avoid the cover charge, have dinner before the first show.

Copacabana

10 E 60th St. (5th Ave.), NY 10022 ☎ *755 – 6010. Map 5N4*
◎ ♩ ♫ ♥ ⚏ AE CB ⓘ CO VISA
Open Mon – Thurs noon – 2am, Fri, Sat noon – 4am. Closed Sun.
Sometimes top Hollywood and Las Vegas performers appear, but this isn't the 'Copa' of the 1940s and 1950s. That it still exists, even in this truncated form, is surprising. A dance band plays upstairs, recorded contemporary sounds downstairs (Fri, Sat only).

Ibis

151 E 50th St. (near Lexington Ave.), NY 10022 ☎ *734 – 3884. Map 5O4* ♩ ♫ ♥ AE CB ⓘ CO VISA *Open 6pm – 2:30am.*
Long an apostle of the splashy floor show with barely draped chorus girls and forgettable blaring music, Ibis now features singing stars of the second magnitude, Eartha Kitt and Della Reese among them. Two shows every night except Mon, with cover and minimum charges. Upstairs, a small room is given over to the ripples and bangles of belly-dancers.

King Cole Room

In the St Regis-Sheraton Hotel, 5th Ave. and 55th St., NY 10022 ☎ *753 – 4500. Map 5N4* ♩ ♫ ≋ AE CB ⓘ CO VISA *Open 6pm – 4am.*
The revues, featuring experienced professionals, are generally built around the music of such legendary composers as Jerome Kern or George Gershwin (no show on Sun). Food is not memorable, but the Maxfield Parrish mural is.

Les Mouches

559 W 26th St. (11th Ave.), NY 10001 ☎ *695 – 5190. Map 4P2*
◎ ♩ ♫ ♥ AE CB ⓘ CO VISA
Open 8pm – 4am. Closed Sun, Mon, Tues.
Slick cabaret acts are the staple, put together to showcase mostly female singers from the Broadway

and pop worlds. These are presented in the dining area, separate from the disco. It isn't cheap to see the show, but it's a good way to cap an exploration of the resurgent Chelsea district.

The New Ballroom
253 W 28th St. (near 8th Ave.), NY 10001 ☎ *244–3005. Map 4P3* ♪♬ ♭ ♪ *AE CD VISA Open Tues–Sun 6pm–2am. Closed Mon.*

The 'Old' Ballroom was in SoHo, and was closed by rent increases. This version has much the same flavor, including a famous mural from the first place. The entertainment policy is eclectic – one week a Broadway singer between plays, the next a campy group reproducing sounds of the 1940s. Above-par food for this sort of enterprise.

Once Upon A Stove
325 3rd Ave. (near 24th St.), NY 10010 ☎ *683–0044. Map 5Q4* ♪♬ ♬ ♭ *CD VISA Open Mon–Sat 7pm–midnight. Closed Sun.*

In a city with so many stage hopefuls 'between engagements,' there is a secondary tradition of restaurants with waiters and waitresses likely to burst into song at any moment. In the Valentine Room, the personable young men and women who bring your dinner and pour wine do just that. Some

nights, they perform a structured revue; on others, outsiders are invited to do their thing.

Rainbow Grill
30 Rockefeller Plaza (RCA Building), NY 10017 ☎ *757–8970. Map 5O4* ♪♬ ♭ ♪ ♬ ♭ *AE CB CD VISA Open 7pm–2:30am. Closed Sun.*

Kicks is the name of the long-running revue, with a Francophile accent. Splendid views from the 65th floor. Across the hall is the Art Deco splendor of the Rainbow Room with live music for dancing.

The Red Parrot
617 W 57th St. (11th Ave.), NY 10019 ☎ *247–1530. Map 4N2* ♪♬ ♭ ♪ ♬ *Open 8pm–4am. Closed Mon, Tues.*

Those who have bemoaned the near death of big band music since rock and roll now take heart with the substantial popularity of this immense new club in the shadow of the West Side Highway. The 15-piece orchestra plays for dancing far into the night, choosing from a repertoire from swing to country.

Sirocco
29 E 29th St. (near Madison Ave.), NY 10016 ☎ *683–9409. Map 5P4* ♪♬ ♭ ♪ ♬ *AE CB CD Open 7pm–3am. Closed Mon.*

Singing, bouzouki and belly dancers, with touch-dancing in between.

Classical music
Avery Fisher Hall (*Lincoln Center* ☎ *874–2424*) is home for the New York Philharmonic. Chamber orchestras, string quartets and instrumentalists are heard at **Alice Tully Hall** (*Lincoln Center* ☎ *362–1911*). The National Orchestra of New York uses **Carnegie Hall** (*57th St. and 7th Ave.* ☎ *247–7459*), while groups and individual artists use the attached **Carnegie Recital Hall** (*performances continue during extensive renovation*).

Other venues are:
Brooklyn Academy of Music   30 Lafayette Ave., Brooklyn ☎ *636–4100*
Merkin Concert Hall   129 W 67th St. ☎ *362–8719*
Town Hall   123 W 43rd St. ☎ *840–2824*

Comedy
As an alternative to cabaret or a show, try standup comedy. Its most typical manifestation is in the form of showcase clubs, in which parades of would-be comics are given opportunities to test their material before live audiences. There tend to be more misses than hits, but that's the nature of the game. Should you attend, don't sit near the stage unless you are prepared to be the object of the performers' jibes. Much of the humor is very local in origin, and non-New Yorkers are apt to find many references obscure.

Catch a Rising Star
*1487 1st Ave. (78th St.), NY
10028* ☎*794–1906. Map 7L5*
🍴 🎵 AE ⦿ *Open 8pm–3am.*
Continuous streams of singers and
comedians, all unpaid, but so
anxious to perform that they line
up every week for auditions. Two
masters of ceremonies keep the
pace brisk.

Comic Strip
*1568 2nd Ave. (near 81st St.),
NY 10028* ☎*861–9386. Map
7L5* 🍴 🎵 AE CB ⦿ ⦿ VISA
Open 6pm–3am.
One of the newer comedy
showcases, with most of the
qualities of the others. The
emphasis is on fledgling comics,
but with some singers. Shows
begin between 8:30 and 9:30.

Dangerfield's
*1118 1st Ave. (near 61st St.), NY
10021* ☎*593–1650. Map 5N5*
🍴 AE ⦿ VISA *Open 8pm–3am.*
Standup comic Rodney
Dangerfield grew weary of life on
the nightclub circuit and so opened
his own place, where he now holds
forth two or three times a night.
When he is away on television, able
comedians fill in. On Sun at 9:30,
the stage is given to aspiring
talents, some of them funny.

Good Times
*449 3rd Ave. (31st St.), NY
10016* ☎*686–4250. Map 5P4*
🍴 🎵 AE ⦿ VISA *Open
10:30pm–2am.*
This is one of several showcase
clubs where young comedians,
singers, ventriloquists and others
can try out their material on a live
audience and pray that a producer

will be sitting there and be
impressed. A few of them make it.
Performances start 9:30pm.

Improvisation
*358 W 44th St. (near 9th Ave.),
NY 10036* ☎*765–8268. Map
403* 🍴 🎵 *Open 8pm–3am.*
The first of the showcase clubs,
and therefore able to boast the
longest list of alumni who went on
to successful careers as comics and
singers. The by-play between
performers and hecklers can get
vicious at times, and it is painful to
watch obvious failures. But people
crowd in to hear the ones who have
true promise.

Monkey Bar
*In Elysee Hotel, 60 E 54th St.
(near Park Ave.), NY 10022*
☎*753–1066. Map 5N4* 🍴 🎵
AE CB ⦿ ⦿ VISA *Open
5:30pm–3am. Closed Sun.*
Most hotel rooms traffic in
soporific piano music, but the
maverick **Elysee** has long chosen to
present comedians, sometimes
standup, sometimes in revue. They
can be risqué, but not unusually so.
There are few breaks, so the laughs
are frequent.

Ted Hook's On Stage
*349 W 46th St. (near 9th Ave.),
NY 10036* ☎*265–3800. Map
403* 🍴 🎵 AE ⦿ ⦿ VISA *Open
6pm–3am.*
The entertainment policy changes
from month to month and from
room to room, with jazz and pop
singers and cabaret acts all taking
their turns. Often, though, there
are comedy improvisation groups
that create songs and skits based on
suggestions from the audience.

Country and western
New Yorkers, who prefer to think of themselves as worldly,
were the last holdouts against this otherwise beloved genre.
Now they support several radio stations and clubs that
specialize in the heart-felt musical plaints of Waylon Jennings
and Delbert McClinton. See also *Pop/folk/rock.*

City Limits
*125 7th Ave. S (10th St.), NY
10014* ☎*243–2242. Map 2R3*
🍴 🎵 🍷 *Open 6pm–4am.*
Foot stompin' and hootin' by
transplanted Texans from Houston
and Brooklyn sets the walls
atremble from 10pm. Music is
virtually continuous, the better to
twirl to the Texas Two-Step and
the Cotton-Eyed Joe. Cover and
minimum charges.

Cody's
*579 6th Ave. (16th St.), NY
10011* ☎*620–0377. Map 5Q4*
🍴 🎵 🍷 AE ⦿ *Open
11am–3am (Fri, Sat 4am).*
Blues and jazz as well as country
draw both listeners and dancers.
Performers usually get to work
around 10pm. Food is available, as
well as limitless popcorn pumping
from two huge machines. The
second bar upstairs has more space.

Eagle Tavern
*355 W 14th St. (9th Ave.), NY
10014* ☎ *924–0275. Map 4Q3*
♀ 🎵 *Open 10pm–4am.*

Distinctions blur here, for it mixes
bluegrass, country, Irish and
British folk music on different
nights. When each is heard and
compared, however, their common
roots are clear. The patrons are
serious (but not solemn)
enthusiasts who pay attention.

Lone Star Cafe
5th Ave. and 13th St., NY 10003
☎ *242–1664. Map 2R4* 🍴 🎵
AE ⊕ CB ⊕ CD *Open daily
6pm–4am. Closed Christmas
and Labor Day.*

It bills itself as "the biggest and
best honky-tonk north of
Abilene," and it has a case. If not
the first country and western bar in
Manhattan, it is certainly the most
popular. Urban cowboy attire is in
evidence, but so are button-down
shirts and three-piece suits. Best
eats are burgers and chili in three
gradations of hotness, washed
down by Lone Star or Dos Equuis
beer. While there are performers of
the classic Hank Snow inclination,
most groups do not so restrict
themselves. Rock, blues and pop

influences are evident. Prior
reservations get admission, if not a
table. Arrive early, and opt for the
upstairs level, for the view can be
obscured on the ground floor. Two
shows by two groups nightly.

O'Lunney's
*915 2nd Ave. (near 38th St.), NY
10017* ☎ *751–5470. Map 5O5*
♀ 🍴 AE ⊕ CD VISA *Open
noon–2am (Sat, Sun 5pm–3am).*

Second only to the **Lone Star Cafe**
in the allegiance of local
aficionados, O'Lunney's hosts the
same or similar groups, although
the audiences include East Side
folk who come to meet as much as
to hear. Calvin Klein's notions of
the Old West dominate, his denims
on the haunches of Texans who
haven't seen Dallas in 10yr. The
bluegrass and outlaw strains are
reasonably authentic, as these
things go.

Sundown
*227 E 56th St. (near 3rd Ave.),
NY 10022* ☎ *755–1725. Map
5N5* 🍴 🎵 ♀ *Open 8pm–4am.*

A new boy on the block, featuring
second-string but quite acceptable
groups and a little room to move
about in. No credit cards.

Discos

Discotheques nearly disappeared after their 1960s heyday, then
came back with a vengeance in the mid-1970s. Some are
cavernous spaces ablaze with multimillion-dollar special effects
that would do credit to *Star Wars*, others are simply cafes that
shove aside a few tables after the dishes are cleared away. Most
are expensive, with cover and minimum charges and stiff prices
for drinks. The few membership-only clubs are not measurably
better than those open to the general public, so none are listed
here.

Adam's Apple
*117 1st Ave. (54th St.), NY
10022* ☎ *371–8650. Map 5N5*
♀ ◑ ♀ AE CB ⊕ CD VISA *Open
4pm–4am.*

One of the survivors, this one has
been around since the 1960s. There
is a bar downstairs, dance floors
upstairs, populated by young
singles.

Electric Circus
*100 5th Ave. (15th St.), NY
10011* ☎ *989–7457. Map 5Q4*
◑ 🍴 🎵 ♀ AE *Open to non-
members Fri, Sat and hols
10pm–4am.*

Not the frantic old East Village
haunt, but a frantic new tri-level
Greenwich Village membership
club that is open to the public Fri,

Sat and hols. Live music, disco,
comedians, jugglers and variations
on the circus theme.

Library
*Barbizon Plaza Hotel, 106
Central Park S (6th Ave.), NY
10019* ☎ *247–7000. Map 5N4*
◑ ♀ AE *Open 4:30pm–3am
(Sat, Sun 9pm–3am).*

Perhaps it persists because it
doesn't strive to be chic. As discos
go, it is almost cozy, with shelves of
real books on the walls. Men
should wear jackets.

Regine's
*502 Park Ave. (49th St.), NY
10022* ☎ *826–0990. Map 5O4*
◑ ♀ AE CB ⊕ CD VISA *Open
6pm–4am. Closed Sun.*

The local branch of the flamboyant Parisienne's international chain. Pretty people and surroundings, but outrageous prices. Dinner is served until midnight, but don't go to eat, and nurse your drinks.

Roseland

239 W 52nd St. (near Broadway), NY 10019 ☎ *247–0200. Map 4N3* ● ♪ ♨
AE VISA *Open Wed, Fri 6pm–2am, Thurs, Sat, Sun 2:30pm–2am.*

Over 60yr old and resisting repeated threats to its existence, this grand old ballroom carries on with two orchestras playing 1930s swing and 1940s Latin American rhythms until 11pm each night. Then it switches to disco. All ages waltz or samba with each other or with professionals. Huge buffet-style restaurant.

Sally's

New York Sheraton Hotel, 870 7th Ave. (56th St.), NY 10019 ☎ *247–8000. Map 4N3* ● ♪ ♨
AE CB ◑ ◐ VISA *Open 9:30pm–2:30am.*

Trendy it isn't, but neither is it threatening, and it charges no cover, no minimum. As it's in the **New York Sheraton Hotel**, the patrons are predominantly visiting businessmen and tourists.

Starbuck's

151 E 45th St. (near Lexington Ave.), NY 10017 ☎ *697–5544. Map 5O4* ● ♪ ♨ AE CB ◑ ◐ VISA *Open noon–4am.*

At this very moment, this might be *the* disco-cabaret in town. Tomorrow, who knows? Its crown slipped a bit when it began to advertise on television. In the meantime, until the mood changes, it's packed to the walls with androgynous models and their fellow-travelers, many of whom affect glittery cowboy garb.

Studio 54

254 W 54th St. (Broadway), NY 10019 ☎ *489–7667. Map 4N3* ● ♨ *Open 8pm–4am.*

This is the one – world-famous, ultra-glamorous, packed with superstars, jetsetters and bizarros, and now in its second incarnation. A mob scene every night at the entrance, and you won't get past the doorman unless you have a friend with connections or fit one of the three aforementioned categories. Maybe not even then.

Wednesday's

210 E 86th St. (near 3rd Ave.), NY 10028 ☎ *535–8500. Map 7L5* ● ♪ ♪ ♨ AE CB ◑ ◐ VISA *Open 6pm–2am, also Sun noon–5pm. Closed Mon.*

One of the first to exploit the emergence of a large class of unmarrieds subsequently described as 'swingles,' this is an underground simulation of a stylized European village. Dance in its 'street,' eat a hamburger or a full meal, listen to live jazz, and watch whatever other amusements the management decides to lay on.

Film

Films are of profound concern to many New Yorkers, often to the point of reverence. In strongmindedly rejecting the foolishness of the notorious Cannes event, for example, the **New York Film Festival** (*Alice Tully Hall, Lincoln Center, mid-Sept to early Oct*) overcompensates on the side of solemnity. No prizes are awarded, no starlets drop their bras, and few outsiders notice that anything happened. Worthwhile films are introduced, nonetheless, some of which go on to limited release. 'Art' films – usually foreign-made and of limited domestic appeal – are showcased by managers who no doubt pray for the occasional hit. A few of these do happen. All are subtitled.

Theaters specializing in such films include:

Art 36 E 8th St. (near University Pl.) ☎ 473–7014
Cinema Studio Broadway (66th St.) ☎ 877–4040
Cinema 3 59th St. (near 5th Ave.) ☎ 752–5959
Film Forum 57 Watts St. (near Greenwich St.) ☎ 431–1590
D. W. Griffith 235 E 59th St. (near 2nd Ave.) ☎ 759–4630
Lincoln Plaza Broadway (near 63rd St.) ☎ 757–2280
Little Carnegie 146 W 57th St. (7th Ave.) ☎ 246–5123

Little Theatre   425 Lafayette St. (near 4th St.) ☎598–7171
Paris   4 W 58th St. (near 5th Ave.) ☎688–2013
68th St. Playhouse   3rd Ave. (68th St.) ☎734–0302

In addition, several theaters specialize in revivals, often in 'festival' or retrospective form. They can be high-minded or high camp, composed of films, foreign or domestic, and anywhere from one to 50yr old.

Such theaters include:
Bleecker St. Cinema   144 Bleecker St. (LaGuardia Pl.)
☎674–2560
Carnegie Hall Cinema   7th Ave. (57th St.) ☎757–2131
Cinema Village   33 E 12th St. (near University Pl.)
☎924–3363
8th St. Playhouse   52 W 8th St. (near 6th Ave.) ☎674–6515
Hollywood Twin Cinema   8th Ave. (47th St.) ☎246–0717
Regency   Broadway (67th St.) ☎724–3700
Thalia   Broadway (95th St.) ☎222–3370
Theatre   80 St. Marks Pl. (near 1st Ave.) ☎254–7400

Several museums have regular film programs, the most comprehensive being at the **Museum of Modern Art** (*11 W 53rd St. (6th Ave,)* ☎956–7070).

Jazz

America's most exportable artform may have been born in New Orleans and journeyed up the Mississippi to Kansas City and Chicago, but the ultimate destination was New York. Jazz musicians were not – *are* not – certain of recognition until they appeared and were accepted here. One of their number was credited with the invention of that celebrated nickname for the metropolis, when he said: "I made it, brother, I'm going to the Big Apple."

Jazz flourished and grew in New York from World War I into the 1950s. It hung on in the face of the onslaught of Elvis, The Beatles and their progeny. Now it is back, more vital than ever, and in all its permutations – Dixieland, swing, fusion, mainstream, bop, progressive, and wildly experimental. It is performed in old-line clubs on the scene for a half-century and in fifth-floor 'lofts' no more settled than Bedouins. Concerts are also mounted in the halls of colleges and churches all over town. Call the **Jazzline** – ☎423–0488 – for a daily recorded announcement. Here are 12 of the 50 possibilities.

Angry Squire
216 7th Ave. (23rd St.), NY 10011 ☎*242–9066. Map* **4** Q3
♪ *Open noon–2am (Fri, Sat noon–4am).*
Another pub-tavern contributing to the Chelsea renaissance, with fittingly British cookery that is at least as authentic as American hamburgers in London. Have a glass of ale from Blighty while attending to mainstream and hard bop.

Bradley's
70 University Pl. (11th St.), NY 10003 ☎*228–6440. Map* **2** R4
♀ ♪ AE ⊕ *Open 11:30am–3pm, 6:30pm–4am.*
Dim, smoky, bubbling with conversation. The burgers are

good and the progressive mainstream duos and trios at the end of the long bar even better. They tune up twice nightly, somewhere around 10pm and midnight. Another jazz pub in the neighborhood is **The Cookery**, just s on University Pl.

Eddie Condon's
144 W 54th St. (near 6th Ave.), NY 10010 ☎*265–8277. Map* **4** N3 ♀ ♪ AE ⊕ ⊕ *Open 10:30am–2pm. Closed Sun.*
Even middle-aged enthusiasts of Dixieland jazz can't remember when their music wasn't presented at some version of Condon's somewhere in the city. Far from reverential, this environment is noisy, crowded, and more

consistent with jazz origins than the hushed halls in which the music is often heard. **Jimmy Ryan's** is a few doors down the street.

The Cookery
21 University Pl. (8th St.), NY 10003 ☎674−4450. Map **2**R4 🎵 💿 🆅🅸🆂🅰 Open 11am−1am.
The Cookery is a light-filled luncheonette with butcher-block tables by day, but it sets out candles at dinner time and brings on piano and bass jazz duos. The incomparable Alberta Hunter is often the attraction, but the other artists are rarely less than first rate. Light meals are high to middle standard. Music is only on Tues−Sat from 8:30pm.

Fat Tuesday's
190 3rd Ave. (17th St.), NY 10003 ☎533−7902. Map **5**Q4 🍸 🎵 💿 🆅🅸🆂🅰 Open 8pm−3am. Closed Sun.
Once upon a time, this was Joe King's Rathskeller, a magnet for generations of collegians. The main floor hasn't changed, in spirit. Singles mingle, burgers are munched, pitchers of beer are quaffed. Downstairs is a separate place. Jazz prevails, largely of the progressive mainstream variety. There is a hefty cover charge, and the minimum is best consumed in liquid form. Sets are usually at 9pm, 11pm and, at weekends, 1am.

Jazzmania Society
40 W 27th St. (near 6th Ave.), NY 10001 ☎532−7666. Map **5**P4 🎵 ✤ Open 8pm−2am. Closed Mon.
This fourth-floor space in a nearly deserted neighborhood is the latest home for large bands of progressive bent. Couches on a raised platform overlook the stand, and there is more elbow room than normally associated with jazz clubs. The kitchen produces passable quiches and salads. There is an entrance fee and a minimum tariff. There is sometimes dancing.

Jimmy Ryan's
154 W 54th St. (near 6th Ave.), NY 10010 ☎664−9700. Map **4**N3 🍸 🎵 🆎 🆅🅸🆂🅰 Open 8pm−3am. Closed Sun, Mon.
Don't expect solicitous treatment. Just push up to the bar and bathe in Dixieland as pure as it gets in these parts. This qualifies as a landmark of the genre. But no food, no cover, no minimum and no warmth.

Michael's Pub
211 E 55th St. (near 3rd Ave.), NY 10022 ☎758−2272. Map **5**N5 🍸 🎵 🆎 💿 💿 🆅🅸🆂🅰 Open noon−1am.
In a dim, woody chain of rooms that suggests some fleeting exposure to the British pub, the music is by such able practitioners as Marian McPartland and George Shearing. On Mon, it shifts to Dixie, and Woody Allen is known to sit in at clarinet when he's in. Music is from 9:30pm.

Sweet Basil
88 7th Ave. (Bleecker St.), NY 10014 ☎242−1785. Map **2**R3 🍸 🎵 🆎 💿 🆅🅸🆂🅰 Open noon−3am.
Mainstream jazz in an attractive brick-and-wood setting, with such artists as Clark Terry and Chris Conner. Music starts at 10pm, or show up for Sun afternoon sessions and avoid the cover charge.

Village Gate
160 Bleecker St. (Thompson St.), NY 10012 ☎475−5120. Map **2**R4 🍸 🎵 ✤ Open Tues−Sat from 2am. Closed Sun, Mon.
Stability is not a characteristic of jazz emporia, but the 'Gate' grooves on, now in its third decade. Performers range from good to unsurpassed, their preferences from be-bop to fusion to salsa. They're housed in a large, comfortable, noisy room. Music starts from 10pm. The multilevel complex also puts on comedy acts, revues, theater, chamber music and anything else that might engage the management's interest.

Village Vanguard
178 7th Ave. (near 11th St.), NY 10011 ☎255−4037. Map **2**R3 🍸 🎵 Open 8pm−2am.
Landmark cellar club approaching its 50th anniversary. Mainstream jazz, mostly, starting 10pm.

West Boondock
114 10th Ave. (17th St.), NY 10011 ☎929−9645. Map **4**Q2 🍸 🎵 🆎 🆑🅱 💿 💿 🆅🅸🆂🅰 Open 6pm−2am.
The crumbling West Side Highway looms overhead and shuttered meat-packing houses glower on all sides − not a gracious setting. But the interior is warm and friendly, and the southern soul food authentic. All that is a backdrop for some of the best mainstream jazz in town.

Nightlife

Opera

Full-scale productions are mounted during extended seasons of the Metropolitan Opera Company and the New York City Opera at the **Metropolitan Opera House** (*Lincoln Center* ☎ *580-9830*) and the **New York State Theater** (*Lincoln Center* ☎ *870-5570*).

Gilbert and Sullivan fans support a year-long season at the **Light Opera of Manhattan** (*334 E 74th St.* ☎ *861-2288*).

Singing principals of these and other companies perform in concerts in other venues around the city, including:

Brooklyn Academy of Music   30 Lafayette Ave. (downtown Brooklyn) ☎636-4100
Carnegie Hall   57th St. and 7th Ave. ☎247-7459
Kaufman Concert Hall   1395 Lexington Ave. ☎427-4410
Town Hall   123 W 43rd St. ☎840-2824

Amateurs and young professionals form the companies of the **Amato Opera Theater** (*319 Bowery* ☎ *228-8200*) and the **Bel Canto Opera** (*220 E 76th St.* ☎ *535-5231*).

Pop/folk/rock

Some of these clubs have survived decades of changing fashions, but most opened yesterday and will close tomorrow. Always call ahead to learn of scheduled acts, prices, dress codes and present policies. See also *Country and western*.

Bottom Line
15 W 4th St. (near Washington Sq.), NY 10003 ☎ *228-7880. Map 2R4* ♩ ♫ *Open 8pm-2am.*

Lines form days in advance for tickets to the celebrated acts, more likely to appear here than anywhere else in the city. One-night stands are the rule for a catholic schedule of top performers leavened with groups the management judges to be on the way up. Any musical persuasion might show up – bluegrass, New Wave, folk, blues, jazz, pop.

CBGB & OMFUG
315 Bowery (Bleecker St.), NY 10012 ☎ *982-4052. Map 2R4* ♥ ♫ *Open 9pm-4am.*

Once the home of imported British punk, this grungy but unintimidating ex-garage now promotes less nihilistic New Wave rockers. For those under 30, a visit now qualifies as a nostalgia trip.

Irving Plaza
17 Irving Pl. (15th St.), NY 10003 ☎ *982-4863. Map 5Q4* ♩ ♫ *Open Fri, Sat only 10pm-4am.*

A relaxed spot as rock palaces go, with room to move about and a balcony from which to view the action. It may be expanding its schedule to other nights, with a menu of reggae, funk, country rock, New Wave, salsa, whatever.

Max's Kansas City
213 Park Ave. (near 17th St.), NY 10003 ☎ *777-7871. Map 5Q4* ♥ ♩ ♫ ♥ AE ⊙ ⊙ VISA *Open 11pm-4am.*

Two floors, two bars, dining downstairs, music upstairs. Max's has survived every social and musical fad of the last two decades – indeed, has helped create the new ones. Expect crowds in often outlandish costumes, and behavior that deviates from community norms.

The Mudd Club
77 White St. (near Broadway), NY 10013 ☎ *227-7777. Map 2T4* ♩ ♫ *Open 11pm-4am.*

Punk music was the reason for the Mudd Club, and at least the purple spiky hair and related accouterments persist. New Wave now dominates, but blues shouters and 'now' musical conceits are also on display. Uptowners swarm to the doors of this far-downtown TriBeCa venue, and admission is not a certainty. Those who make it inside needn't leave until dawn.

The Other End
147 Bleecker St. (near La Guardia Pl.), NY 10012 ☎ *673-7030. Map 2R4* ♩ ♫ ♥ *Open 3pm-4am (Sat, Sun 3pm-3am).*

Since the 1960s, when it was 'The Bitter End' and showcased Bob Dylan and Joni Mitchell, this has been one of the most influential rooms in New York. It is still snug and plain, but with an unusually good sound system and acoustics. Genres represented run from folk to jazz to rock and their subspecies. Shows are usually at 9pm and midnight, but call ahead.

Peppermint Lounge

128 W 45th St. (near Broadway), NY 10036 ☎*796–3176. Map 4O3* ● ♫ 🍸 *Open 10pm–4am. Closed Mon, Tues.*

The *numero uno* rock-and-roll club in town – at this very instant. The name lives as the birthplace of the 'Twist' (for those who can remember). Now it favors New Wave and allied forms. When entrance can be wangled, the live shows start up around midnight and continue until dawn.

The Ritz

119 E 11th St. (Park Ave. S), NY 10003 ☎*228–8888. Map 2R4* ♫ ♫ 🍸 *Open 8pm–4am.*

One of the new strain of big rock palaces that care how they look as well as sound. This Art Deco lounge is the place for ageing rock fans (i.e. the over 30s) who don't want to be the oldest people in the room. Attractions are up-and-coming New Wave bands and reggae groups. Shows don't start until midnight.

Tramps

125 E 15th St. (near Irving Pl.), NY 10003 ☎*777–5077. Map 5Q4* ♫ ♫ AE CO VISA *Open 8pm–4am.*

Blues in all its variations is the staple, although experimental jazz features from time to time. Comfortable tavern atmosphere.

Theater

Broadway, the avenue, long ago gave its name to Broadway, the theater district. Few of the approximately 40 theaters actually front on to that thoroughfare, however. Rather, they cluster around Times Sq, the intersection of Broadway and 7th Ave. Here are the lavish musicals, popular intimate comedies and, against heavy odds, occasional serious dramas.

Economics mitigated against experimentation, so that role was traditionally assumed by what came to be known as 'Off-Broadway' – smaller houses with lower overheads and greater daring. Many of these are found in and near Greenwich Village, but they are also located throughout Manhattan. In recent years they have grown somewhat more wary, in effect serving as a pre-Broadway tryout circuit, although few productions manage the long step into the big time. Alternative theater, often raw and wildly avant-garde, is known as 'Off-Off-Broadway.' These productions – happenings – are mounted in garages, churches, lofts, back rooms of restaurants, galleries, anywhere.

Good seats at a hit musical are extremely expensive; and seats are not cheap even at the back of the auditorium. There are ways to reduce the bite, however. Productions nearing the end of their runs issue 'twofer' passes to shops and hotels: take these to the box office of the appropriate theater and receive two tickets for the price of one. Or, visit the **TKTS** booth at the N end of Times Sq. after 3pm on the day you wish to attend. Last-minute cancellations and unsold seats are made available at substantial discounts, although not for all plays, of course.

Many theaters sell tickets through **Chargit** (☎*944–9300 and have a major credit card ready*), a service which takes the card number, adds a small service charge, and advises the box office to have the tickets ready for you at a specified time. Some theaters will do this directly. There are also dozens of **Ticketron** outlets throughout the city and suburbs at which tickets can be purchased for most Broadway and Off-Broadway productions (and concerts and sports events, too). Ticket brokers and hotel concierges can handle requests, but make certain that their handling fee will not exceed the going rate.

Shopping

All the world's goods pour into Manhattan. There is no material need, and few of the psychic kind, that is not supplied by its shops and stores. Many objects and services are offered at heart-stopping prices, but more often at costs equal to or below those of the countries of origin. Peruvian folk art to Japanese video recorders, Belgian lace to Colombian emeralds, Florentine leather to Chinese porcelain – if it isn't here, somewhere, it probably isn't worth having. Those who shop as a form of recreation cannot exhaust the possibilities for diversion. Those who regard it as a chore can, with prior research, march into a single shop and emerge minutes later with the precise product required.

At this center of the nation's garment industry, clothing is available in bewildering profusion. Milanese and Parisian couture are represented, of course, often in salons devoted exclusively to the work of a single house. Native designers challenge them on every front, especially in sportswear and ready-to-wear. Part of the success of Calvin Klein, Bill Blass, Geoffrey Beene, Halston, Ralph Lauren and Anne Klein is attributable to their willingness to design for broader markets. While custom tailoring is still available, careful sizing in both men's and women's ready-to-wear garments largely eliminates the need. The better shirts, for example, are calibrated in both neck and sleeve size, and dresses are proportioned to body type – petite, junior, misses, women's – as well as size.

Photographic and home electronic equipment is consistently sold below list price. High volume permits this and heavy competition requires it. Many camera dealers bypass the US distributors, for example, to purchase directly from Japanese manufacturers, thereby eliminating intermediate price rises. With over 90% of the nation's publishers quartered here, discounting of new books is widespread, all languages are represented, and rare and out-of-print volumes are quickly located. Specialization reigns, as with shops that concentrate exclusively on Marxism, homosexuality, feminism, travel or detective novels. Jewelry and unset gems, musical instruments, kitchenware and fashion accessories are of the highest quality and at accessible prices.

The picture is not entirely blue sky and clear sailing, of course. Objects of substantial age, such as antiques or Oriental carpets, are available in quantity, but are invariably overpriced. Be wary, too, of stores that proclaim in foot-high letters that they are going out of business: some of them have had those signs up for years. Check labels and identifications carefully, especially of watches and electronic equipment. Unknown brands aren't worth the risk, and some are made to look like products of reputable companies, right down to names with only one letter changed. Street vendors peddle scarves, umbrellas, belts, almost anything portable. Their prices are low, but remember that they move about and might not be at the same site tomorrow.

Weekday mornings are the best times to shop, lunch hours and Sat the worst. The only days on which virtually everything is closed are Thanksgiving (last Thurs in Nov), Christmas and New Year's Day. Other holidays are used as an excuse for sales. Although Sun is still usually a day off, many large stores now open on Sun afternoon. As a rule, midtown shops are open from 9:30 or 10am until 6pm, Mon–Sat, with late closing, 8 or 9pm, on Thurs eve. Elsewhere, the hours reflect the religious convictions or lifestyles of the communities. In Bohemian Greenwich Village and SoHo, doors may not open until noon, but close as late as midnight. Jewish-owned businesses of the Lower East Side are closed Fri afternoon and Sat, but open Sun. In the nine-to-five world of the Wall St. area, many shops close Sat as well as Sun.

Sales personnel, being New Yorkers, can be brusque or helpful, irritable or patient. For no obvious reason, assistants in camera stores and luxury clothing emporia are testy and/or indifferent in undue proportions. Generally, however, encounters will be pleasant and informative. While department stores are logical first stops in the quest of two or more unrelated items, they are frequently under-staffed and the wait can be long at the payment and wrapping counter. Items of a more specific or unusual nature are more easily found in smaller shops. Their owners, fearing crime, often keep their doors locked, buzzing them open only after making snap judgements of potential clients. On that subject, incidentally, take care never to leave a handbag or wallet on a counter while signing a sales slip or examining goods. They can be snatched in an instant.

Credit cards are widely accepted, even in the smallest shops, although a minimum purchase price might be stipulated. Travelers cheques are *not* regarded as simply another form of money. Supplementary identification is often required, and cheques drawn in another currency are invariably refused. Personal checks from out-of-town banks are not welcomed, but individual managers can sometimes be persuaded to take them, with two or more types of identification, if the customer appears trustworthy.

While diversity prevails – a florist next to a hardware store next to a travel agency – certain streets and neighborhoods have taken on distinct commercial identities, with regard to either cost or similarity of merchandise. Even casual window-shoppers gravitate to the stretch of 5th Ave. from about 47th St. to 57th St., a half-mile of world-famous clothiers, jewelers, booksellers and purveyors of superior luggage and shoes. The same distinction applies along 57th St., especially between 1st Ave. and 5th Ave. Antique hunters and art lovers will want to explore Madison Ave., from 57th St. to 80th. Tucked between the galleries are scores of boutiques trafficking in leather goods, pet supplies, lingerie, materials for needlework, and clothing geared to expectant mothers, debutantes, urban cowboys and country squires.

Before settling on **Tiffany's** or **Cartier**, stroll both sides of 47th St. between 5th Ave. and 6th Ave. for a boggling pageant of jewelry and precious stones of every description and price. For art galleries, see *Guide to the galleries* in *Culture, history and background*. For discount designer and mass clothing, make the excursion to Orchard St. (see *Walk 4* in *Planning*). For photographic equipment, head for 34th St. near Herald Sq. or for Lexington Ave. between 42nd St. and 52nd St. Crafts and offbeat articles of clothing are apparent on a gallery tour of SoHo and along the blocks of W 4th St. and Greenwich Ave., just W of 7th Ave. in Greenwich Village. The compilation that follows in the next few pages does no more than sketch the highlights.

Shops are open normal hours (9:30 or 10am to 6pm) unless otherwise stated.

Antiques

If rarity and distinction are your criteria and cost is not, there
are dozens of exclusive dealers along 57th St., Madison Ave.
and the adjoining blocks. For 17th–19thC porcelain,
look at:

Antique Porcelain Company   48 E 57th St. (near Park Ave.)
☎758–2363
Robert E. Mann   1050 2nd Ave. (near 56th St.) ☎838–4301
Sarah Potter Conover   17 E 64th St. ☎861–0515
James Robinson   12 E 57th St. (near 5th Ave.) ☎752–6166

Fine European furniture of the same period can be
viewed at:
French & Co.   17 E 65th St. (near 5th Ave.) ☎535–3330
Old Versailles   152 E 52nd St. (near Lexington Ave.)
☎753–4479
Gene Tyson   19 E 69th St. (near 5th Ave.) ☎744–5785

Overseas visitors may be more interested in early American
furnishings, quilts, funky tat and folk arts. Among shops
focusing on these are:
American Hurrah   316 E 70th St. (near 2nd Ave.)
☎535–1930
Bashful Bear   95 E 10th St. (near 3rd Ave.) ☎533–1465
Equator   459 Broome St. (in SoHo) ☎925–5905
Inglenook Antiques   529 Hudson St. (in Greenwich Village)
☎675–0890
Poor Richard's Antiques   369 2nd Ave. (near 23rd St.)
☎677–6064
Somethin' Else   182 9th Ave. (in Chelsea) ☎924–0006
Spirit of America   269 W 4th St. (in Greenwich Village)
☎255–3255

The multi-floored antique galleries of London and Paris have
their counterparts here, too. While rewards for the diligent do
not qualify as bargains, there can be good buys, somewhat
below the stratospheric price ranges of the shops already
mentioned. Dealers in silver, enamel, crystal, music boxes,
vintage clothing, china, paperweights, brassware and every
category of bric-a-brac lease space at:
Manhattan Art and Antiques Center   1050 2nd Ave. (56th St.)
☎355–4400 (85 stalls)
New York Antique and Flea Market   145 E 23rd St. (near
Lexington Ave.) ☎777–9609 (20 shops)
SoHo Canal Flea Market   369 Canal St. (near W. Broadway)
☎266–8724 (45 stalls)

Auction houses

Auctions are a source of enlightenment and entertainment even
for those who have no intention of bidding. For a recorded
announcement of the week's sales at these and other auction
houses ☎977–2579.

Christie's
504 Park Ave. (near 59th St.), NY 10022 ☎546–1000. Map **5N4**.
Closest in stature to **Sotheby Parke Bernet**, Christie's is also a British
house and nearly as comprehensive in its offerings.

Sotheby Parke Bernet
1334 York Ave. (72nd St.), NY 10021 ☎472–3400. Map
7M5.
This result of a merger of British and American firms continues to hold
center stage. It deals in snuff boxes, folk arts, antiquities, Oriental
carpets, Impressionist paintings, toys, Judaica, Art Nouveau –
everything.

Beauty salons and hairdressers

Once the exclusive province of women, both skin-care centers and hairstylists now cater to men as well. The former retain their markedly feminine decor and emphasis, despite the fact that as much as 40% of their clientele is male. Hairdressers are increasingly uni-sexual (one might say multi-sexual) in character.

Facial treatments typically take an hour to an hour and a half. Inevitably, there are soft-sell efforts by attendants to sign you up for repeat sessions and costly cleansers, creams and lotions. Advance booking is essential. Among the salons that serve both men and women are:

Gabriel   15 Park Ave. (35th St.) ☎683–1639
Anne Keane   16 W 57th St. (near 5th Ave.) ☎586–2803
Georgette Klinger   501 Madison Ave. (52nd St.) ☎838–3200
Klisar   18 E 53rd St. (near 5th Ave.) ☎838–4422
Lea Schorr   527 Madison Ave. (54th St.) ☎486–9670
Christine Valmy   767 5th Ave. (58th St.) ☎752–0303

For shampoo, cut and blow-dry, try the following hairstylists. Appointments are not always required, but call ahead for hours and rates.

Bob Bent   204 Waverly Pl. (near 10th St.) ☎255–6473
Michael Kazan   16 E 55th St. (near 5th Ave.) ☎688–1400
Kenneth   19 E 54th St. (near 5th Ave.) ☎752–1800
Larry Mathews   536 Madison Ave. (near 54th St.)
☎246–6100
Vidal Sassoon   767 5th Ave. (near 58th St.) ☎535–9200

Books and records

Barnes and Noble
600 5th Ave. (near 48th St.), NY 10017 ☎*765–0590. Map **5**O4* AE CD VISA *Open also Sun noon–5pm.*
One of a chain, this outlet concentrates on recent books at a discount. The selection is limited, but there are many bargains.

Brentano's
586 5th Ave. (near 47th St.), NY 10036 ☎*757–8600. Map **5**O4* AE CD VISA
The substantial stocks of books are supplemented by gifts, posters, games and records.

Doubleday
724 5th Ave. (57th St.), NY 10019 ☎*397–0550. Map **5**N4* AE CB ◊ CD VISA *Open until midnight.*
Large three-level store. Every category is covered, with a marked emphasis on the performing arts. The shop sells records, too.

Sam Goody
666 3rd Ave. (near E 43rd St.), NY 10017 ☎*986–8480. Map **5**O4* AE ◊ CD VISA *Open also Sun noon–5pm.*
Records and tapes in all categories,

and at a discount. Audio equipment, musical instruments and sheet music are also on sale. Another branch at 235 W 49th St.

King Karol
126 W 42nd St. (near Broadway), NY 10036 ☎*354–6880. Map **4**O3* AE CD VISA *Open also Sun 11am–8pm.*
With a comprehensive stock of old and new records in all cateories; what it does not have it can quickly obtain.

Murder Ink
271 W 87th St. (near West End Ave.), NY 10024 ☎*362–8905. Map **6**K2* CD VISA
Bookshop dealing exclusively in crime mysteries.

New York Bound Bookshop
43 W 54th St. (near 5th Ave.), NY 10019 ☎*245–8106. Map **5**N4.*
Although it specializes in rare and out-of-print books about New York, what attracts clients to this shop is its axonometric maps of midtown Manhattan, on which buildings are reproduced right down to the steps and construction cranes.

Rizzoli
*712 5th Ave. (near 56th St.), NY
10019* ☎ *397–3700. Map* **5**N4
AE O CB VISA
The New York outlet of the
prestigious Italian publisher, with
books in several European
languages and classical
background music in keeping with
its studied elegance.

Scribner's
*597 5th Ave. (near 48th St.), NY
10017* ☎ *486–4070. Map* **5**O4
AE CB VISA
A retail subsidiary of the
publishers of Hemingway and
Fitzgerald, in a handsome space
with a balcony and high ceiling. In
front, the hardbacks concentrate
on art history, travel and children's
books. There is a paperback gallery
in the rear.

Strand
*828 Broadway (12th St.), NY
10003* ☎ *473–1452. Map* **2**R4.
Open also Sun 11am–5pm.
Rack after rack and shelf after shelf
of mostly used books in a gratifying
clutter that ensnares book lovers
for hours. Reviewers and critics
sell off their advance copies, which
are thus available here at discounts.

Cameras and photographic equipment
Sales and discounts are the rule in this enormously competitive
field. Check the full-page ads in the Sun *New York Times* before
setting out. Profit margins are slashed to the bone, which makes
some floor managers irritable when you inquire if they will
match the lower price for the same lens or projector at a store
down the street. Ask anyway. When making a purchase, be
certain it is handed over in a sealed factory carton. Most shops
below are open seven days a week, and take major credit cards.

Camera World
104 W 32nd St. (near 6th Ave.), NY 10001 ☎ *563–8770. Map* **5**P4.
Nearly as well-stocked as **Willoughby's**, and holding frequent sales. It
makes a point of carrying electrical products in foreign voltages.

Grand Central Cameras
420 Lexington Ave. (near 44th St.), NY 10017 ☎ *986–2270. Map*
5O4.
The personnel have proved consistently helpful and the prices are good.

Hirsch Photo
699 3rd Ave. at 44th St., NY 10017 ☎ *557–1150. Map* **5**O4.
Prides itself on its attentiveness to individual needs.

Willoughby's
Main branch at 110 W 32nd St. (near 7th Ave.), NY 10001
☎ *564–1600. Map* **4**P3.
The largest of the photographic stores. Willoughby's accept trade-ins
and members of staff speak several languages.

Clothing and shoes for men

Barney's
7th Ave. and 17th St., NY 10011
☎ *929–9000. Map* **4**Q3 💻 AE
CB VISA
Within the memory of most of its
customers, Barney's was an out-of-
the-way discount house that drew
them to inconvenient Chelsea with
promises of bargains. Those low-
priced days are gone, but now men
of every shape, height and girth
come for the unrivaled range of
garments in all sizes and fashions.
They have installed a coffee shop in
which to consider whether the Wall
St. or Via Condotti look is for you.

Brooks Brothers
*346 Madison Ave. (44th St.), NY
10017* ☎ *682–8800. Map* **5**O4
AE
In an aberrant world, there is
Brooks. Tradition cleaves to its
stately spaces. This is the 165yr-old
home of the natural-shoulder suit
preferred by American business
leaders and those who aspire to
succeed them. The classic detailing
is altered in deference to current
fashion only by quarter-inches,
and the trenchcoat purchased in
1959 is much the same as the one
bought yesterday.

Custom Shop
*555 Lexington Ave. (50th St.),
NY 10022* ☎ *759–7480. Map
5O4* AE ⊙ CB VISA
Men of proportions that don't
quite fit off-the-shelf shirts – thick
neck, short arms; thin neck, long
arms – can stop here for made-to-
measure cottons and cotton blends
that cost little more than average,
depending on fabric and collar
style. There is a minimum order of
four, however. Buy your ties
somewhere else.

Dunhill Tailors
*65 E 57th St. (near Park Ave.),
NY 10022* ☎ *355–0050. Map
5N4* AE CB VISA
It also sells ready-made suits, but
its reputation is for custom
tailoring in English cuts and
fabrics. That Cary Grant has been a
steady client should be sufficient
recommendation. Expect to pay
handsomely for a suit that will last
decades.

The Gap
*145 E 42nd St. (near 3rd Ave.),
NY 10017* ☎ *286–9490. Map
5O4* VISA *Open also Sun
noon–6pm.*
This and seven other branches
throughout Manhattan purvey
jeans in every style, color and size –
but from reputable manufacturers,
not overpriced, shoddy, bootleg
products – also some tops and
related sportswear.

Merns Mart
*525 Madison Ave. (near 54th
St.), NY 10022* ☎ *371–9175.
Map 5N4* CB VISA *Closed Sat,
Sun.*
Discounts of 25%–50% on
American and European menswear
of middle quality, with some
surprising buys (and some
regrettable errors) to be found
among racks of shirts, slacks,
jeans, sports jackets and suits. It
also offers shoes, belts and a
selection of women's clothes.

Paul Stuart
*Madison Ave. and 45th St., NY
10017* ☎ *682–0320. Map 5O4*
AE ⊙ CB VISA
For the British-American or mid-
Atlantic look, Paul Stuart has suits

and sports jackets in a subdued
palette of checks, herringbones,
flannels and twills. The armholes
are higher than those of the equally
traditional **Brooks Brothers**, the
shoulders are squared, the waists
ever-so-slightly more suppressed.
Most are of natural fibers, but
there are some blends. Shirts come
in an unusually broad range of
sizes. There is a small women's
department. The prices are
middling to high.

A. Sulka
*711 5th Ave. (55th St.), NY
10022* ☎ *980–5200. Map 5N4*
AE ⊙ CB VISA
Made-to-measure silk shirts are the
ultimate luxury in this exclusive
shop, but there are also suits, coats
and accessories of comparably high
standard. Monogrammed
handkerchiefs make an affordable
gift, custom cashmere bathrobes
do not.

Sym's
*45 Park Pl. (near Church St.), NY
10007* ☎ *791–1199. Map 2T4.*
One of the more prominent
discount men's stores by virtue of
its insistent TV advertising, Sym's
takes a center path in fashion and
delivers good value. The labels are
left in the garments so the customer
can have an idea of their origins,
and the original list price is
followed on the tag with the Sym's
price. Those willing to examine
carefully three floors of racks and
counters can emerge with twice as
much clothing as the same
expenditure would obtain
midtown, and that is the
temptation.

Victory Shirt Company
*345 Madison Ave. (near 45th
St.), NY 10017* ☎ *687–6375.
Map 5O4* AE ⊙ CB VISA
A boon to the odd-size man or
woman who doesn't care to pay for
custom tailoring. Victory makes
100% cotton shirts of made-to-
measure quality at ready-made
prices. Some sweaters and ties are
available, all in natural fibers.
Monograms and alterations are
extra. There are two more
branches at 10 Maiden Lane and 96
Orchard St.

Clothing and shoes for women

Betsey, Bunky and Nini
*746 Madison Ave. (near 65th
St.), NY 10021* ☎ *744–6716.*

Map 7M4 AE CB VISA
With a name like that, one expects
something adorable, and gets it,

with peachy tones, flower-
stenciled walls and rather more
ruffles and flounces than are
absolutely necessary. Individual
separates are sleek and well-
constructed, however, with
examples both from the house
designer and from others.

Boutique Valentino
*677 5th Ave. (near 53rd St.), NY
10022* ☎*421–7550. Map* **5***N4*
AE O CB VISA

The nearly legendary Valentino
permits us to gaze on his trend-
anticipating lines of dresses,
sweaters and separates, and to
marvel at fabrics and sartorial
details; and at very high prices.

Fiorucci
*125 E 59th St. (near Park Ave.),
NY 10022* ☎*751–5638. Map*
5*N4* AE CB VISA

Have an espresso while
contemplating startling,
imaginative and often popularly
priced clothes that bear no
allegiance to any fashion schools.
Everyone calls it 'fun'; and
certainly no-one who walks out in
one of these zingy tops or slacks
will lack attention.

Gucci
*685 5th Ave. (54th St.), NY
10022* ☎*826–2600. Map* **5***N4*
AE CB VISA

Despite the not-unwarranted
reputation of the sales staff for
sullenness, flocks of moneyed
patrons storm these four floors
daily (not Sun). They are men and
women who admire fine Italian
craftsmanship in leather goods –
shoes, belts, handbags and luggage
– and don't mind wearing someone
else's initials – the famed double G.

Halston
*813 Madison Ave. (68th St.), NY
10021* ☎*744–9033. Map* **7***M4*
AE VISA

Halston, arguably America's high
fashion doyen, and certainly the
designer closest in sensibility to the
Paris houses, lets nothing in the
way of clothes and accessories
escape his attention. Resort wear to
evening dress, gloves to perfumes –
all are supplanted four or five times
a year with fresh ideas.

Charles Jourdan
*700 5th Ave. (55th St.), NY
10022* ☎*541–8440. Map* **5***N4*
AE O CB VISA

Imported French shoes of
frolicsome panache – wispy
sandals, and shoes in frothy hues,
lighter than air but remarkably
long-lived. There are men's shoes,
too, but they are much more
traditional. All are expensive.

Emilio Pucci
*24 E 64th St. (near Madison
Ave.), NY 10021* ☎*752–8957.
Map* **7***M4* AE O CB VISA

'Signature' blouses, bags, etc., in
sprightly tints; also perfumes.

Saint Laurent Rive Gauche
*855 Madison Ave. (near 70th
St.), NY 10021* ☎*988–3821.
Map* **7***M4* AE O CB VISA

From the striking front to the
metal-and-leather interior, this
boutique sizzles with the products of
the restless mind of the
celebrated French designer.
Shirts, trousers, shoes, dresses,
suits, belts are at the leading edge
of fashion.

Yves St Tropez
*4 W 57th St. (near 5th Ave.), NY
10019* ☎*759–3784. Map* **5***N4*
AE CB VISA

Ethereal *crêpe de chine*, buttery-soft
cottons, silks that feel like baby's
skin, furs tinted pearl and rose – all
the ingredients of the wardrobe for
a jet-setting weekend beneath this
year's Alp.

Unique Clothing Warehouse
*718 Broadway (Washington
Pl.), NY 10003* ☎*674–1767.
Map* **2***R4* AE O CB *Open also
on Sun noon–5:45pm.*

As an antidote to the jasmine and
musk air of the 5th Ave. boutiques,
or simply because it's Sunday,
drop down to Greenwich Village.
This repository of rugged working
man's apparel and military
uniforms was the first, it is said, to
recognize the inherent chic of such
things. A few years later, the
Parisian and Milanese couturiers
were turning out their own
versions for the Côte d'Azur. The
prices are good, but the quality
is variable so choose carefully.

Department stores

B. Altman & Co
5th Ave. and 34th St., NY 10016
☎*679–7800. Map* **5***P4* AE

Open Thurs until 8pm.
Perhaps it hasn't the cachet of
other stores farther N along 5th

Ave., but this long-established emporium (founded in 1865) manages to display similar goods at slightly less inflated prices. As a bonus, the staff are as courteous and as helpful as any in the city. Go there primarily for home furnishings and clothing.

Henri Bendel
10 W 57th St. (near 5th Ave.), NY 10019 ☎*247–1100. Map 5N4* AE CB VISA
While it avoids the flashy, Bendel's is at the forefront of fashion trends, at least among department stores. A step inside the door and a peek at size labels reveals that the cautious and/or amply proportioned shopper would best spend time elsewhere. Clothes boutiques take up the first floor, but there are five more floors above in which to consider stationery, table linens, shoes, cosmetics, household ware.

Bergdorf Goodman
754 5th Ave. (57th St.), NY 10022 ☎*752–0303. Map 5N4* AE *Open Thurs until 8pm.*
On what is perhaps the most glamorous corner in New York, Bergdorf's follows through with unrivaled service and products. Furs, lingerie, fragrances, linens are of the highest order. To a degree, the store is shelter to the glossy boutiques of Givenchy, Halston, Saint Laurent and their like. Men who can afford the tariffs are drawn to the Turnbull & Asser counter for shirts.

Bloomingdale's
1000 3rd Ave. (59th St.), NY 10022 ☎*355–5900. Map 5N5* AE *Open Mon, Thurs until 9pm.*
Multitudes of New Yorkers and suburbanites slavishly follow the dictates of the great guru Bloomingdale, denying all the while that their sitting rooms are replicas of those in the store, that they dress like the models in the Sat newspaper ads, that the food they eat imitates the delights of the gourmet shops on the ground floor. They need not be defensive, for they could hardly find a better model to follow. In the evening and on Sat they are as likely to drop in just to watch people similarly afflicted as to buy anything.

Gimbel's
Broadway and 33rd Sts., NY 10001 ☎*564–3300. Map 5P4* AE CB VISA *Open Mon, Thurs, Fri to 8:30, Sun noon–5pm.*
The traditional rival to **Macy's**, across Herald Sq., Gimbel's has fallen behind in recent years. Product lines and prices are still competitive, but it lacks the perkiness of its competitor, which is forever seeking ways to keep its name before the public. There is, in addition, another branch of Gimbel's (*86th St. in the Upper East Side*) which partially succeeds in closing the gap between the two rivals.

Lord & Taylor
424 5th Ave. (39th St.), NY 10016 ☎*391–3344. Map 5O4* AE *Open Thurs until 8pm.*
Whether you want a cashmere sweater or a chair, curtain fabric or a crystal bowl, buy it here and it will remain a classic until its natural demise. That might be later than your own, for Lord & Taylor has been around well over a century, and it has no intention of alienating coming generations. Known mainly for sportswear, it also employs interior decorators to advise on renovations both modest and ambitious. Decisions can be made in comfort over soup and salad in one of the store's three cafés.

Macy's
Broadway and 34th St., NY 10001 ☎*695–4400. Map 5P4* AE *Open Mon, Thurs, Fri until 8:30pm, Sun noon–5pm.*
In recent years, Macy's has moved to occupy the area between the bland middle ground and the snappy upper-middle ground represented by **Bloomingdale's**. Most welcome innovations are the repository of kitchenware and gourmet foods called The Cellar, and an uncanny reproduction of the trendy Irish saloon, **P. J. Clarke's**. The largest store in the world (so they claim) has something for everyone, from antiques to puppet shows, high fashion to tableware.

Saks Fifth Avenue
611 5th Ave. (50th St.), NY 10022 ☎*753–4000. Map 5O4* AE CB *Open Thurs until 8:30pm.*
Scrupulously choreographed and relentlessly edited, Saks contrives to retain its classic image without allowing itself to descend into dowdiness. Clothes are its particular strength, from sports to formal wear, as delineated by Bill Blass, Oscar de la Renta and similar luminaries.

Food and kitchenware

New Yorkers have always been interested in food and cooking, if only to reproduce the cuisines of their homelands. The recent enthusiasm for gourmet cookery has intensified that concern, and these shops are booming. Try to avoid Sat.

Balducci's

422 6th Ave. (near 9th St.), NY 10011 ☎ *673–2600. Map 2R4* ⓐⓔ *Open daily 7am–8:30pm.*
Enter Balducci's immediately after a large meal, or your eyes will grow round as billiard balls and you will be seized with a compulsion to sweep up chunks of everything in sight. You will be in competition with milling throngs anxious to get their hands on the very same cheeses, pastries, choice vegetables, thick slabs of prime meats, ringlets of homemade sausages, smoked fishes, or lobsters. Absolute freshness of produce and ingredients in cooked or baked products is the norm. It is always busy.

Bridge Kitchenware

214 E 52nd St. (near 2nd Ave.), NY 10022 ☎ *688–4220. Map 5N5* ⓒ ⓥⓘⓢⓐ
The shelves are packed with quality utensils for the serious cook. Pick through stainless carbon knives by several manufacturers, food processors, graters, coffee grinders, bowls of steel and ceramic, copper molds, crystal. The prices are neither exorbitant nor low, they are simply fair.

Caviarteria

29 E 60th St. (near Madison Ave.), NY 10022 ☎ *759–7410. Map 5N4* ⓐⓔ ⓒ ⓥⓘⓢⓐ *Open also Sun 9am–6pm except July, Aug.*
Unprepossessing inside and out, this small shop is easy to dismiss. But the distractedly helpful proprietor deals in the essentials of a calculated seduction or a dinner designed to impress. His caviar is Iranian, Russian and American. The last is a Californian experiment that appears to be succeeding, and at half the price of the imports. He also stocks smoked salmon, cheeses and related delicacies, and enjoys a large mail order trade.

Dean & DeLuca

121 Prince St. (SoHo), NY 10012 ☎ *254–7774. Map 2S4. Open also Sun 10am–6pm.*
Expensive, yes, but not unconscionably so, and the mark-up is justified merely by the aroma encountered at the front door: coffee, freshly baked bread, cheeses, fresh produce all contribute. At the squared counter in the center are baskets of exotic mushrooms, pâtés and terrines. Along one wall, an extraordinary selection of herbs; on the other, honeys and jams. And at the back, racks of kitchen utensils, including whisks and cast-iron pans and oven-usable stoneware. At Christmas, the management brings in fresh-killed rabbits, game birds and haunches of venison.

E.A.T.

869 Madison Ave. (72nd St.), NY 10021 ☎ *772–1586. Map 7M4* ⓐⓔ *Open also Sun 9am–5pm.*
This newer, larger branch is in a Gothic town house and the decor complements the architecture with checkered marble floors and ornamental balustrades. Prepared dishes and baked goods are made on the premises, from sourdough to pâtés to stuffed breast of chicken. Teas, jams, salmon and cheeses are imported. Visit the original store (*1064 Madison Ave.*), or there is an E.A.T. enclave in the **Henri Bendel's** department store.

Zabar's

2245 Broadway (near 80th St.), NY 10024 ☎ *787–2000. Map 6L2* ⓐⓔ ⓒ ⓓ ⓥⓘⓢⓐ *Open Mon–Thurs 8am–7:30pm, Fri until 10pm, Sat until midnight, Sun until 7pm.*
Balducci's and Zabar's are perennial contenders for the throne of gourmet shops, but Zabar's may have pulled ahead by virtue of its recent second-floor expansion for kitchenware. Absolute kitchen essentials – fish poachers and duck presses – take their place among food mills and copper pots. On the ground floor, cheese, coffee, caviar, smoked fish, prepared terrines and entrées, pumpernickel bread, ice cream, coffee cake, chopped liver, herring, and all manner of intoxicating sights and aromas battle for customers' attention.

Jewelry

From the waiting limousines to the understated window displays and the hushed, almost ecclesiastical interiors, **Cartier**, **Harry Winston**, **Tiffany & Co.** and **Van Cleef & Arpels**, the Titans of the retail trade in gold, gems, silver and watches, breathe an ever-tasteful opulence. Dress for the occasion. All of them have a well-crafted trinket or two at modest cost for recipients back home who are impressed by the name on the gift box.

Department-store marketing techniques are used by **Fortunoff**, and its stock is supplemented with crystal, flatware, clocks, antique jewelry and pewter. There are four floors and prices are reasonable, as these things go.

While all these shops are within a few steps of each other, true comparison shopping is best undertaken along 47th St., between 5th Ave. and 6th Ave. Every imaginable sort of jewelry is on hand in shoulder-to-shoulder (and floor-upon-floor) shops that sell nothing else. Start at the **International Jewelers Exchange**, with its dealers installed in 84 cubicles, then work w along 47th St., crossing to the opposite side and returning E. Prices are often negotiable, so it's best to delay purchase until several trays of the desired object have been examined.

Cartier   5th Ave. and 52nd St. ☎753–0111
Fortunoff   681 5th Ave. (near 54th St.) ☎758–6000
International Jewelers Exchange   5th Ave. and 47th St.
☎869–8600
Tiffany & Co.   5th Ave. and 57th St. ☎755–8000
Van Cleef & Arpels   5th Ave. and 57th St. ☎644–9500
Harry Winston   718 5th Ave. (near 56th St.) ☎245–2000

Museum shops

Cultural curiosity and the acquisitive impulse are handily combined in the gift and bookshops of all the major museums and most of the smaller ones. While selections naturally reflect the concerns of the museums in which they are located – seafaring motifs at the *South Street Seaport Museum*, folk art at the *Brooklyn Museum* – they interpret their missions with broad strokes. Given their auspices, trashy merchandise rarely slips onto the shelves. For the same reason, expect fair prices but no bargains. See *Sights and places of interest* for addresses and telephone numbers.

Predictably, the shop of the *Metropolitan Museum of Art* is largest, with excellent reproductions of many items in the collections as well as art books and illustrated catalogues. The *Museum of the American Indian* has handcrafted 'squash-blossom' necklaces, silver belt buckles, 'concha' belts, and Navajo rugs. Reproductions of Egyptian jewelry and authentic Latin American ceramics and dolls are the specialty of the *Brooklyn Museum*. Books and posters dominate at the *Museum of Modern Art* shop, but its design collection inspires exquisite glassware, pottery, flatware, cigarette lighters, garden shears and clocks. At the *Jewish Museum*, even Gentiles are drawn to the brass candlesticks and *menorahs*, *mezuzah* boxes, and the jewelry. Finally, there are quilts and crafts, antique and contemporary, to be enjoyed at the *Museum of American Folk Art*.

Pharmacies

Despite their fanciful European imitations, not all American drugstores resemble supermarkets. Most concentrate on the sale of cosmetics, perfumes, toiletries, assorted sickroom and surgical devices and, of course, prescription and non-prescription drugs. Be sure to bring along your doctor's prescription. Two of the oldest pharmacies in New York are **Caswell-Massey** (established 1752) and **Bigelow Pharmacy** (established 1838). The **Duane Reade** chain, with locations all over town, is noted for its discounts.

Bigelow Pharmacy
414 6th Ave. (near 8th St.), NY 10011 ☎ *533–2700. Map 2R4.*
Still in its original quarters, and open every day.

Caswell-Massey
518 Lexington Ave. (near 48th St.), NY 10017 ☎ *755–2254. Map 5O4. Closed Sun.*
Caswell-Massey blended soaps and colognes for George Washington and Sarah Bernhardt, and its products make good souvenirs.

Kaufman Pharmacy
Lexington Ave. and 50th St., NY 10022 ☎ *755–2266. Map 5O4.*
Open 24hr a day, seven days a week.

Sports and camping equipment

Athlete's Foot
16 W 57th St. (near 5th Ave.), NY 10022 ☎ *586–1936. Map 5N4.*
Runners stop here, or at one of its six branches, for its full line of footwear and warmup suits.

Herman's
Midtown branches at 135 W 42nd St. (near Times Sq.), NY 10036 ☎ *730–7400. Map 4O3. And 845 2nd Ave. (near E 51st St.), NY 10022* ☎ *688–4603. Map 5N5.*
One of the largest general sporting goods stores.

Hudson's
3rd Ave. and 13th St., NY 10003 ☎ *473–7321. Map 2R4.*
For camping and outdoor equipment.

Paragon
867 Broadway (near E 18th St.), NY 10003 ☎ *255–8036. Map 5Q4.*
Large stock of general sporting goods.

Spiegels
Nassau St. and Ann St., NY 10005 ☎ *227–8400. Map 2U4.*
For all sports goods in lower Manhattan.

Toys

It is tempting to begin and end with **F.A.O. Schwarz**, but there are other shops too. All of them will wrap and ship.

Childcraft Center
150 E 58th St. (Lexington Ave.), NY 10022 ☎ *753–3196. Map 5N4.*
Focuses on sturdy educational toys.

Penny Whistle
1281 Madison Ave. (near 91st St.), NY 10028 ☎ *369–3868. Map 7K4.*
Young patrons are actually encouraged to play with the dolls and games.

F.A.O. Schwarz
5th Ave. and 58th St., NY 10022 ☎ *644–9400. Map 5N4.*
A wonderland of fantasies even for the most cynical adult, it qualifies as a not-to-be-missed sight of the same order as the Empire State Building. Imagine 10ft-high stuffed giraffes, storybook villages complete with

dogs and street lamps, childsize cars that really work, marionettes,
electric trains and, of course, a vast selection of dolls, books and games
. . . . three floors of them.

Westside Toy Center
2305 Broadway (near 83rd St.), NY 10024 ☎*877–2060. Map* **6**L2.
Another leading toyshop.

Wines and spirits

Equidistant from the vineyards of France and California, New
York samples the vintages of Old World and New. Special sales
are frequent, sometimes of wine from unexpected countries –
Lebanon, Chile, Yugoslavia. Their advantage is price, of
course. Choices can be bewildering, but the sales people at the
following shops are helpful, and their wares are exemplary for
price and/or variety.

All are closed Sun and none accept credit cards. Most make
deliveries.

Astor Wines & Spirits   12 Astor Pl. (near Lafayette St.)
☎674–7500
Cork & Bottle   1158 1st Ave. (near 63rd St.) ☎838–5300
Embassy Liquors   796 Lexington Ave. (near 61st St.)
☎838–6551
Morrell & Co.   307 E 3rd St. (near 2nd Ave.) ☎688–9370
Sherry-Lehmann   679 Madison Ave. (near E 61st St.)
☎838–7500
Sokolin   178 Madison Ave. (near 34th St.) ☎ 532–5893

Clothing sizes

New Yorkers buying clothes with European labels, as well as
European visitors to the city, will find the following chart of
clothing sizes useful.

Clothing sizes
When shops give clothing sizes in inches or centimetres, use
the following conversion scale to determine the correct size

12 in	16	20	24	28	32	36	40	44	48
30 cm	40	50	60	70	80	90	100	110	120

When standardized codes are used, although these may be found
to vary considerably, the following provides a useful guide.

Women's clothing sizes

UK/US sizes	8/6	10/8	12/10	14/12	16/14	18/16
Bust in/cm	31/80	32/81	34/86	36/91	38/97	40/102
Hips in/cm	33/85	34/86	36/91	38/97	40/102	42/107

Men's clothing sizes

European code (suits)	44	46	48	50	52	54	56
Chest in/cm	34/86	36/91	38/97	40/102	42/107	44/112	46/117
Collar in/cm	13½/34	14/36	14½/37	15/38	15½/39	16/41	16½/42
Waist in/cm	28/71	30/76	32/81	34/86	36/91	38/97	40/102
Inside leg in/cm	28/71	29/74	30/76	31/79	32/81	33/84	34/86

Men's and women's shoe sizes

UK/US sizes	3/4½	4/5½	5/6½	6/7½	7/8½	8/9½	9/10½	10/11½	11/12½
European	36	37	38	39	40	41	42	43	44

Biographies

One of the most cosmopolitan of cities, New York has a history rich in memorable characters – among them the following are a representative selection.

Allen, Woody (born 1935)

The writer-actor-comedian-satirist-director is said to get the bends whenever he ventures beyond the city limits of New York. Nevertheless, by his own account, a Brooklyn childhood and an aborted career at New York University gave him little joy but much material for his *New Yorker* magazine essays and his films *Annie Hall* and *Manhattan*.

Beecher, Henry Ward (1813–87)

A minister, lecturer, author and firebrand abolitionist, he was also the older brother of Harriet Beecher Stowe, who wrote *Uncle Tom's Cabin*. His pulpit was the Plymouth Church on Orange St. in Brooklyn Heights.

Booth, Edwin (1833–93)

Often cited as the first important American actor, Booth made his permanent home in New York. His career was blighted after his brother, John Wilkes, killed Abraham Lincoln.

Bryant, William Cullen (1794–1878)

Best known as a poet, Bryant made his living as a reform-minded editor of the *Evening Post* (1826–78). He is credited with prodding the city into the development of Central Park.

Burr, Aaron (1756–1836)

In a checkered political career that saw him lose as many elections as he won, Burr's highest post was Vice-President to Thomas Jefferson. The image of Burr as an amoral schemer gained strength from his shooting of Alexander Hamilton in a duel and from the plan, attributed to him, to establish an independent republic in the southwest. He was tried for treason and acquitted, but never re-entered public life.

Fulton, Robert (1765–1815)

Talented and energetic, Fulton's curiosity led him to careers in painting, gunsmithing, civil engineering and the invention of ambitious mechanical devices. Although he was not the creator of the steamboat, as is widely believed, his *Clermont* (1807) was the first profitable version.

Greeley, Horace (1811–72)

After his arrival in New York at the age of 21, Greeley worked as a printer, editor and newspaper columnist. He founded *The New Yorker* (1834) and the *Tribune* (1841) and edited them, in various combinations, for over 30yr. Although initially considered a conservative, he advocated women's suffrage, abolition of slavery, labour unions and experiments in communal living, all daring stands at that time.

Hamilton, Alexander (1755–1804)

Born out of wedlock in the West Indies, Hamilton came to New York to study at King's College in 1773. His anonymous writings on behalf of the Revolutionary cause drew much attention, as did his service on the battlefield and as General Washington's aide. An influential delegate to the Continental Congress at 25, he was one of the leading proponents of the Constitution drafted by Jefferson. Undeniably brilliant, he nevertheless made many enemies. One of them, **Aaron Burr**, mortally wounded him in a duel in 1804.

Henry, O. (1862–1910)

The pen name of William S. Porter, a short-story writer noted for his tight plots and surprise endings, exemplified in *Gift of the*

Magi. He began writing in prison, to which he was sentenced for embezzlement. Most of his literary production was in the last 10yr of his life, spent in New York.

Hopper, Edward (1882–1973)

Born in a small town on the Hudson River, Hopper moved in young adulthood to Greenwich Village. The muted, melancholy cityscapes of this Realist painter began to gain favour in the 1920s, although they ran against Modernist trends. In later years, his studio was at 3 Washington Sq. North.

Irving, Washington (1783–1859)

Diplomat, biographer, satirist and author – of *Rip Van Winkle* and *The Legend of Sleepy Hollow* among other tales – Irving was born in New York. His estate in nearby Tarrytown is open to the public.

Koch, Edward (born 1924)

Child of immigrant parents, Koch narrowly won election as mayor of New York in 1977; and despite, or because of, his propensity for speaking his mind, he soon established himself as the most popular mayor since LaGuardia. In 1981, as the candidate of both the Democrat and Republican parties, he was returned to office by an overwhelming vote.

LaGuardia, Fiorello Henry (1882–1947)

Probably the most beloved mayor in the city's history – serving from 1935–45 for an unprecedented three terms – the 'Little Flower' gave luster and color to an office celebrated for both the flamboyance and corruptibility of its incumbents.

Millay, Edna St Vincent (1892–1950)

The popular lyric poet was a leader of the Greenwich Village Bohemian group that founded the Provincetown Players.

Minuit, Peter (1580–1638)

The famous $24 purchase of Manhattan was negotiated by Minuit, who was then appointed Director General (1626–31) of the new colony by the Dutch West India Company.

Morgan, John Pierpont (1837–1913)

Beginning with the fortune accumulated by his father, J. P. used it as seed money to build a financial empire that is said to have exceeded even that of the first Rockefeller. Along the way, he bought out industrialists Andrew Carnegie and Henry Frick. All of them spent their declining years in New York and engaged in good works.

Morse, Samuel F. B. (1791–1872)

While a member of the arts faculty at New York University, Morse perfected his telegraph device and the code to be used with it. A demonstration was given at Castle Clinton in 1842. Morse was also a pioneer in the development of photography.

Olmsted, Frederick Law (1822–1903)

Travel writer and landscape architect, Olmsted designed Central Park, Prospect Park (Brooklyn) and Riverside Park, all in collaboration with Calvert Vaux.

O'Neill, Eugene (1888–1953)

The work of the playwright who fashioned *The Iceman Cometh* and *Mourning Becomes Electra* is the standard against which all American dramatists must be measured. One of his finest plays, *Long Day's Journey into Night*, was discovered among his papers after his death. O'Neill was awarded the Nobel Prize in 1936.

Parker, Dorothy (1893–1967)

Renowned for the razor-sharp wit she directed as readily at herself as at others, Parker employed that gift in verse, plays, films, essays and short stories. Much of her work appeared in *The New Yorker* magazine.

Perelman, S. J. (*1904–79*)
Brooklyn-born Perelman wrote for *The New Yorker* magazine
from 1934 almost until his death. Essentially a humorist and
satirist, his interests focused on the inanities of advertising and
Hollywood. He also wrote film scripts and plays in the 1930s
and 1940s, often in association with such luminaries as the Marx
Brothers, Ogden Nash and George S. Kaufman. His affection
for the elaborate pun was legendary, apparent in such book
titles as *The Road to Miltown*, or *Under the Spreading Atrophy*.

Poe, Edgar Allen (*1809–49*)
Impoverished for most of his adult life, having alienated his
wealthy foster father through repeated alcoholism and
gambling, Poe moved to New York with his child bride in 1844.
Their cottage in the Fordham section of The Bronx is now a
museum. He finally achieved recognition for his poetry with
The Raven, which led to fame for such mystery stories as *The
Gold Bug*, and *The Murders in the Rue Morgue*.

Pollock, Jackson (*1912–56*)
Although contemporaries were working in similar directions,
the seminal work of this innovative artist heralded the explosion
of post-War creativity now known as the New York School.
Inspired by Picasso and impatient with the academic
techniques he mastered in his early years, he applied paint to
vast canvasses by splashing, dribbling, thrusting and pouring in
a method later labelled 'action painting.'

Porter, Cole (*1893–1964*)
The enduring sophistication of Porter's lyrics is remarkable. He
penned both words and music of over 400 songs, for such stage
musicals as *Can-Can*, *Silk Stockings* and *Kiss Me, Kate*.

Pulitzer, Joseph (*1847–1911*)
Hungarian-born Pulitzer emigrated to the USA in 1864 and
became a journalist, editor and publisher in short order. He
bought the *New York World* in 1883 and in competition with
William Randolph Hearst permitted it to plummet to the nadir
of 'yellow journalism.' After the Spanish-American War
(1898), his newspapers altered course to become relatively
dignified. His will bequeathed money for the establishment of
the Columbia University School of Journalism. Annual prizes
for journalistic excellence are given in his name.

Rauschenberg, Robert (*born 1925*)
Rauschenberg first attracted attention with an exhibition of
entirely black canvasses, but then moved on to 'combine-
paintings' – assemblages of pigment, collage and such three-
dimensional objects as stuffed goats and rubber tyres. Born in
Texas, he is nonetheless an exemplar of the New York School.

Rockefeller, John D. Jr. (*1874–1960*)
The son of the incalculably wealthy oil magnate and financier
was granted control of his father's interests at the age of 37. To a
large extent, this involved philanthropic activities, many of
which benefited New York. Among the projects he inspired or
helped underwrite were Riverside Church, the Cloisters of the
Metropolitan Museum of Art and Rockefeller Center.

Rockefeller, Nelson Alrich (*1908–79*)
After able participation in both Democrat and Republican
federal administrations during World War II and after, Nelson
defeated W. Averell Harriman for the governorship of the State
of New York in 1958. His subsequent bids for the Republican
presidential nomination were unsuccessful, but he was
re-elected governor three times and was appointed Vice-
President for the brief term of Gerald Ford (1974–77). He

made substantial contributions to New York's cultural and educational institutions, as did his siblings.

Roosevelt, Theodore (1858–1919)
The 28th and youngest President passed the first 15yr of his extraordinarily active life at 28 E 20th St., near Gramercy Park. Hunter and environmentalist, rancher and author, statesman and chauvinist, peacemaker and militarist, explorer and politician, he pursued these contradictory interests vigorously until his death.

Runyon, Damon (1884–1946)
Born in Manhattan (the one in the state of Kansas), this popular journalist came to New York, where he quickly mastered the patois of the criminal fringe and transferred that knowledge to a long string of evocative and humorous short stories, which provided the basis of the musical *Guys and Dolls*.

Ruth, George Hermon (1895–1948)
A near-legendary athlete, 'Babe' Ruth played for the New York Yankees professional baseball team from 1920–35. Most of his pitching and batting records went unchallenged for decades, and some still stand.

Stuyvesant, Peter (1610–72)
A harshly autocratic man intolerant of religious and political dissent, this Director General of New Amsterdam held power from 1647–64. In 1664 he surrendered the colony to an English naval force and retired to his farm, near the present Lower East Side.

Tweed, William Marcy (1823–78)
The undisputed leader of Tammany Hall, which controlled the city and state Democrat Party, 'Boss' Tweed ruled the city from 1857 until the early 1870s. He died in prison, having defrauded taxpayers and contractors of unaccounted millions in bribes, kickbacks and related schemes.

Warhol, Andy
No-one is certain when he was born (about 1930), or where (probably Philadelphia), but there is no question of his primacy in the Pop Art movement of the 1960s. Through repeated prints of commonplace objects – cows, soup cans, movie stars – he endeavored to elevate the mundane and overexposed into subjects worthy of serious consideration. He went on to found a 'factory' that produced films of elusive intent, a magazine of celebrity interviews and autobiographical books that celebrate banality.

White, Stanford (1853–1906)
As the most celebrated partner of the architectural firm of McKim, Mead & White, he probably received more credit than his due for their collective achievements. Many of their buildings have been lost, but a rich heritage remains. These include Washington Arch, the Villard Houses, the portico of St Bartholomew's Church, three buildings at Columbia University and three more at the former Bronx campus of New York University, in all of which White had a hand.

Whitman, Walt (1819–92)
The innovative free verse of *Leaves of Grass* drew mostly negative reaction on its first appearance in 1855, but many 20thC scholars regard Whitman as America's finest poet.

Wolfe, Thomas Clayton (1900–38)
The haunted author of *Look Homeward, Angel* and *You Can't Go Home Again* joined the English faculty at New York University in 1924 and spent most of the last years of his life in the city.

177

New York for children

From boat trips to children's zoos, New York is a city packed with interest for children. The following are the most accessible suggestions.

Boat trips

Circle Line (*Pier 83, w 43rd St.* ☎ *563–3200*). Three-hour trips around Manhattan Island may be a trifle long for the very young, but there are few dull moments for everyone else. Cruises depart at least ten times a day, weather and demand permitting, during Apr–Nov from 9:45am–5:30pm. Half-price for children under 12.

Ellis Island Ferry (*Battery Park, Lower Manhattan* ☎ *269–5755*). Ferries to the famous old immigrant processing centre leave daily during May–Nov at 9:30am, 11:45am, 2pm and 4:15pm. The fare includes a 1hr guided tour of the poignant national monument.

Staten Island Ferry (*Battery Park, Lower Manhattan* ☎ *248–8097*). The double-decker ferry leaves Whitehall St. pier every 20–30min. It passes the Statue of Liberty and provides unparalleled views of bridges, harbor traffic and an imposing skyline.

Statue of Liberty Ferry (*Battery Park, Lower Manhattan* ☎ *269–5755*). Spectacular views from the crown of the famous lady and the ride from the city are included in the fare. Keep in mind the long walk up from the base.

Children's theater

Courtyard Playhouse (*39 Grove St.* (*near 7th Ave. S*) ☎ *765–9540*). Productions such as *Flash Gordon Saves the Universe* and *Wilbur the Christmas Mouse* are representative of the fare offered by the **Little People's Theater Company**, usually on Sat and Sun at 11am and 3pm. Admission is inexpensive, but reservations are essential.

First All Children's Theater (*37 W 65th St.* (*near Central Park W*) ☎ *873–6400*). Musical productions with casts of children are usually held during Oct–May on Sat and Sun only, but there are more frequent performances during school vacations. Telephone for details and reservations.

Hartly House Theater (*413 W 46th St.* (*near 9th Ave.*) ☎ *246–9885*). The **On Stage, Children!** company mounts four plays a year, including such classics as *Androcles and the Lion*. Shows during Sept–May at 1pm and 3:30pm on Sat. Inexpensive, but reservations are necessary.

Jan Hus Playhouse (*351 E 74th St.* (*near 2nd Ave.*) ☎ *772–9180*). Plays and musicals are presented on an irregular schedule, sometimes two in an afternoon. Inexpensive.

Magic Towne House (*1026 3rd Ave.* (*near 60th St.*) ☎ *752–1165*). Magic shows are leavened with laughs and cute animals, and 'assistants' are recruited from the audience. Reservations are required, and no adults are allowed without children. Shows are on Sat and Sun at 1pm, 2:30pm, 4pm.

New Media Repertory Company (*203 E 88th St.* (*near 3rd Ave.*) ☎ *860–8679*). Unpredictable entertainments performed by the **Children's Improvisational Company** on Sat at 3:30pm during the school year. Inexpensive.

13th Street Repertory Company (*50 W 13th St.* (*near 5th Ave.*) ☎ *675–6677*). Plays with music, based upon children's stories on Sat at 3pm, Sun at 1pm. Call in advance to confirm times.

Truck and Warehouse Theater (*79 E 4th St. (near 2nd Ave.)* ☎ *254–5060*). A long-running rock 'n' roll musical fantasy called *Captain Boogie and the Kids from Mars* is performed during Oct–June on Sat and Sun at 3:30pm.

Christmas decorations

The luxury shops and large department stores are ablaze with holiday lights and window-dressing from late Nov to late Dec, and midtown 5th Ave. is a spectacle of dizzying amplitude. The centerpiece is the 70ft tree with myriad winking lights looming above the skating rink at the foot of the **RCA Building**. The **Channel Gardens** that lead into Rockefeller Center from 5th Ave. are transformed by stylized novas and silvery angels. Shop windows and interior displays of invariable delight are those of **B. Altman & Co.** (*34th St.*), **Lord & Taylor** (*38th St.*), **Saks Fifth Avenue** (*50th St.*), and **F.A.O. Schwarz** (*58th St.*).

Elsewhere in Manhattan, a Christmas tree is framed within Washington Arch in **Greenwich Village**, wreaths encircle the necks of the lions outside the **42nd St. Library**, an elaborate tableau of castles and elves fills the lobby of the **Museum of the City of New York** and a tree in the Medieval Hall of the **Metropolitan Museum of Art** emphasizes the spiritual origins of the holiday, supplemented by a panorama of 200 18thC figures gathered about the birthplace of the Christ child.

Comedy and revue

Several nightclubs set aside afternoon sessions for children. But inevitably some clubs change policy and others close, so telephone for schedules and prices.

The **Comic Strip** (*1568 2nd Ave. (near 81st St.)* ☎ *861–9386, Sat 5pm, Sun 5:30pm*) spotlights professional youngsters appearing in current TV and stage shows. Similar showcases are arranged by **Something Different** (*1488 1st Ave. (near 78th St.)* ☎ *570–6666, Sat 7pm, Sun 3pm, 5:30pm*), and by **Improvisation** (*358 W 44th St. (near 9th Ave.)* ☎ *765–8268, Sun 2:30pm*). In TriBeCa, the **Ones** disco (*111 Hudson St. (near N Moore St.)* ☎ *925–0011*) turns over the floor to pre-teenagers on Sun (*1–5pm*).

Concerts for young people

The American Symphony Orchestra and the New York Philharmonic give irregularly scheduled concerts of classical music directed at ages 6–16. Most are performed in the fall and winter at **Carnegie Hall** (☎ *247–7459*) or **Avery Fisher Hall** (☎ *874–2424*). Check newspapers for full details.

Events and entertainments

Big Apple Circus. This is New York's very own one-ring circus in a tent, modeled after the intimate European troupes that have no other equivalent in the US. Clowns cavort, aerialists execute the fabled triple somersault, elephants dance, jugglers and acrobats twirl and tumble, all to the delightful cacophony of a tiny band. Prices are variable but low for this not-for-profit enterprise; operation is most likely in summer and the Christmas season. A frequent site is Damrosch Park in the **Lincoln Center**, but it moves through all the boroughs.
Citicorp Center (*Lexington Ave. and 53rd St.* ☎ *559–4259*). The atrium has free entertainment most days, but Sat afternoon is for children, with music, magic, jugglers and puppets.
Gimbels Department Store (*Broadway and 33rd St.*

☎ *564–3300*). The famous store underwrites free shows for children on Sun at 1:30pm.

July 4th (Independence Day) festivities. An awesome fireworks display is put on by Macy's Department Store, set off from barges in the Hudson River and best seen from **Riverside Park** *(from 80th St. to 100th St.)*. Be there by 9pm. The 'Old New York' celebrations take place at **Battery Park** in lower Manhattan, with street performers and suitable ceremonies from noon to dusk.

Storytelling in Central Park. At the **Hans Christian Andersen Memorial** *(near 5th Ave. and 72nd St.)* stories are read to children, some of whom sit in the bronze lap of the master, during May–Sept on Wed and Sat at 11am.

Hotels

Various discounts and incentives help keep costs within reason when children are in tow. At least a dozen hotels permit children under 12 (or 14, or even 17) to stay with their parents for free. Most will roll in an extra bed or cot at an additional but not excessive charge, making a substantial saving over the alternatives of a suite or separate rooms.

Reception desks or concierges normally have lists of babysitters available for hire.

Swimming pools are an important feature for children, and the following Manhattan hotels and motels have them: **Best Western Skyline** (indoor), **Halloran House, Harley, Holiday Inn-Coliseum, Parker Meridien, Ramada Inn-Midtown, Sheraton City Squire** (indoor), **United Nations Plaza** (indoor), and **Vista International**. See *Hotels* for addresses and telephone numbers.

Museums and exhibitions

Brooklyn Children's Museum *(145 Brooklyn Ave. (between Eastern Parkway and Atlantic Ave.)* ☎ *735–4432, open Mon, Wed–Fri 1–5pm, Sat, Sun 10am–5pm* 🖾*)*. The oldest (1899) children's museum in the US is in a new building. Exhibits cover basic technologies, social and natural history. Handling and participation are encouraged. Several levels support waterwheels, ladders, a windmill, a steam engine, hydraulic devices, plants, animals, and thousands of other objects and displays.

Junior Museum of the Metropolitan Museum of Art *(5th Ave. and 82nd St.* ☎ *879–5500, ext 351, open Tues 10am–8:45pm, Wed–Sat 10am–4:45pm, Sun and hols 11am–4:45pm)*. Somehow it manages to be intellectually accessible to children under 12 without patronizing them. Exhibits, from the permanent collections and outside sources, introduce the arts and inspire a thirst for further exposure in the galleries upstairs. There is also a lively program of workshop demonstrations, films, and gallery tours.

Manhattan Laboratory Museum *(314 W 54th St. (near 8th Ave.)* ☎ *752–7684, open Tues–Fri 11am–5pm, Sat noon–5pm* 🖾*)*. Despite the name, this modest new museum does not concentrate solely on science. Rather, it emphasizes hands-on participation by children in games, displays and workshops concerned with natural history, conservation, culture and society.

In addition to these three, many of the city's museums have presentations and programs of interest for children. For

addresses and opening times, and fuller details, see
individual museums in *Sights and places of interest*.
American Museum of Natural History. The reassembled
dinosaur skeletons and dioramas of mounted animals and birds
in simulated habitats are long-time favorites, but they seem
bland beside the vivid and detailed depictions of the peoples
and cultures of Asia, Central America and Africa. Several
rooms are set aside for schoolchildren to rouse their curiosity
about the larger concerns of the museum through participatory
exhibitions, games, performers, films, story hours and guided
tours. The **Hayden Planetarium** is part of the facility, and on
Sat during the school year (Oct–June), it mounts a 'Young
People's Sky Show' which includes realistic overhead
projections of galaxies and constellations accompanied by
music and narration.
Aunt Len's Doll and Toy Museum. Hundreds of antique toys,
dolls and miniature houses crowd every inch of space in this
refreshingly informal museum. Visits by appointment only.
Brooklyn Museum. After-school programs on Wed–Sat
introduce youngsters aged 6–12 to various parts of the
collections through talks and demonstrations that do not abuse
attention spans.
Fire Department Museum. Antique equipment and
firefighting memorabilia housed in an old firehouse provide a
break in a walking tour of the Financial District.
Guinness World Records Exhibit Hall. Excess fascinates, and
this set of tableaux of the longest, highest, shortest, fattest,
oldest, youngest and most bizarre creations of man and nature
never fails to grab attention.
Metropolitan Museum of Art. Apart from the **Junior Museum**
on the basement level, the most alluring items in the many
collections seem to be the Egyptian tombs and mummies and
the medieval arms and armor; older children are drawn to the
special shows of the **Costume Institute**. The recorded cassette
tours are attractive.
Museum of Broadcasting. Children can enjoy tapes and
kinescopes of radio and TV shows of the 'olden times.' Adults
are usually as intrigued, but some might wish to wait in Paley
Park, next door.
Museum of the City of New York. Puppet shows on Sat during
Nov–Apr are the incentive to join in various 'please touch'
demonstrations of objects related to the history of the area.
Museum of Holography. Ghostly three-dimensional images
produced by laser technology represent a glimpse of the 21stC.
New York Experience. This multi-media extravaganza is short
and slick enough to give an impression of the city without a
single stifled yawn.
New York Historical Society. A scale-model of a Noah's Ark
populated by 300 animals dominates the collection of vintage
toys and dolls on the 2nd floor.
Richmondtown Restoration (Staten Island). Costumed
guides and craftsmen bring history to life in this re-created
village with demonstrations of weaving, wool-spinning, basket-
making, leatherwork, and cooperage.
Songwriters' Hall of Fame. Times Square can be daunting for
children, but this casual museum encourages them to take a toot
or a strum on a number of musical instruments and forget for a
while the dismaying barrage of noise and electric signs on the
streets below.
South Street Seaport Museum. The authentic tall ships of this

open-air museum are diverting for all ages, and special events include folk singers and a theater designed for children. Youngsters can take part in lectures and browse in shops concerned with toys, ship models and games of nautical bent.

Observation decks

Empire State Building (*350 5th Ave. (34th St.)* ☎ *736–3100*). There are two decks, on the 86th and 102nd floors, open daily at 9:30am–midnight, except Christmas and New Year's Day. Children under 12 half-price.
RCA Building (*30 Rockefeller Plaza (between 49th St. and 50th St.)* ☎ *489–2947*). Not quite as high as the others, its wrap-around vistas and midtown location give a better sense of the New York topography. The 70th floor deck is open daily during Apr–Oct at 10am–8:45pm, and during Nov–Mar at 10:30am–7pm. Children under 12 half-price.
World Trade Center (*2 World Trade Center, Lower Manhattan* ☎ *466–7377*). An enclosed deck is on the 107th floor, with an open deck on the 110th. On a clear day, it is easy to imagine that you can see the curvature of the earth. Open daily from 9:30am to 7:30pm. Children 6–12 about half-price, under 6 free.

Closer to sea-level (and free) are the pedestrian walkways of the **Brooklyn Bridge** and the **George Washington Bridge**, as well as the **Brooklyn Heights** esplanade.

In addition, there are several restaurants with sky-high venues. As long as one does not inspect the bill or what appears on the plate too critically, the following can be pleasant: **Act One** (*1 Times Sq.*), **Copter Club** (*Pan Am Building*), **Rainbow Room** (*RCA Building*), **The Terrace** (*Butler Hall, Columbia University*), **3 Mitchell Place** (*49th St. and 1st Ave.*), **Top of the Sixes** (*666 5th Ave.*), **Windows on the World** (*1 World Trade Center*).

Parades

For youngsters, the big one is the **Macy's Thanksgiving Day Parade** on the last Thurs in Nov, with its huge floating balloons of comic-book heroes and the Muppets. The longest and most eagerly anticipated is the **St Patrick's Day Parade** on Mar 17, but that has become rowdy in recent years with roving bands of intoxicated teenagers. Most months have a parade of some kind in some part of the city, but 5th Ave. has several events in autumn. See *Calendar of events* in *Planning*.

Playgrounds

Numerous conventional playgrounds dot New York. But the ones suggested below are described as adventure playgrounds, with stacked wooden blocks, rope nets, sections of concrete tubes, and comparable combinations of shapes and materials intended to be transformed into whatever can be inspired in a child's imagination.
Central Park   Central Park West and 68th St.; Central Park West, near 85th St.; 5th Ave. and 85th St.; 5th Ave. and 71st St.
Gramercy Park   2nd Ave. and 19th St.
Greenwich Village   Washington Square Park, between 5th Ave. and University Pl.; Abingdon Square Park at Hudson St. and Bleecker St.
Upper East Side   1st Ave. near 67th St.; East End Ave. and 84th St.
Upper West Side   W 45th St. near 10th Ave.; W 90th St. near Columbus Ave.

Puppets and marionettes

First Moravian Church (*154 Lexington Ave. at 30th St.*
☎ *254–9074*). Participatory puppet shows every weekend on
Sat at 2pm. Admission is inexpensive, but reservations are
wise.

Greenwich House Music School (*46 Barrow St. at 7th Ave. S*
☎ *924–4589*). Puppet shows staged each weekend on Sat and
Sun at 3:30pm. A modest admission fee is charged, but book
ahead.

Museum of the City of New York (*1220 5th Ave. at 103rd St.*
☎ *534–1672*). Shows conducted during Nov–Apr on Sat at
1:30pm. Inexpensive.

New York Stageworks (*15 W 18th St. at 5th Ave.*
☎ *691–9106*). The **Nicolo Marionettes** perform at weekends
during Sept–May on Sat at 1pm, Sun at 1pm and 3pm.
Inexpensive, but reserve in advance.

Origami Center (*31 Union Sq. W at E 16th St.* ☎ *255–0469*).
Weekend performances of **Alice May's Puppets** during
Nov–May on Sun at 2pm. Inexpensive, but reservations are
necessary.

F.A.O. Schwarz (*5th Ave. and 58th St.* ☎ *644–9400*). The
famous toy store has free puppet shows Mon–Fri at 2:30pm.

South Street Seaport Museum (*16 Fulton St. at South St.*
☎ *766–9020*). Shipboard puppet shows and related
entertainments on Sun at 2pm.

Swedish Cottage Marionette Theater (*81st St. and Central
Park West* ☎ *988–9093*). Performances on Sat and Sun
afternoons, but call ahead for times. Inexpensive entry;
reservations required.

Restaurants

Apart from their prohibitive cost, the shrines of *haute cuisine* set
children to squirming and are unlikely to have available the
simple fare they prefer. There are many moderately priced
restaurants catering to families, however, with special
children's menus, highchairs, and speedy service. The
following tend to be large and rather touristy, but they go to
considerable lengths to amuse young patrons.

Benihana Palace (*15 W 55th St.* ☎ *688–3690*). Diners sit in
groups of six or eight around a horseshoe counter that encloses a
sizzling grill. A cook in *toque blanche* arrives and, with a showy
clatter, swoops over piles of shrimp, zucchini and beef, slicing,
flipping, sautéing, serving. It may not be Japanese, but it is
theatrical.

The Cattleman (*5 E 45th St.* ☎ *661–1200*). A crowded, gaudy
Hollywood version of a Wild West saloon, the cuts of beef are
large if tenderized, and there is a horse-drawn stagecoach for
rides around the block. Lady magicians and singers circulate
among diners.

Copenhagen (*68 W 58th St.* ☎ *688–3690*). No flash, no
strolling performers, but a sumptuous *smorgasbord* permits
everyone to pick helpings of whatever they want, as often as
they want.

Gaylord (*50 E 58th St.* ☎ *759–1710*). The chef at the tandoori
oven is fun to watch, and they'll keep the seasonings mild for
young palates, but the big treat is a palm reader.

Mamma Leone's (*239 W 48th St.* ☎ *586–5151*). Plates are
heaped high, the walls and ceilings of the cavernous rooms are
encrusted with Neapolitan kitsch, fiddle players stroll, flash
bulbs pop. Boredom is not permitted.

Sports
See also *Sports and activities*.
Bicycling
Bicycles can be rented from many shops, and the **Loeb Boathouse** (*in Central Park, near E 72nd St.* ☎ *288 – 7707*).
Horse riding
The **Claremont Riding Academy** (*175 W 89th St.* ☎ *724 – 5100*) rents horses by the hour and offers classes for children in its indoor ring. Trails are in Central Park.
Ice-skating
The rink at the base of the **RCA Building** is open to all, despite the style of many of its skaters. Less exhibitionistic youngsters may prefer the **Wollman Memorial Rink** (*in Central Park, near 5th Ave. at 64th St., open approximately late Oct to late Mar*). Admission fees are modest but vary.
Model boats
Miniature boats both humble and elaborate, radio-controlled or sail-powered, are seen nearly every day of the year on the **Conservatory Pond** (*in Central Park, near 5th Ave. and 72nd St.*).
Rowboats
The **Loeb Boathouse** (*in Central Park, near E 72nd St.* ☎ *288 – 7707*) has rowboats for hire by the hour to persons over 16yr.

Television shows
A number of game shows and variety specials originate in New York. Tickets are free, and sources are:
American Broadcasting Company 1330 6th Ave. ☎ 581 – 7777
Columbia Broadcasting System 51 W 52nd St. ☎ 581 – 4321
National Broadcasting Company 30 Rockefeller Plaza, ☎ 664 – 3055
New York Convention and Visitors Bureau 2 Columbus Circle, ☎ 397 – 8222
Children between 6 and 18 must be accompanied by adults.

Zoos and aquarium
For addresses and opening times, see individual entries in *Sights and places of interest*.
Bronx Zoo. The new Children's Zoo, within the larger park, has gentle animals for petting and camels and pony carts for riding, and is open Apr – Oct. Kids also enjoy the monorail that circles the 'Wild Asia' preserve, the aerial tram that glides over the recreated 'African Plains,' and the tractor train that tours the entire park.
Central Park Zoo. Next to the 64th St. entrance is a merry-go-round, and inside are pony rides. The hub is the seal pool. To the N is the Children's Zoo on a triangle of land on 5th Ave. between 65th St. and 66th St. Open seven days a week, all year round.
New York Aquarium. From May – Oct, there are performances by dolphins, whales, and sea-lions. Most winter in Florida, but there are still indoor tanks featuring fish that resemble floating flowers and others, even stranger, that inspire shudders.
Prospect Park Zoo. This compact zoo also features pony rides and a section of small farm animals set aside for children.
Staten Island Zoo. The comprehensive reptile collection is the big attraction, supplemented by a children's zoo and pony rides. Admission free on Wed.

Sports and activities

The following guide to sport and leisure in and around New York offers ideas for spectators and participants.

Spectator sports

Arenas and stadiums

Baker Field (*W 218th St. and Broadway* ☎ *567–7423*).
Football as played by Columbia University, one of the members of the Ivy League; Sept–Nov.

Byrne Arena (*Meadowlands Sports Complex, E Rutherford, NJ* ☎ *(201) 935–8222*). Since its opening in 1981, this facility has been the venue for the professional basketball Nets and college teams, as well as rock concerts, circuses, and other events. Get there by bus from Port Authority Bus Terminal on 8th Ave.

Giants Stadium (*Meadowlands Sports Complex, E Rutherford, NJ* ☎ *(201) 935–8222*). Crowds invariably fill the superb arena on Sun afternoons from late Aug to early Dec to watch professional football by the venerable Giants; tickets are nearly impossible to obtain. The Cosmos play soccer here from Apr–Sept.

Madison Square Garden (*8th Ave. and 33rd St.* ☎ *564–4400*).
This is the home of New York Rangers ice hockey (Oct–Apr), Knicks basketball (Oct–Apr), college basketball (Nov–Apr) and indoor soccer with the Arrows (Nov–Mar). Boxing and wrestling matches and such special events as the circus, the Ice Capades, dog and horse shows, and rock concerts are also held here at various times of year.

Nassau Coliseum (*Uniondale, Long Island* ☎ *(516) 794–9100*).
Special musical and entertainment events are presented, as are the ice hockey games of the successful Islanders.

National Tennis Center (*Flushing Meadows-Corona Park, Queens* ☎ *592–9300*). These courts are the site of the annual US Open Championships in early Sept.

Shea Stadium (*126th St. and Roosevelt Ave., Queens*). The professional baseball Mets play here from Apr–Sept (☎ *672–3000*); the football Jets from Sept–Dec (☎ *421–6600*).

Yankee Stadium (*River Ave. and W 161st St., The Bronx* ☎ *293–6000*). Frequent champions and one of the oldest teams in professional baseball, the Yankees perform here Apr–Sept.

Racetracks

Aqueduct (*108th St. and Rockaway Blvd., Queens* ☎ *641–4700*). The 'Big A' features thoroughbred flat racing from Jan–May, Oct–Dec. It can be reached by subway. For routes and fares ☎ *330–1234*.

Belmont Park (*Elmont, Long Island* ☎ *641–4700*).
Thoroughbred racing from May–July, Sept–Oct. The Long Island Railroad, departing from Penn Station, has special trains and fare-admission packages ☎ *739–4200* for information.

Meadowlands (*Meadowlands Sports Complex, E Rutherford, NJ* ☎ *(201) 935–8500*). Most of the grandstands are enclosed at this new track, permitting comfortable viewing of Thoroughbreds from Sept–Dec, and of trotters from Jan–Aug. Races are in the evening, and can be watched from the full-service diningroom called Pegasus.

Roosevelt Raceway (*Westbury, Long Island* ☎ *(516) 222–2000*). Evening trotters go through their paces from Jan–Mar, June–Aug, Oct–Dec. Package fares on the

Long Island Railroad from Penn Station include coach transfers and track admission.

Yonkers Raceway (*Yonkers, NY* ☎ 968–4200). Easily accessible off the Gov. Thomas E Dewey Thruway, just N of The Bronx. The track is devoted to trotting races Mar–Apr, June–July, Sept–Oct and Dec. Special buses leave from Port Authority Bus Terminal on 8th Ave.

Participant sports
Baseball
The national game can be played on diamond-shaped fields all over New York. Many are reserved at various times by amateur and semi-professional leagues, but 'pick-up' teams come together for a few innings whenever a sufficient number of enthusiasts gather. Contact the **Heckscher Ballfields** (*Central Park, E of Central Park W at about 64th St.*), or ☎ 397–3100 for the location of the nearest field.

Basketball
There are courts within a few blocks of nearly every address in Manhattan. These are usually occupied by local youngsters or ageing executives who take the game very seriously ☎ 397–3100 for the closest court. Branches of the **YMCA** (*215 W 23rd St.* ☎ 741–9220; *224 E 47th St.* ☎ 755–2410; *and 5 W 63rd St.* ☎ 787–4400) have gymnasiums, but a membership card from a hometown 'Y' is usually required.

Bicycling
Shops in most neighborhoods rent bicycles by the hour, day, or week – consult the telephone directory Yellow Pages under *Bicycles*. City streets are intimidating for any but unflappable native cyclists, so consider Central Park on weekends, when roads in it are closed to cars. The **72nd St. Boathouse in Central Park** (☎288–7707) has bicycles for rent.

Boating and sailing
Rowboats are available at the **72nd St. Boathouse in Central Park** (☎288–7707). Sailing instruction is offered by the **New York Sailing School** (*City Island, The Bronx* ☎864–4472), and the **Offshore Sailing School** (*at 820 2nd Ave.* ☎986–4570).

Bowling
All the boroughs have bowling alleys, although they are least obvious in Manhattan. **Madison Square Garden Bowling Center** (*7th Ave. and W 31st St.* ☎ 563–8160, open 9.00–1.00), with 48 lanes, also has instructors.

Cricket
While it is not a sport that fires the imagination of the local citizenry, immigrants from the British West Indies keep the imperial heritage alive on pitches in **Flushing Meadows-Corona Park** (*in Queens* ☎ 520–5311), and in **Van Cortlandt Park** (*W 250th St. and Broadway* ☎822–4711).

Diving
Instruction in scuba is given by the **Aqua-Lung School of New York** (*1089 2nd Ave.* ☎582–2800), **Atlantis II** (*498 6th Ave.* ☎924–7556), and **Scuba Plus** (*201 E 34th St.* ☎689–0035), all in Manhattan. They also arrange diving trips throughout the

area for qualified divers. There are a number of intriguing wrecks in offshore waters.

Fishing
Anglers over 16 must obtain a license to use the freshwater lakes and rivers of New York City and State, but these are available for a small fee at many sporting goods stores. Anyone can fish in salt water without a permit. Lakes within **Central Park**, **Prospect Park** (*Brooklyn*), and **Van Cortlandt Park** (*The Bronx*) contain such gullible species as catfish, bluegills and carp. Charters and party boats (on which each passenger pays a fare) are available at **City Island** (*The Bronx*) and **Sheepshead Bay** (*Brooklyn*).

Golf
While there are no golf courses in Manhattan, the outlying boroughs have 13 owned and operated by New York City. Expect to wait for a tee-off time. For information:

The Bronx ☎822–4711
Brooklyn ☎965–6511
Queens ☎520–5311
Staten Island ☎422–7640

Handball
For the location of the nearest city-owned court in Manhattan ☎397–3100.

Horse riding
Instruction and rent-by-the-hour are available at:
Claremont Riding Academy 175 W 89th St. ☎724–5100
Clove Lake Stables 1025 Clove Rd. in Staten Island ☎448–1414
Van Cortlandt Park Stables Broadway and W 254th St. in The Bronx ☎549–6200

The trails for the **Claremont** wind through Central Park, and it has an indoor ring as well.

Ice skating
The rink at the base of the **RCA Building** in the Rockefeller Center has a constant crowd of spectators and so is used primarily by skilled and/or exhibitionistic skaters. Central Park has two outdoor rinks: **Lasker** (*near 110th St.*) and **Wollman** (*near the Zoo*). All are open Nov–Apr.

The **Sky Rink** (*450 W 33rd St.* ☎695–6555) is large, indoors and on the 16th floor. Open all year, it has disco skating on Fri and Sat nights.

Skating is also permitted on natural lakes and ponds when there is safe ice cover, but it is wise to stick to the artificial rinks.

Racquetball
So popular it threatens to eclipse tennis, racquetball is normally available only at membership clubs. But some are open to the public, at least on an occasional basis. Among these are:
Gramercy Tennis & Racquetball Club 708 6th Ave. ☎691–0110
Grand Central Racquetball Club 25 Vanderbilt Ave. ☎883–0994
Manhattan Plaza Racquet Club 45 W 45th St. ☎594–0554
Manhattan Squash & Racquetball Club 41 W 42nd St. ☎869–8969

187

Sports and activities

Racquetball Fifth Avenue   25 W 39th St. ☎944–0144

Usually they are open every day from 7am to midnight.
Equipment is sold and rented at each, and credit cards are
accepted. Reserve courts well in advance. Hotels that have
courts include the **Parker Meridien** and the **Vista
International**.

Roller skating

Skates can be rented at many shops, among them:

Dream Wheels   295 Mercer St. ☎677–0005
New York Skate   113 W 10th St. ☎929–0630
Skate Connection   349 W 14th St. ☎243–6343
Sportiva Sporthaus   145 E 47th St. ☎421–7466
US Roller World   160 5th Ave. ☎691–2680

Indoor rinks in Manhattan include:

Metropolis Roller Skate Club   241 W 55th St. ☎586–4649
Riverroll Rollerskating   312 E 23rd St. ☎673–0950
Roxy Roller Rink   515 W 18th St. ☎675–8300

Most of these have disco nights.

Running

New York runners are a hardy breed, seen on every street, at all
hours, in any weather. Non participants might question the
description of running as a 'sport', but its benefits to fitness and
the modest cost of equipment are unquestionable. A morning
jog or a serious 10-mile effort can follow any route, but certain
areas and pathways are favored for their even road surfaces,
lack of vehicles and crowds, and relative freedom from air
pollution.

Obviously these requirements point to the parks, especially
Central Park. Its 30-plus miles of roads provide substantial
variety in distances and difficulty. Suggested routes are detailed
below.

The fenced reservoir slightly N of the mid-point of the park
has two cinder tracks. Enter the park at **Engineer's Gate**, at 5th
Ave. and E 90th St. The inner track is 1.57 miles long.

Slightly S of the reservoir is **The Great Lawn Oval**, with a
measured circumference of half a mile and markers at 220yd
(200m) intervals.

A 6-mile loop follows the main drive around the perimeter of
the park, with frequent opportunities to cut E or W for runs of 1,
2 or 4 miles. Enter at **Engineer's Gate**, or at W 66th St. beyond
the Tavern On The Green restaurant, or just beyond the Zoo.

Less crowded parks are **Fort Tryon** (*Brooklyn*), **Prospect**,
Riverside, and **Van Cortlandt** (*The Bronx*). **The New York
Botanical Garden** (*also in The Bronx*) is ideal for runners, and is
a worthy destination by itself.

For river vistas, try the elevated **West Side Highway**,
presently closed to traffic below 42nd St., or the promenades
along the East River, with easy access S from **Carl Schurz Park**.

Road races of varying lengths are held every month in the
city. Contact the **New York Road Runners Club** (*9 E 89th St.*
☎ 860–4455) for dates, times and registration details.

The following is a list of indoor tracks:

McBurney YMCA   215 W 23rd St. ☎741–9224
92nd St. YMHA   1395 Lexington Ave. ☎427–6000
West Side YMCA   5 W 63rd St. ☎787–4400

Skiing

Cross-country skiing, with rolling terrain and gentle slopes, is

available in **Prospect Park** (*Brooklyn* ☎ 965–6511) and at **Van
Cortlandt Park** (*The Bronx* ☎ 543–4595). Equipment rental,
instruction, and tours to upstate and New England ski centers
are available at **Scandinavian Ski Shop** (*40 W 57th St.*
☎ 757–8524) and **Sportiva Sporthaus** (*145 E 47th St.*
☎ 421–7466).

Soccer
Enthusiasts might be invited to join a game in **Central Park** (*at
W 81st St.* ☎ 397–3110), or in **Van Cortlandt Park** (*The Bronx*
☎ 822–4599).

Squash
Most of the racquetball clubs listed on the preceding pages also
have squash courts.

Swimming
Municipally owned pools in the five boroughs are open from
late May to early Sept. They tend to be shabby, crowded, and
sometimes rowdy. Visitors are likely to prefer the pools at the
following hotels, some of which are open to outsiders as well as
guests: **Best Western Skyline** (indoor), **Halloran House**,
Harley, **Holiday Inn-Coliseum**, **Parker Meridien**, **Ramada
Inn-Midtown**, **Sheraton City Squire** (indoor), **United Nations
Plaza** (indoor), and **Vista International**. See *Hotels* for
addresses.

    Jones Beach State Park (*on the s side of Long Island*) has the
finest public beach and related facilities in the region, and is less
than an hour by car (*via Southern State Parkway, exiting s on
Wantagh State Parkway*) or special bus from the Port Authority
Bus Terminal. Municipal beaches are nearly always crowded
and the color of the water is often suspect, even though certified
safe for bathing, but most are within reach of public transport.
Coney Island Beach (*S Brooklyn*) is best known, but
Rockaway Beach, to the E, is three times as long with a tenth of
the humanity. At its western end is **Jacob Riis Park**, for long a
haunt of uninhibited male homosexuals. **Orchard Beach** (*near
City Island in The Bronx*), and **Great Kills Park** (*Staten Island*)
are also popular.

Tennis
Commercial tennis clubs usually have equipment shops,
lounges, instructors, and lockers available. Many also offer
saunas, air conditioning, swimming pools, weekend brunches
and evening parties. Indoor courts are offered by:
Crosstown Tennis   14 W 31st St. ☎ 947–5780
Gramercy Tennis & Racquetball Club   708 6th Ave.
☎ 691–0110
The Midtown Tennis Club   341 8th Ave. ☎ 989–8572
Tower Tennis Courts   1725 York Ave. ☎ 860–2464
Turtle Bay Tennis & Swim Club   1 United Nations Plaza
☎ 355–3400
Wall Street Racquet Club   Wall St. (at East River) ☎ 952–0760
    These are normally open seven days a week from 7am to
midnight. You should always call ahead to book a court and, if
alone, to arrange a game. All boroughs have municipal courts,
but season permits are required and red tape slows the process.
Fanatics are pleased to know of the **Stadium Tennis Center** (*11
E 162nd St. in The Bronx* ☎ 293–2386), which is open 24hr a
day, Oct–May.

Excursions

Unlike the capitals of Europe, New York has no medieval cathedrals or ancient university towns within easy reach. Beyond the inner ring of bleak smaller cities, however, the countryside is dotted with hamlets of Colonial serenity, inviting inns, dairy farms, and a surprising number of stately homes. These places are found in a great variety of natural settings, from hushed valleys to surf-pounded shores. For the following tours a car is essential.

A taste of New England
105 miles round trip NE. One day, preferably with an overnight stop.

Leave the city via the West Side Highway, which goes through several name changes and two toll booths. After the second toll, take the first exit onto the Cross County Expressway. This merges eventually with the Hutchinson River Parkway, heading towards Connecticut. Leave it at Exit 27, turning left, N, on Route 120 (Purchase St.).

At the next traffic signal, turn right, E, on Anderson Hill Rd. and follow it to the next crossroad, Route 120A (King St.). Turn left, N. Continue past the entrance to the Westchester County Airport on the left. Keep a sharp lookout for Cliffdale Rd. on the right and turn into it. It winds down a steep hill into a bosky gorge with a tumbling brook, and leads on through a neighborhood of luxurious estates. After a mile, Cliffdale Rd. ends at Route 433 (Riversville Rd.). Turn left, N.

At the intersection with John St., about a mile farther on, is the tall, chunky steeple of the **N Greenwich Congregational Church**, erected in 1896. On the opposite corner is an **Audubon Center**, with nature trails open to the public. Continue N on Route 433 to the first traffic signal, and turn right on Route 22. Just beyond a large modern furniture store is **Smith's Tavern** (*open Wed–Sat 1–3:30pm*). Built at the time of the Revolutionary War, it is now a modest museum of such items as antique dollhouses and quilts.

Route 22 rolls on over rising and falling hills past country clubs and examples of residential architecture dating back three centuries. Eventually there is **Bedford Village**, settled in 1680 by pioneers from New England. At the fork in the road, park near the tiny schoolhouse (1829) which is now a museum of local history (*open Wed–Sun 2–5pm, often closed from Christmas to mid-Feb*). Across the street is a white clapboard Methodist Church (1806) now headquarters of the Bedford Historical Society. The adjacent burial ground was established in 1681.

Bedford deserves an exploratory stroll. Around the triangular village green are the **Bedford Free Library** (1807), the **Courthouse** (1787), and **Post Office** (1838). Side streets have homes of the Dutch Colonial and Greek Revival styles. Most date from after 1779, when a British commander burned all but one of the then existing houses in retribution for rebel resistance. Some of the historic buildings are open to the public (*usually open Wed–Sun 2–5pm*) but they are dependent upon volunteers so might be closed at unpredictable times.

You will soon have an opportunity to picnic, and good wholesome fare can be purchased at the delicatessen next to the Post Office or at the **Bedford Gourmet** take-out shop, which is opposite the movie theater. Then continue by car through the

village on Route 22. Just beyond, bear right at the junction on
Route 121, N. If a picnic does not strike your fancy, there is
Nino's, with good if unremarkable veal, pastas and mussels.
Continue on Route 121, which eventually passes the Cross
River Reservoir, part of New York City's water system.

Just before the junction with Route 35 is the entrance to the
Ward Pound Ridge Reservation, 4,750 acres of hiking trails
and camping grounds. If you did decide on a picnic, this is the
place, but drive around to choose a spot. There are tables, stone
barbecues and fields in which to fling Frisbees. In cooler
months, deer and racoon are often sighted and cross-country
skiing is popular. Return then to Route 35. After about 2 miles,
look for the 'State Police' sign and turn left into **South Salem**
(settled 1731). Although the hamlet is of mild interest, the
primary reason for the detour is to note for future reference the
Horse and Hound restaurant (*dinner only; for reservations*
☎*(914)763–3108*), where the chef-owner specializes in game
dishes. Follow the street through town, turning left back on to
Route 35.

Soon, this crosses into Connecticut and the town of
Ridgefield. On the left is the **Inn at Ridgefield**, which offers
lodgings and lunch and dinner (*Wed–Sun*). Turn left on Main
St., an avenue of majestic trees and splendid 19thC homes. On
the right is the **Aldrich Museum of Contemporary Art** (*open
Sat, Sun, Wed 1–5pm*). Sculptures monumental and whimsical
are placed about the lawn, and these are on view every day.
They and the works within are primarily those by Americans
since 1945. There are frequent special shows and equally
frequent vacations. Should it happen to be open, a visit is a
must. Continue N through the village on Main St. About 2 miles
farther on, at the flashing traffic signal, turn right on Haviland
Rd. At the next traffic signal, turn right again on Route 7. After
half a mile, make a sharp right turn for **Stonehenge**
(☎*(203) 438–6511*) – not a megalithic monument, but the
finest restaurant in the area. It serves imaginative game dishes
and quick-poached trout taken straight from the kitchen's own
holding tank. Reservations are essential for weekend dinners
and necessary if you want to stay in one of the eight cozy
bedrooms overlooking the inn's geese-filled pond. Should this
be fully booked or time limited, return to New York via Route 7
and Interstate 95.

Fishing village in the metropolis
40 miles round trip NE. Minimum of half a day.

Pack a bathing suit. Take the West Side Highway to Interstate
95 (E), following that highway as far as exit 8B (City
Island–Orchard Beach). The road passes a wildlife refuge as
you bear S to **City Island**. A reassuringly ramshackle enclave
that is not the slightest bit chic, it has room only for one main
thoroughfare, City Island Ave., with short side streets of sturdy
detached frame houses for people who live there all year. On the
block between Hawkins St. and Carroll St., there are stores full
of offbeat antiques, bric-a-brac, and unclassifiable discards.
There are also coffee houses intended for leisurely drop-ins.
The Hippie's Place is one. Another, particularly memorable, is
the **Black Whale** (*even in summer it is only open Thurs–Sun,
usually 8:30am–midnight*). There is a patio out back where 15
kinds of tea are served, as well as *espresso* and *cappuccino* coffee
and a wickedly tempting chocolate angel food cake.

There are numerous seafood restaurants of varying quality.

Those at the foot of the main avenue are bargains with bonus views of the bay and a hazy Manhattan skyline, but they and many others close during the coldest months. **Anna's Harbor** and **Thwaite's Inn** (see *Restaurants*), at the N end of the avenue, are open all year.

After lunch and a stroll, leave by the same road, now following the signs to **Orchard Beach**. This is one of the finest public strands within the city, normally less crowded and littered than the others. There are changing rooms, a playground, snack bars, and ample parking. It takes less than a half hour to return to town by the same route.

The Hudson River Valley

150 miles round trip N. Minimum one long day, preferably two days.

Travel N on the West Side Highway, which becomes the Henry Hudson Parkway and then the Saw Mill River Parkway after it crosses the city line into Westchester County. It is designated Route 9A all the way. Continue through the city of Yonkers and the town of Hastings-on-Hudson, taking exit 17 in Dobbs Ferry, W on Ashford Ave. until it joins with Broadway (Route 9). Turn right, N, and drive on past the commercial district of the village of Irvington. Four blocks beyond Main St., turn left, W, on Sunnyside Lane. At the end, just before the railroad tracks and the Hudson, is **Sunnyside** (◪ *open 10am – 5pm*), the home of Washington Irving (1783 – 1859), author, diplomat and scholar. He always returned to this region, which he called 'Sleepy Hollow' in his novels and stories. The house, gardens and outbuildings have been scrupulously restored, with guides in appropriate 19thC garb. This is part of the Sleepy Hollow Restorations, a group of historic buildings which includes **Philipsburg Manor** and **Van Cortlandt Manor** (see below). Combination tickets can be purchased for all three at a substantial saving.

Return to Route 9 (S. Broadway) and go N, to reach a Gothic Revival mansion called **Lyndhurst** (◪ *open May – Oct, Wed – Sun 10am – 5pm*), constructed in 1838 by a mayor of New York, and purchased by the railroad tycoon Jay Gould in 1880. Many original furnishings are in place, generally complementing the vaulted ceilings and stained-glass windows. There are very popular summer concerts in the grounds (☎ *(914) 631 – 0046 for information*). Picnicking is permitted.

Back on Route 9, proceed N 2 miles beyond the Dewey Thruway, watching for signs to **Philipsburg Manor** (◪ *open 10am – 5pm*). Frederick Philipse, a late 17thC Dutch immigrant, was clearly a businessman and entrepreneur of exceptional acumen. This bustling complex of dam, gristmill, granary, bakery, stockyards, shipping wharf, and farmland was only part of his holdings, which at one time totaled 90,000 acres on both banks of the Hudson. Costumed attendants give demonstrations of Colonial cooking, millwork, weaving, and agricultural trades and crafts. You can go on a guided tour, beginning with a short film and then visiting the farmhouse, mill and barn. The **Old Dutch Church** across the street was built by Philipse in 1697. Washington Irving is buried in the nearby cemetery.

Route 9 passes N through Ossining and arrives after 8 miles in Croton-on-Hudson. Turn right at Croton Point Ave., continue to the first traffic signal, and turn right again on S. Riverside Ave. **Van Cortlandt Manor** (*open 10am – 5pm*), the third part of Sleepy Hollow Restorations, is about 100yd down the road. The main house began as a modest lodge erected in the late 1600s and was expanded to its present size by subsequent generations of the wealthy and influential Van Cortlandt family, who lived on this land for over 260yr. The original 86,000 acres have shrunk to 20, but they are well-tended, and the manor has been restored to its 18thC splendor.

Down by the river, past flourishing gardens and fruit trees, is the Ferry House, an inn of the same period that served passengers of the ferry operated by the Van Cortlandts. George Washington stopped by frequently, as did many other prominent figures of the Revolutionary War period. As at the other Sleepy Hollow Restorations, appropriately attired guides and craftspeople give demonstrations of home and farm skills. Frequent special events include a Christmas Candlelight Tour and the Autumn Crafts and Tasks Festival.

Late lunch can be taken in the suitably old-fashioned atmosphere of the 1761 **Bird & Bottle Inn** (*near Route 9, 4 miles N of Garrison* ☎ *(914) 424–3000, open for lunch and dinner Wed–Sun, closed Mon, Tues*). Afterwards drive w on Route 301, s on Route 9D to **Boscobel** (☎ *open Apr–Oct, Wed–Mon 9:30am–5pm, Mar, Nov, Dec, Wed–Mon 9:30am–4pm, closed Jan, Feb*). This is an early 18thC mansion in the Federalist manner, but with overtones of Neoclassicism. Many furnishings are original. There are informative guided tours of house and gardens.

Drive N on Route 9D, through Hudson Highlands State Park, joining with Route 9 again a mile N of Wappingers Falls. This leads into the river port town of Poughkeepsie. If time and interest permit, turn E on Route 55 to the **Vassar College** campus. One of the first institutions of higher education for women (opened 1865) and a member of the prestigious 'Seven Sisters' group, it turned coeducational in 1968. The **Taylor Art Gallery** (*open Mon–Sat 9am–5pm, Sun 2pm–5pm during the academic year*) is the highpoint, but the other buildings present an attractive and interesting variety of architectural styles. Afterward, return to Route 9 and turn N.

For evening refreshment at the end of a full day, drive about 16 miles on to Rhinebeck and stop at the **Beekman Arms** (*open all year, meals and room rates moderate*), dating from 1700 and claiming to be one of the two oldest inns in continuous operation in the United States.

Should the next day be a Sat or Sun (May–Oct only), you can see an airshow featuring vintage planes at the **Old Rhinebeck Aerodrome** (☎ *(914) 758–8610 to check times*), reached by driving N on Route 9. On other days (or in addition), there are the historic sites in Hyde Park, to the s on Route 9. Near the center of that sleepy village is the 1898 **Vanderbilt Mansion** (☎ *(914) 229–9115, open June–Aug 9am–6pm, Sept–May 9am–5pm*). Most of the works of art and furnishings in it are original. A mile or two s on Route 9 is the entrance to **the home of Franklin Delano Roosevelt** (*times as for Vanderbilt Mansion*). Parts of the house date from 1826, F.D.R. was born there in 1882, and he and his wife are buried in the rose garden.

Two miles farther s on Route 9 is an unusual educational institution sometimes called "the other CIA," The **Culinary Institute of America** (☎ *(914) 471–6608 for information and bookings*). The student-chefs operate a coffee shop and a restaurant called the Escoffier Room, both open to the public.

Continue s on Route 9 to Poughkeepsie and take the Mid-Hudson Bridge, picking up Route 9W on the opposite side of the river. In Newburgh is **Hasbrouck House** (*open Wed–Sun 9am–5pm*), once Washington's headquarters and now restored to an approximation of its original condition. Return to 9W. Just s of town pick up Route 218 through Cornwall, a winding but especially scenic drive high above the Hudson. This road ends at the Washington Gate of the **US Military Academy**, the officers' training college better known as **West Point**. The campus is open to the public all year round. Ask for directions at the **Visitors' Information Center** (*open Apr–Nov daily 8:30am–4:30pm, Dec–Mar Wed–Sun 8:30am–4:30pm*). The **military museum** exhibits uniforms and weaponry from the 18thC to the present, and dioramas depict important battles. Be sure to stop at the belvedere overlooking the Hudson.

Exit from the main gate at the s end of the reservation, driving through the village and on to Route 9W once again. This passes **High Tor State Park** (🏊 *open June–Sept*) in Haverstraw, with hiking trails, swimming, and picnic facilities. After about 3 miles, watch for the right turn on to Route 303. If it is mealtime, take that road to the **Bully Boy Chop House** (☎ *(914) 268–6555, open for lunch Mon–Fri, and dinner daily*), for uncommonly generous portions of non-gimmicky American food. Alternatively, continue s on 9W, detouring into the business district of Nyack, with antique and bric-a-brac shops.

Pick up Route 97 (the Dewey Thruway) at the edge of town, driving E across the Tappan Zee Bridge and s into the city.

Shakers and Berkshires
290 miles NE. Minimum two days.

There are numerous opportunities for swimming, hiking, and picnicking along this route, so dress and pack accordingly.

Leave Manhattan via the West Side Highway. This becomes the Henry Hudson Parkway, which joins the Saw Mill River Parkway. Follow the latter to Hawthorne Circle, transferring to the Taconic State Parkway, N, which passes through a sparsely settled countryside of meadows, groves, and green and tawny land with folds like a rumpled blanket. Leave the Parkway at the Route 44 exit, heading E towards **Millbrook**. Watch for the junction with Route 82. Just beyond is Tyrrell Rd. Turn right, s, and follow signs to **Innisfree Garden** (🏊 ☎ *(914) 677–8000, open May–Oct Wed–Sun 10am–4pm*), the creation of a painter by the name of Walter Beck. A gallery contains a selection of Beck's paintings.

Return to Route 44 and turn right, E, through the small village of Millbrook, an antique hunter's haven. Continue about 10 miles to Amenia, there picking up Route 363 E towards **Sharon**, a charming Connecticut town with white clapboard frame houses beneath sheltering elms and maples. Two miles s on Route 4 is an **Audubon Center** (🏊 ☎ *(203) 364–5826, open Wed–Sat 9am–5pm, Sun 1–5pm*), a wildlife sanctuary with miles of nature walks, a museum, and a herb garden. When you leave, return to the center of Sharon and pick up Route 41, N, to Lakeville. Once there, turn left, w, on Route 44, crossing once again into New York State and arriving in Millerton. Look for **McArthur's Smokehouse**, by the railway tracks, where superior sausages and other smoked meats are sold. With supplementary supplies from the nearby grocery store, the ingredients of a memorable picnic can be assembled; and the perfect place to eat it is nearby.

To find the spot, take Route 22, N, and after about 8 miles look for the inconspicuous sign directing you to **Boston Corners**, then look for signs to **Bash Bish Falls Reservation**. From the designated parking lot, a woodland path rises toward the gap between two peaks, a brook tumbling by on the right. After less than a mile, a slender waterfall plunges 50ft into a large clear pool, spilling into a series of smaller rock clefts and crevices. Man-made intrusions do not detract from the primitive grandeur of the place.

The road from the parking lot up to a vantage above the falls is a worthwhile detour. Afterwards, return to Route 22 and drive N to **Hillsdale**. At the juncture with Route 23 is **L'Hostellerie Bressane** (☎ *(518) 325–3412 for information and bookings*), an ambitious (and costly) inn of classical Provençal leanings. Only dinner is served, and it is closed at unpredictable times. Turn right, E, on Route 23. This leads back to Massachusetts and through the pretty hamlet of South Egremont, eventually connecting with Route 7. Turn left, N, through Great Barrington and on to **Stockbridge**, 6 miles farther on.

On most counts a quintessential New England village, Stockbridge stops short of touristy clutter. Turn right, E, into Main St. (Route 102). At that corner is the **Red Lion Inn** (☎ *(413) 298–5545* �📶 ✆ *108, advance booking essential*). The dining room serves three meals daily, and there is a convivial tap room downstairs with live music most weekend evenings. The revered illustrator Norman Rockwell lived in Stockbridge much of his life, and many of his paintings are on view at the 18thC **Corner House** (📷 *open Wed–Mon 10am–5pm*), just down the street. Two blocks in the other direction, W, is the **Mission House** (📷 ☎ *(413) 298–3383, open late May to early Oct, Tues–Sat 10am–5pm*), built in 1739 and maintained as a museum of domestic Colonial life. The estate of the sculptor Daniel Chester French is 2 miles away, N on Route 102, then S on Route 183. There are daily guided tours of his **house and studio** (📷 *open 10am–5pm, late May to early Oct*).

The southern Berkshires host a multitude of cultural activities every summer. In Stockbridge, the **Berkshire Playhouse** presents classics and some pre-Broadway tryouts from June–Oct. The **Boston Symphony Orchestra** and other musical ensembles perform at **Tanglewood**, an open-sided 'shed' in spacious grounds in nearby Lenox. The town of Lee is known for the annual **Jacob's Pillow Dance Festival**, in a theater created by Martha Graham and Ted Shawn. In winter, there are several popular ski resorts, including Bousquet, Brodie, and Jiminy Peak near Pittsfield and Butternut Basin near Great Barrington.

When ready to leave for New York, drive N on Route 7 to Pittsfield, then W on Route 20. Five miles from the center of Pittsfield is **Hancock Shaker Village** (☎ *(413) 433–0188, open June–Oct 9:30am–5pm*), one of the former settlements of the celibate religious sect founded as an offshoot of the Quakers in the 18thC. In accordance with their beliefs, their houses and furnishings were crisp and exquisitely simple. This painstakingly restored village illustrates their crafts and trades, from cookery to 'spirit painting,' with admirable clarity. Don't miss it.

Drive W on Route 20, then turn left, S, on Route 22. At Hillsdale, take Route 23 right, W, to the Taconic State Parkway for the return to New York.

Index

General index 196
Gazetteer of street names 204

Individual hotels, restaurants and shops have not been indexed, because they appear in alphabetical order within their appropriate sections. The sections themselves, however, have been indexed. Streets are listed in the gazetteer and not the index.

Page numbers in bold type indicate the main entry.

Index

Index

Index

Gazetteer of street names

Numbers after the street name refer to pages on which the street is mentioned in the book. Map references refer to the maps that follow this gazetteer.

Streets are listed alphabetically. Numbered avenues (1st Avenue, 2nd Avenue, etc) are listed under **A**. Numbered streets (3rd St., 4th St., etc) are listed in numerical sequence at the end of the gazetteer.

It has not been possible to label every street drawn on the maps, although all major streets and most smaller ones have been named. Some streets that it has not been possible to label on the maps have been given map references in this gazetteer, however, because this serves as an approximate location, which will nearly always be sufficient for you to find your way.

A

Amsterdam Avenue, 14; 112th St., 64; Map 8I3
Ann St., 172; Map 2U4
Audubon Terrace, 35, 53, 55–7, 83–4, 95, 101; Map 8F2
Avenue of the Americas *see* 6th Avenue; Maps 2, 5
1st Avenue, 8, 10, 15, 109, 136, 141, 143, 152, 155, 156, 173, 179, 182; Maps 3Q-R5, 5M-R5, 7I-N5, 9I-J5
2nd Avenue, 30, 84, 103, 108, 136, 141, 142, 143, 146, 153, 155, 156, 164, 172, 179, 182, 186; Maps 3R5, 5N-Q5, 7K-L4-5, 9I-J5
3rd Avenue, 94, 139, 148, 152, 154, 155, 159, 165, 166, 169, 172, 173, 178; Maps 2Q-R4, 5N-Q5, 7L-M5
5th Avenue, 10, 12, 14, 15, 30, 31, 32, 35, 36, 42, 45, 46, 47, 48, 65, 67, 74, 76, 79, 82, 83, 84, 85, 88, 89, 90, 93, 94, 95, 99, 102, 103, 107, 111, 115, 118, 123, 125, 142, 152, 153, 156, 163, 165, 166, 167, 168, 169, 170, 171, 172, 179, 180, 182, 183, 184; Maps 2R4, 5M-R4, 7J-N4
6th Avenue (Avenue of the Americas), 9, 10, 12, 14, 36, 43, 44, 63, 98, 102, 121, 155, 170, 171, 184, 186, 187; Maps 2R-S4, 5P-R4
7th Avenue, 10, 15, 30, 43, 66, 79, 107, 122, 124, 125, 154, 155, 156, 157, 158, 159, 163, 166, 185, 186; Maps 2Q-R3, 4N-Q3

8th Avenue, 9, 10, 12, 14, 30, 88, 107, 119, 123, 155, 189; Maps 2Q-R3, 4N-Q3, 6I3, 8E-I3
9th Avenue, 15, 30, 66, 164; Maps 2Q3, 4N-R3
10th Avenue, 116, 159; Map 4N-O2
11th Avenue, 10, 152; Map 4N-O2

B

Bank St.; Map 2R3
Hudson St., 148; Map 2R3
Barclay St., 108; Map 2T4
Barrow St., 43; Map 2R3
7th Ave, 183; Map 2R3
Battery Place, 57, 58; Map 2U4
Bayard St.; Map 3T5
Mulberry St., 148; Map 2T4
Bedford St., 43, 151; Map 2R3
Beekman Place, 74; Map 5O5
Beekman St., 106; Map 2T4
Belt Parkway, 110; Map 13E5
Bleecker St., 42, 43, 182; Map 2R4
LaGuardia Pl., 155, 160; Map 2R4
Thompson St., 159; Map 2R4
Boardwalk (Coney Island); Map 12F3
8th St., 98; Map 12F3
'Bobkin Lane', 42; Map 2R4
Bowery, The, 40, 57, 67, 87, 160; Maps 2R4, 3S–T5
Bleecker St., 160; Map 2R4
Broad St., 38; Map 2U4
Broadway, 10, 14, 15, 17, 32, 37, 39, 55, 56, 57,

58, 64, 68, 71, 74, 80, 84, 104, 105, 106, 107, 108, 112, 145, 154, 161, 166, 168, 169, 170, 172, 173, 179, 185, 186, 187; Maps 2R-U4, 4N-O3, 5P-Q4, 6I-M2-3, 8F-I2, 10B2
E Broadway, 42; Map 3S5-6
W Broadway, 27, 105, 152; Map 2T4
Thomas St., 141; Map 2T4
Brooklyn Avenue, 180; Map 12E3
Brooklyn Bridge, 19, 21, 37, 39, 50, 60, 61, 106, 182; Map 3T-U5
Brooklyn-Battery Tunnel, 60; Map 2V4
Brooklyn-Queens Expressway, 50; Map 3U-V6
Broome St., 27, 40, 164; Map 2S4

C

Cadman Plaza W, 50; Map 3U6
Canal St., 34, 40, 41, 67, 84, 87, 105, 108; Map 2S3–4
W Broadway, 164; Map 2S4
Central Park, 10, 12, 184, 186; Maps 6-7J-N3-4
Central Park S, 46, 116, 120, 121, 122, 123, 156; Maps 4-5M-N3-4
Central Park W, 14, 46, 53, 55, 98, 110, 120, 147, 182, 183; Maps 4M-N3, 6L-M3
Chambers St., 37, 39; Map 2T4
Charles St., 43; Map 2R3
Christopher St., 152; Map 2R3

204

Gazetteer

Gazetteer

NEW YORK

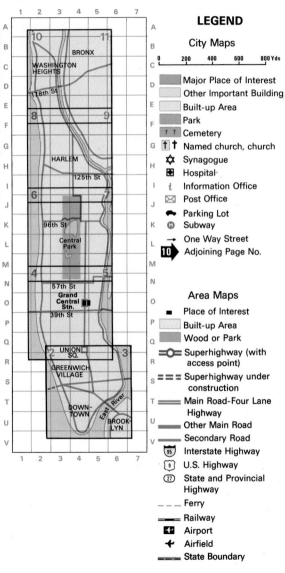

LEGEND

City Maps

| | |
0   200   400   600   800 Yds

- Major Place of Interest
- Other Important Building
- Built-up Area
- Park
- † † Cemetery
- † † Named church, church
- ✡ Synagogue
- ✚ Hospital
- ℹ Information Office
- ✉ Post Office
- ☎ Parking Lot
- Ⓜ Subway
- → One Way Street
- **10** Adjoining Page No.

Area Maps

- ■ Place of Interest
- Built-up Area
- Wood or Park
- =O= Superhighway (with access point)
- = = = Superhighway under construction
- Main Road-Four Lane Highway
- Other Main Road
- Secondary Road
- ⑮ Interstate Highway
- ⑨ U.S. Highway
- ㉗ State and Provincial Highway
- - - - Ferry
- Railway
- ✈ Airport
- ✦ Airfield
- State Boundary

BRONX

WASHINGTON HEIGHTS

178th St

HARLEM

125th St

96th St

Central Park

57th St

Grand Central Stn.

39th St

UNION SQ.

GREENWICH VILLAGE

East River

DOWN-TOWN

BROOK-LYN

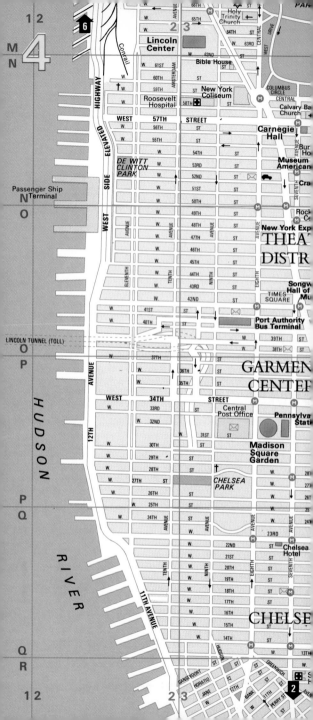

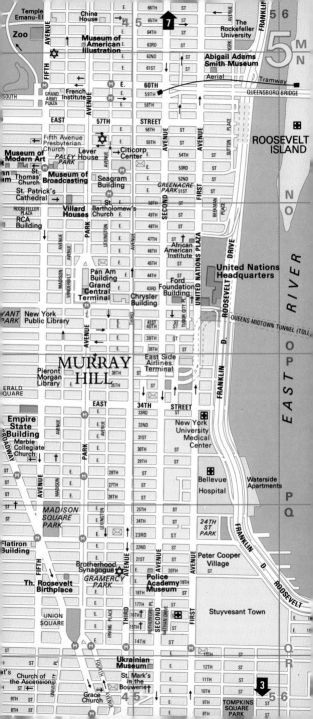

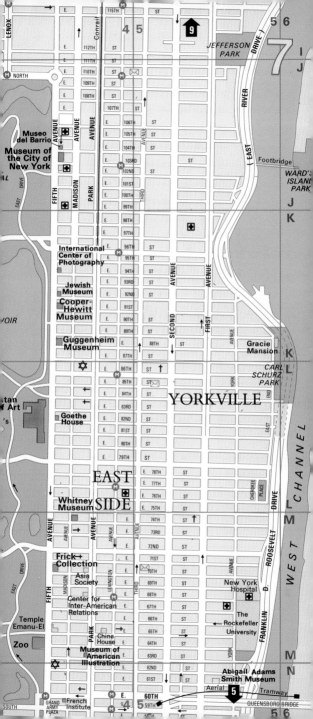

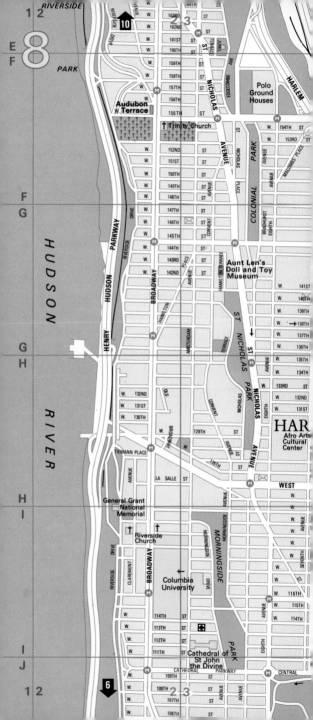

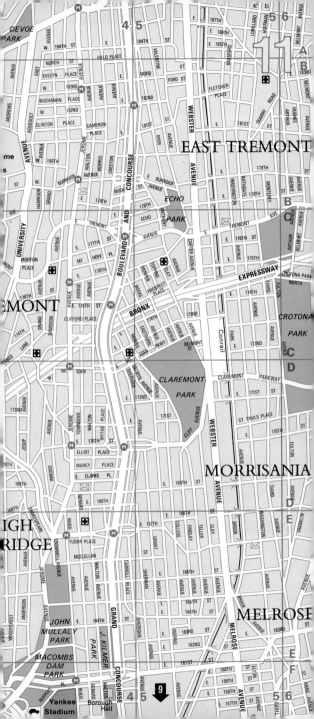

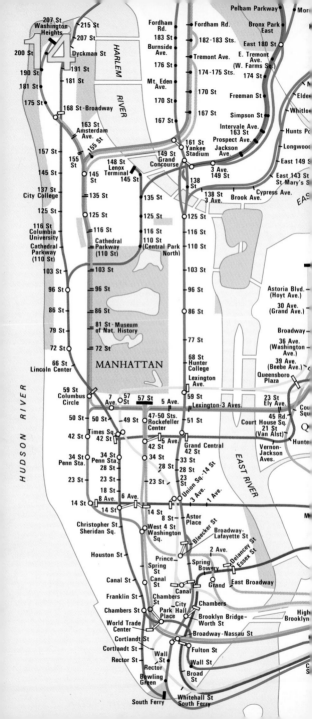

NEW YORK SUBWAY SYSTEM

15

ROUTES

Broadway - 7th Ave.
(Local/Express/Shuttle)

Lexington Ave.
(Express/Local/Local Pelham Express)

Flushing
(Local/Express)

J.F.K.
(Express)

8th Ave.
(Local/Express/Rockaway Shuttle)

Ave. of Americas (6th Ave.)
(Local/Express/Shuttle)

Brooklyn/Queens
(Crosstown)

Nassau St.
(Local/Shuttle)

14 St-Canarsie
(Local)

Broadway
(Local/Express/Shuttle/
Nassau St Local)

Terminal

Local Stop

Express Stop

Express & Local Stop

Free Transfers

Special Rush Hour
Express Service

BRONX

r Sq.
Ave.

Castle Hill Ave.
177 St
chester
ce Ave.
d

46 St.

Northern Blvd.

82 St.
74 St-Broadway
Jackson Heights
65 St.
Elmhurst Ave.
69 St.-Jackson Heights
61 St.-Woodside
52 St. (Lincoln Ave.)
46 St. (Bliss St.)
40 St. (Lowery St.)
awson St.

103 St-Corona Plaza
Junction Blvd.
90 St-Elmhurst Ave.
Grand Ave. Newtown
Woodhaven Blvd. Slattery Plaza
63 Drive Rego Park
67 Ave.
71 Continental Aves. Forest Hills
75 Ave.
Roosevelt Ave. Jackson Heights

Metropolitan Ave.
Fresh Pond Rd.
Forest Ave.
Seneca Ave.
Myrtle Ave.
Wilson Ave.

Forest Parkway
Elderts Lane
Cypress Hills
Crescent St

nt Ave.
ssau Ave.
Ave.

Lorimer St.
Graham Ave.
Grand Ave.
Montrose Ave.
Morgan Ave.
Jefferson St.
DeKalb Ave.
Halsey St.
Knickerbocker Ave.
Wyckoff Ave.
Central Ave.
Chauncey St.
Halsey St.
Gates Ave.

Bushwick Ave. Aberdeen St.
Broadway Junction Eastern Parkway
Norwood Ave.
Cleveland St
Van Siclen Ave.
Alabama Ave.

Broadway-East New York
Rockaway Ave.
Atlantic Ave. Liberty Ave.
Sutter Ave.
Van Siclen Ave.
Livonia Ave.

Hewes St.
Broadway
Lorimer St.
Flushing Ave.
Flushing Ave.
Myrtle Ave.
Kosciusko St.
Ralph Ave.
Junius St.

BROOKLYN

Myrtle-Willoughby Aves.
Bedford-Nostrand Aves.
Classon Ave.
Clinton-Washington Aves.
Nostrand Ave.
Franklin Ave.
Kingston-Throop Aves.
Utica Ave.
Rockaway Ave. Saratoga Ave.
Sutter Ave. Rutland Rd.

rough Hall
Lawrence St.
DeKalb Ave.
Fulton St.
Hoyt St.
Nevins
Pacific St.
Hoyt-Schermerhorn Sts.
Bergen St.
Union St.
Smith-9 Sts.
9 St.
4 Ave.
7 Ave.
Grand Army Plaza
Clinton-Washington Ave.
Lafayette Ave.
Franklin Ave.
Eastern Pkwy. Brooklyn Museum
Prospect Park
Nostrand Ave. President St.
Sterling St.
Winthrop St.
Church Ave.
Kingston Ave.
Utica Ave.
Atlantic Ave.

A selection of crosstown and uptown routes

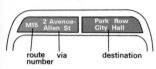

route number   via   destination

UPTOWN

M1 5th & Madison Aves
(8 St/4 Ave & 146 St/Lenox Ave)

M4 5th & Madison Aves
(32 St/7 Ave & 193 St/Ft Washington Ave)

M5 5th Ave & 6th Ave
(Houston St/W.B'way & 178 St/B'way)

M6 7th Ave/B'way & 6 Ave
(59 St/6 Ave & South Ferry)

M10 7th & 8th Aves
(Houston St/7 Ave & 159 St/8 Ave)

M11 9th & 10th Aves
(12 St/Hudson St & 133 St/B'way)

M15 1st & 2nd Aves
(South Ferry & 126 St/2 Ave)

M101 3rd & Lexington Aves
(6 St/3 Ave & †93 St/Amsterdam Ave)

M104 Broadway
(42 St/1 Ave & 129 St/Amsterdam Ave)

CROSSTOWN

M19 96th St
(1 Ave/96 St & West End Ave/96 St)

M18 86th St
(York Ave/91 St & West End Ave/86 St)

M17 79th St
(East End Ave/79 St & West End Ave/79 St)

M103 59th St
(York Ave/61 St & B'way/72 St)

M28 57th St
(Sutton Place/55 St & 12 Ave/55 St)

M27 49th & 50th Streets
(1 Ave/47 St & 12 Ave/42 St)

M106 42nd St
(1 Ave/42 St & 12 Ave/42 St)

M16 34th St
(1 Ave/34 St & 12 Ave/42 St)

M14 14th St
(FDR Drive/Delancey St & 10 Ave/15 St)

M13 8th St
(Ave D/10 St & West St/Christopher St)

M21 Houston St
(1 Ave/27 St & Hudson St/Van Dam St)

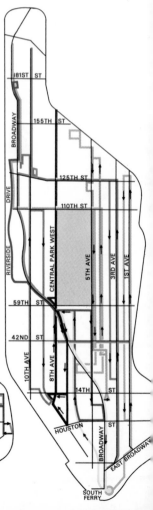